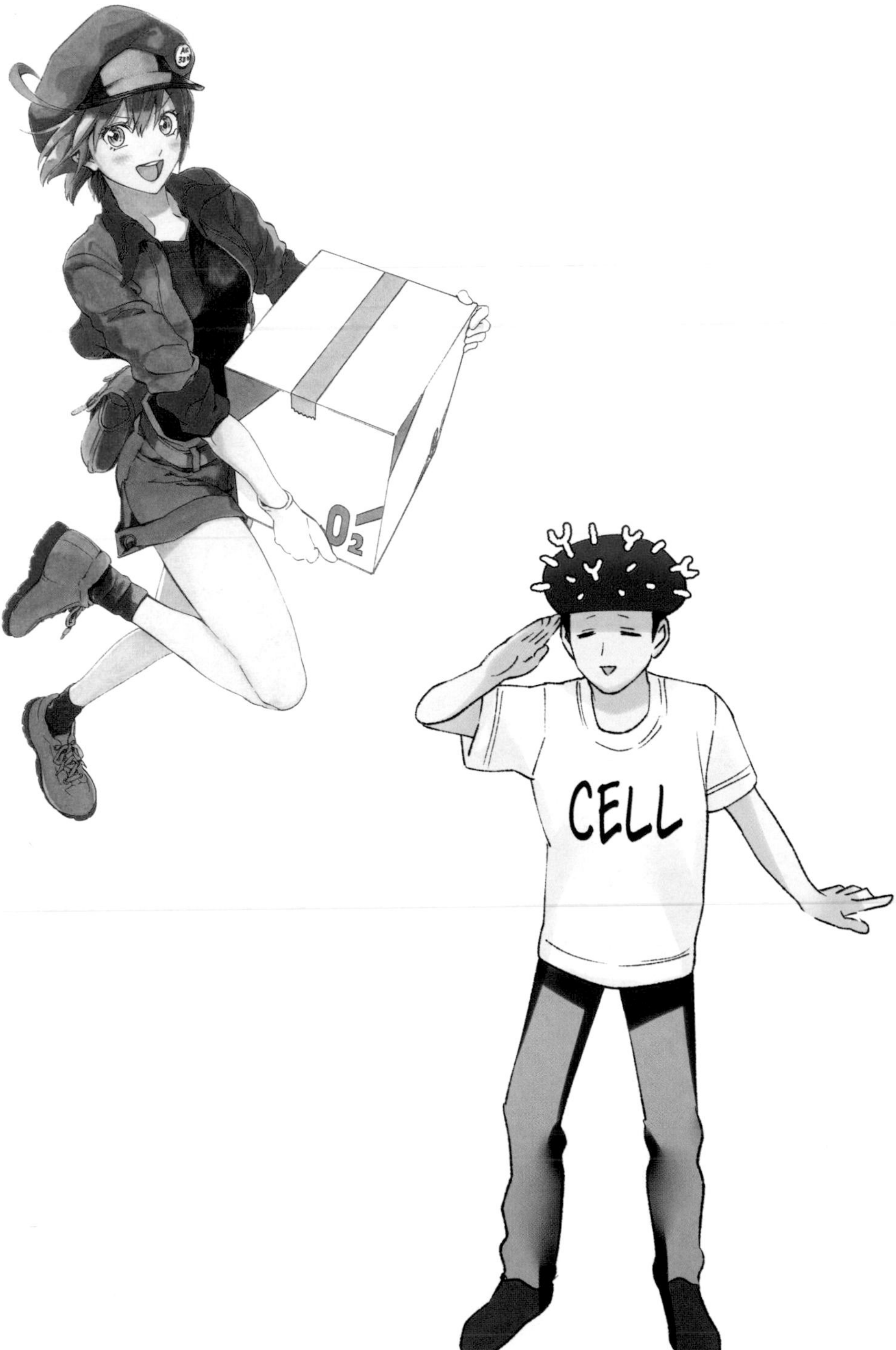
O2
CELL

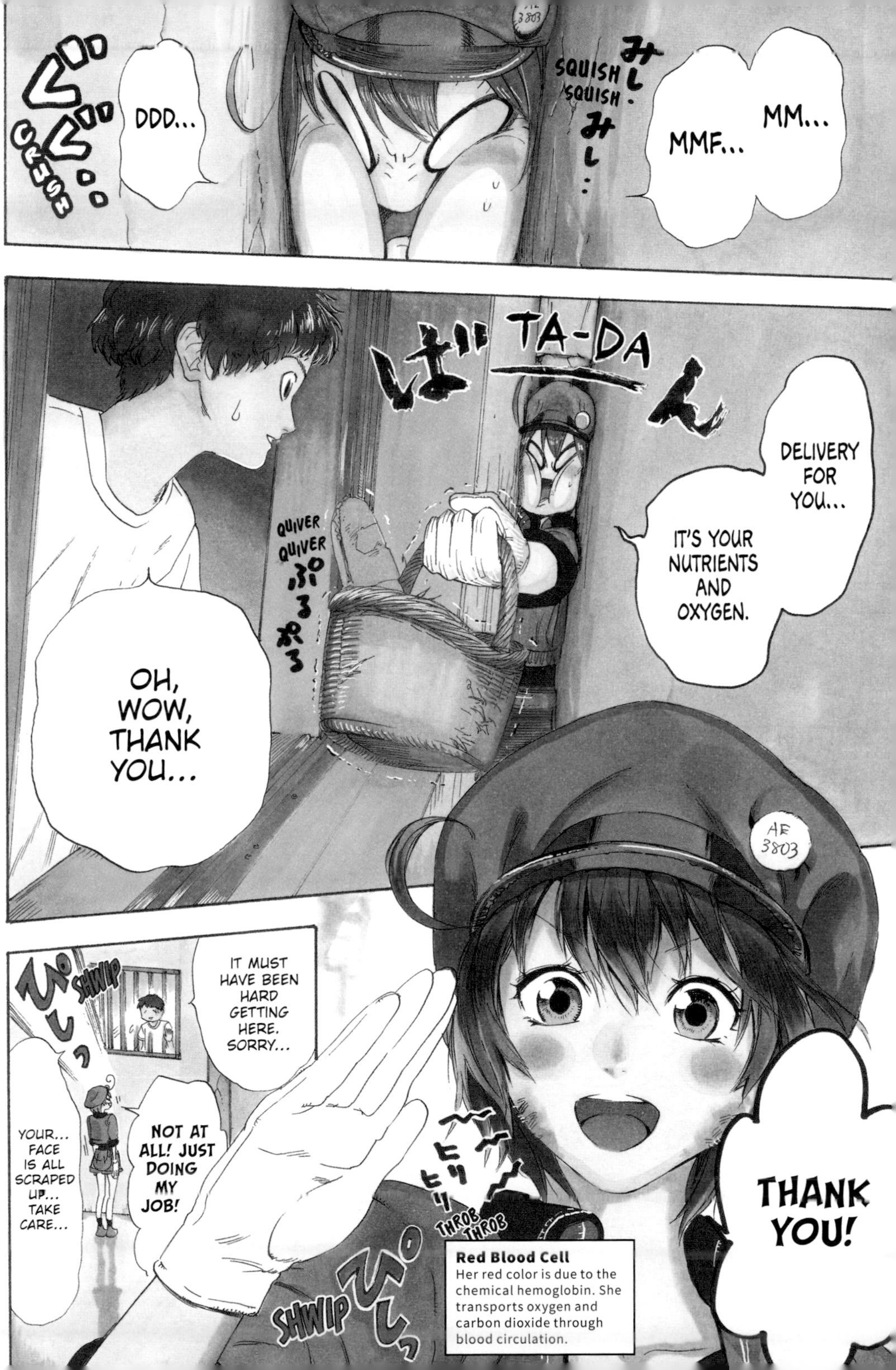
MM...
MMF...
SQUISH SQUISH
みし・みし・・
DDD...
CRUSH
TA-DA
DELIVERY FOR YOU...
IT'S YOUR NUTRIENTS AND OXYGEN.
QUIVER QUIVER
ぷるぷる
OH, WOW, THANK YOU...
AE 3803
THANK YOU!
ヒリ ヒリ
THROB THROB
Red Blood Cell
Her red color is due to the chemical hemoglobin. She transports oxygen and carbon dioxide through blood circulation.
SHWIP
ぴっ
IT MUST HAVE BEEN HARD GETTING HERE. SORRY...
SHWIP
ぴっ
NOT AT ALL! JUST DOING MY JOB!
YOUR... FACE IS ALL SCRAPED UP... TAKE CARE...

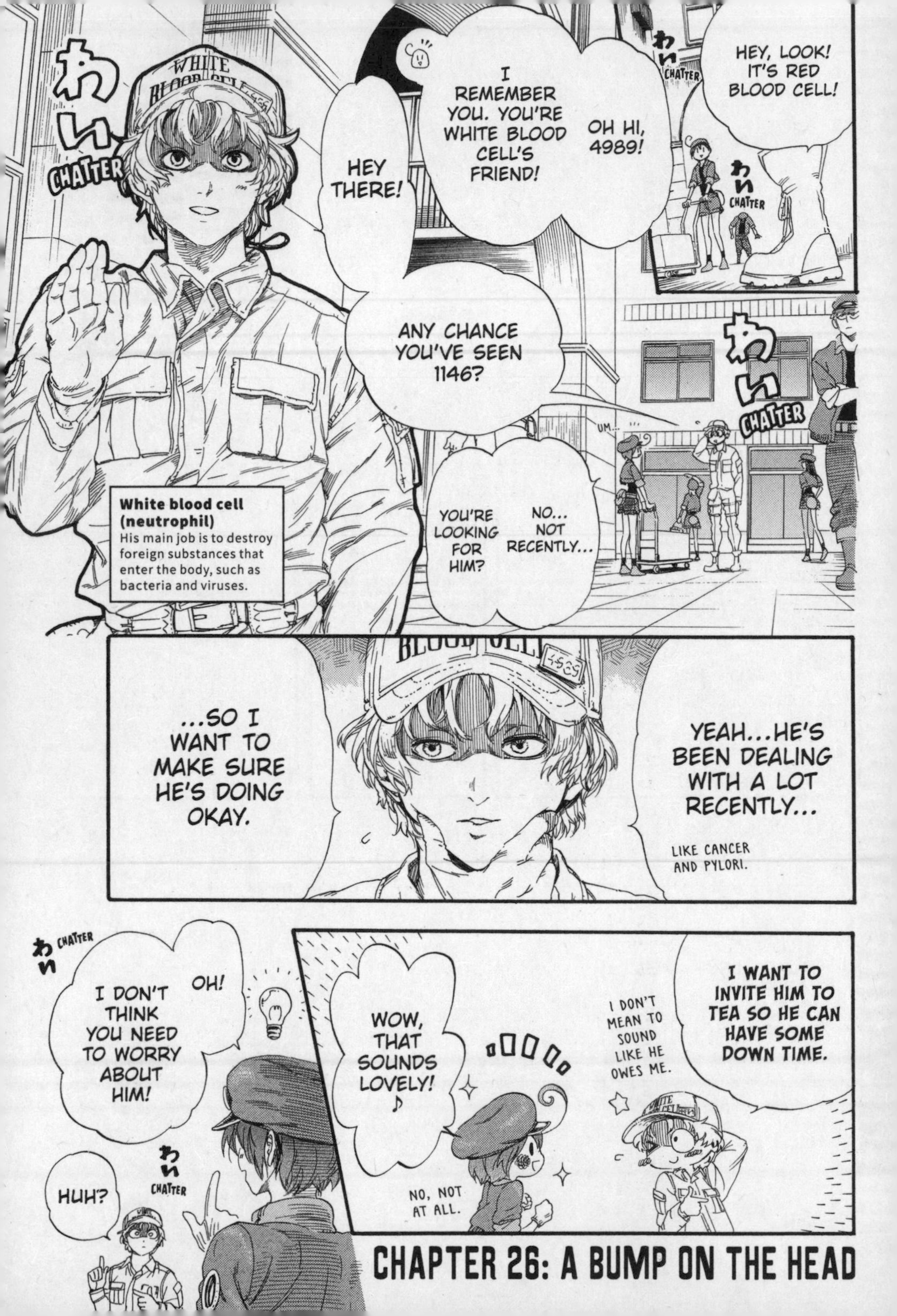
わい CHATTER
HEY, LOOK! IT'S RED BLOOD CELL!
わい CHATTER
わい CHATTER
OH HI, 4989!
I REMEMBER YOU. YOU'RE WHITE BLOOD CELL'S FRIEND!
HEY THERE!
わい CHATTER
わい CHATTER
ANY CHANCE YOU'VE SEEN 1146?
UM...
NO... NOT RECENTLY...
YOU'RE LOOKING FOR HIM?
White blood cell (neutrophil)
His main job is to destroy foreign substances that enter the body, such as bacteria and viruses.
YEAH...HE'S BEEN DEALING WITH A LOT RECENTLY...
LIKE CANCER AND PYLORI.
...SO I WANT TO MAKE SURE HE'S DOING OKAY.
I WANT TO INVITE HIM TO TEA SO HE CAN HAVE SOME DOWN TIME.
I DON'T MEAN TO SOUND LIKE HE OWES ME.
WOW, THAT SOUNDS LOVELY! ♪
NO, NOT AT ALL.
わい CHATTER
OH!
I DON'T THINK YOU NEED TO WORRY ABOUT HIM!
わい CHATTER
HUH?

CHAPTER 26: A BUMP ON THE HEAD

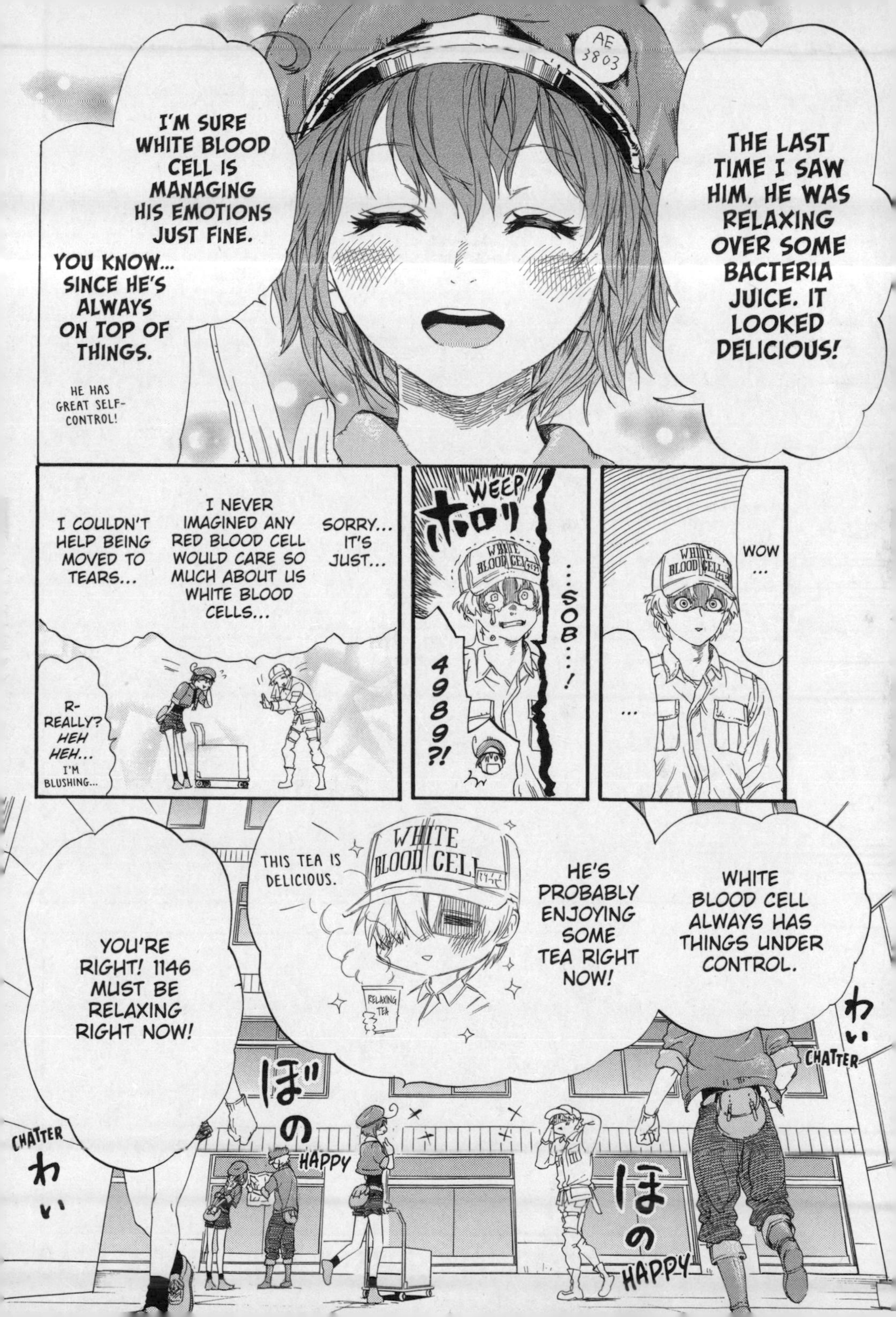
AE 3803
THE LAST TIME I SAW HIM, HE WAS RELAXING OVER SOME BACTERIA JUICE. IT LOOKED DELICIOUS!
I'M SURE WHITE BLOOD CELL IS MANAGING HIS EMOTIONS JUST FINE.
YOU KNOW... SINCE HE'S ALWAYS ON TOP OF THINGS.
HE HAS GREAT SELF-CONTROL!
WOW...
...
WEEP
ホロリ
WHITE BLOOD CELL
4989?!
...SOB...!
SORRY... IT'S JUST...
I NEVER IMAGINED ANY RED BLOOD CELL WOULD CARE SO MUCH ABOUT US WHITE BLOOD CELLS...
I COULDN'T HELP BEING MOVED TO TEARS...
R-REALLY? HEH HEH... I'M BLUSHING...
WHITE BLOOD CELL ALWAYS HAS THINGS UNDER CONTROL.
HE'S PROBABLY ENJOYING SOME TEA RIGHT NOW!
WHITE BLOOD CELL
THIS TEA IS DELICIOUS.
RELAXING TEA
YOU'RE RIGHT! 1146 MUST BE RELAXING RIGHT NOW!
わい CHATTER
ほの HAPPY
ぼの HAPPY
CHATTER わい

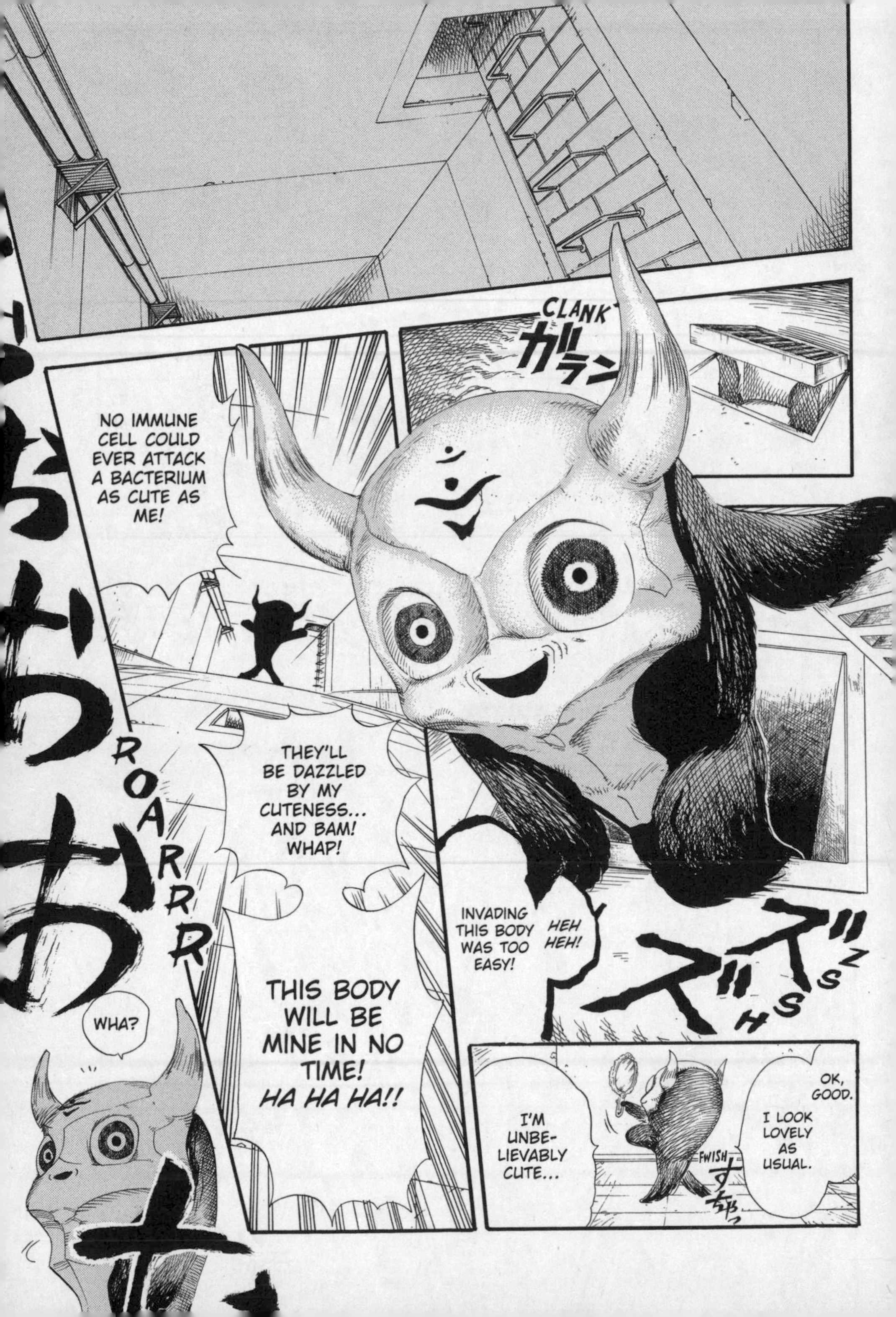
CLANK
ガラン
INVADING THIS BODY WAS TOO EASY!
HEH HEH!
ズズ
SHSS
OK, GOOD.
I LOOK LOVELY AS USUAL.
I'M UNBE-LIEVABLY CUTE...
FWISH
すちゃっ
NO IMMUNE CELL COULD EVER ATTACK A BACTERIUM AS CUTE AS ME!
THEY'LL BE DAZZLED BY MY CUTENESS... AND BAM! WHAP!
THIS BODY WILL BE MINE IN NO TIME! HA HA HA!!
ROARRR
WHA?

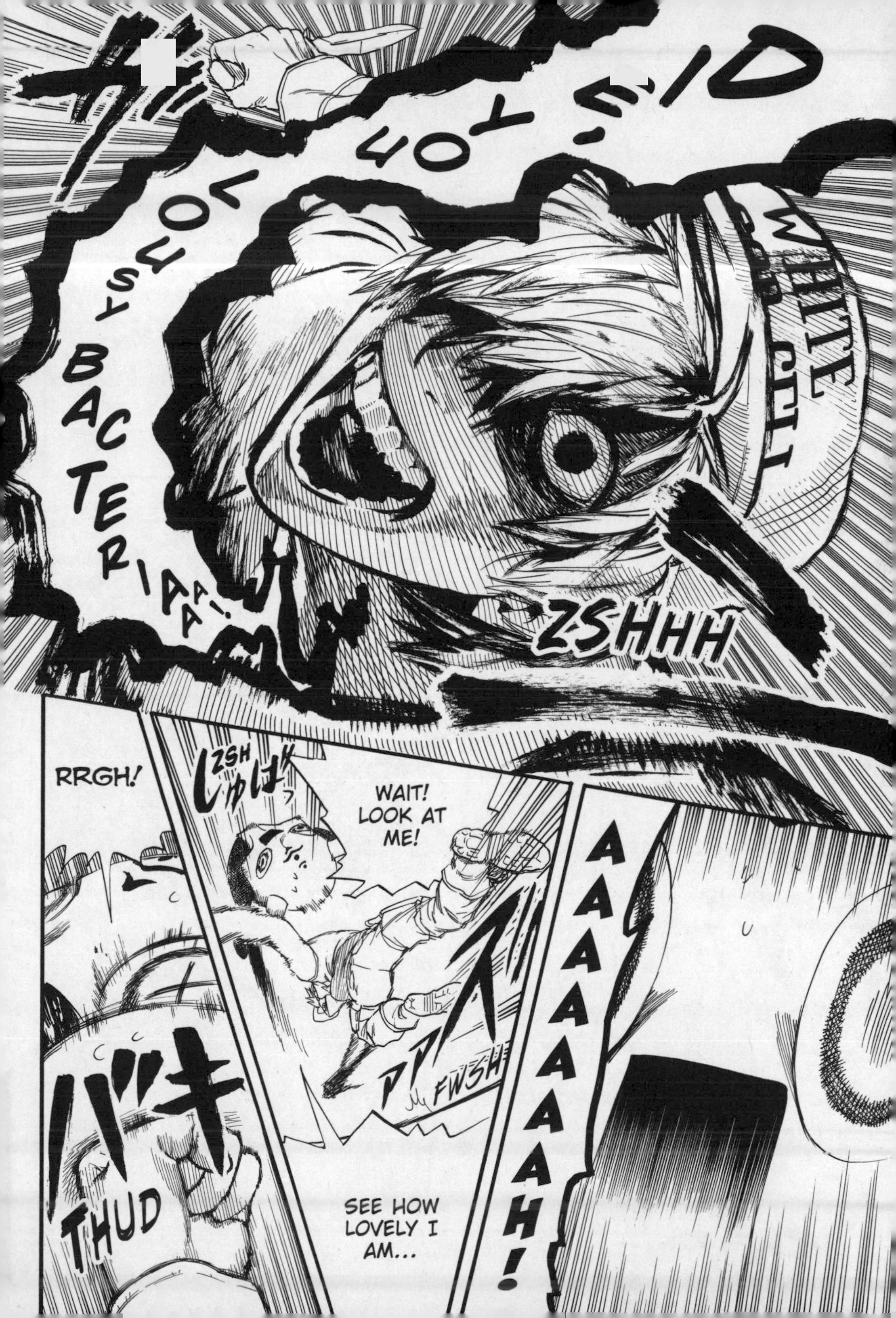
DIE, YOU LOUSY BACTERIAAA!
WHITE
ZSHHH
AAAAAAAAAH!
ZSH
WAIT! LOOK AT ME!
FWSH
SEE HOW LOVELY I AM...
RRGH!
THUD

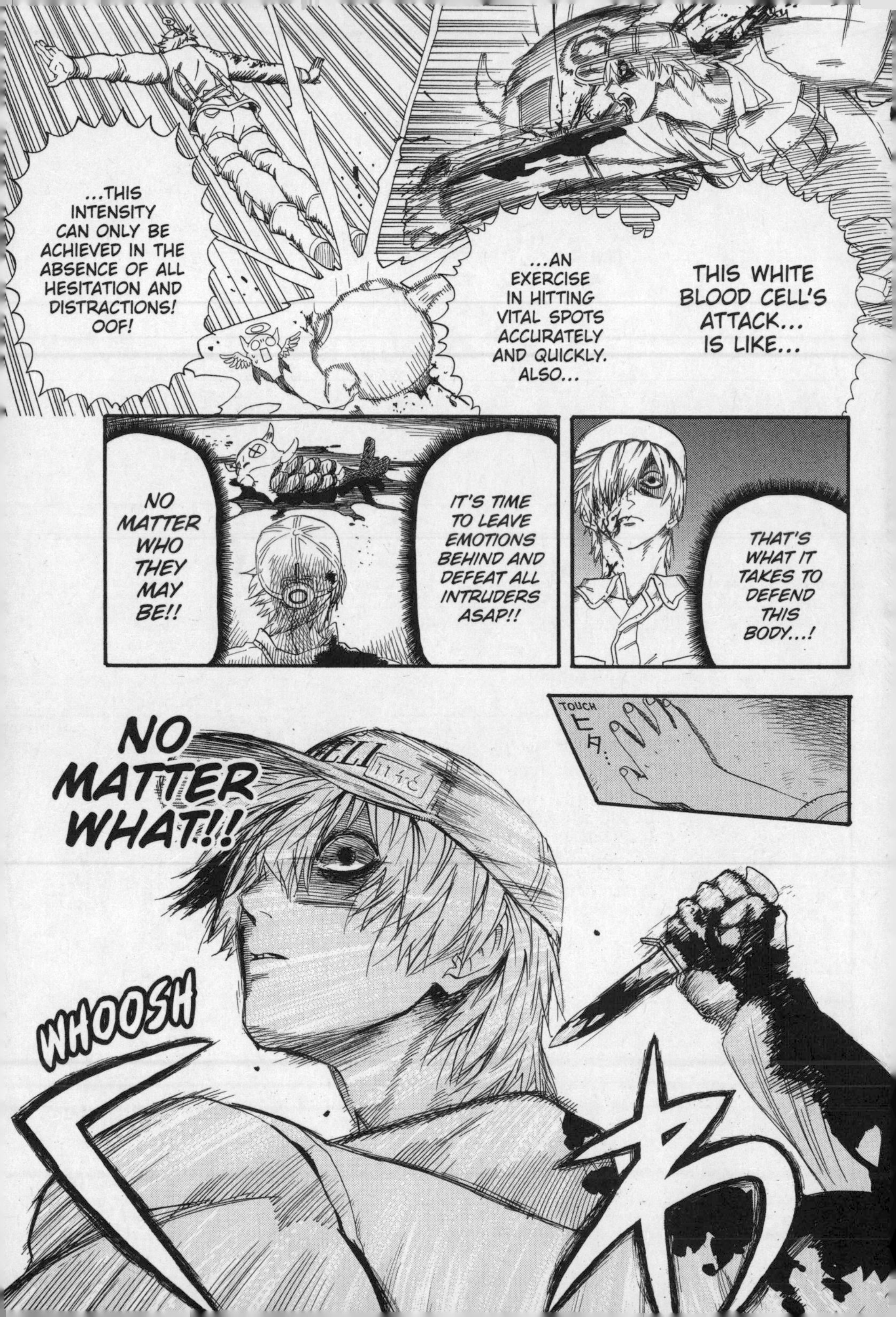
THIS WHITE BLOOD CELL'S ATTACK... IS LIKE...
...AN EXERCISE IN HITTING VITAL SPOTS ACCURATELY AND QUICKLY. ALSO...
...THIS INTENSITY CAN ONLY BE ACHIEVED IN THE ABSENCE OF ALL HESITATION AND DISTRACTIONS! OOF!
THAT'S WHAT IT TAKES TO DEFEND THIS BODY...!
IT'S TIME TO LEAVE EMOTIONS BEHIND AND DEFEAT ALL INTRUDERS ASAP!!
NO MATTER WHO THEY MAY BE!!
TOUCH
NO MATTER WHAT!!
WHOOSH

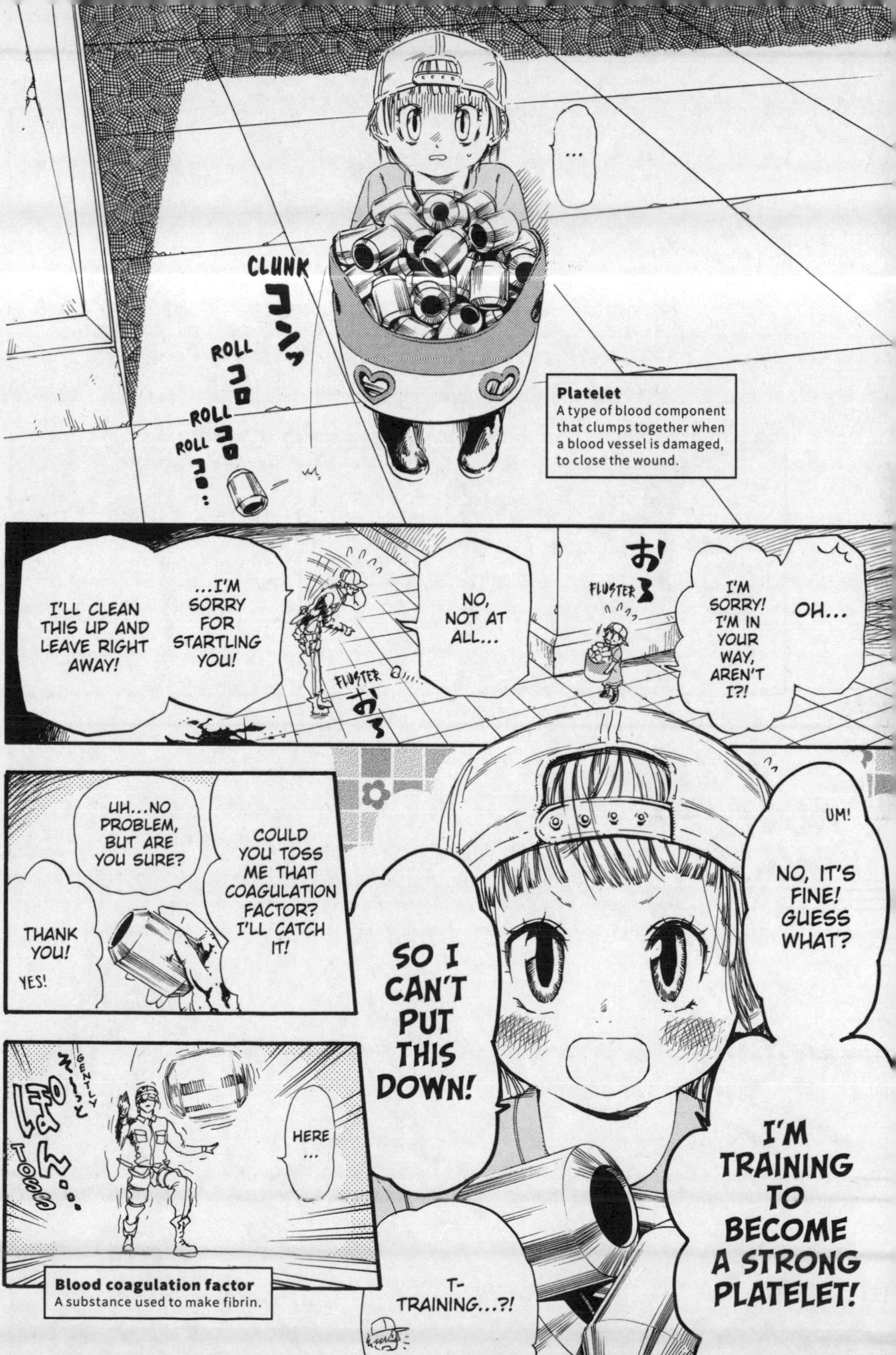
...
CLUNK コンッ
ROLL コロ
ROLL コロ
ROLL コロ..
Platelet
A type of blood component that clumps together when a blood vessel is damaged, to close the wound.
OH...
I'M SORRY! I'M IN YOUR WAY, AREN'T I?!
FLUSTER おろ
NO, NOT AT ALL...
FLUSTER おろ
...I'M SORRY FOR STARTLING YOU!
I'LL CLEAN THIS UP AND LEAVE RIGHT AWAY!
UM!
NO, IT'S FINE! GUESS WHAT?
I'M TRAINING TO BECOME A STRONG PLATELET!
SO I CAN'T PUT THIS DOWN!
T-TRAINING...?!
COULD YOU TOSS ME THAT COAGULATION FACTOR? I'LL CATCH IT!
UH...NO PROBLEM, BUT ARE YOU SURE?
THANK YOU!
YES!
HERE...
GENTLY そ〜っと
TOSS ぽん...
Blood coagulation factor
A substance used to make fibrin.

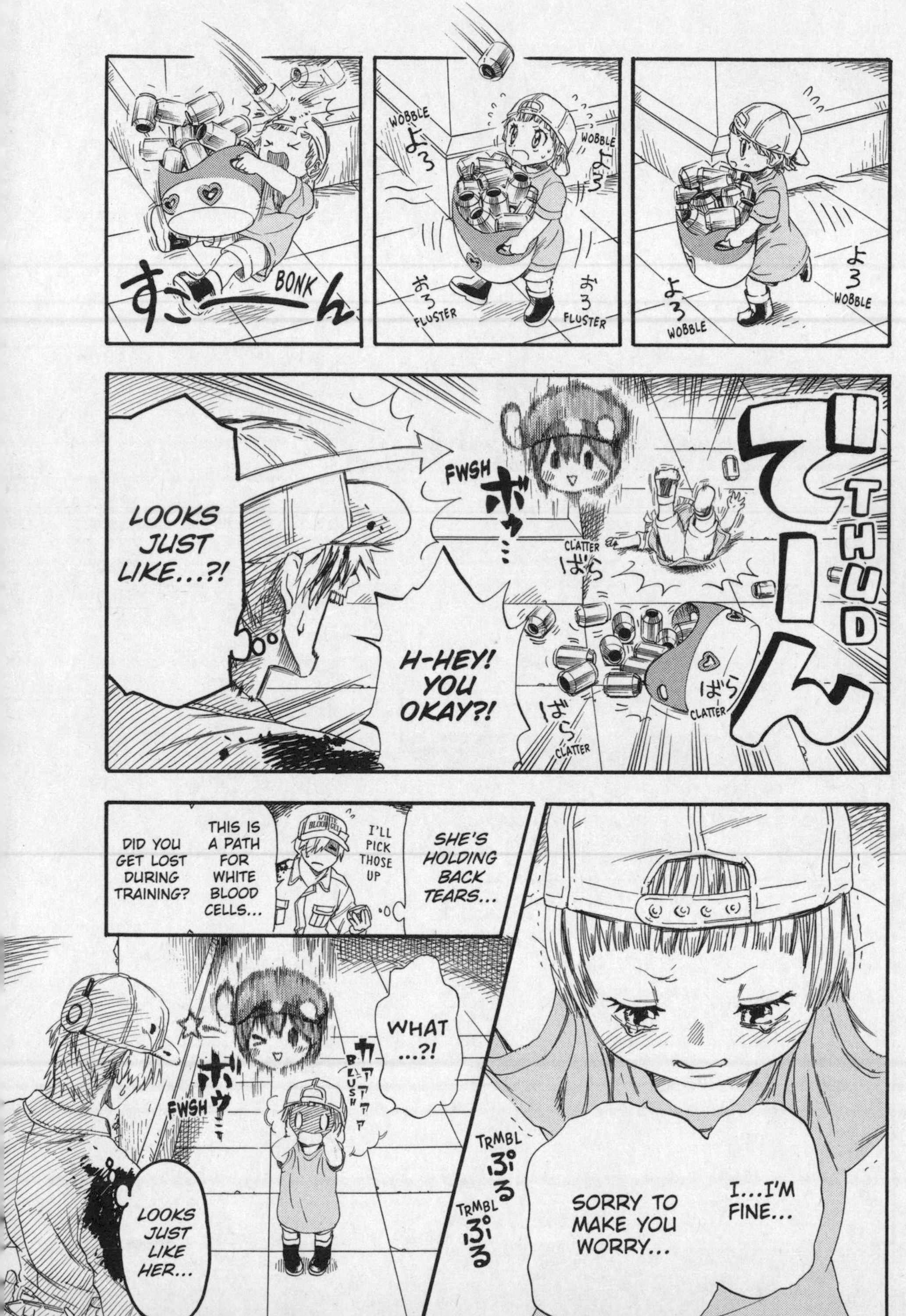
よろ
WOBBLE
よろ
WOBBLE
よろ
WOBBLE
よろ
WOBBLE
おろ
FLUSTER
おろ
FLUSTER
すこーん
BONK
でーん
THUD
ボッ
FWSH
ばら
CLATTER
ばら
CLATTER
ばら
CLATTER
LOOKS JUST LIKE...?!
H-HEY! YOU OKAY?!
I...I'M FINE...
SORRY TO MAKE YOU WORRY...
ぷる
TRMBL
ぷる
TRMBL
SHE'S HOLDING BACK TEARS...
I'LL PICK THOSE UP
THIS IS A PATH FOR WHITE BLOOD CELLS...
DID YOU GET LOST DURING TRAINING?
WHAT ...?!
カァァァァ
BLUSH
ボウッ
FWSH
LOOKS JUST LIKE HER...

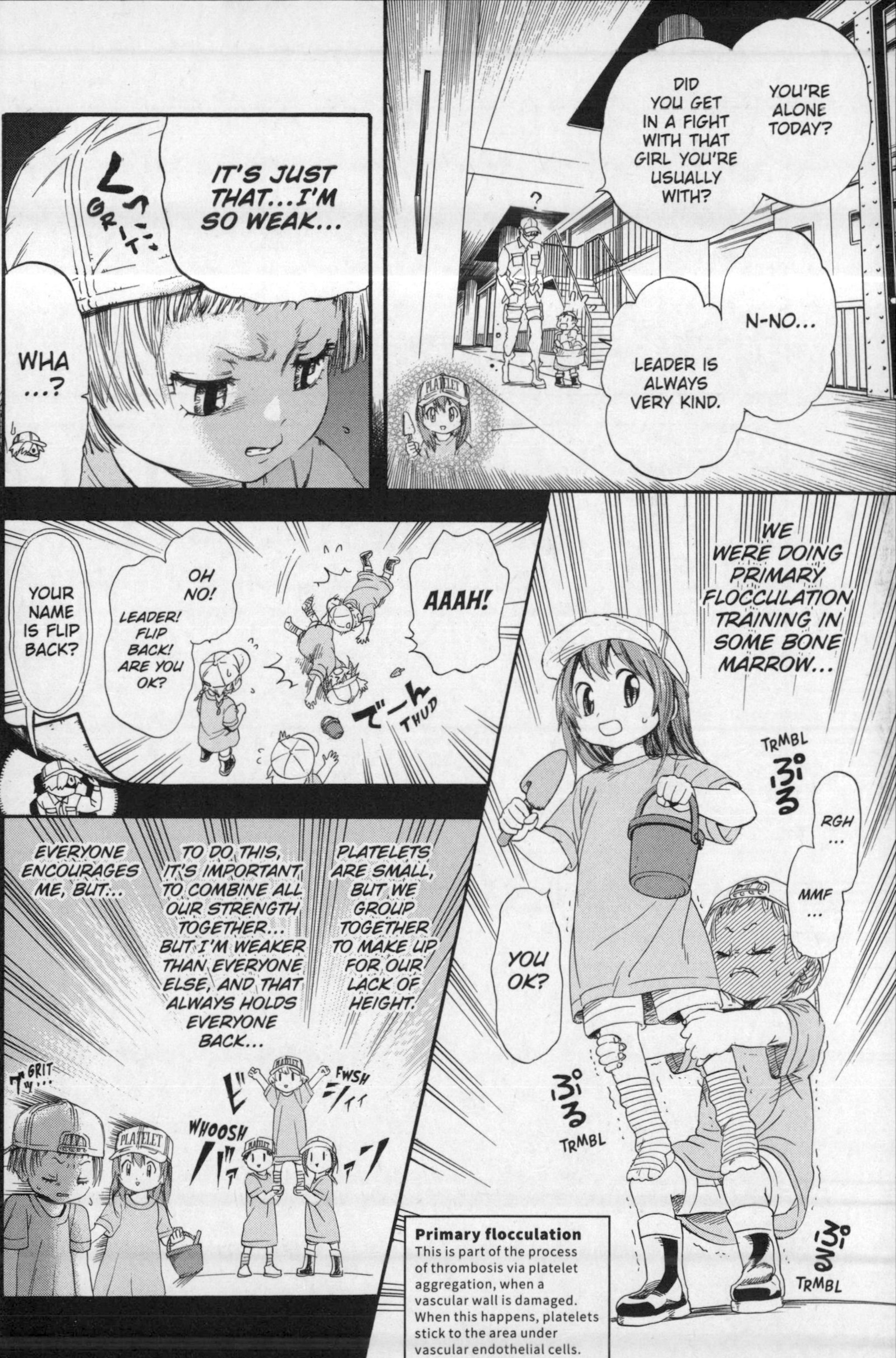
YOU'RE ALONE TODAY?
DID YOU GET IN A FIGHT WITH THAT GIRL YOU'RE USUALLY WITH?
?
N-NO...
LEADER IS ALWAYS VERY KIND.
IT'S JUST THAT...I'M SO WEAK...
GRIT
WHA ...?
WE WERE DOING PRIMARY FLOCCULATION TRAINING IN SOME BONE MARROW...
TRMBL
RGH ...
MMF ...
YOU OK?
TRMBL
TRMBL
AAAH!
OH NO!
LEADER! FLIP BACK! ARE YOU OK?
THUD
YOUR NAME IS FLIP BACK?
PLATELETS ARE SMALL, BUT WE GROUP TOGETHER TO MAKE UP FOR OUR LACK OF HEIGHT.
TO DO THIS, IT'S IMPORTANT TO COMBINE ALL OUR STRENGTH TOGETHER... BUT I'M WEAKER THAN EVERYONE ELSE, AND THAT ALWAYS HOLDS EVERYONE BACK...
EVERYONE ENCOURAGES ME, BUT...
FWSH
WHOOSH
GRIT...

Primary flocculation
This is part of the process of thrombosis via platelet aggregation, when a vascular wall is damaged. When this happens, platelets stick to the area under vascular endothelial cells.

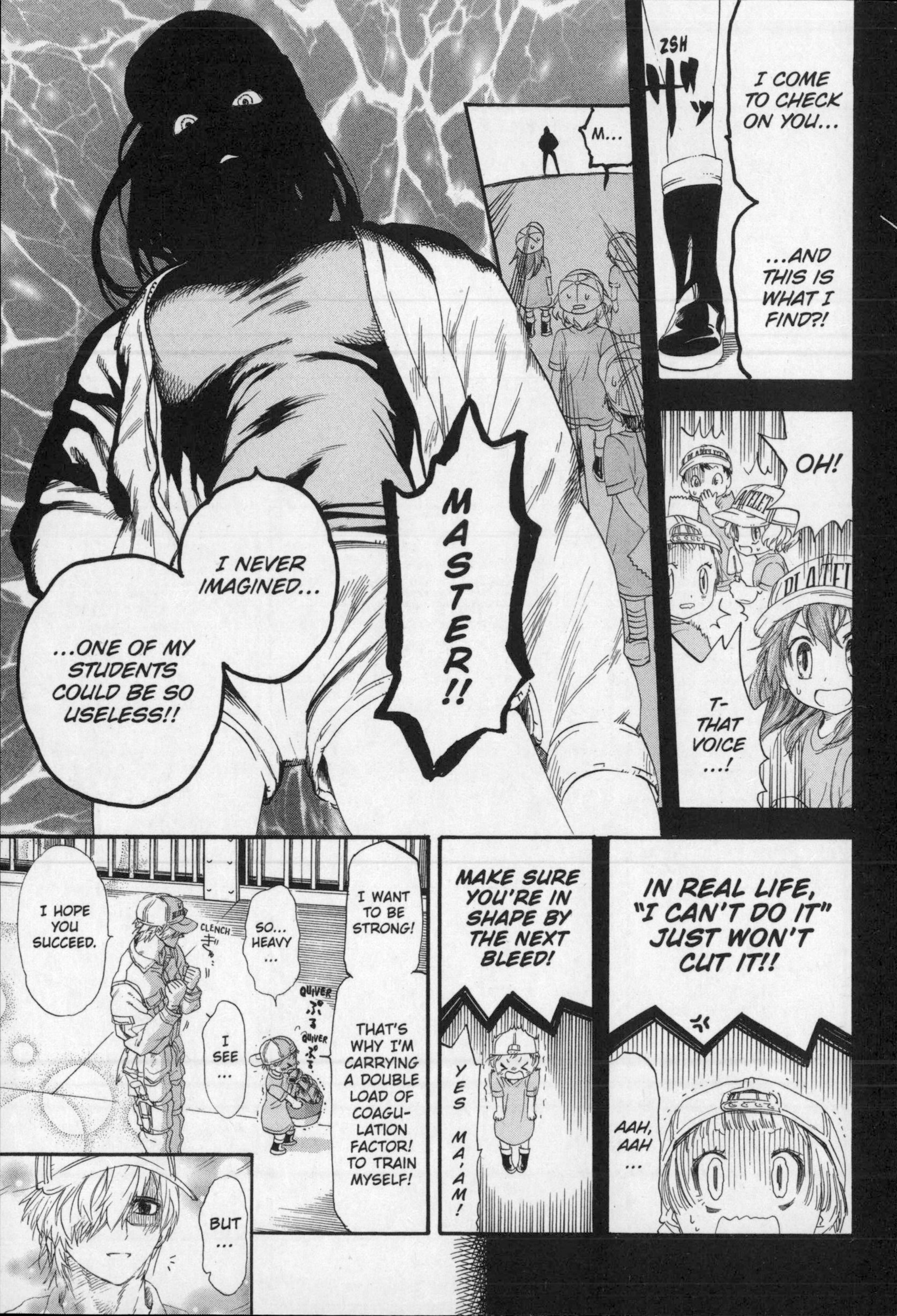
ZSH
I COME TO CHECK ON YOU...
...AND THIS IS WHAT I FIND?!
M...
OH!
T-THAT VOICE...!
MASTER!!
I NEVER IMAGINED...
...ONE OF MY STUDENTS COULD BE SO USELESS!!
IN REAL LIFE, "I CAN'T DO IT" JUST WON'T CUT IT!!
AAH, AAH...
MAKE SURE YOU'RE IN SHAPE BY THE NEXT BLEED!
YES MA'AM!
I WANT TO BE STRONG!
SO... HEAVY...
CLENCH
I HOPE YOU SUCCEED.
QUIVER
QUIVER
THAT'S WHY I'M CARRYING A DOUBLE LOAD OF COAGULATION FACTOR! TO TRAIN MYSELF!
I SEE...
BUT...

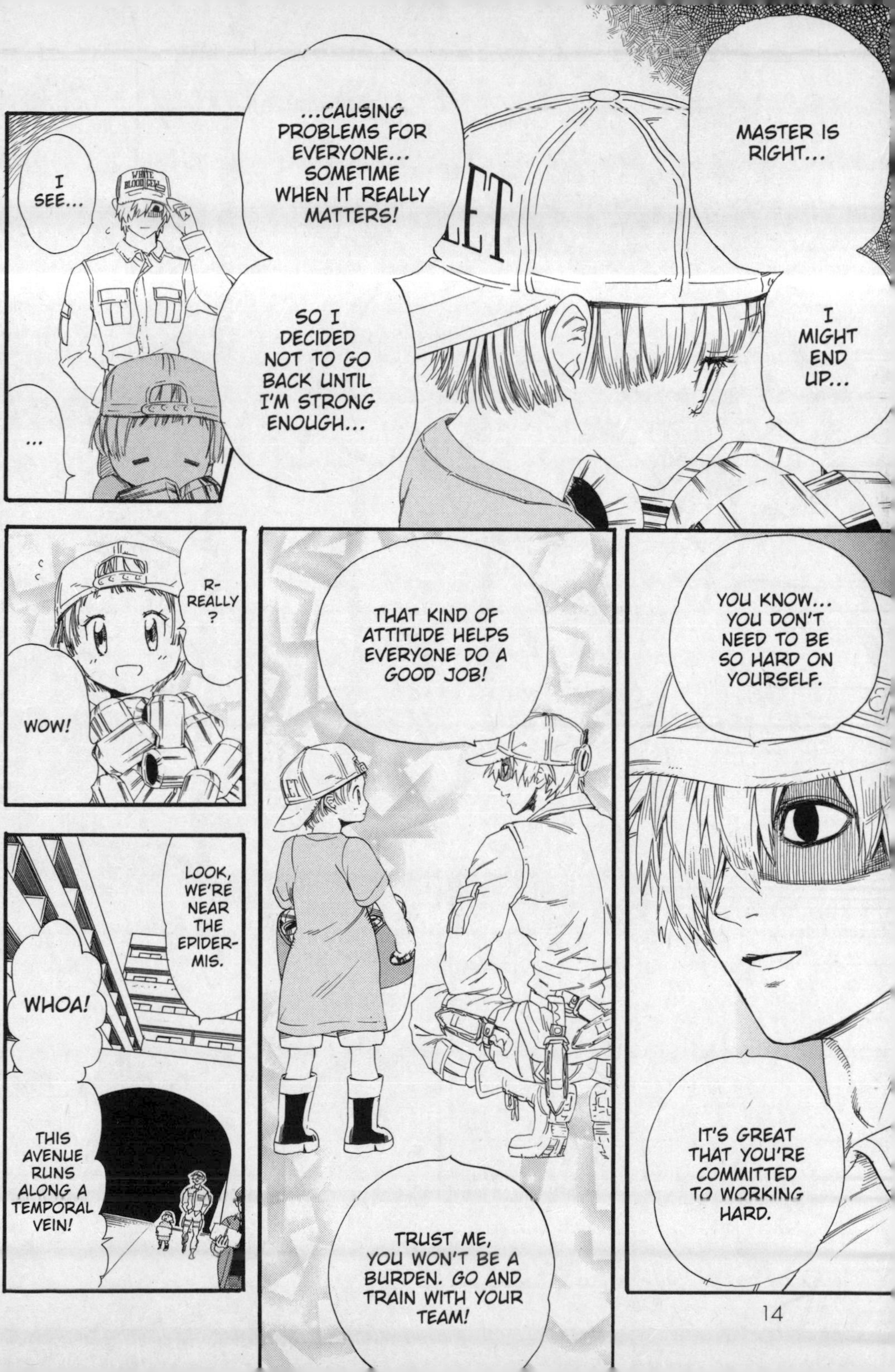
MASTER IS RIGHT...
I MIGHT END UP...
...CAUSING PROBLEMS FOR EVERYONE... SOMETIME WHEN IT REALLY MATTERS!
SO I DECIDED NOT TO GO BACK UNTIL I'M STRONG ENOUGH...
I SEE...
...
YOU KNOW... YOU DON'T NEED TO BE SO HARD ON YOURSELF.
IT'S GREAT THAT YOU'RE COMMITTED TO WORKING HARD.
THAT KIND OF ATTITUDE HELPS EVERYONE DO A GOOD JOB!
TRUST ME, YOU WON'T BE A BURDEN. GO AND TRAIN WITH YOUR TEAM!
R-REALLY?
WOW!
LOOK, WE'RE NEAR THE EPIDER-MIS.
WHOA!
THIS AVENUE RUNS ALONG A TEMPORAL VEIN!

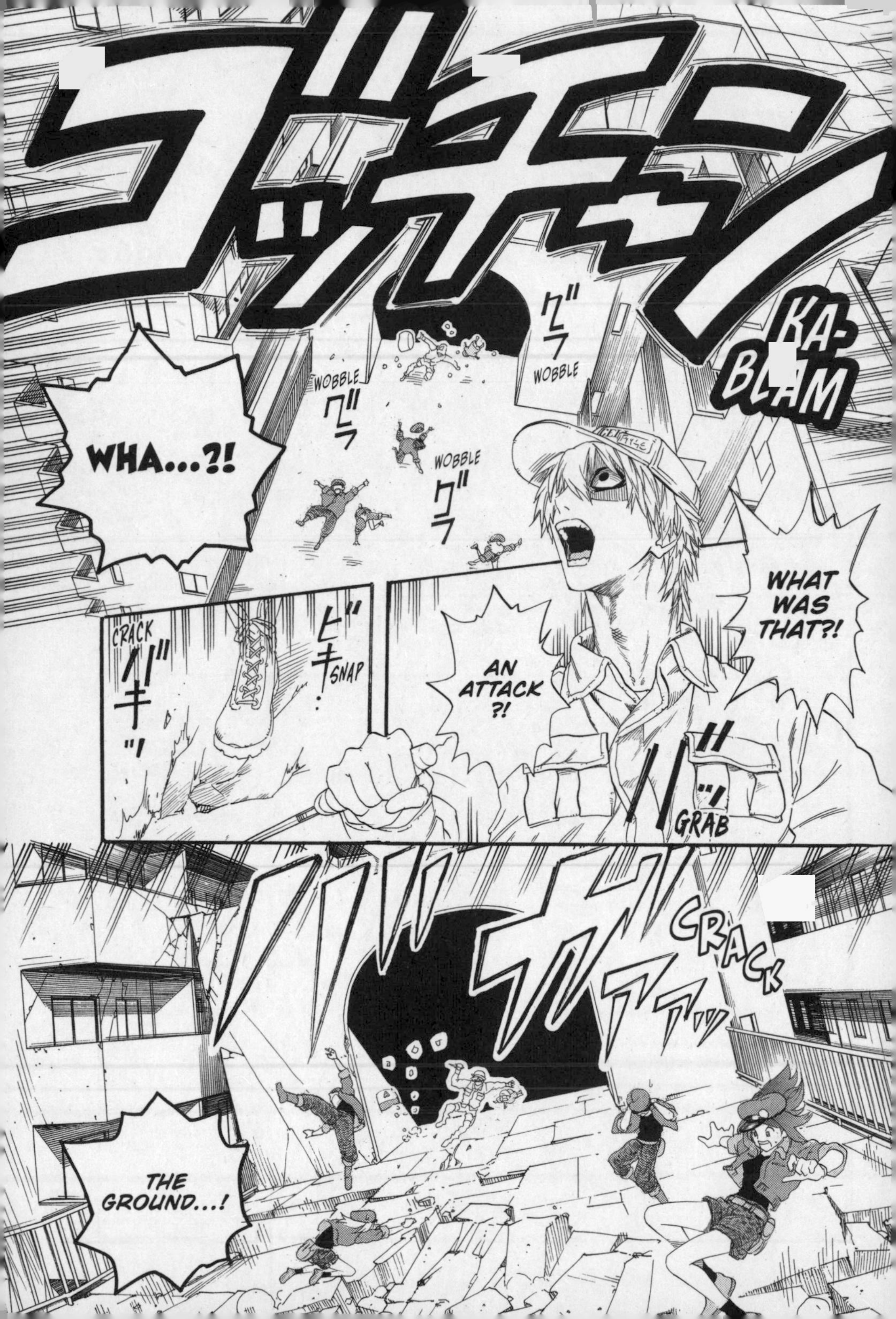
KA-BLAM
WOBBLE
WOBBLE
WOBBLE
WHA...?!
WHAT WAS THAT?!
AN ATTACK?!
GRAB
SNAP
CRACK
CRACK
THE GROUND...!

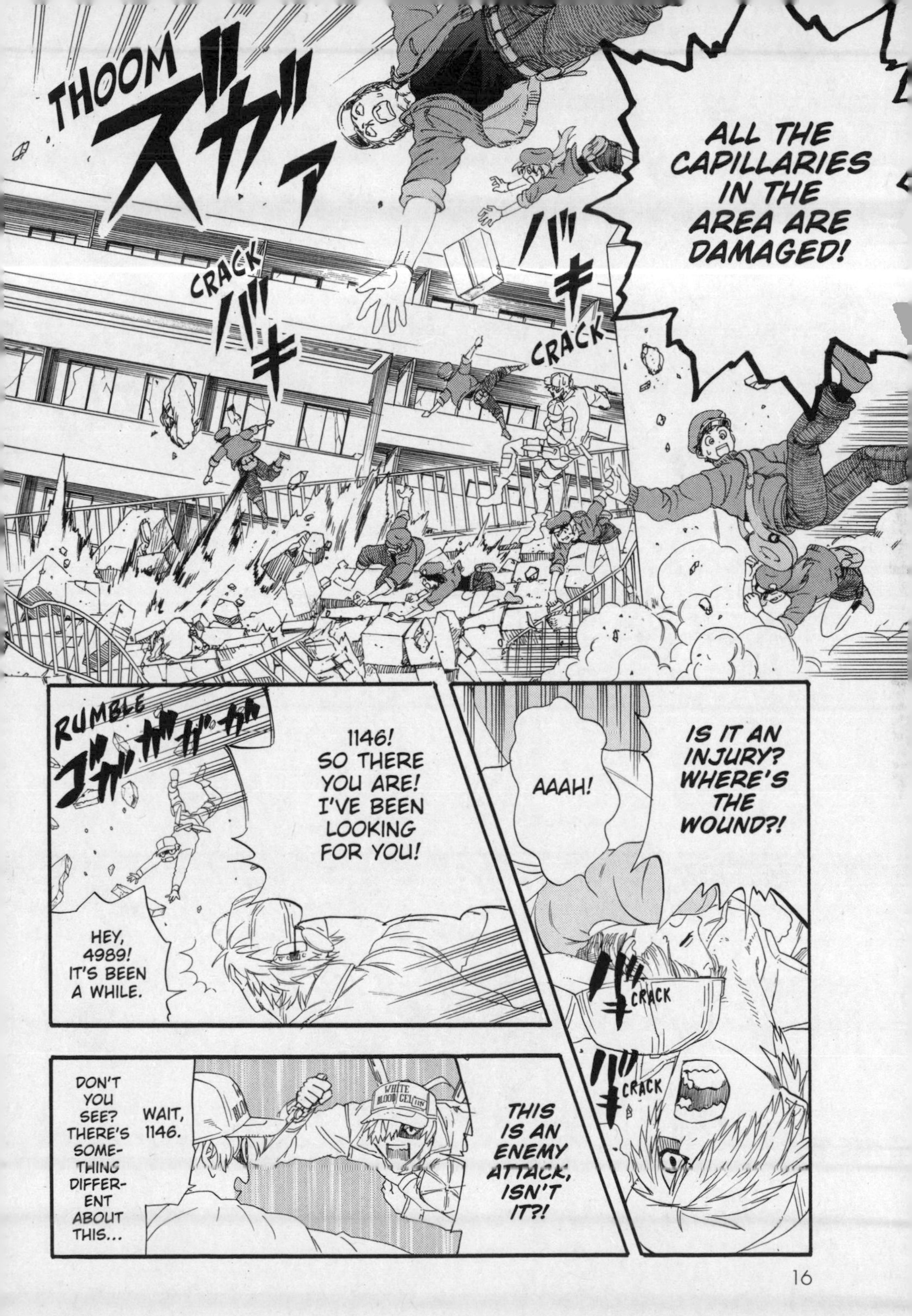
ALL THE CAPILLARIES IN THE AREA ARE DAMAGED!
THOOM
ズガァ
バキ
CRACK
CRACK
バキ
IS IT AN INJURY? WHERE'S THE WOUND?!
AAAH!
バキ
CRACK
バキ
CRACK
THIS IS AN ENEMY ATTACK, ISN'T IT?!
RUMBLE
1146! SO THERE YOU ARE! I'VE BEEN LOOKING FOR YOU!
HEY, 4989! IT'S BEEN A WHILE.
WHITE BLOOD CELL 1146
WAIT, 1146.
DON'T YOU SEE? THERE'S SOME-THING DIFFER-ENT ABOUT THIS...

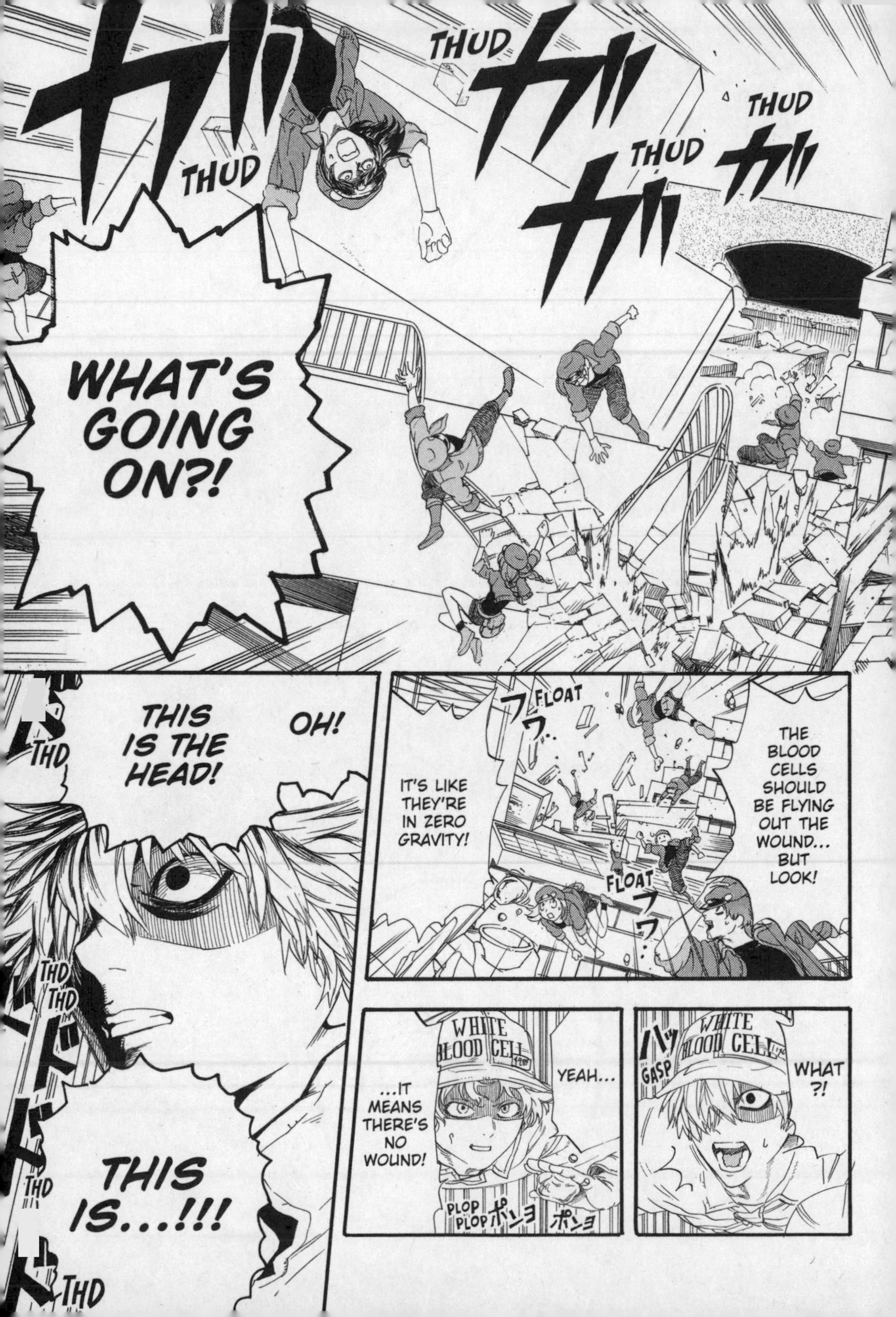
THUD
THUD
THUD
THUD
WHAT'S GOING ON?!
THE BLOOD CELLS SHOULD BE FLYING OUT THE WOUND... BUT LOOK!
IT'S LIKE THEY'RE IN ZERO GRAVITY!
FLOAT
FLOAT
WHAT ?!
GASP
YEAH...
...IT MEANS THERE'S NO WOUND!
PLOP PLOP
WHITE BLOOD CELL
OH!
THIS IS THE HEAD!
THD
THD
THD
THD
THIS IS...!!!
THD

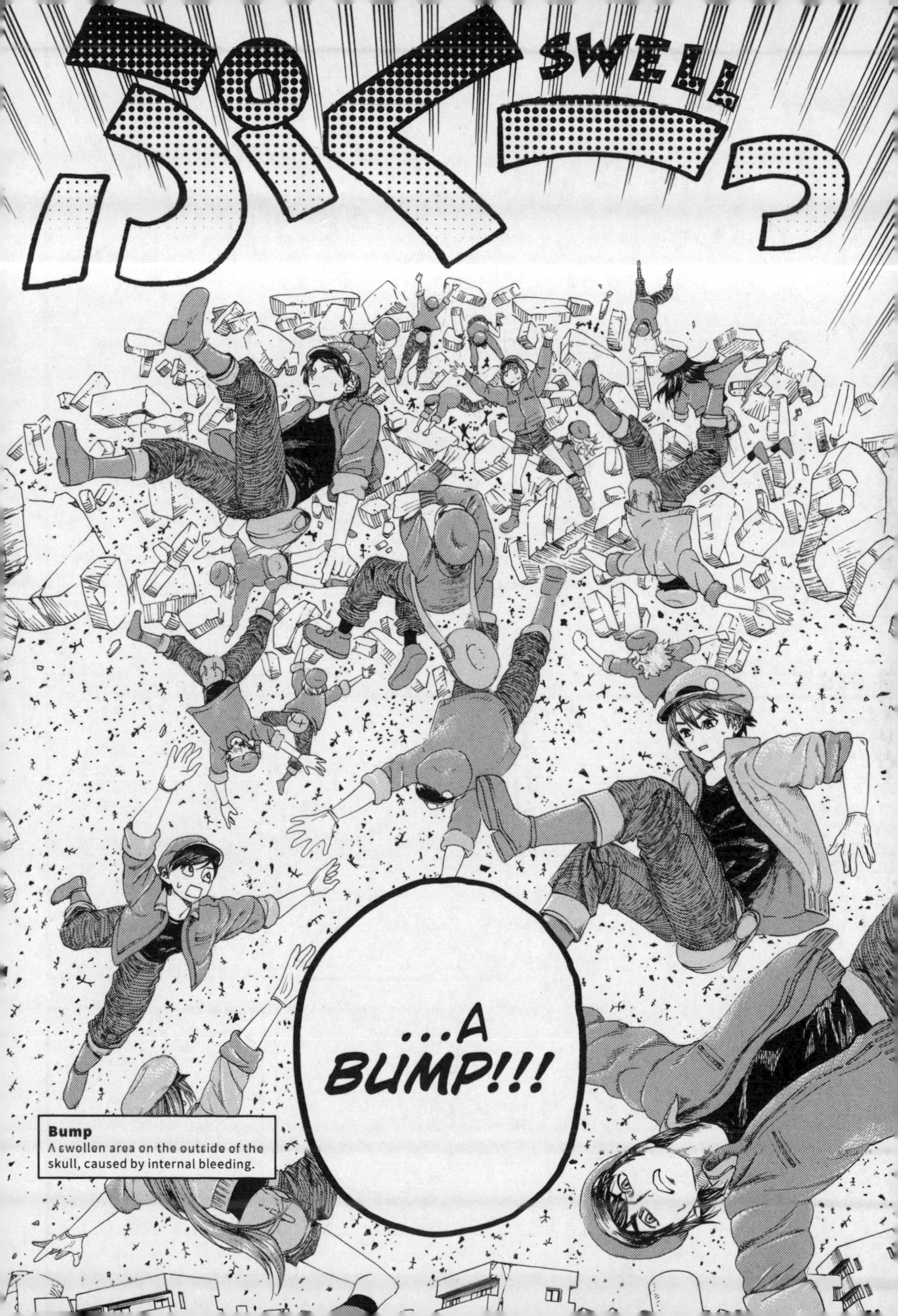
ぷくーっ
SWELL
...A BUMP!!!
Bump
A swollen area on the outside of the skull, caused by internal bleeding.

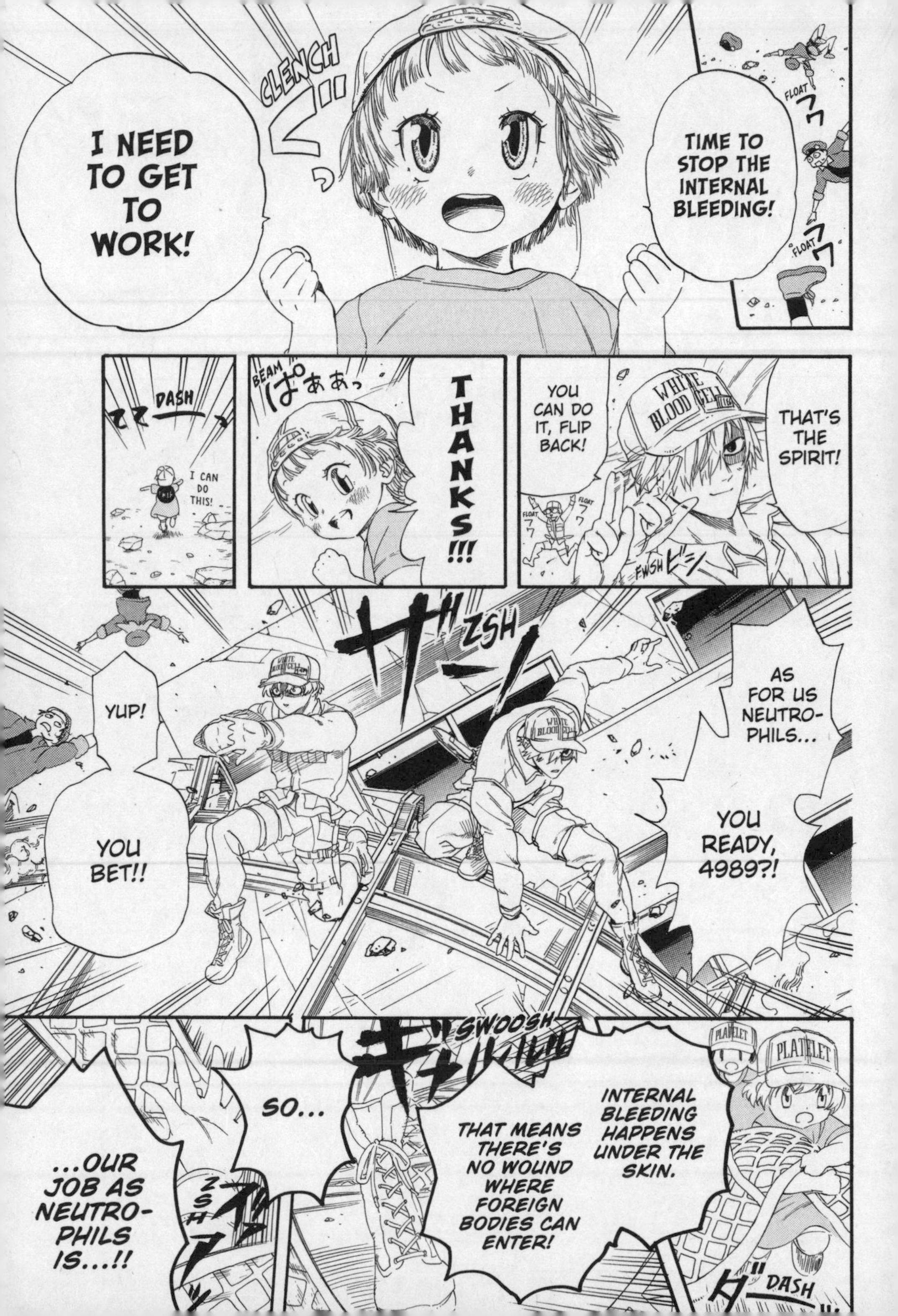
FLOAT
FLOAT
TIME TO STOP THE INTERNAL BLEEDING!
CLENCH
I NEED TO GET TO WORK!
THAT'S THE SPIRIT!
YOU CAN DO IT, FLIP BACK!
FLOAT
FLOAT
FWSH
THANKS!!!
BEAM
DASH
I CAN DO THIS!
AS FOR US NEUTROPHILS...
YOU READY, 4989?!
ZSH
YUP!
YOU BET!!
INTERNAL BLEEDING HAPPENS UNDER THE SKIN.
DASH
SWOOSH
THAT MEANS THERE'S NO WOUND WHERE FOREIGN BODIES CAN ENTER!
SO...
ZSH
...OUR JOB AS NEUTROPHILS IS...!!

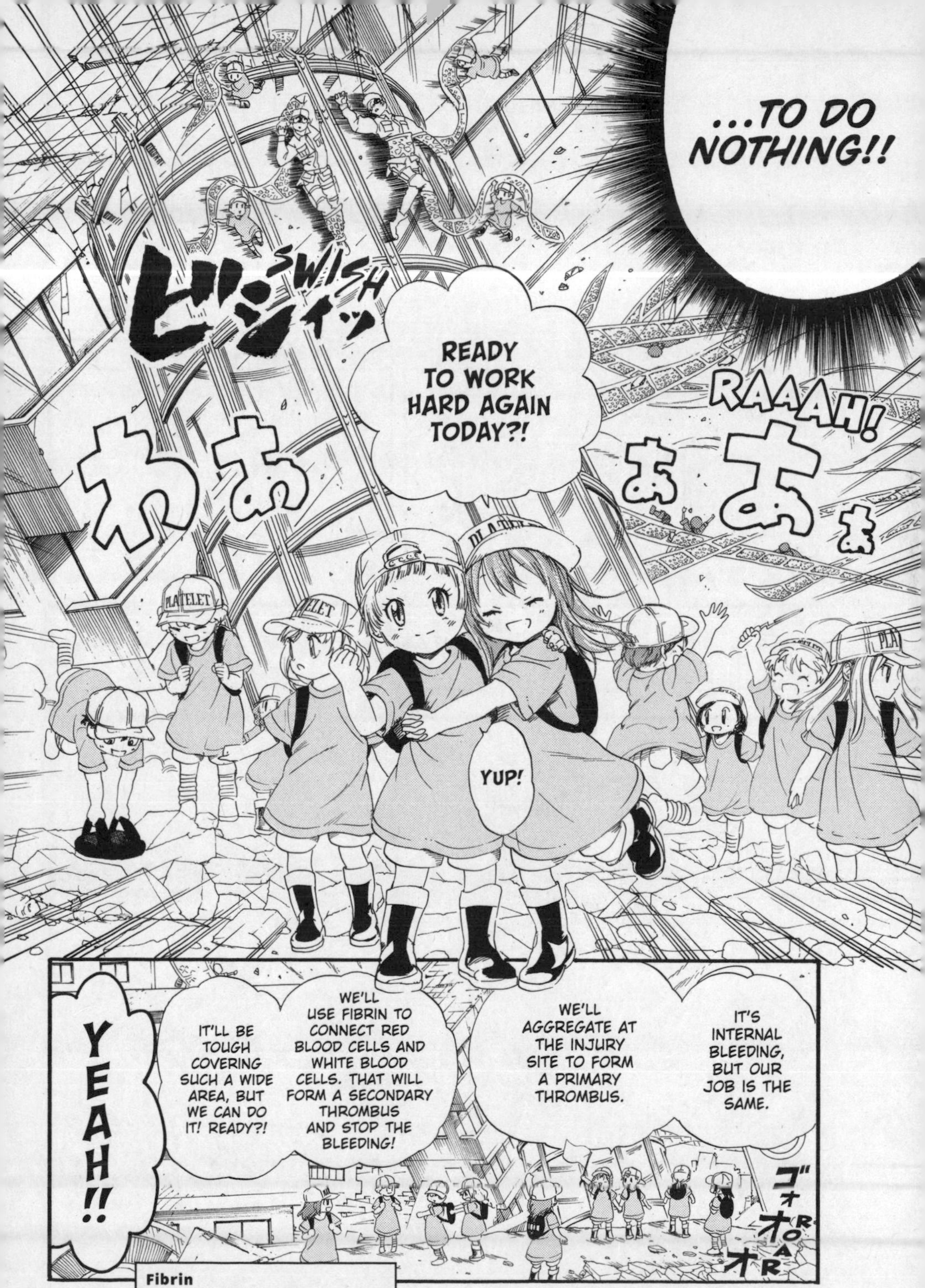

...TO DO NOTHING!!
RAAAH!
READY TO WORK HARD AGAIN TODAY?!
SWISH
YUP!
ROAR
IT'S INTERNAL BLEEDING, BUT OUR JOB IS THE SAME.
WE'LL AGGREGATE AT THE INJURY SITE TO FORM A PRIMARY THROMBUS.
WE'LL USE FIBRIN TO CONNECT RED BLOOD CELLS AND WHITE BLOOD CELLS. THAT WILL FORM A SECONDARY THROMBUS AND STOP THE BLEEDING!
IT'LL BE TOUGH COVERING SUCH A WIDE AREA, BUT WE CAN DO IT! READY?!
YEAH!!

Fibrin
Protein involved in blood coagulation.

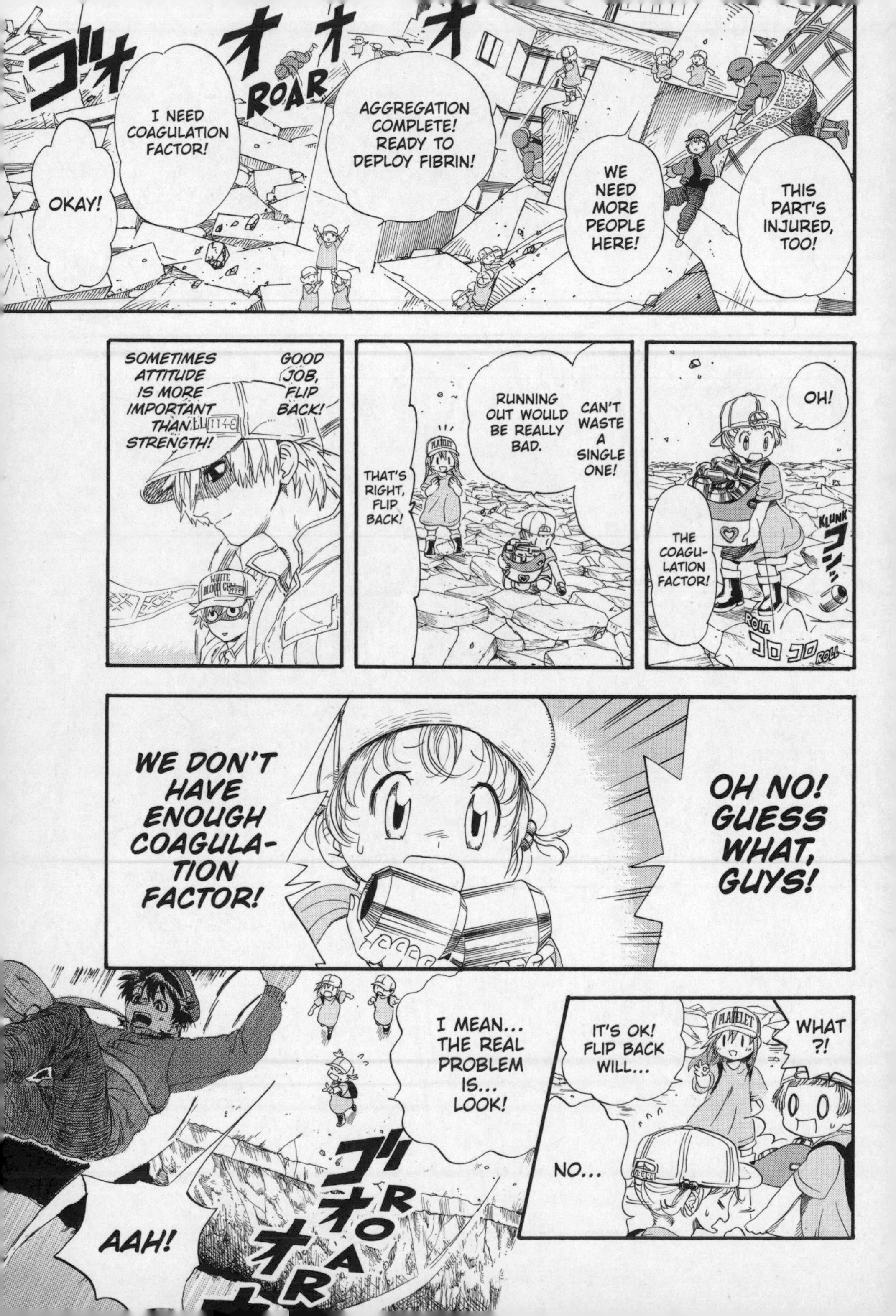
THIS PART'S INJURED, TOO!
WE NEED MORE PEOPLE HERE!
AGGREGATION COMPLETE! READY TO DEPLOY FIBRIN!
ゴオオオオ
ROAR
I NEED COAGULATION FACTOR!
OKAY!
OH!
THE COAGULATION FACTOR!
KLUNK
ROLL
ROLL
CAN'T WASTE A SINGLE ONE!
RUNNING OUT WOULD BE REALLY BAD.
THAT'S RIGHT, FLIP BACK!
GOOD JOB, FLIP BACK!
SOMETIMES ATTITUDE IS MORE IMPORTANT THAN STRENGTH!
OH NO! GUESS WHAT, GUYS!
WE DON'T HAVE ENOUGH COAGULATION FACTOR!
WHAT?!
IT'S OK! FLIP BACK WILL...
NO...
I MEAN... THE REAL PROBLEM IS... LOOK!
ROAR
AAH!

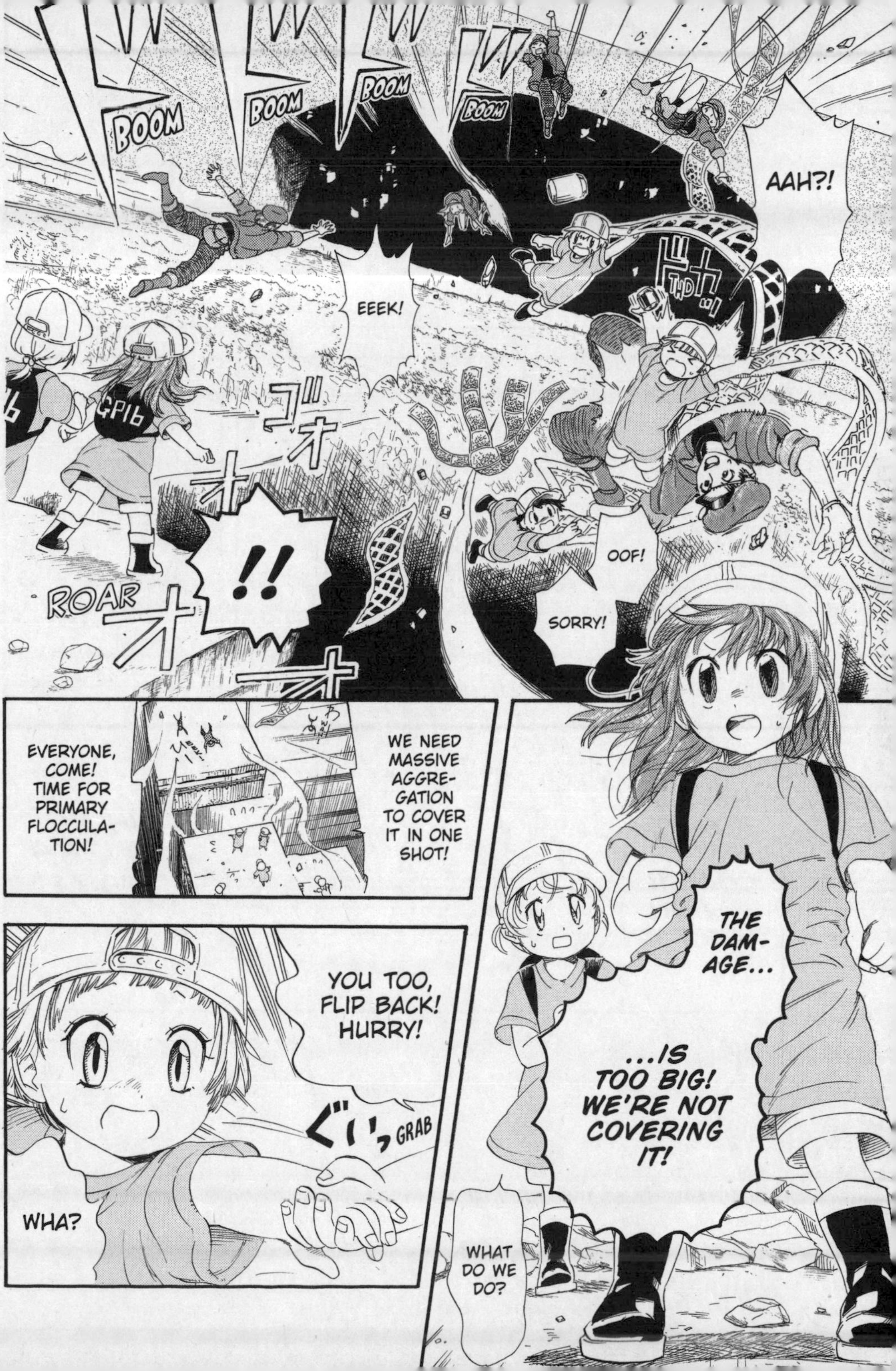
AAH?!
BOOM
BOOM
BOOM
BOOM
EEEK!
OOF!
SORRY!
!!
ROAR
THE DAMAGE...
...IS TOO BIG! WE'RE NOT COVERING IT!
WHAT DO WE DO?
WE NEED MASSIVE AGGREGATION TO COVER IT IN ONE SHOT!
EVERYONE, COME! TIME FOR PRIMARY FLOCCULATION!
YOU TOO, FLIP BACK! HURRY!
GRAB
WHA?

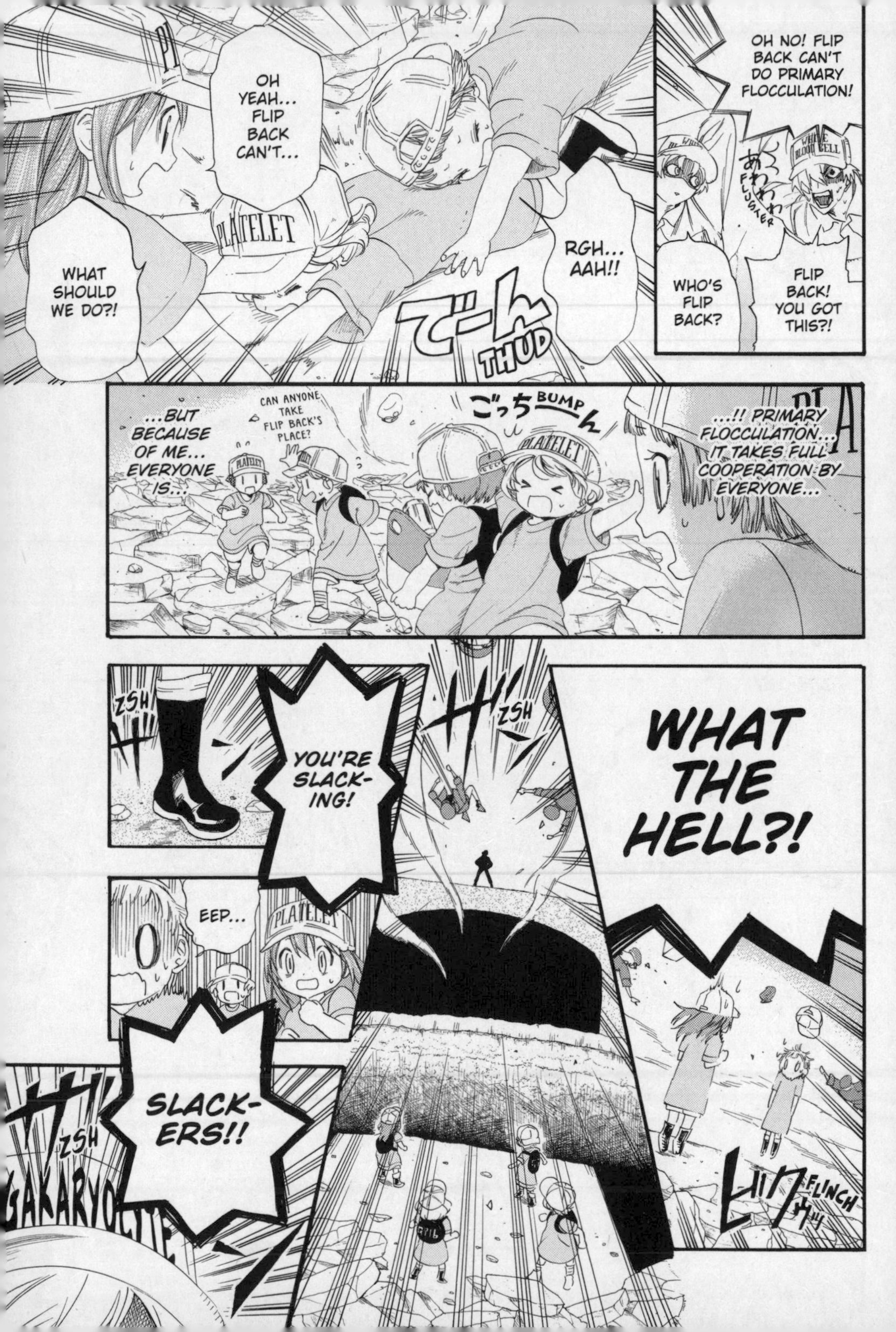
OH NO! FLIP BACK CAN'T DO PRIMARY FLOCCULATION!
あわわわ
FLUSTER
FLIP BACK! YOU GOT THIS?!
WHO'S FLIP BACK?
OH YEAH... FLIP BACK CAN'T...
RGH... AAH!!
でーん
THUD
WHAT SHOULD WE DO?!
...!! PRIMARY FLOCCULATION... IT TAKES FULL COOPERATION BY EVERYONE...
ごっちん
BUMP
CAN ANYONE TAKE FLIP BACK'S PLACE?
...BUT BECAUSE OF ME... EVERYONE IS...
WHAT THE HELL?!
ザッ
ZSH
YOU'RE SLACKING!
ザッ
ZSH
ビクッ
FLINCH
EEP...
SLACKERS!!
ザッ
ZSH

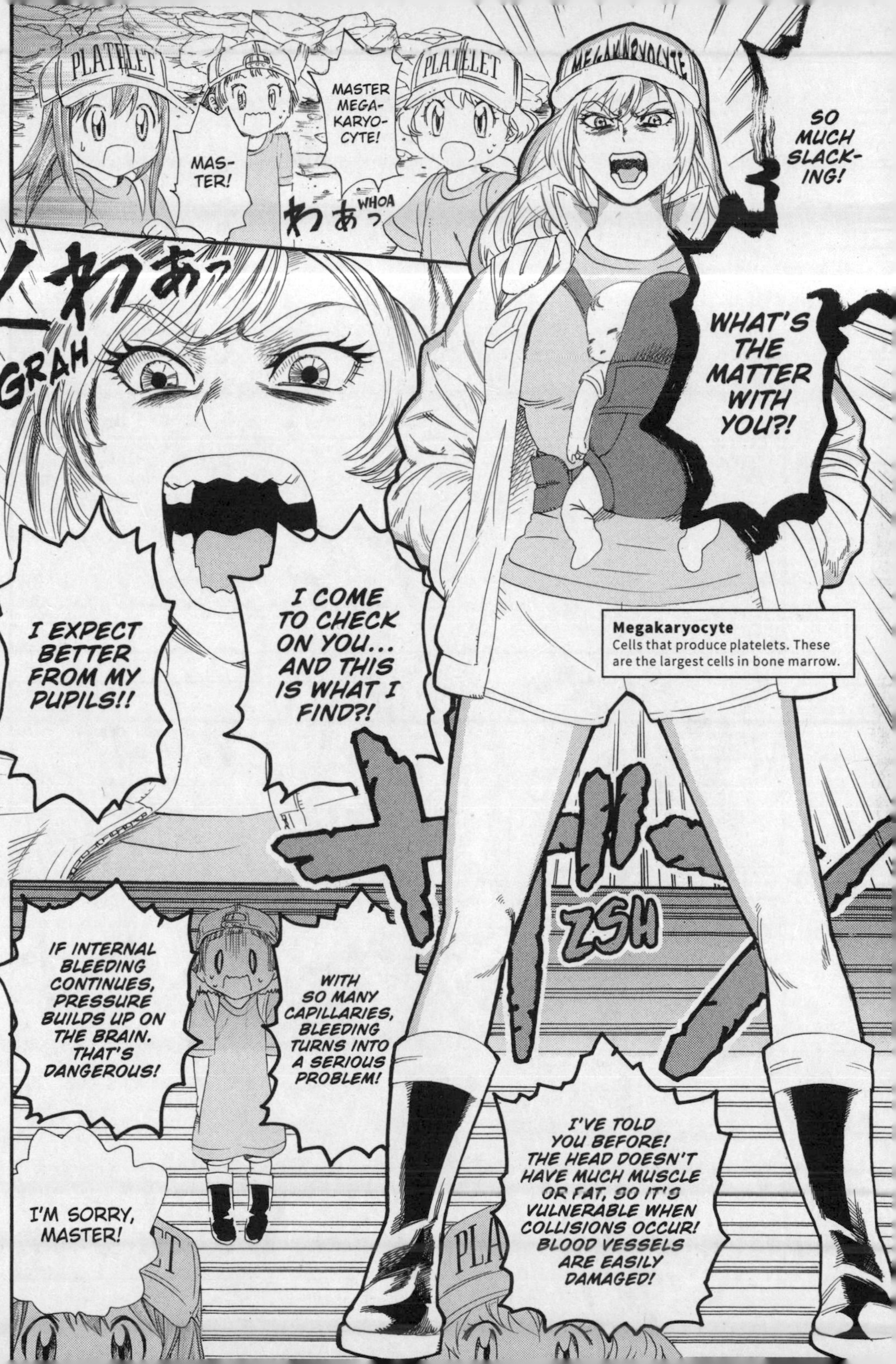
SO MUCH SLACKING!
WHAT'S THE MATTER WITH YOU?!
Megakaryocyte
Cells that produce platelets. These are the largest cells in bone marrow.
ZSH
I'VE TOLD YOU BEFORE! THE HEAD DOESN'T HAVE MUCH MUSCLE OR FAT, SO IT'S VULNERABLE WHEN COLLISIONS OCCUR! BLOOD VESSELS ARE EASILY DAMAGED!
MASTER MEGA-KARYO-CYTE!
MAS-TER!
わあっ WHOA
わあっ GRAH
I COME TO CHECK ON YOU... AND THIS IS WHAT I FIND?!
I EXPECT BETTER FROM MY PUPILS!!
WITH SO MANY CAPILLARIES, BLEEDING TURNS INTO A SERIOUS PROBLEM!
IF INTERNAL BLEEDING CONTINUES, PRESSURE BUILDS UP ON THE BRAIN. THAT'S DANGEROUS!
I'M SORRY, MASTER!

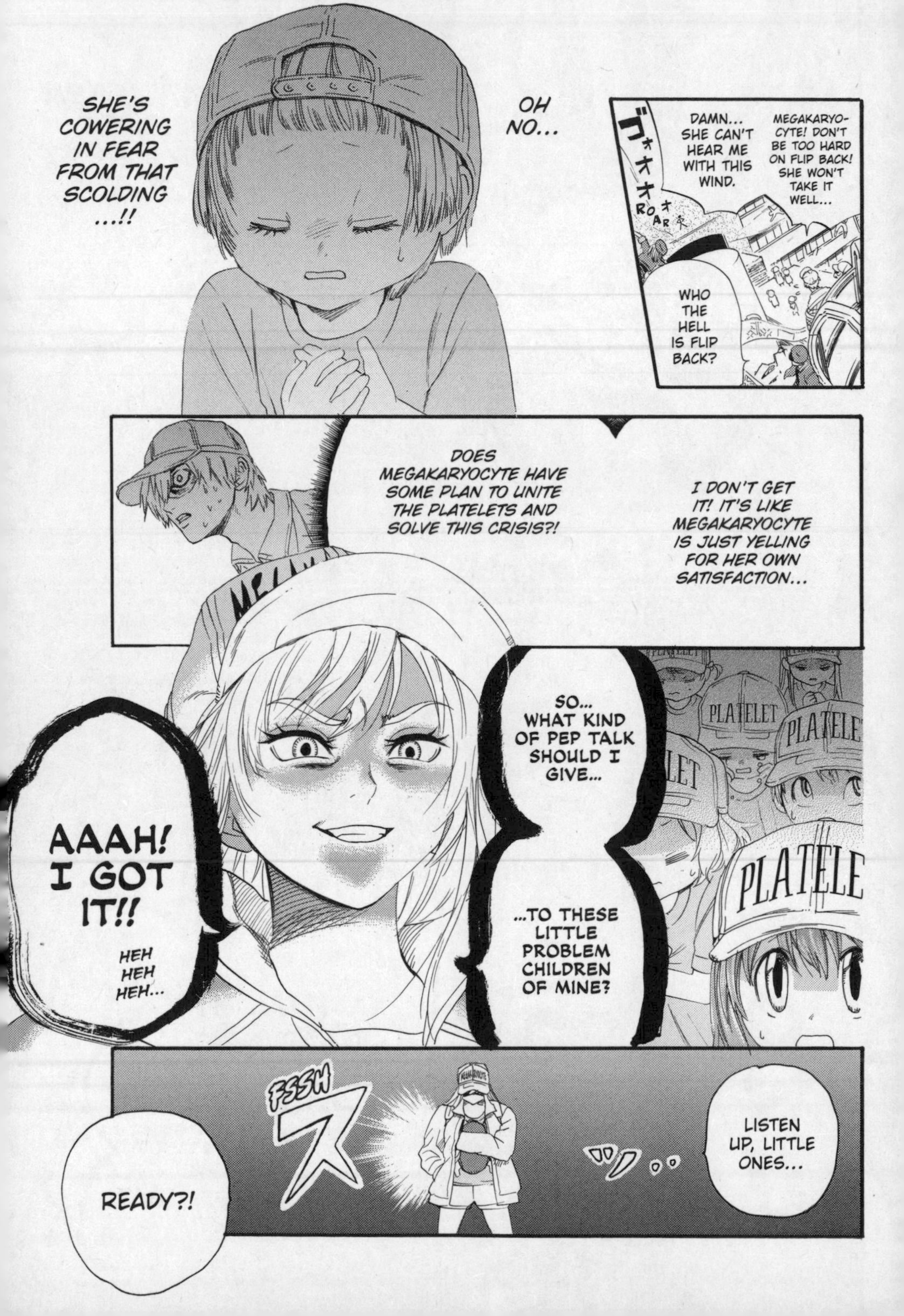
MEGAKARYOCYTE! DON'T BE TOO HARD ON FLIP BACK! SHE WON'T TAKE IT WELL...
DAMN... SHE CAN'T HEAR ME WITH THIS WIND.
ゴォォォ ROAR
WHO THE HELL IS FLIP BACK?
OH NO...
SHE'S COWERING IN FEAR FROM THAT SCOLDING ...!!
I DON'T GET IT! IT'S LIKE MEGAKARYOCYTE IS JUST YELLING FOR HER OWN SATISFACTION...
DOES MEGAKARYOCYTE HAVE SOME PLAN TO UNITE THE PLATELETS AND SOLVE THIS CRISIS?!
SO... WHAT KIND OF PEP TALK SHOULD I GIVE...
...TO THESE LITTLE PROBLEM CHILDREN OF MINE?
AAAH! I GOT IT!!
HEH HEH HEH...
LISTEN UP, LITTLE ONES...
FSSH ス
READY?!

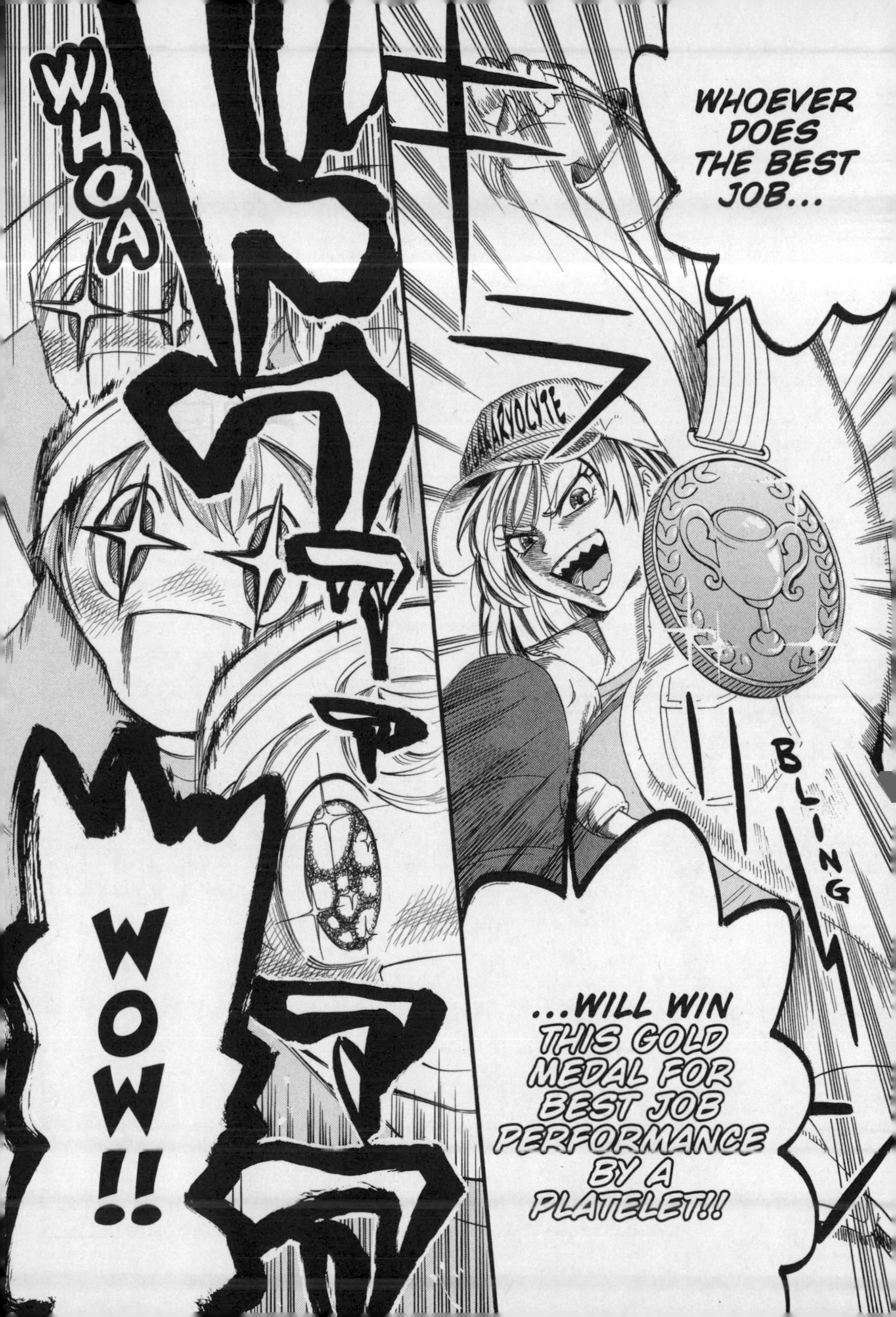
WHOEVER DOES THE BEST JOB...
BLING
...WILL WIN THIS GOLD MEDAL FOR BEST JOB PERFORMANCE BY A PLATELET!!
WHOA
WOW!!

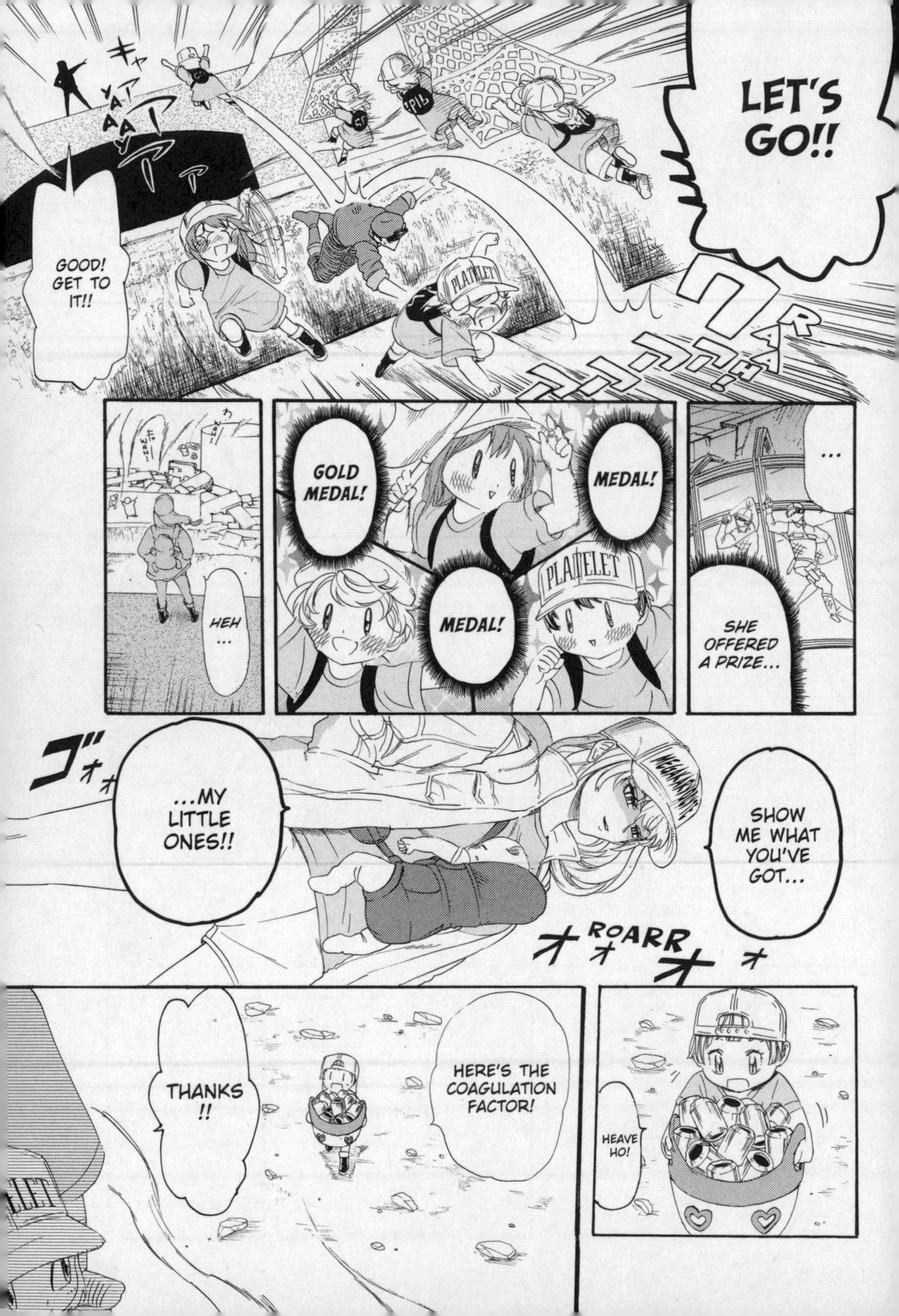
LET'S GO!!
RAAH!
GOOD! GET TO IT!!
YAAAAY!
...
SHE OFFERED A PRIZE...
MEDAL!
GOLD MEDAL!
MEDAL!
WAH!
HEH...
SHOW ME WHAT YOU'VE GOT...
...MY LITTLE ONES!!
ROARR
HEAVE HO!
HERE'S THE COAGULATION FACTOR!
THANKS!!

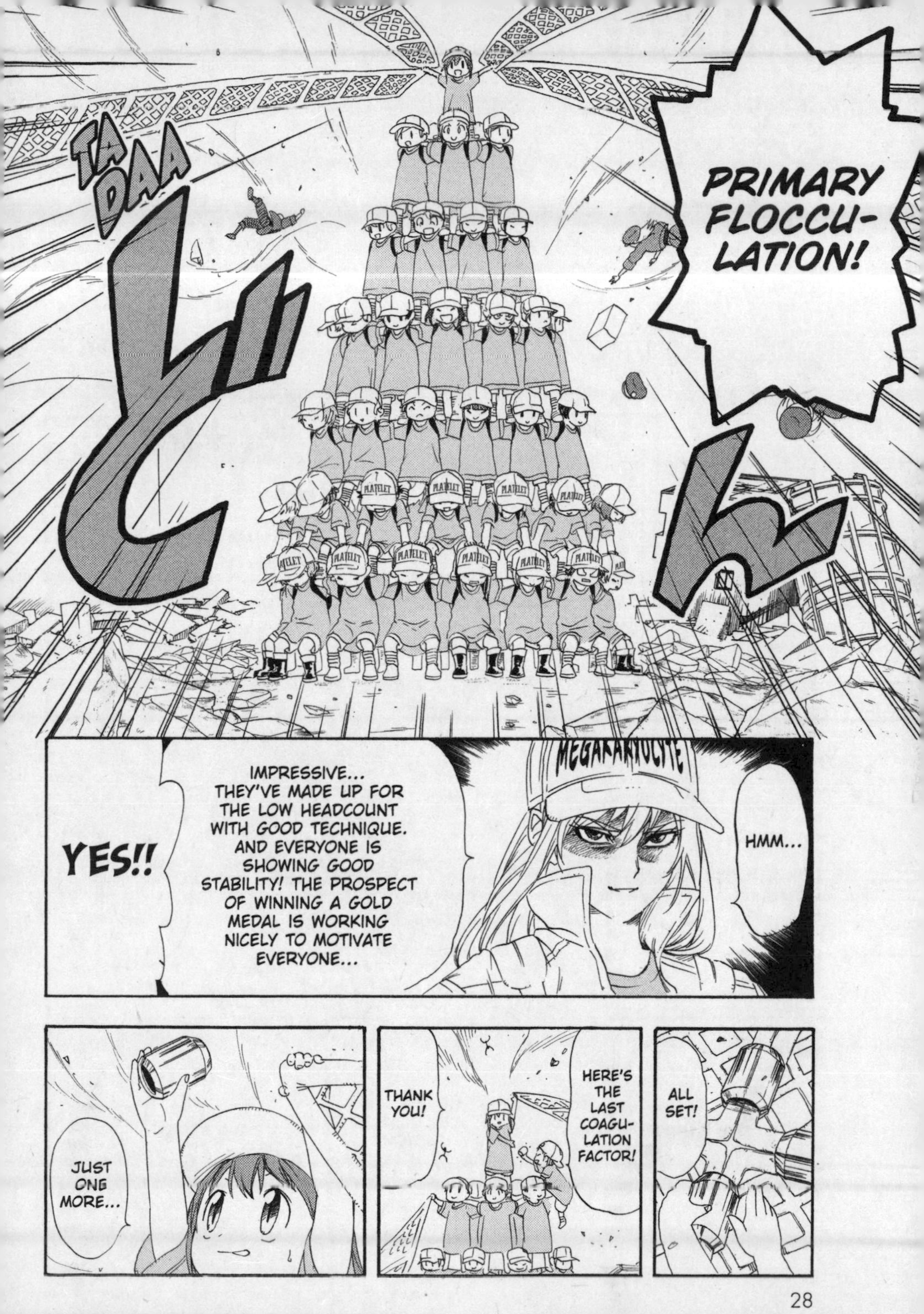
PRIMARY FLOCCU-LATION!
TA DAA
HMM...
IMPRESSIVE... THEY'VE MADE UP FOR THE LOW HEADCOUNT WITH GOOD TECHNIQUE. AND EVERYONE IS SHOWING GOOD STABILITY! THE PROSPECT OF WINNING A GOLD MEDAL IS WORKING NICELY TO MOTIVATE EVERYONE...
YES!!
ALL SET!
HERE'S THE LAST COAGU-LATION FACTOR!
THANK YOU!
JUST ONE MORE...

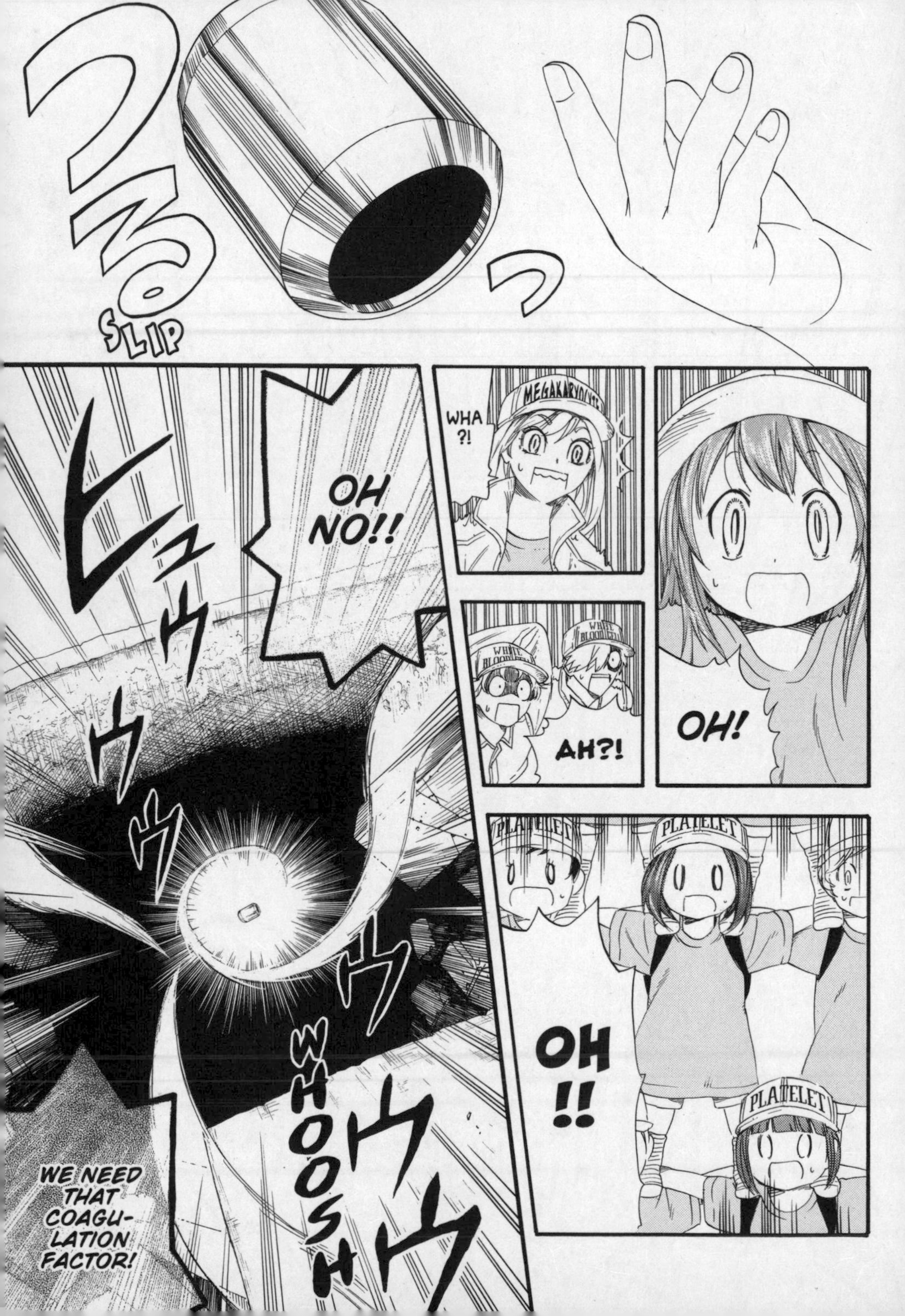
SLIP
OH!
WHA ?!
AH?!
OH !!
OH NO!!
WHOOSH
WE NEED THAT COAGU-LATION FACTOR!

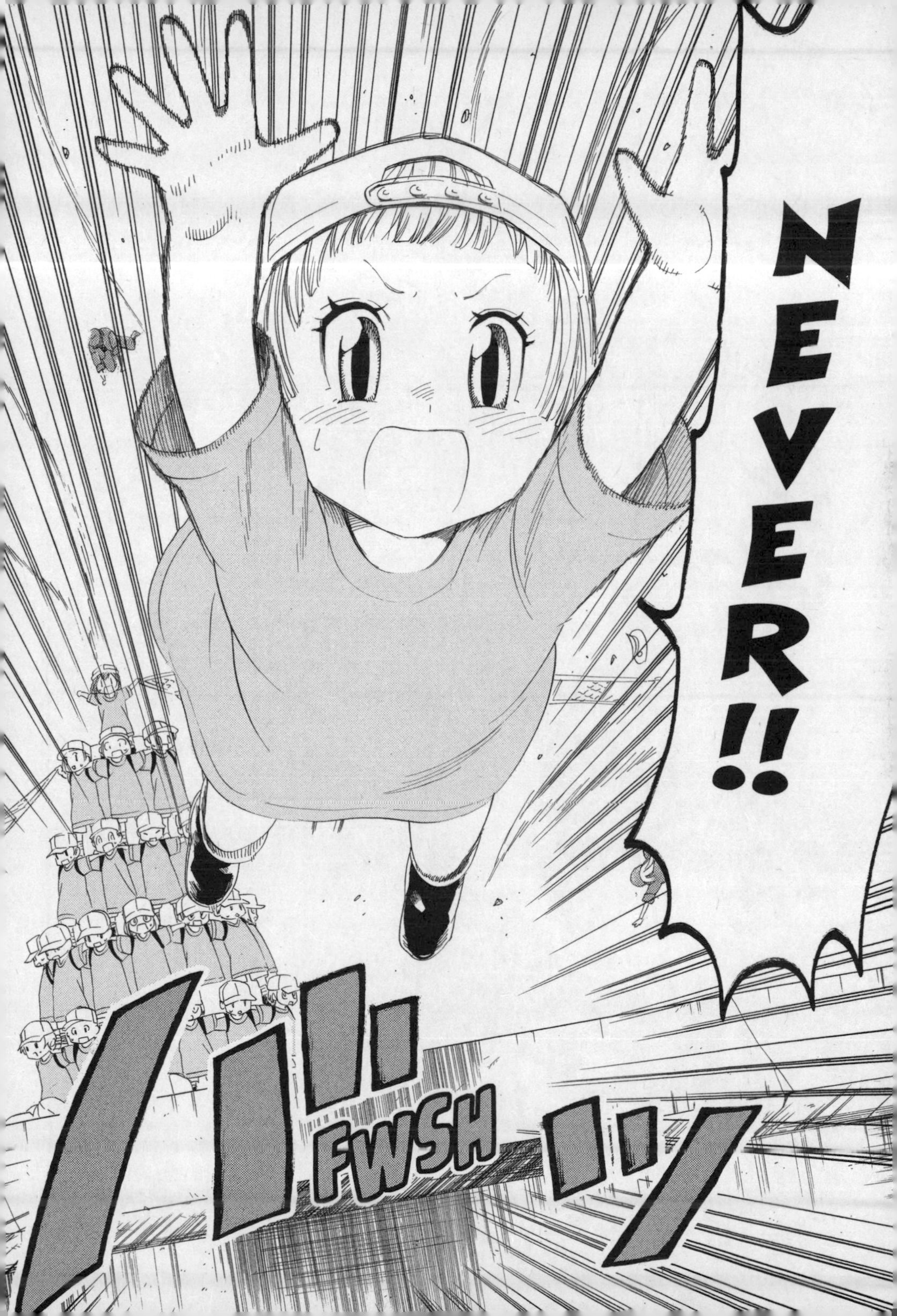
NEVER!!
FWSH

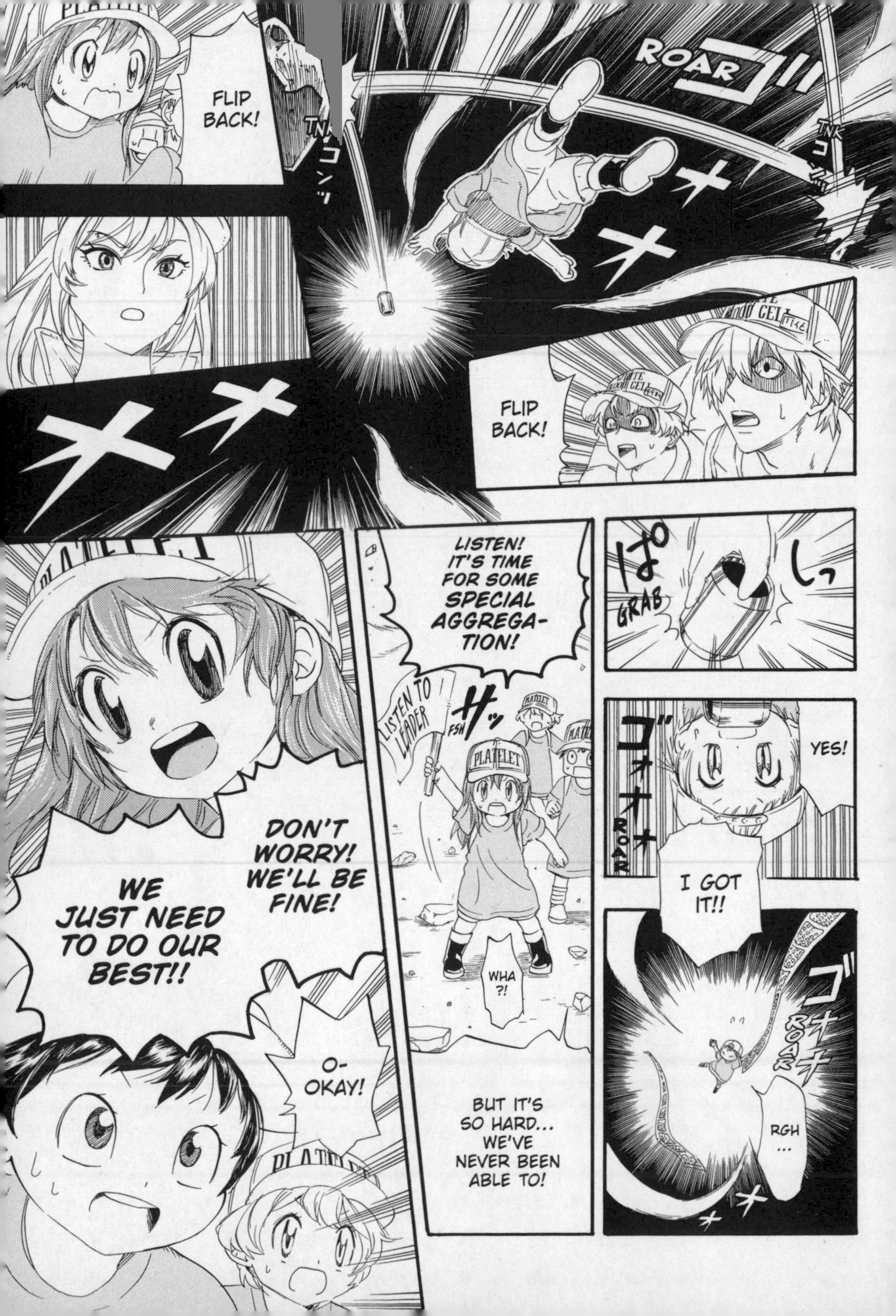
ROAR
TNK
TNK
FLIP BACK!
FLIP BACK!
GRAB
ROAR
YES!
I GOT IT!!
ROAR
RGH ...
LISTEN! IT'S TIME FOR SOME SPECIAL AGGREGA-TION!
LISTEN TO LEADER
FSH
WHA ?!
BUT IT'S SO HARD... WE'VE NEVER BEEN ABLE TO!
DON'T WORRY! WE'LL BE FINE!
WE JUST NEED TO DO OUR BEST!!
O-OKAY!

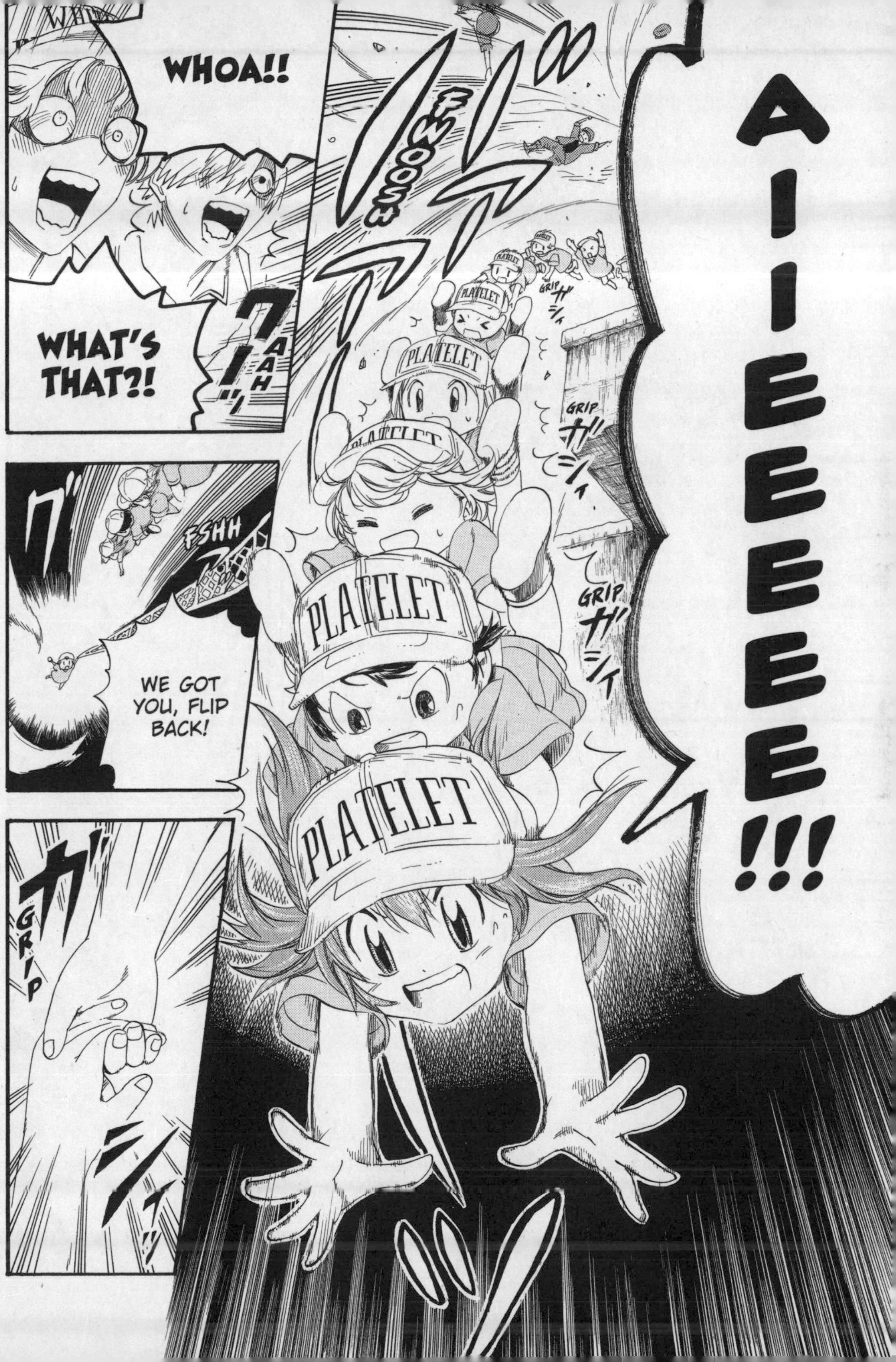
AIIEEEEE!!!
FWOOSH
GRIP
GRIP
GRIP
WHOA!!
WHAT'S THAT?!
AAH
FSHH
WE GOT YOU, FLIP BACK!
GRIP

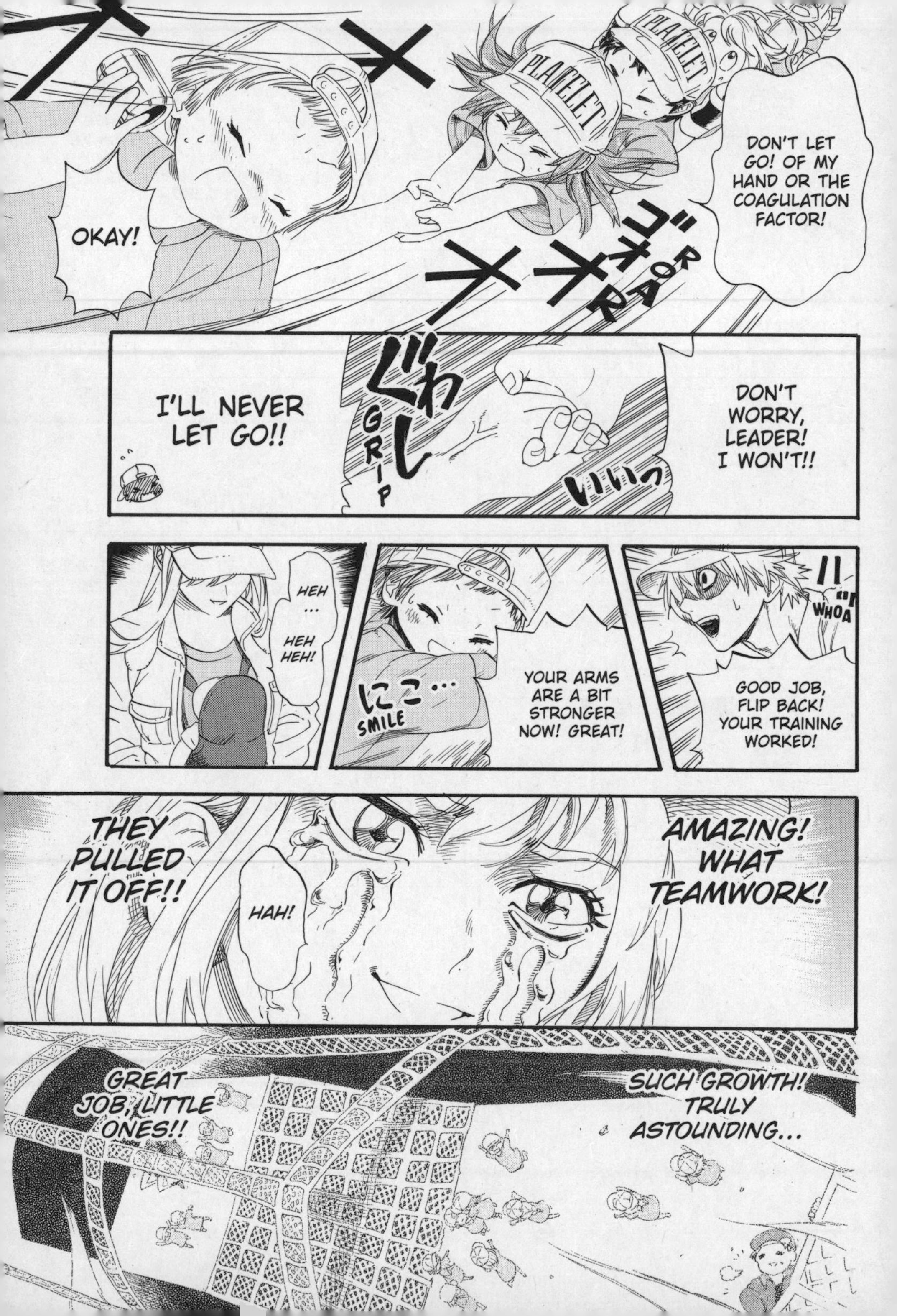
DON'T LET GO! OF MY HAND OR THE COAGULATION FACTOR!
ゴオオ
ROAR
OKAY!
DON'T WORRY, LEADER! I WON'T!!
いいっ
ぐわし
GRIP
I'LL NEVER LET GO!!
!!
WHOA
GOOD JOB, FLIP BACK! YOUR TRAINING WORKED!
YOUR ARMS ARE A BIT STRONGER NOW! GREAT!
にこ…
SMILE
HEH ... HEH HEH!
AMAZING! WHAT TEAMWORK!
HAH!
THEY PULLED IT OFF!!
SUCH GROWTH! TRULY ASTOUNDING...
GREAT JOB, LITTLE ONES!!

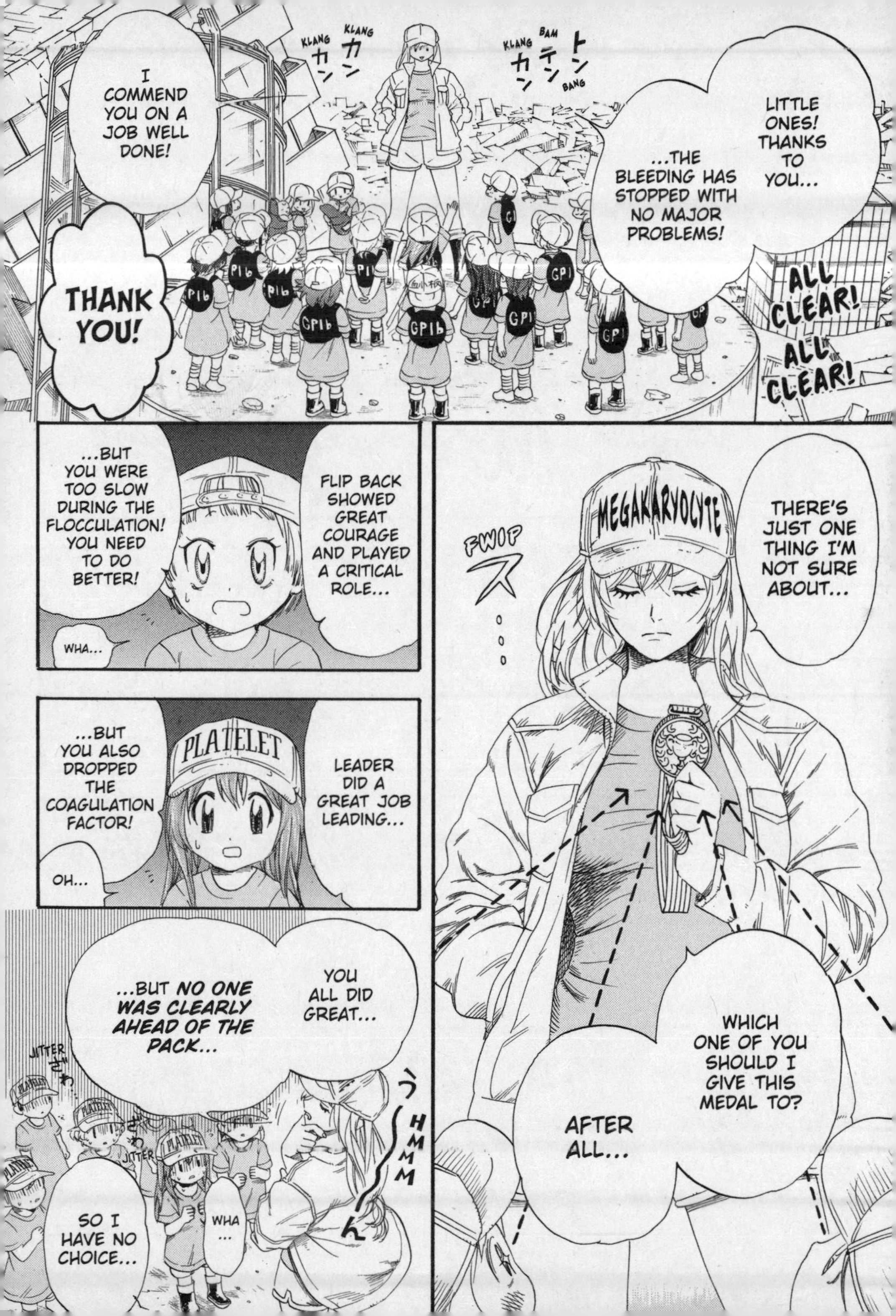
LITTLE ONES! THANKS TO YOU...
...THE BLEEDING HAS STOPPED WITH NO MAJOR PROBLEMS!
BAM
BANG
KLANG
ALL CLEAR!
ALL CLEAR!
KLANG
KLANG
I COMMEND YOU ON A JOB WELL DONE!
THANK YOU!
THERE'S JUST ONE THING I'M NOT SURE ABOUT...
FWIP
WHICH ONE OF YOU SHOULD I GIVE THIS MEDAL TO?
AFTER ALL...
FLIP BACK SHOWED GREAT COURAGE AND PLAYED A CRITICAL ROLE...
...BUT YOU WERE TOO SLOW DURING THE FLOCCULATION! YOU NEED TO DO BETTER!
WHA...
LEADER DID A GREAT JOB LEADING...
...BUT YOU ALSO DROPPED THE COAGULATION FACTOR!
OH...
YOU ALL DID GREAT...
...BUT NO ONE WAS CLEARLY AHEAD OF THE PACK...
HMMM
JITTER
JITTER
WHA ...
SO I HAVE NO CHOICE...

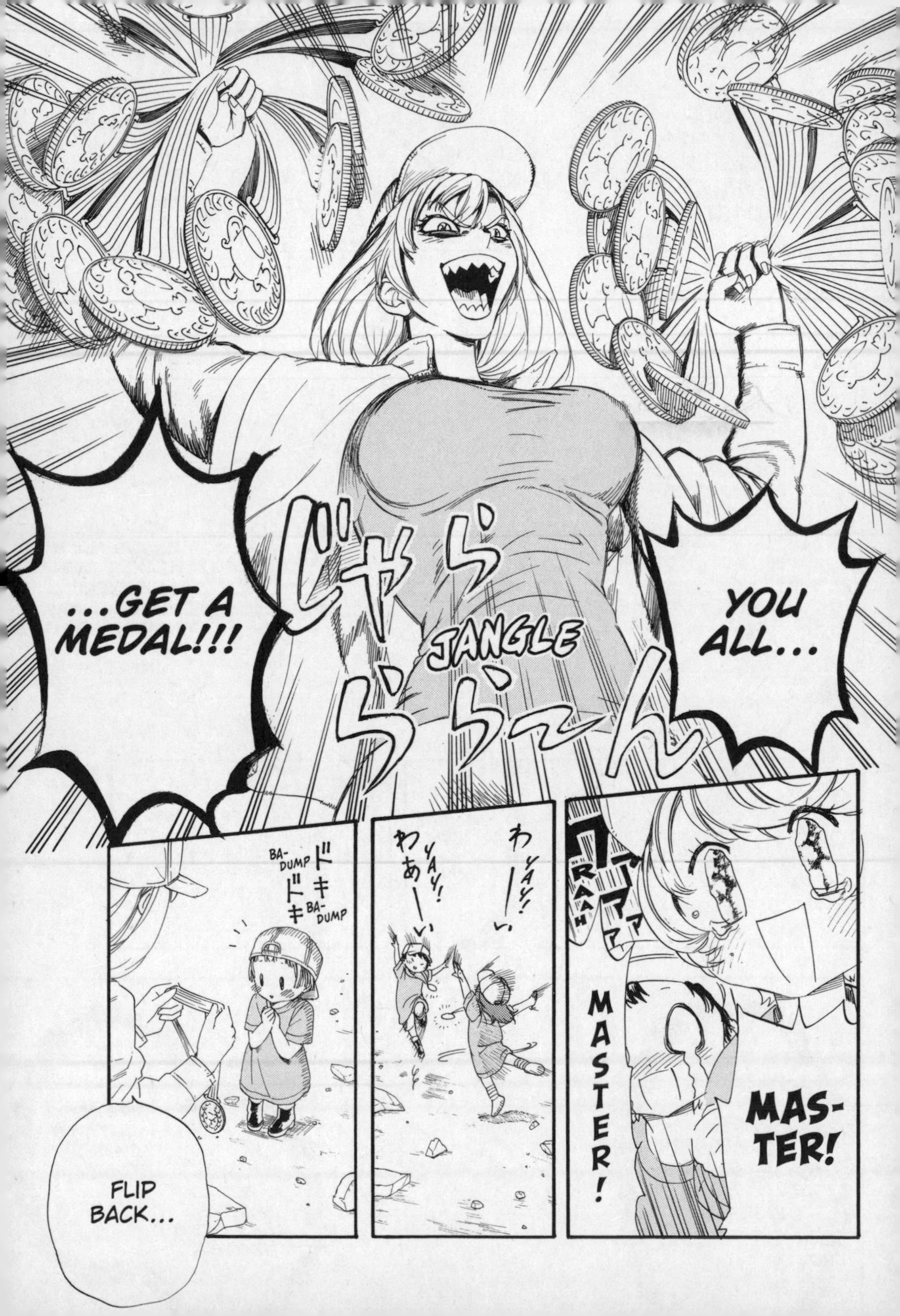
YOU ALL...
JANGLE
...GET A MEDAL!!!
MAS-TER!
MASTER!
RAAH
アアア
わーい
YAY!
わあーい
YAY!
ドキドキ
BA-DUMP BA-DUMP
FLIP BACK...

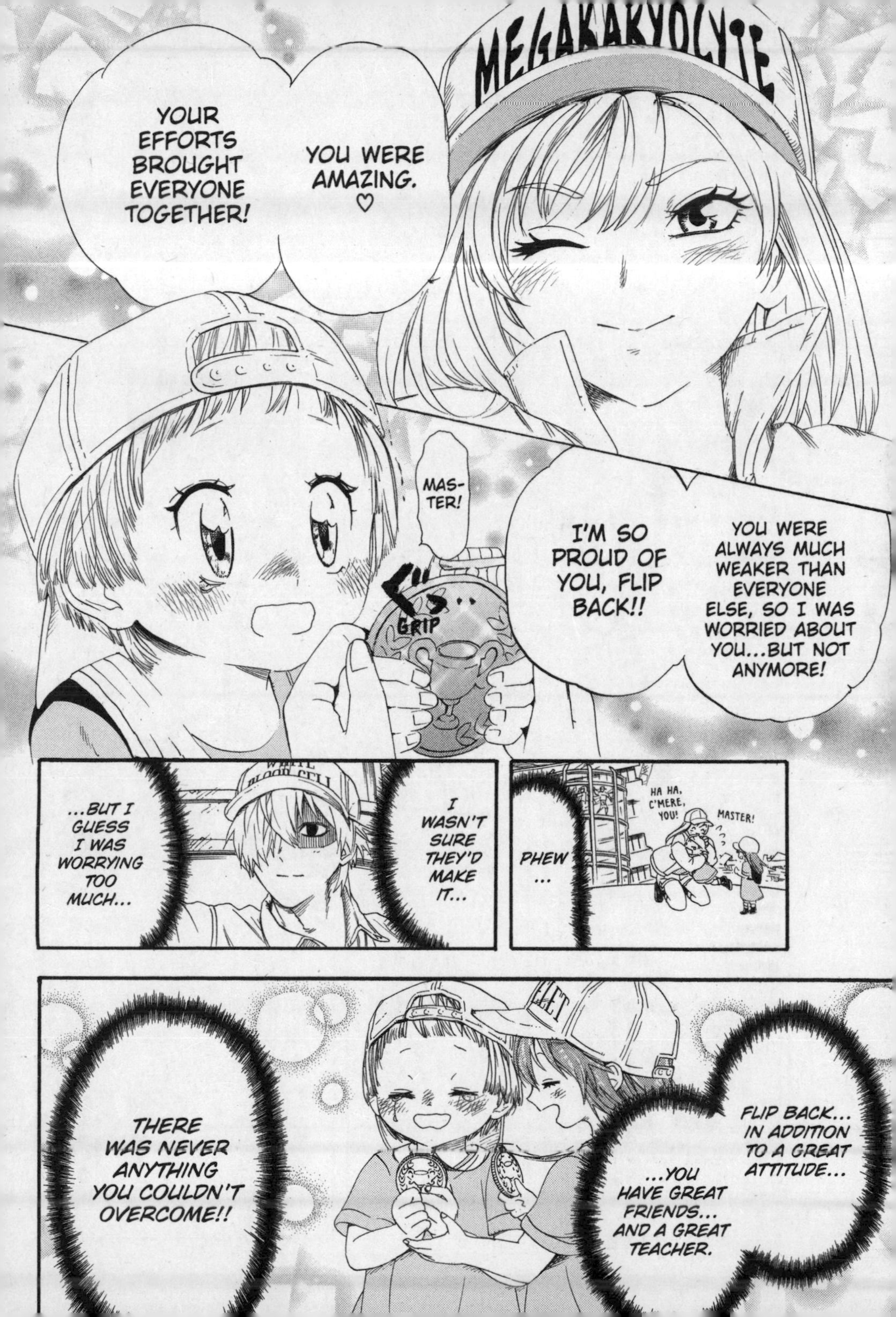
YOUR EFFORTS BROUGHT EVERYONE TOGETHER! YOU WERE AMAZING. ♡
I'M SO PROUD OF YOU, FLIP BACK!! YOU WERE ALWAYS MUCH WEAKER THAN EVERYONE ELSE, SO I WAS WORRIED ABOUT YOU...BUT NOT ANYMORE!
MAS-TER!
GRIP
PHEW...
HA HA, C'MERE, YOU!
MASTER!
I WASN'T SURE THEY'D MAKE IT...
...BUT I GUESS I WAS WORRYING TOO MUCH...
FLIP BACK... IN ADDITION TO A GREAT ATTITUDE...
...YOU HAVE GREAT FRIENDS... AND A GREAT TEACHER.
THERE WAS NEVER ANYTHING YOU COULDN'T OVERCOME!!

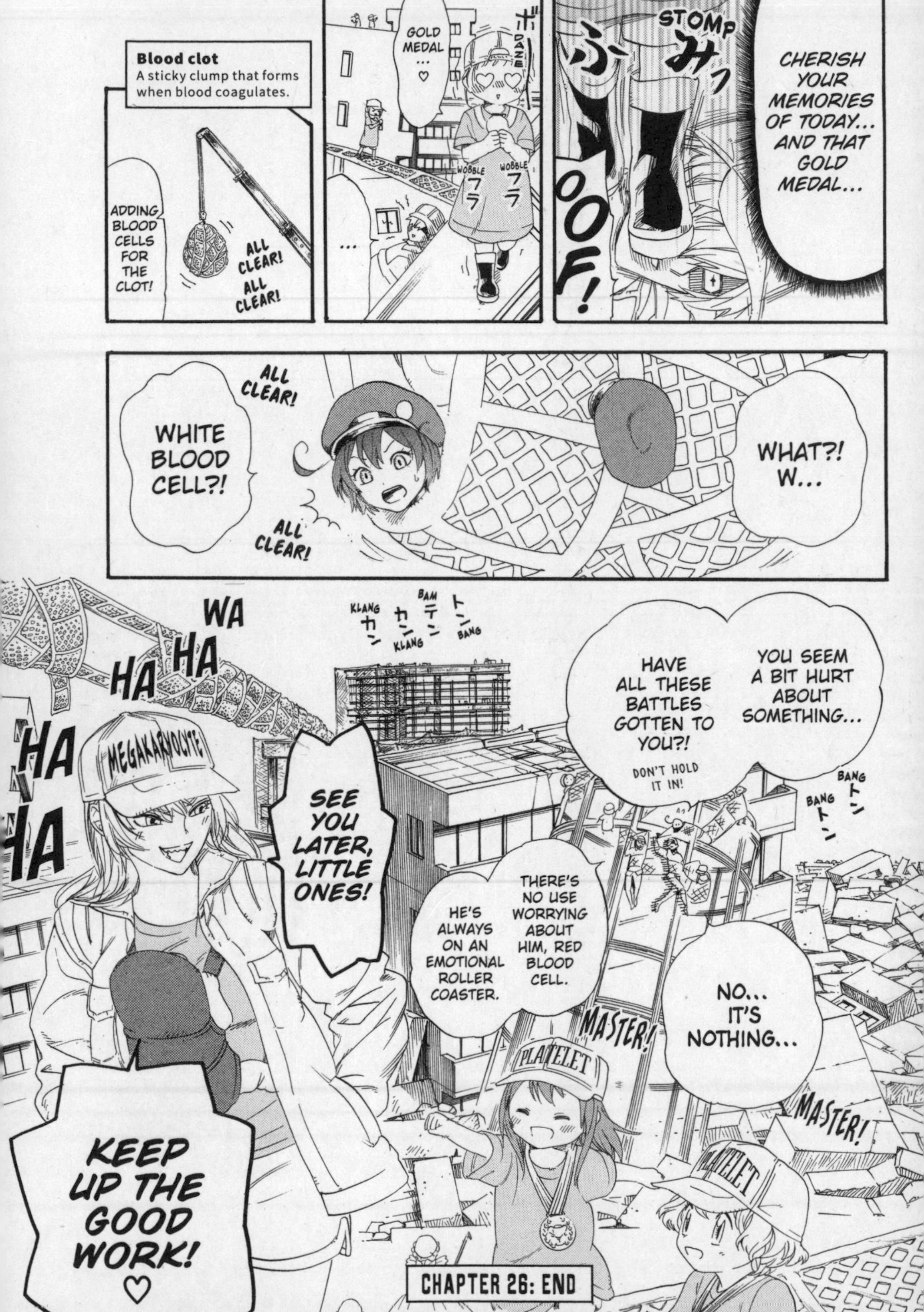
STOMP ふみっ
CHERISH YOUR MEMORIES OF TODAY... AND THAT GOLD MEDAL...
OOF!
DAZE ボ
GOLD MEDAL... ♡
WOBBLE フラ WOBBLE フラ
...
Blood clot
A sticky clump that forms when blood coagulates.
ADDING BLOOD CELLS FOR THE CLOT!
ALL CLEAR!
ALL CLEAR!
WHAT?! W...
ALL CLEAR!
WHITE BLOOD CELL?!
ALL CLEAR!
YOU SEEM A BIT HURT ABOUT SOMETHING...
HAVE ALL THESE BATTLES GOTTEN TO YOU?!
DON'T HOLD IT IN!
BANG トン
BANG トン
NO... IT'S NOTHING...
THERE'S NO USE WORRYING ABOUT HIM, RED BLOOD CELL.
HE'S ALWAYS ON AN EMOTIONAL ROLLER COASTER.
MASTER!
MASTER!
BAM テン BANG トン
KLANG カン KLANG カン
SEE YOU LATER, LITTLE ONES!
WA HA HA HA HA
KEEP UP THE GOOD WORK! ♡

CHAPTER 26: END

Medical Advisor: Tomoyuki Harada

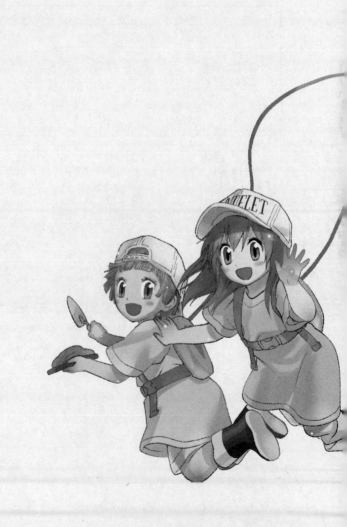

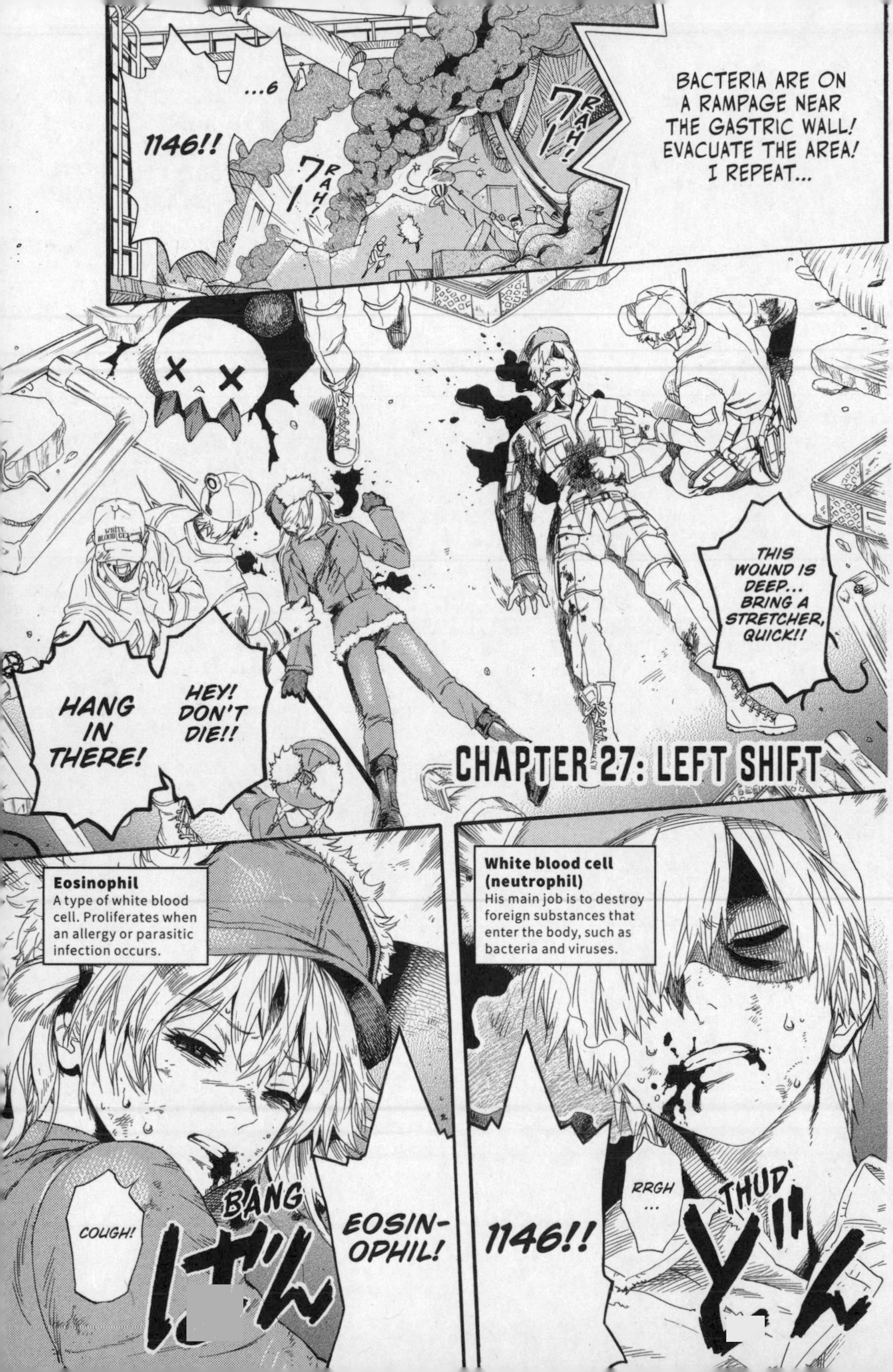
BACTERIA ARE ON A RAMPAGE NEAR THE GASTRIC WALL! EVACUATE THE AREA! I REPEAT...
RAH!
RAH!
...6
1146!!
THIS WOUND IS DEEP... BRING A STRETCHER, QUICK!!
CHAPTER 27: LEFT SHIFT
HEY! DON'T DIE!!
HANG IN THERE!
White blood cell (neutrophil)
His main job is to destroy foreign substances that enter the body, such as bacteria and viruses.
RRGH ...
THUD
1146!!
Eosinophil
A type of white blood cell. Proliferates when an allergy or parasitic infection occurs.
EOSIN-OPHIL!
BANG
COUGH!

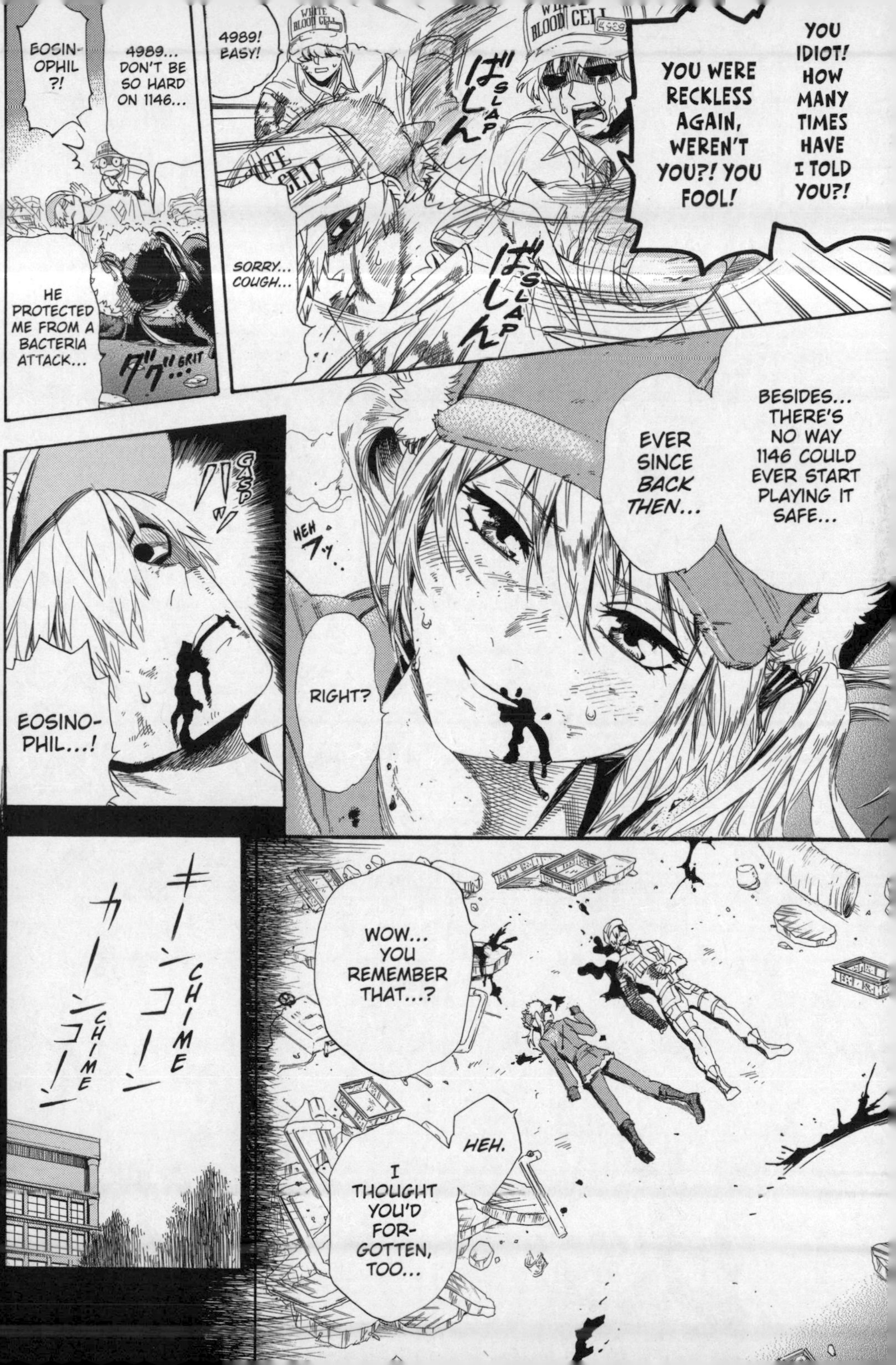
YOU IDIOT! HOW MANY TIMES HAVE I TOLD YOU?!
YOU WERE RECKLESS AGAIN, WEREN'T YOU?! YOU FOOL!
ばしん SLAP
ばしん SLAP
SORRY... COUGH...
4989! BASY!
4989... DON'T BE SO HARD ON 1146...
EOSINOPHIL?!
HE PROTECTED ME FROM A BACTERIA ATTACK...
グッ GRIT
BESIDES... THERE'S NO WAY 1146 COULD EVER START PLAYING IT SAFE...
EVER SINCE BACK THEN...
HEH フッ...
RIGHT?
ハッ GASP
EOSINOPHIL...!
WOW... YOU REMEMBER THAT...?
HEH.
I THOUGHT YOU'D FORGOTTEN, TOO...
キーンコーン CHIME
カーンコーン CHIME

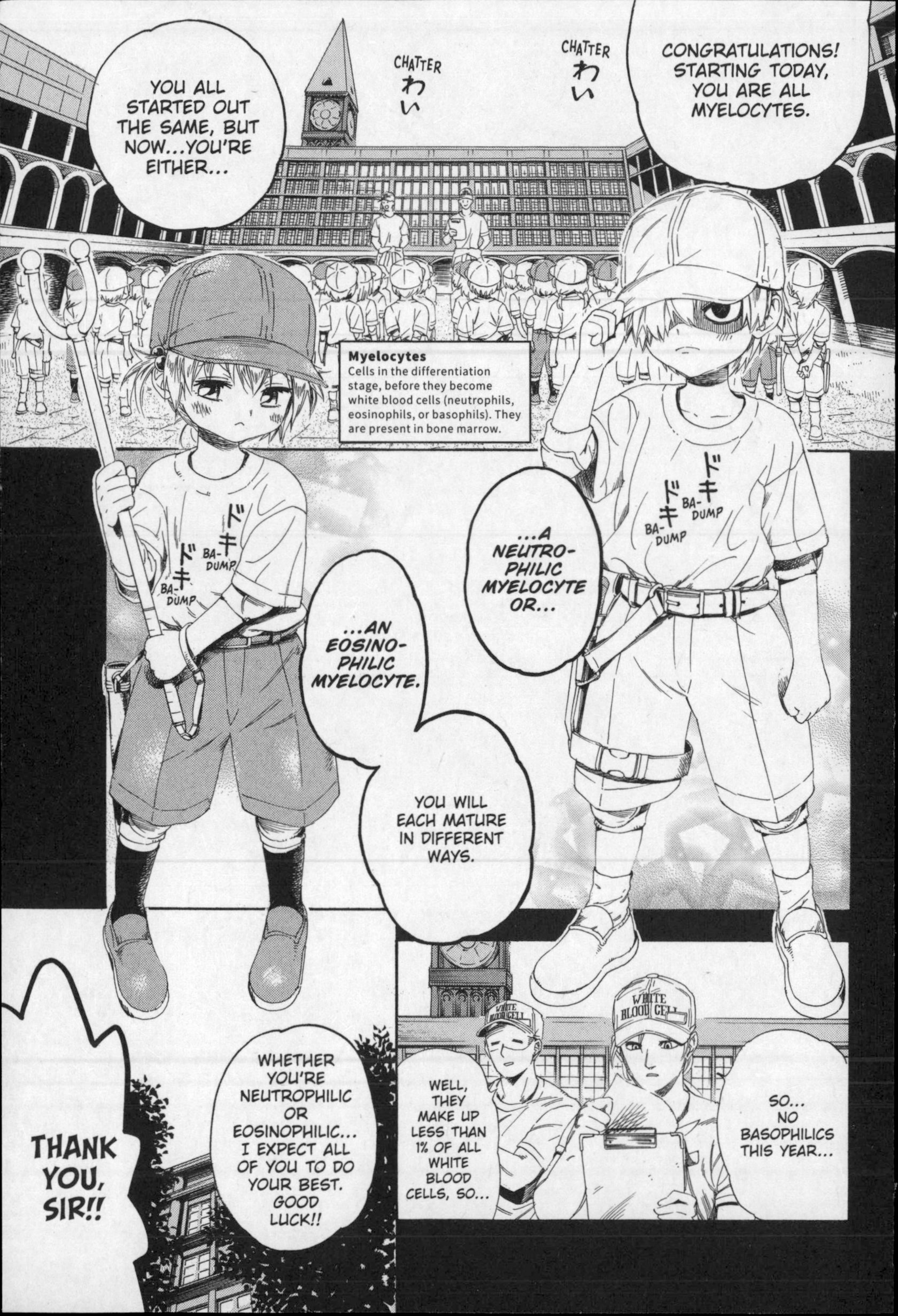
CONGRATULATIONS! STARTING TODAY, YOU ARE ALL MYELOCYTES.
CHATTER わい
CHATTER わい
YOU ALL STARTED OUT THE SAME, BUT NOW...YOU'RE EITHER...
Myelocytes
Cells in the differentiation stage, before they become white blood cells (neutrophils, eosinophils, or basophils). They are present in bone marrow.
ドキ BA-DUMP
ドキ BA-DUMP
...A NEUTROPHILIC MYELOCYTE OR...
...AN EOSINOPHILIC MYELOCYTE.
ドキ BA-DUMP
ドキ BA-DUMP
YOU WILL EACH MATURE IN DIFFERENT WAYS.
WHITE BLOOD CELL
WHITE BLOOD CELL
SO... NO BASOPHILICS THIS YEAR...
WELL, THEY MAKE UP LESS THAN 1% OF ALL WHITE BLOOD CELLS, SO...
WHETHER YOU'RE NEUTROPHILIC OR EOSINOPHILIC... I EXPECT ALL OF YOU TO DO YOUR BEST. GOOD LUCK!!
THANK YOU, SIR!!

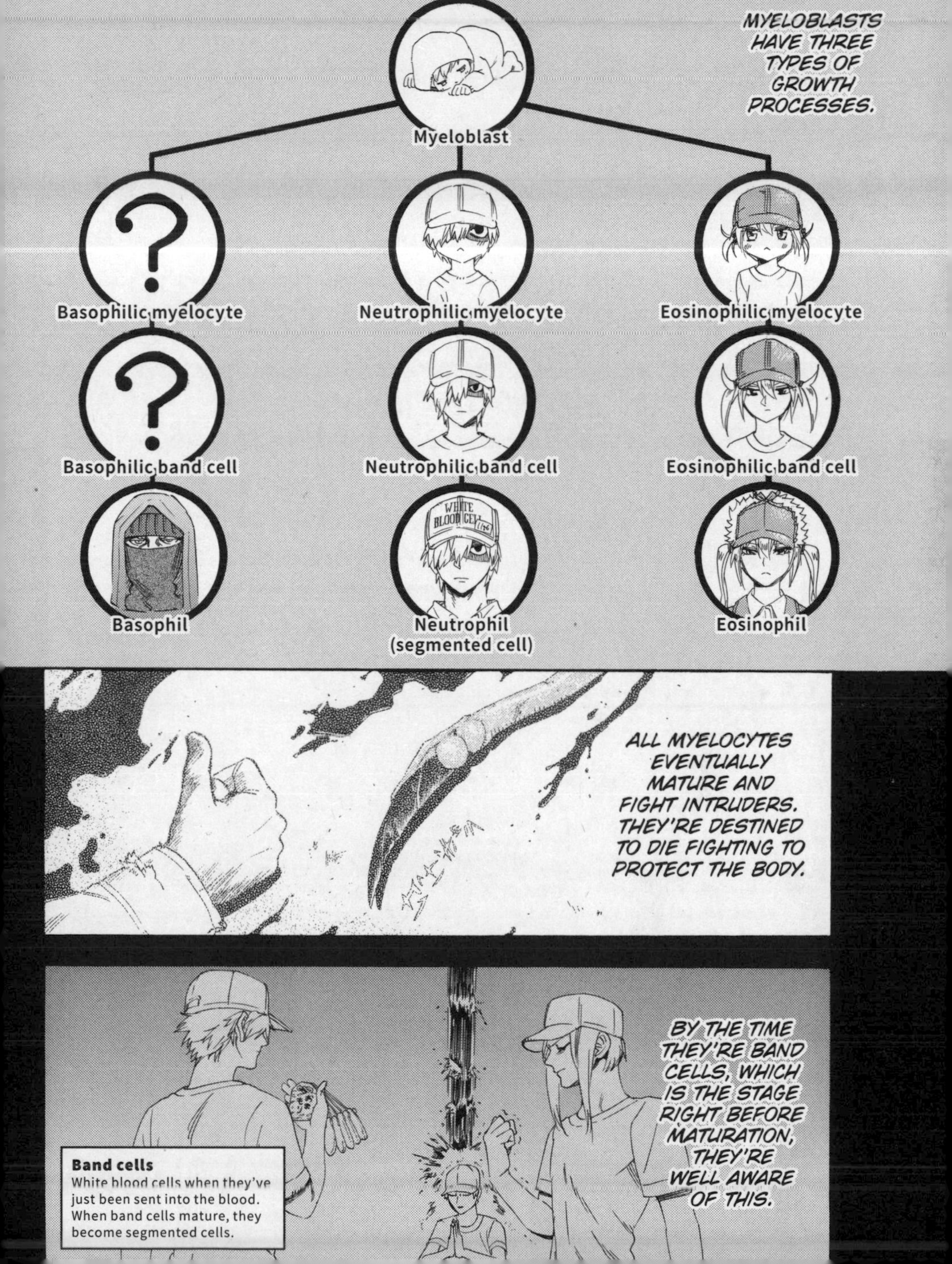
MYELOBLASTS HAVE THREE TYPES OF GROWTH PROCESSES.
Myeloblast
Basophilic myelocyte
Neutrophilic myelocyte
Eosinophilic myelocyte
Basophilic band cell
Neutrophilic band cell
Eosinophilic band cell
Basophil
WHITE BLOOD CELL 1146
Neutrophil (segmented cell)
Eosinophil
ALL MYELOCYTES EVENTUALLY MATURE AND FIGHT INTRUDERS. THEY'RE DESTINED TO DIE FIGHTING TO PROTECT THE BODY.
BY THE TIME THEY'RE BAND CELLS, WHICH IS THE STAGE RIGHT BEFORE MATURATION, THEY'RE WELL AWARE OF THIS.
Band cells
White blood cells when they've just been sent into the blood. When band cells mature, they become segmented cells.

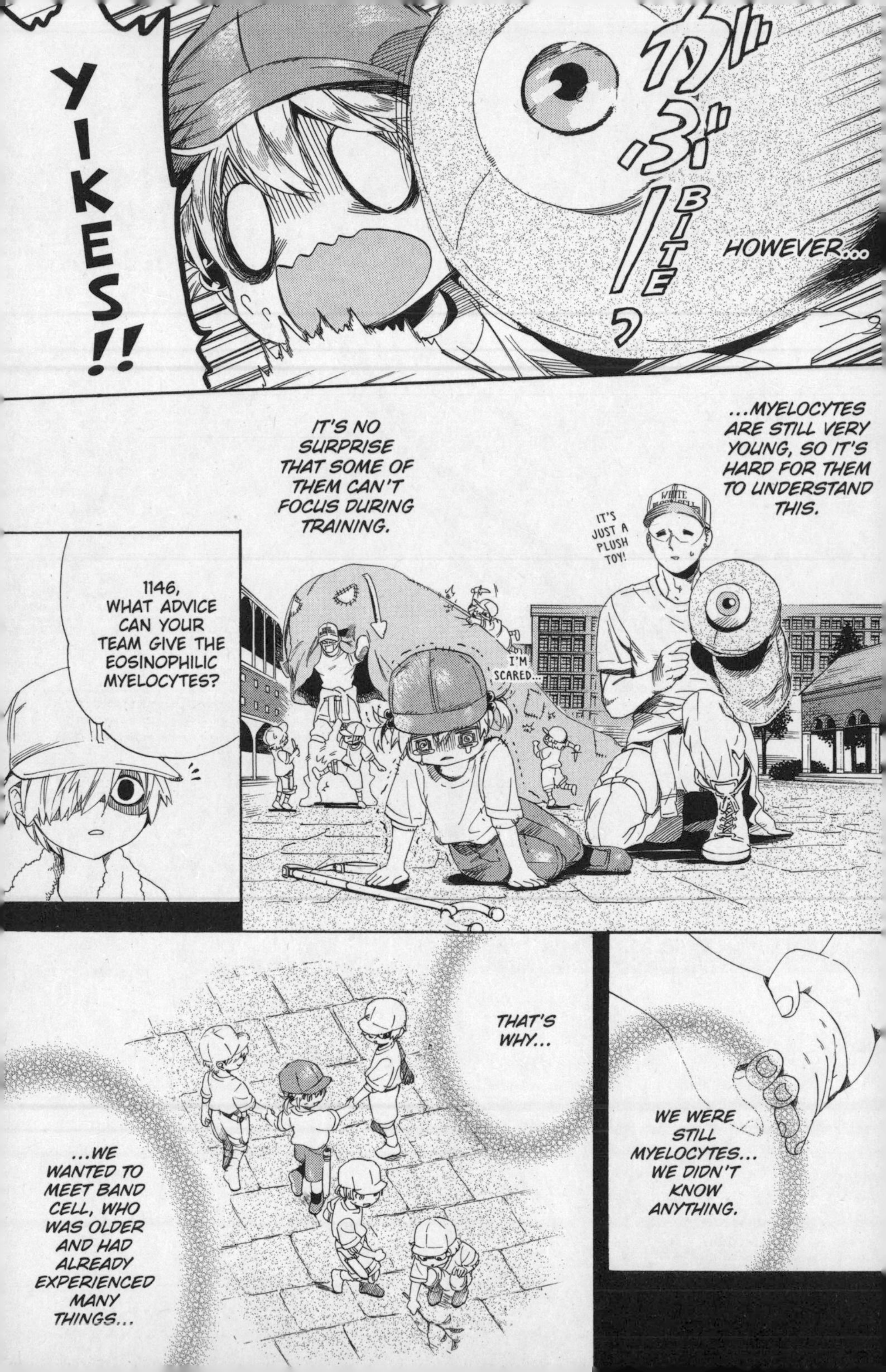
HOWEVER...
BITE
YIKES!!
...MYELOCYTES ARE STILL VERY YOUNG, SO IT'S HARD FOR THEM TO UNDERSTAND THIS.
IT'S JUST A PLUSH TOY!
I'M SCARED...
IT'S NO SURPRISE THAT SOME OF THEM CAN'T FOCUS DURING TRAINING.
1146, WHAT ADVICE CAN YOUR TEAM GIVE THE EOSINOPHILIC MYELOCYTES?
WE WERE STILL MYELOCYTES... WE DIDN'T KNOW ANYTHING.
THAT'S WHY...
...WE WANTED TO MEET BAND CELL, WHO WAS OLDER AND HAD ALREADY EXPERIENCED MANY THINGS...

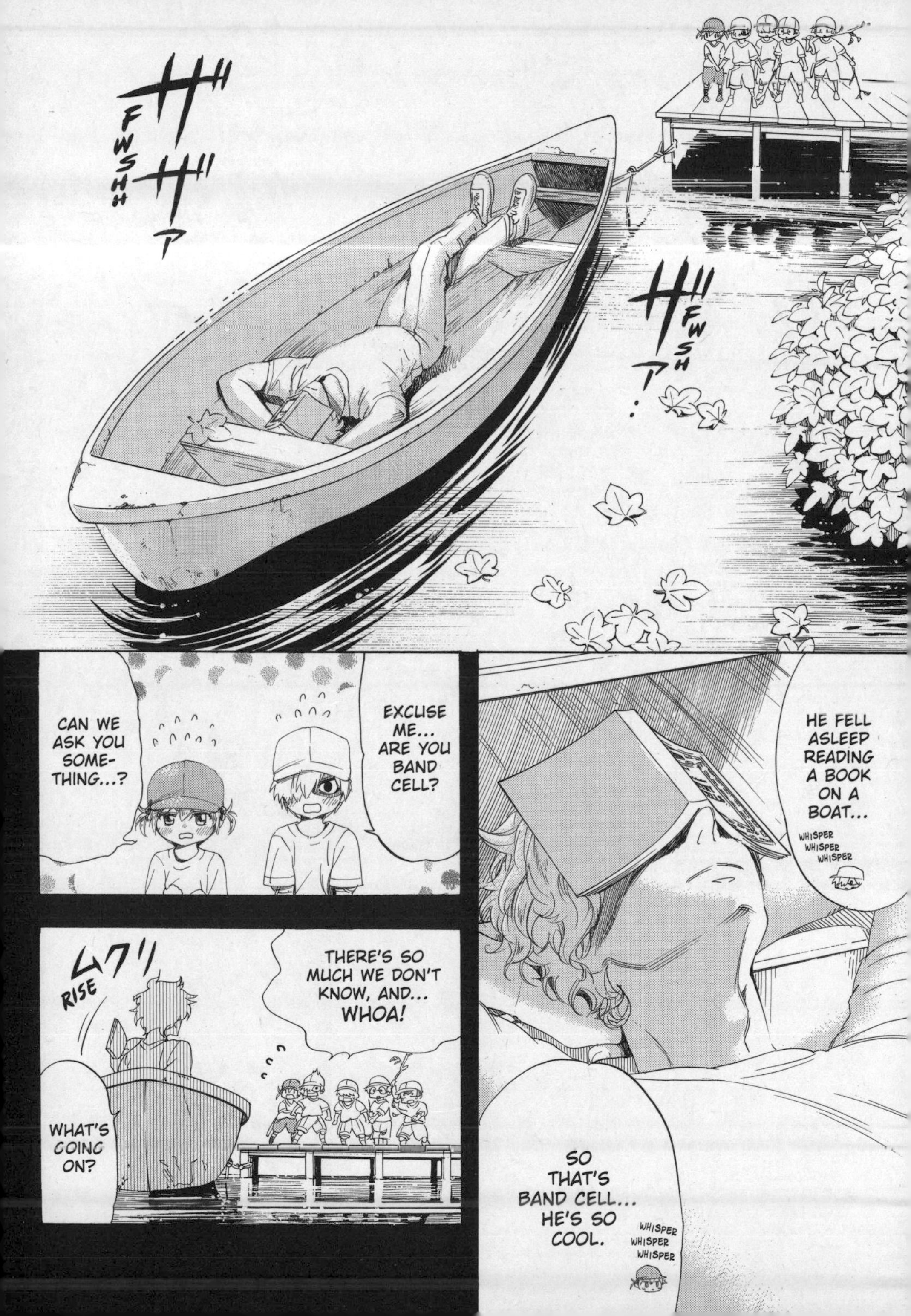
ザザァ
FWSHH
ザァ..
FWSH
HE FELL ASLEEP READING A BOOK ON A BOAT...
WHISPER WHISPER WHISPER
SO THAT'S BAND CELL... HE'S SO COOL.
WHISPER WHISPER WHISPER
EXCUSE ME... ARE YOU BAND CELL?
CAN WE ASK YOU SOME-THING...?
THERE'S SO MUCH WE DON'T KNOW, AND... WHOA!
ムクリ
RISE
WHAT'S COING ON?

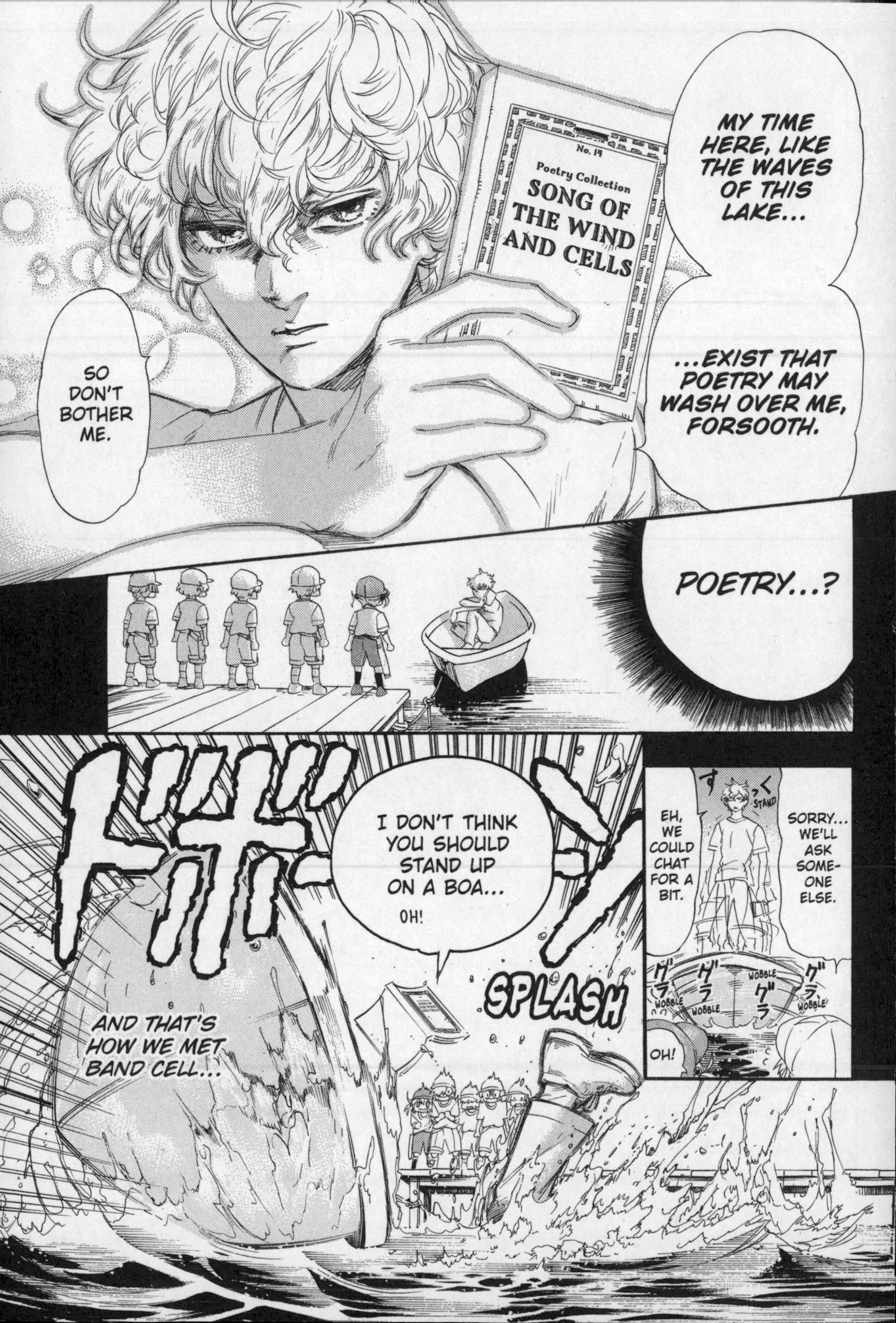
MY TIME HERE, LIKE THE WAVES OF THIS LAKE...
No. 14
Poetry Collection
SONG OF THE WIND AND CELLS
...EXIST THAT POETRY MAY WASH OVER ME, FORSOOTH.
SO DON'T BOTHER ME.
POETRY...?
すっく
STAND
SORRY... WE'LL ASK SOME-ONE ELSE.
EH, WE COULD CHAT FOR A BIT.
グラ WOBBLE
グラ WOBBLE
グラ WOBBLE
OH!
ドボーン
I DON'T THINK YOU SHOULD STAND UP ON A BOA...
OH!
SPLASH
AND THAT'S HOW WE MET BAND CELL...

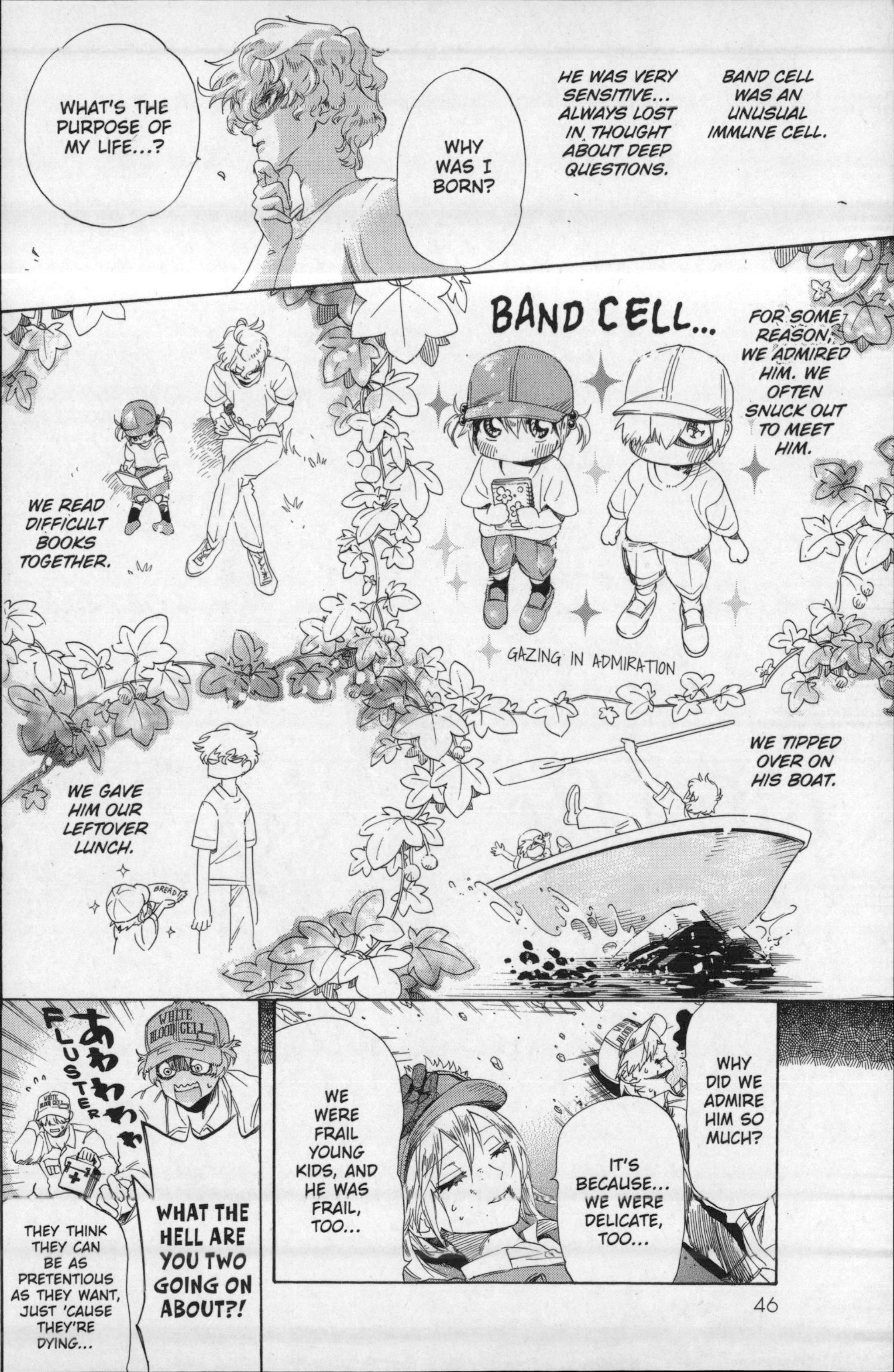
BAND CELL WAS AN UNUSUAL IMMUNE CELL.
HE WAS VERY SENSITIVE... ALWAYS LOST IN THOUGHT ABOUT DEEP QUESTIONS.
WHY WAS I BORN?
WHAT'S THE PURPOSE OF MY LIFE...?
BAND CELL...
FOR SOME REASON, WE ADMIRED HIM. WE OFTEN SNUCK OUT TO MEET HIM.
GAZING IN ADMIRATION
WE READ DIFFICULT BOOKS TOGETHER.
WE TIPPED OVER ON HIS BOAT.
WE GAVE HIM OUR LEFTOVER LUNCH.
BREAD
WHY DID WE ADMIRE HIM SO MUCH?
IT'S BECAUSE... WE WERE DELICATE, TOO...
WE WERE FRAIL YOUNG KIDS, AND HE WAS FRAIL, TOO...
あわわわわ
FLUSTER
WHITE BLOOD CELL
WHAT THE HELL ARE YOU TWO GOING ON ABOUT?!
THEY THINK THEY CAN BE AS PRETENTIOUS AS THEY WANT, JUST 'CAUSE THEY'RE DYING...

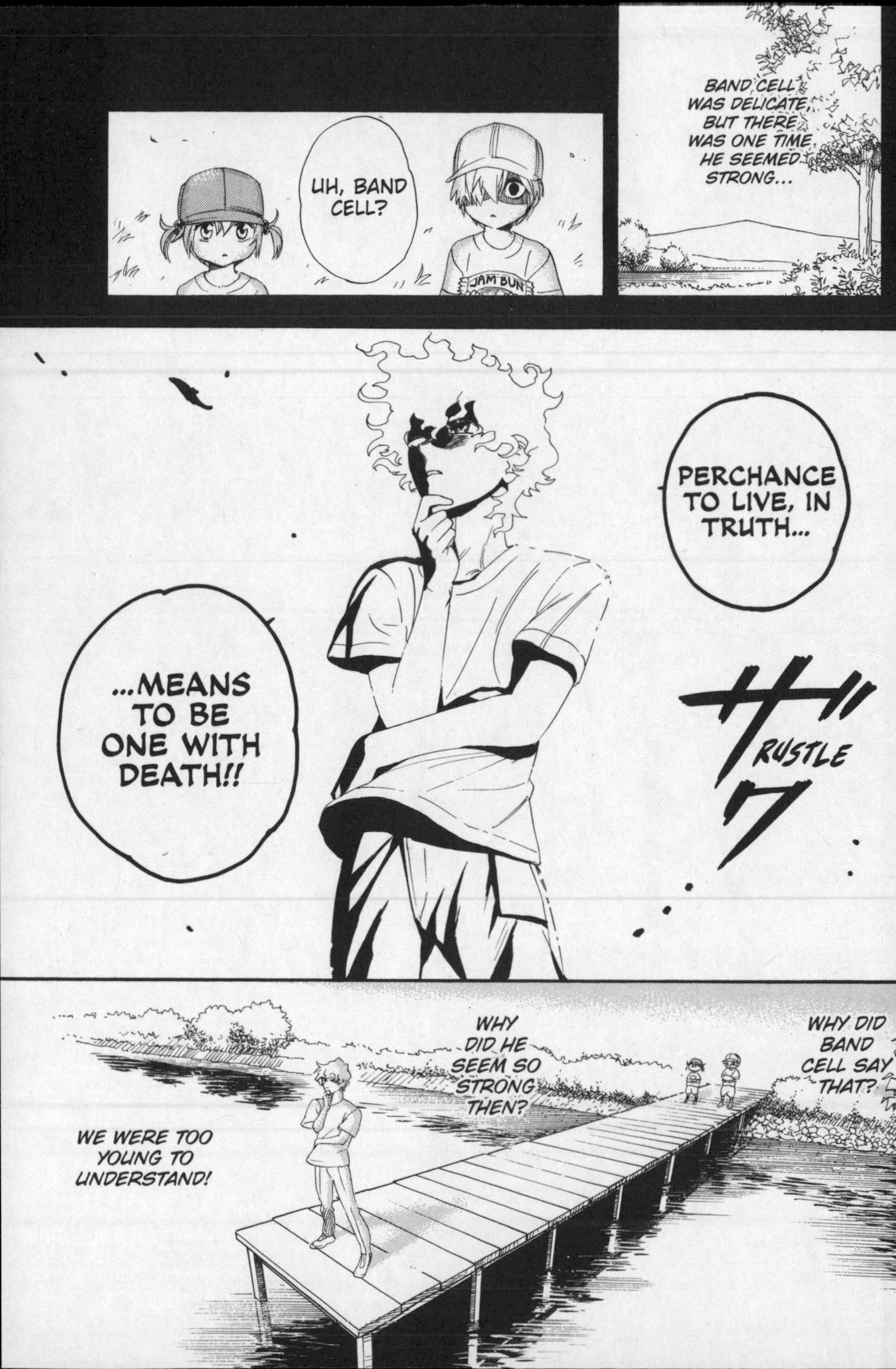
BAND CELL WAS DELICATE, BUT THERE WAS ONE TIME HE SEEMED STRONG...
UH, BAND CELL?
PERCHANCE TO LIVE, IN TRUTH...
...MEANS TO BE ONE WITH DEATH!!
RUSTLE
WHY DID BAND CELL SAY THAT?
WHY DID HE SEEM SO STRONG THEN?
WE WERE TOO YOUNG TO UNDERSTAND!

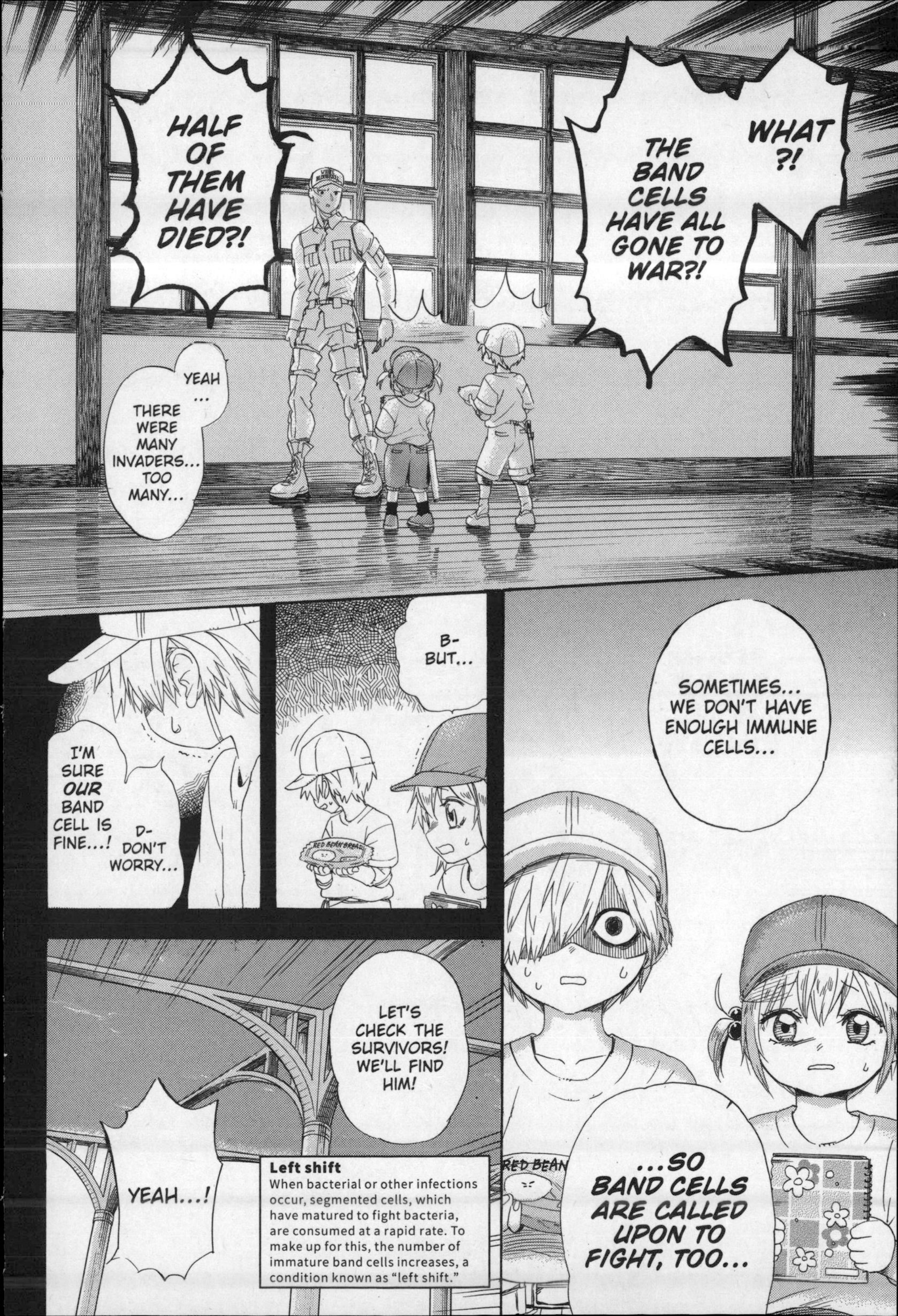
WHAT ?!
THE BAND CELLS HAVE ALL GONE TO WAR?!
HALF OF THEM HAVE DIED?!
YEAH ... THERE WERE MANY INVADERS... TOO MANY...
SOMETIMES... WE DON'T HAVE ENOUGH IMMUNE CELLS...
...SO BAND CELLS ARE CALLED UPON TO FIGHT, TOO...
RED BEAN
B- BUT...
RED BEAN BREAD
I'M SURE OUR BAND CELL IS FINE...!
D- DON'T WORRY...
LET'S CHECK THE SURVIVORS! WE'LL FIND HIM!
YEAH...!
Left shift
When bacterial or other infections occur, segmented cells, which have matured to fight bacteria, are consumed at a rapid rate. To make up for this, the number of immature band cells increases, a condition known as "left shift."

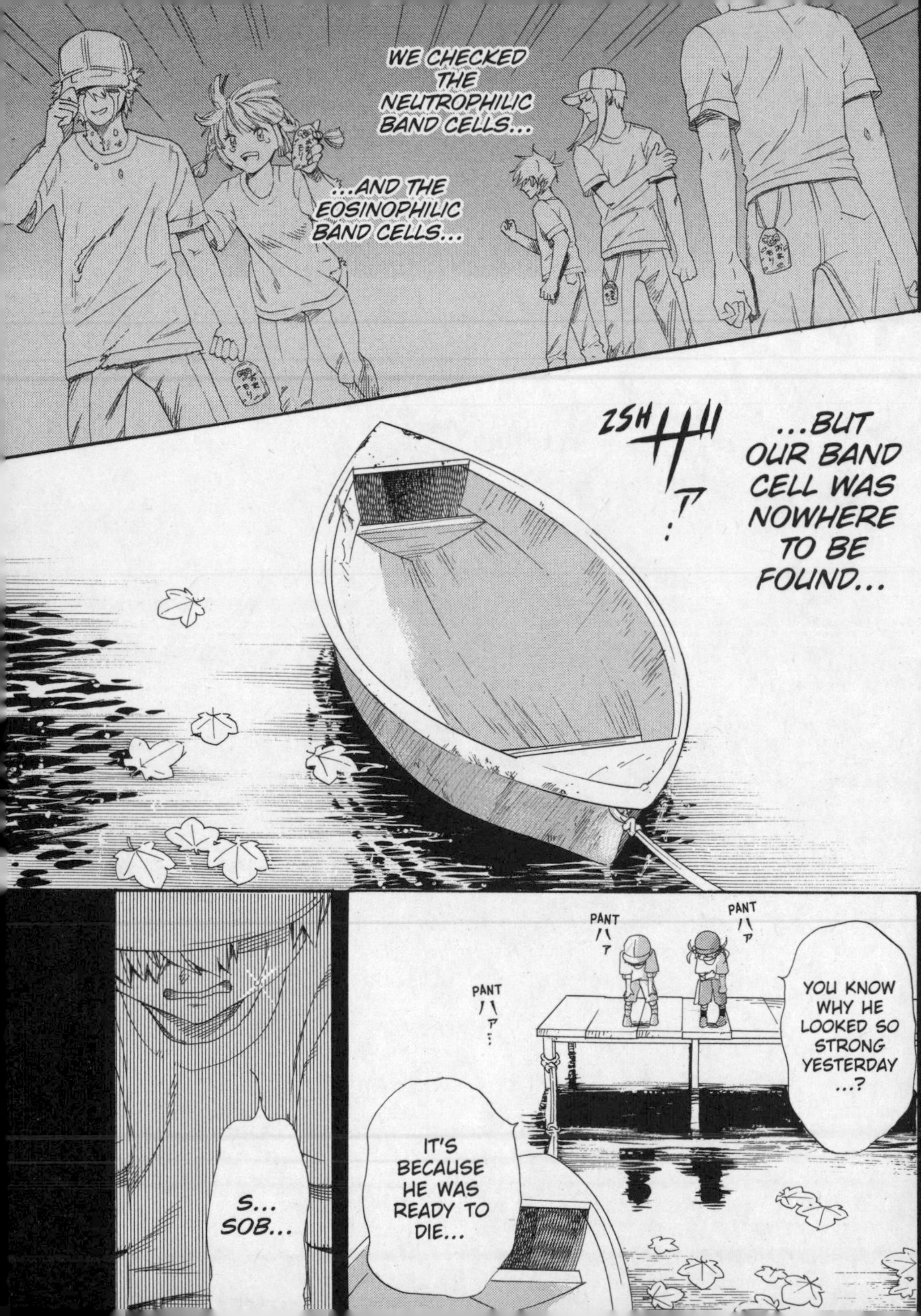
WE CHECKED THE NEUTROPHILIC BAND CELLS...
...AND THE EOSINOPHILIC BAND CELLS...
...BUT OUR BAND CELL WAS NOWHERE TO BE FOUND...
ZSH
PANT
PANT
PANT
YOU KNOW WHY HE LOOKED SO STRONG YESTERDAY ...?
IT'S BECAUSE HE WAS READY TO DIE...
S... SOB...

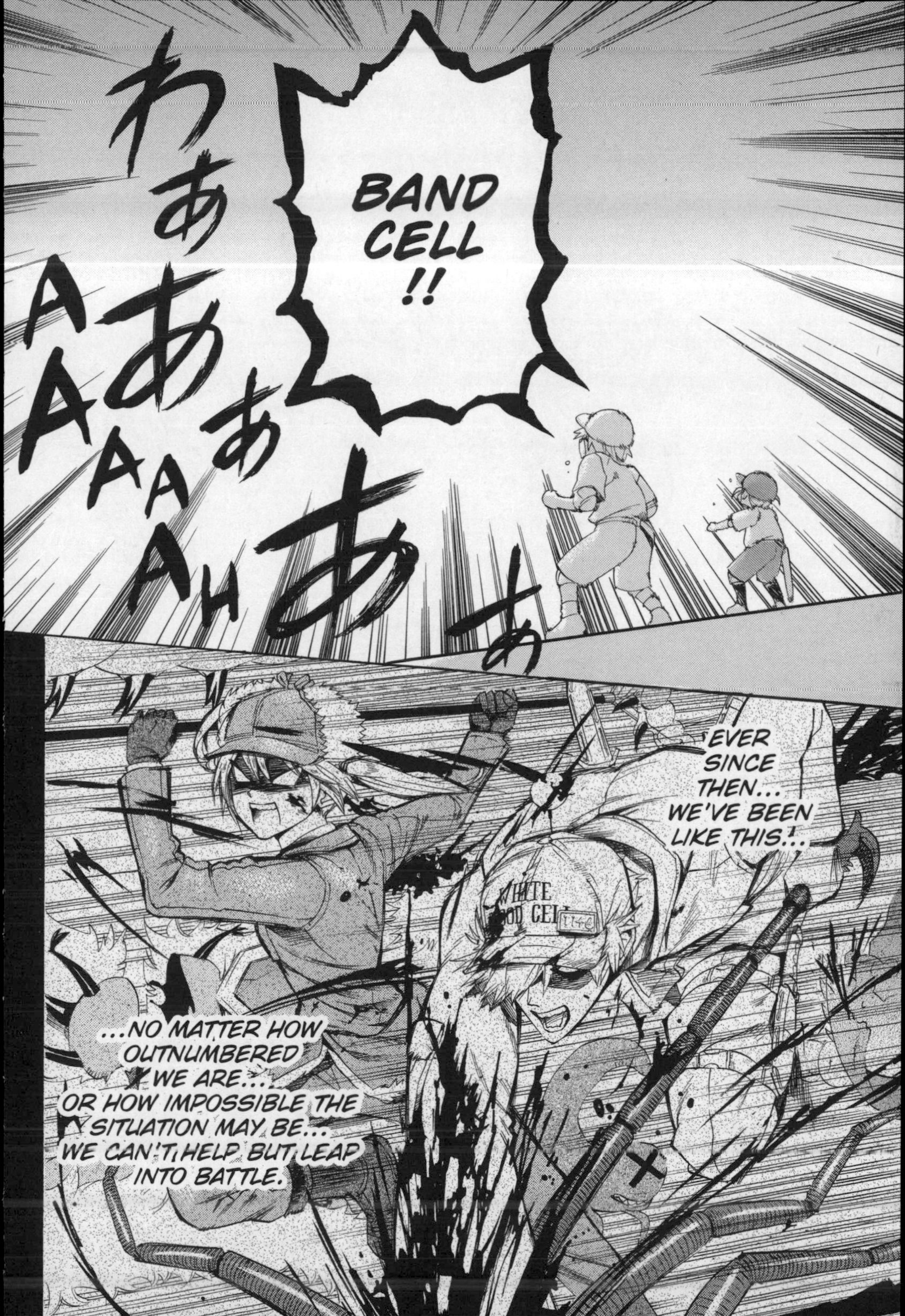
BAND CELL!!
わあああああ
AAAAAH
EVER SINCE THEN... WE'VE BEEN LIKE THIS...
...NO MATTER HOW OUTNUMBERED WE ARE... OR HOW IMPOSSIBLE THE SITUATION MAY BE... WE CAN'T HELP BUT LEAP INTO BATTLE.

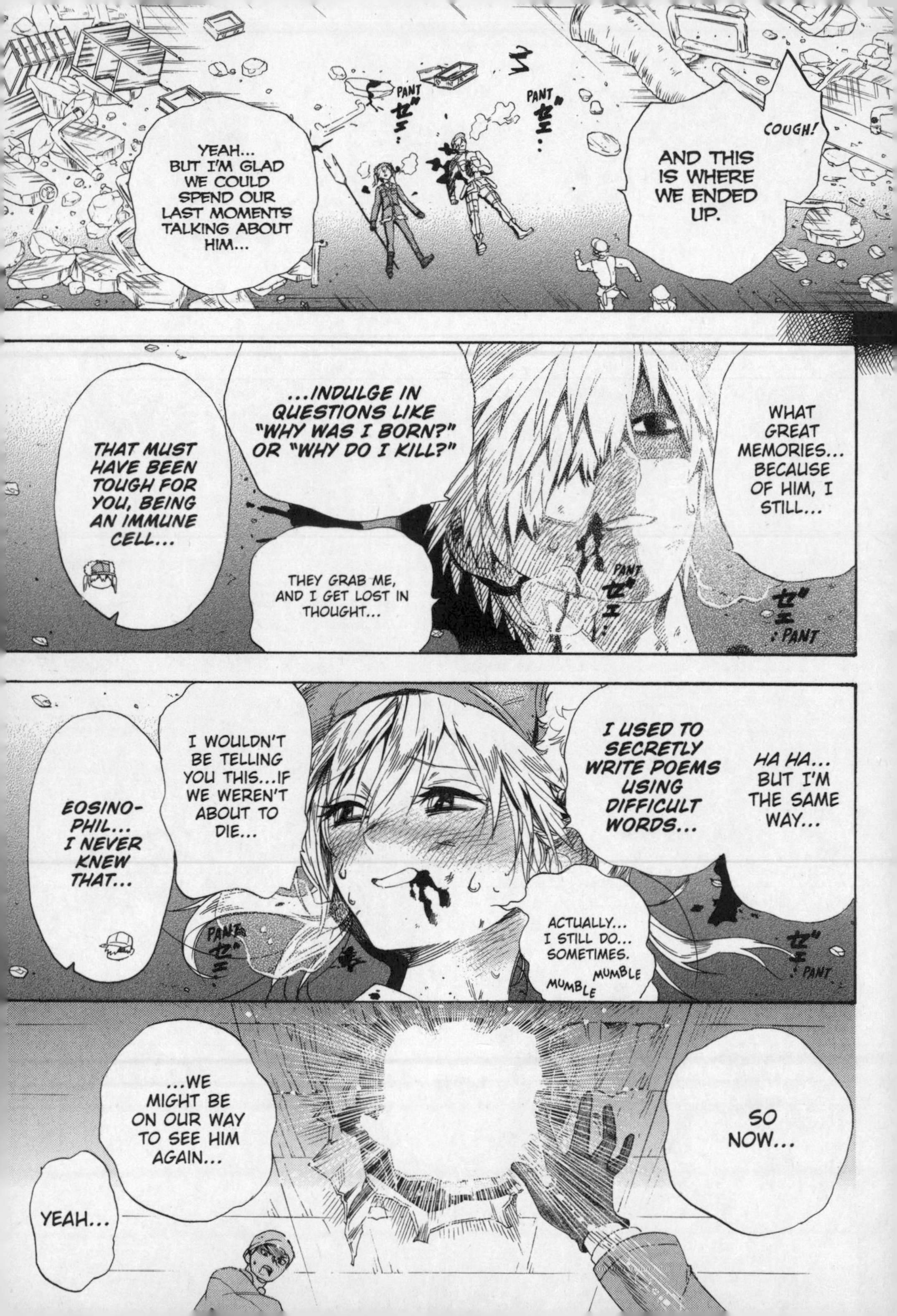
COUGH!
AND THIS IS WHERE WE ENDED UP.
PANT
PANT
YEAH... BUT I'M GLAD WE COULD SPEND OUR LAST MOMENTS TALKING ABOUT HIM...
WHAT GREAT MEMORIES... BECAUSE OF HIM, I STILL...
PANT
PANT
...INDULGE IN QUESTIONS LIKE "WHY WAS I BORN?" OR "WHY DO I KILL?"
THEY GRAB ME, AND I GET LOST IN THOUGHT...
THAT MUST HAVE BEEN TOUGH FOR YOU, BEING AN IMMUNE CELL...
HA HA... BUT I'M THE SAME WAY...
I USED TO SECRETLY WRITE POEMS USING DIFFICULT WORDS...
PANT
ACTUALLY... I STILL DO... SOMETIMES.
MUMBLE MUMBLE
I WOULDN'T BE TELLING YOU THIS...IF WE WEREN'T ABOUT TO DIE...
PANT
EOSINO-PHIL... I NEVER KNEW THAT...
SO NOW...
...WE MIGHT BE ON OUR WAY TO SEE HIM AGAIN...
YEAH...

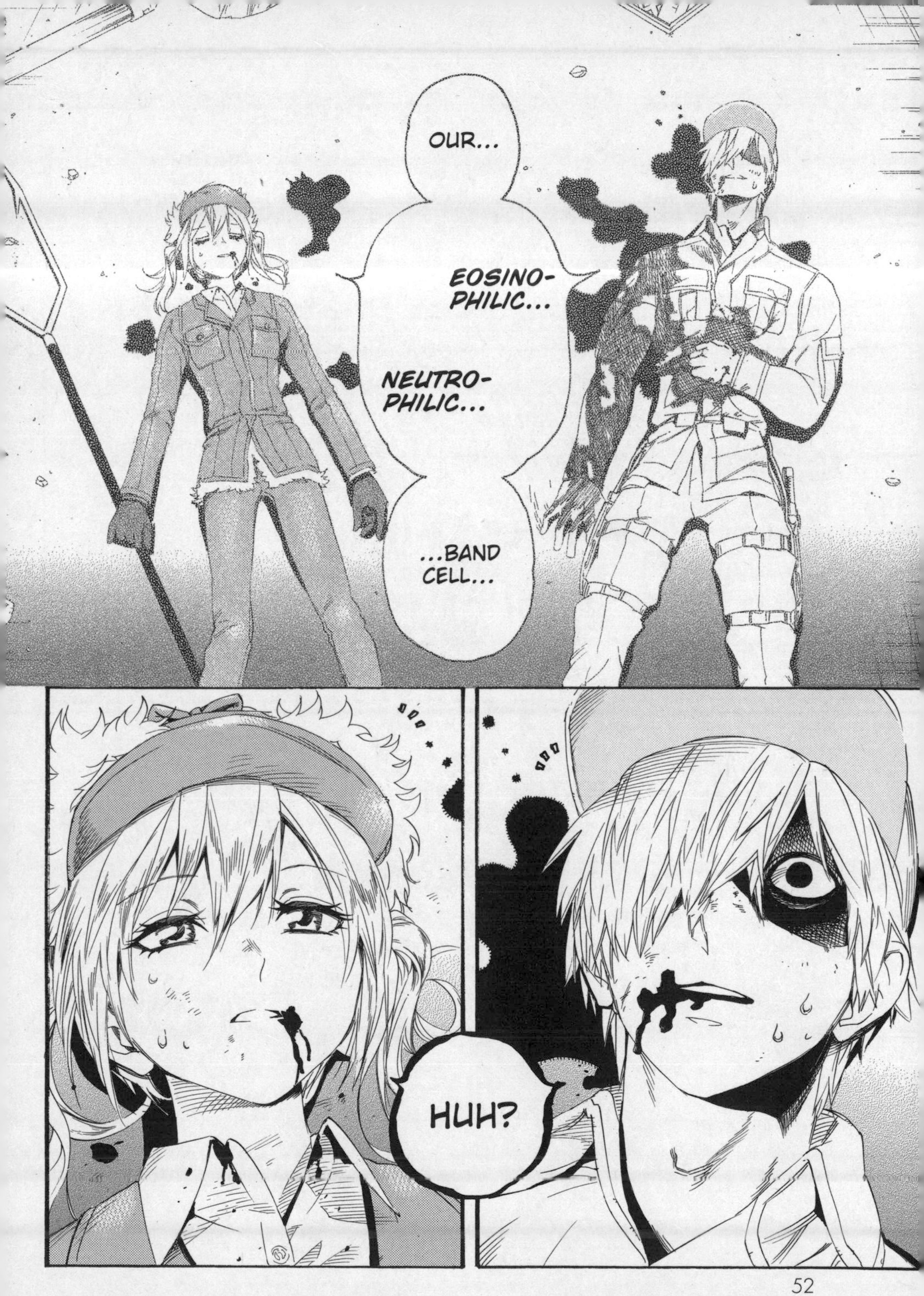
OUR...
EOSINO-
PHILIC...
NEUTRO-
PHILIC...
...BAND
CELL...
HUH?

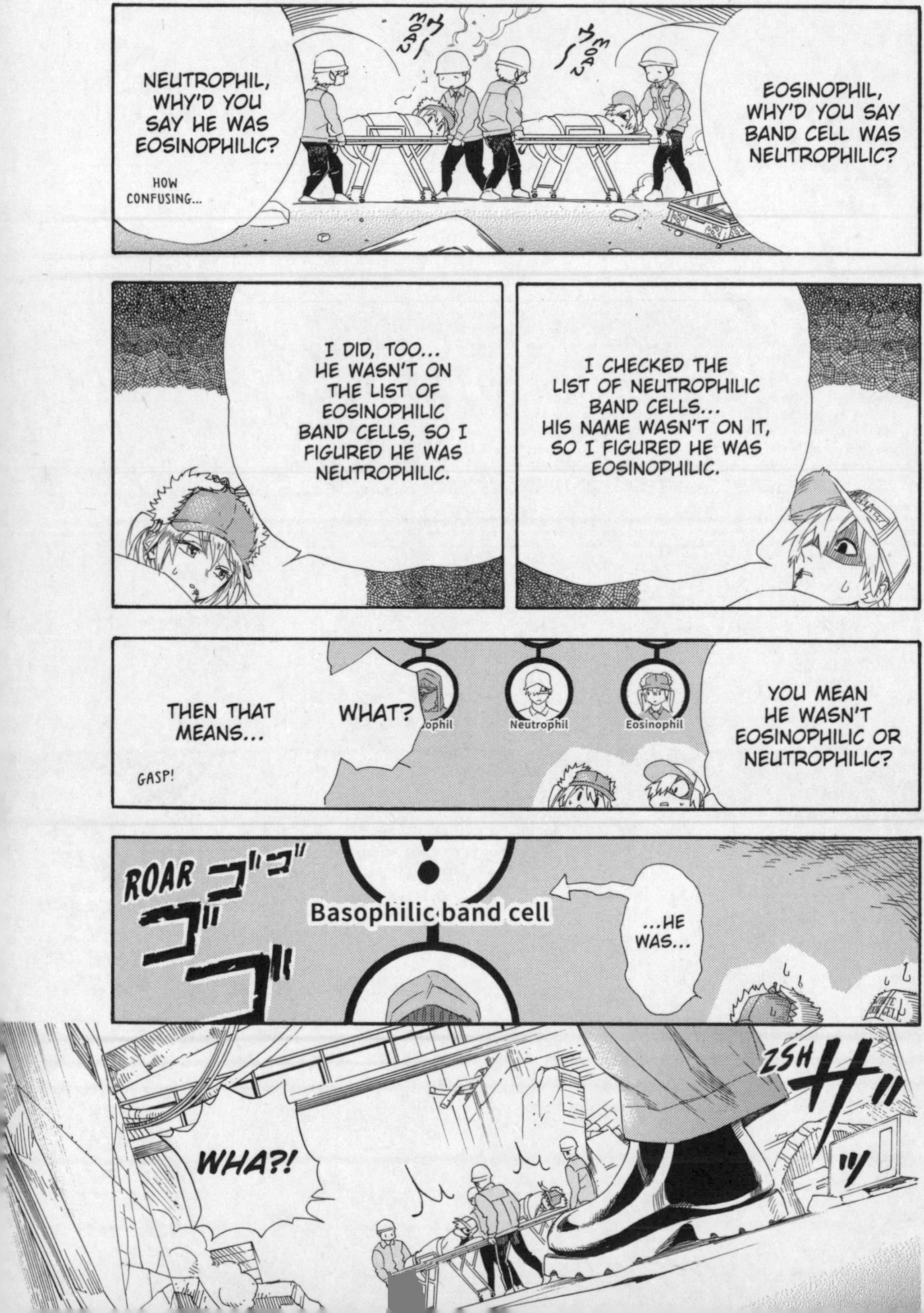
MOAN
MOAN
EOSINOPHIL, WHY'D YOU SAY BAND CELL WAS NEUTROPHILIC?
NEUTROPHIL, WHY'D YOU SAY HE WAS EOSINOPHILIC?
HOW CONFUSING...
I CHECKED THE LIST OF NEUTROPHILIC BAND CELLS... HIS NAME WASN'T ON IT, SO I FIGURED HE WAS EOSINOPHILIC.
I DID, TOO... HE WASN'T ON THE LIST OF EOSINOPHILIC BAND CELLS, SO I FIGURED HE WAS NEUTROPHILIC.
YOU MEAN HE WASN'T EOSINOPHILIC OR NEUTROPHILIC?
Eosinophil
Neutrophil
WHAT?
THEN THAT MEANS...
GASP!
...HE WAS...
Basophilic band cell
ROAR
ZSH
WHA?!

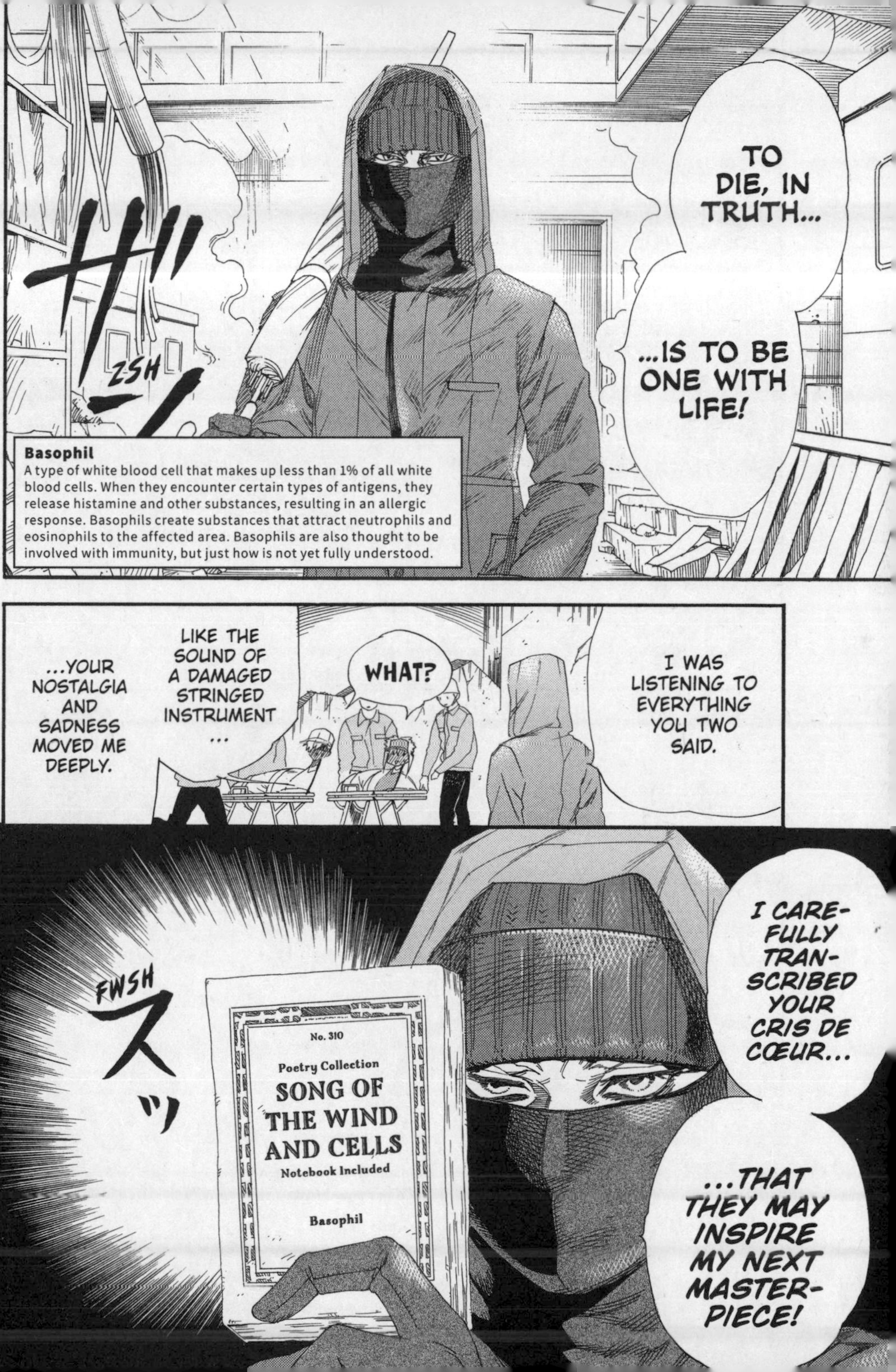
TO DIE, IN TRUTH...
...IS TO BE ONE WITH LIFE!
ZSH
Basophil
A type of white blood cell that makes up less than 1% of all white blood cells. When they encounter certain types of antigens, they release histamine and other substances, resulting in an allergic response. Basophils create substances that attract neutrophils and eosinophils to the affected area. Basophils are also thought to be involved with immunity, but just how is not yet fully understood.
I WAS LISTENING TO EVERYTHING YOU TWO SAID.
WHAT?
LIKE THE SOUND OF A DAMAGED STRINGED INSTRUMENT...
...YOUR NOSTALGIA AND SADNESS MOVED ME DEEPLY.
I CAREFULLY TRANSCRIBED YOUR CRIS DE CŒUR...
...THAT THEY MAY INSPIRE MY NEXT MASTERPIECE!
FWSH
No. 310
Poetry Collection
SONG OF THE WIND AND CELLS
Notebook Included
Basophil

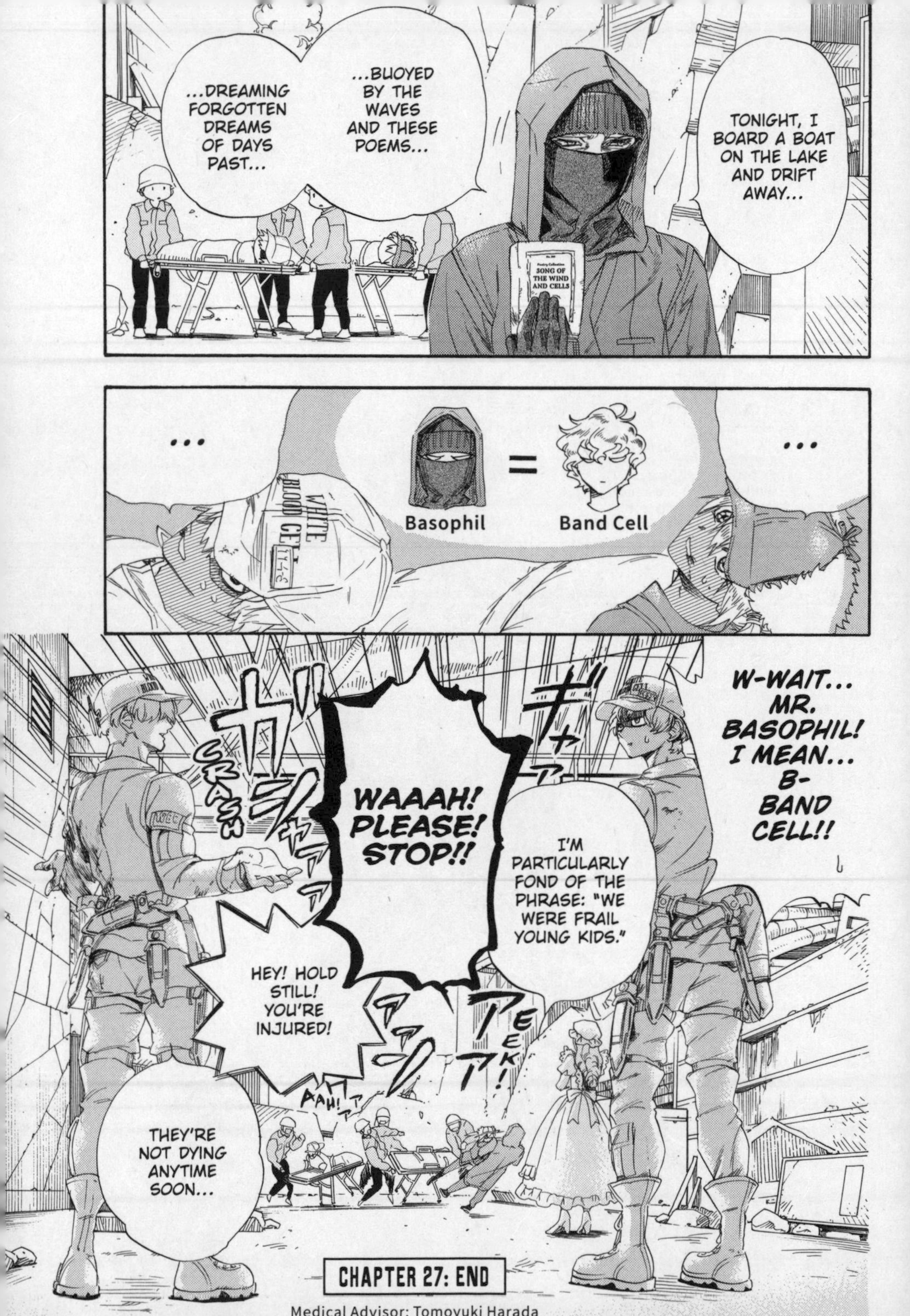
TONIGHT, I BOARD A BOAT ON THE LAKE AND DRIFT AWAY...
...BUOYED BY THE WAVES AND THESE POEMS...
...DREAMING FORGOTTEN DREAMS OF DAYS PAST...
Poetry Collection SONG OF THE WIND AND CELLS
...
Basophil
=
Band Cell
...
WHITE BLOOD CELL
W-WAIT... MR. BASOPHIL! I MEAN... B-BAND CELL!!
I'M PARTICULARLY FOND OF THE PHRASE: "WE WERE FRAIL YOUNG KIDS."
WAAAH! PLEASE! STOP!!
CRASH
EEK!
HEY! HOLD STILL! YOU'RE INJURED!
AAH!
THEY'RE NOT DYING ANYTIME SOON...
CHAPTER 27: END

Medical Advisor: Tomoyuki Harada

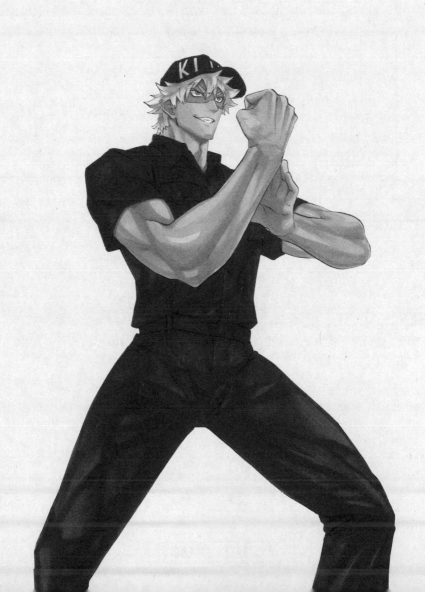

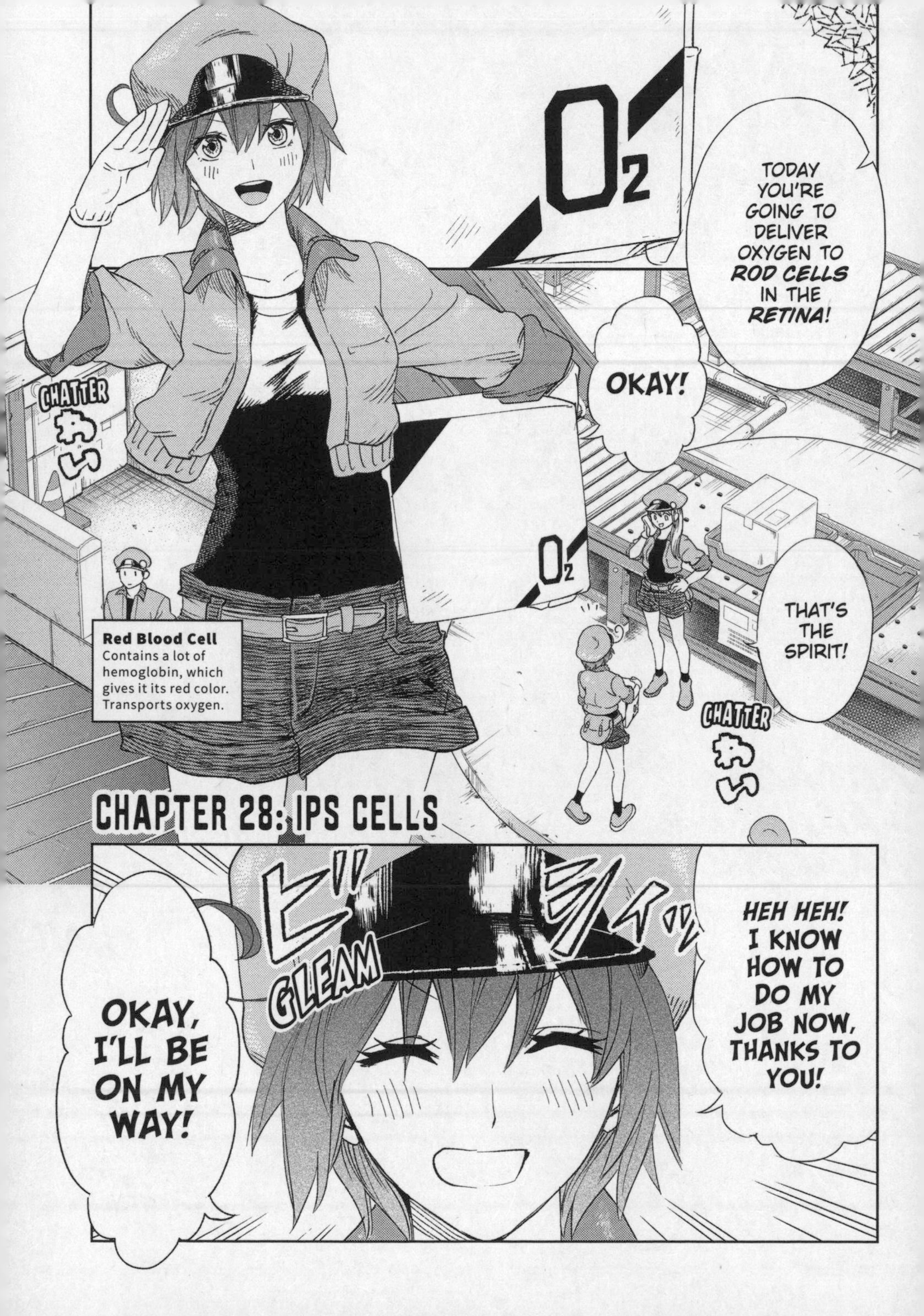
TODAY YOU'RE GOING TO DELIVER OXYGEN TO ROD CELLS IN THE RETINA!
O_2
OKAY!
THAT'S THE SPIRIT!
CHATTER
わい
CHATTER
わい
Red Blood Cell
Contains a lot of hemoglobin, which gives it its red color. Transports oxygen.
CHAPTER 28: IPS CELLS
HEH HEH! I KNOW HOW TO DO MY JOB NOW, THANKS TO YOU!
GLEAM
OKAY, I'LL BE ON MY WAY!

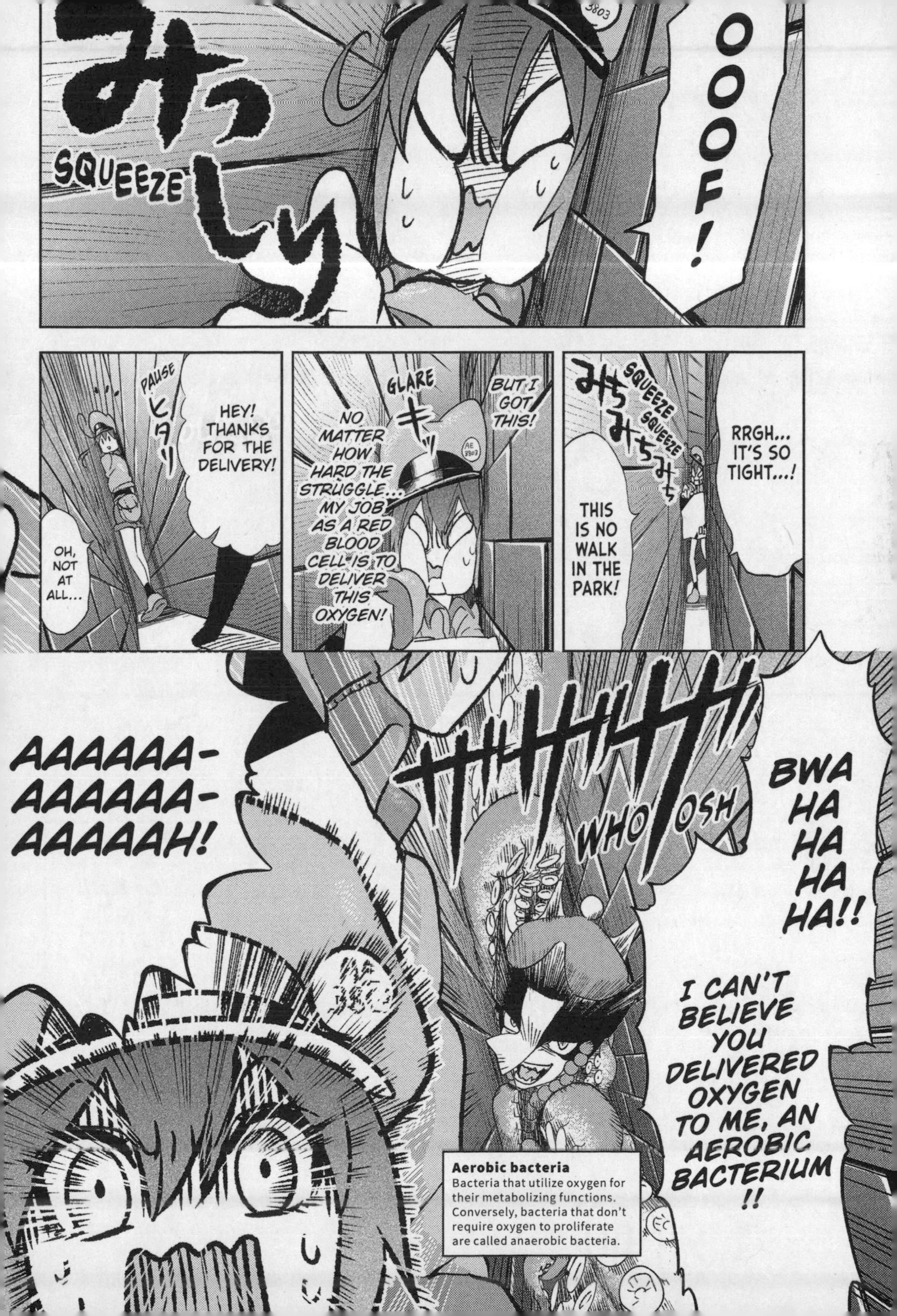
OOOF!
みっしり
SQUEEZE
みちみちみち
SQUEEZE SQUEEZE
RRGH... IT'S SO TIGHT...!
THIS IS NO WALK IN THE PARK!
BUT I GOT THIS!
GLARE
NO MATTER HOW HARD THE STRUGGLE... MY JOB AS A RED BLOOD CELL IS TO DELIVER THIS OXYGEN!
PAUSE
HEY! THANKS FOR THE DELIVERY!
OH, NOT AT ALL...
BWA HA HA HA HA!!
I CAN'T BELIEVE YOU DELIVERED OXYGEN TO ME, AN AEROBIC BACTERIUM!!
WHOOSH
AAAAAA-AAAAAA-AAAAAH!
Aerobic bacteria
Bacteria that utilize oxygen for their metabolizing functions. Conversely, bacteria that don't require oxygen to proliferate are called anaerobic bacteria.

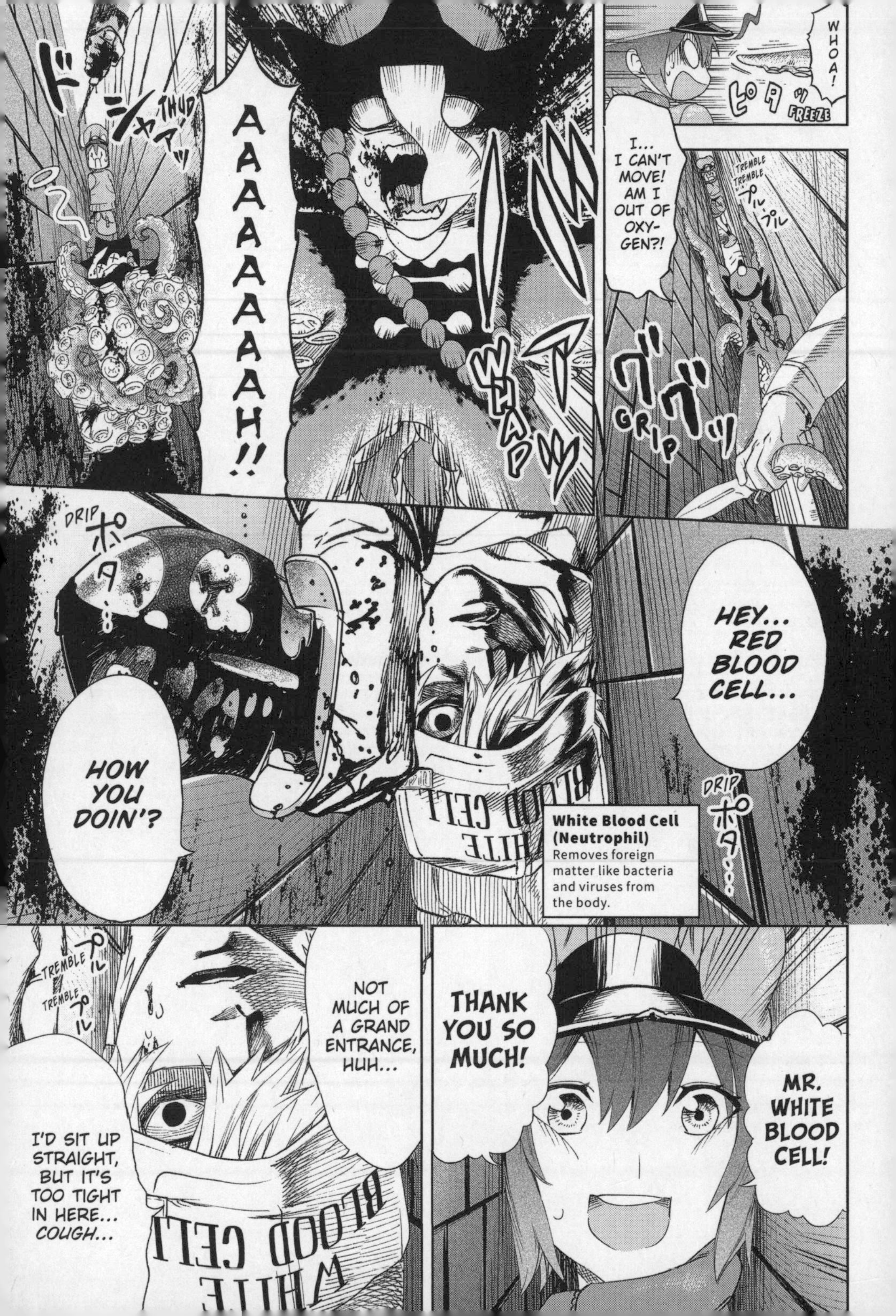
WHOA!
FREEZE
I... I CAN'T MOVE! AM I OUT OF OXYGEN?!
TREMBLE TREMBLE
GRIP
WHAP
THUD
AAAAAAAAH!!
HEY... RED BLOOD CELL...
DRIP
White Blood Cell (Neutrophil)
Removes foreign matter like bacteria and viruses from the body.
HOW YOU DOIN'?
DRIP
MR. WHITE BLOOD CELL!
THANK YOU SO MUCH!
NOT MUCH OF A GRAND ENTRANCE, HUH...
I'D SIT UP STRAIGHT, BUT IT'S TOO TIGHT IN HERE... COUGH...
TREMBLE
TREMBLE

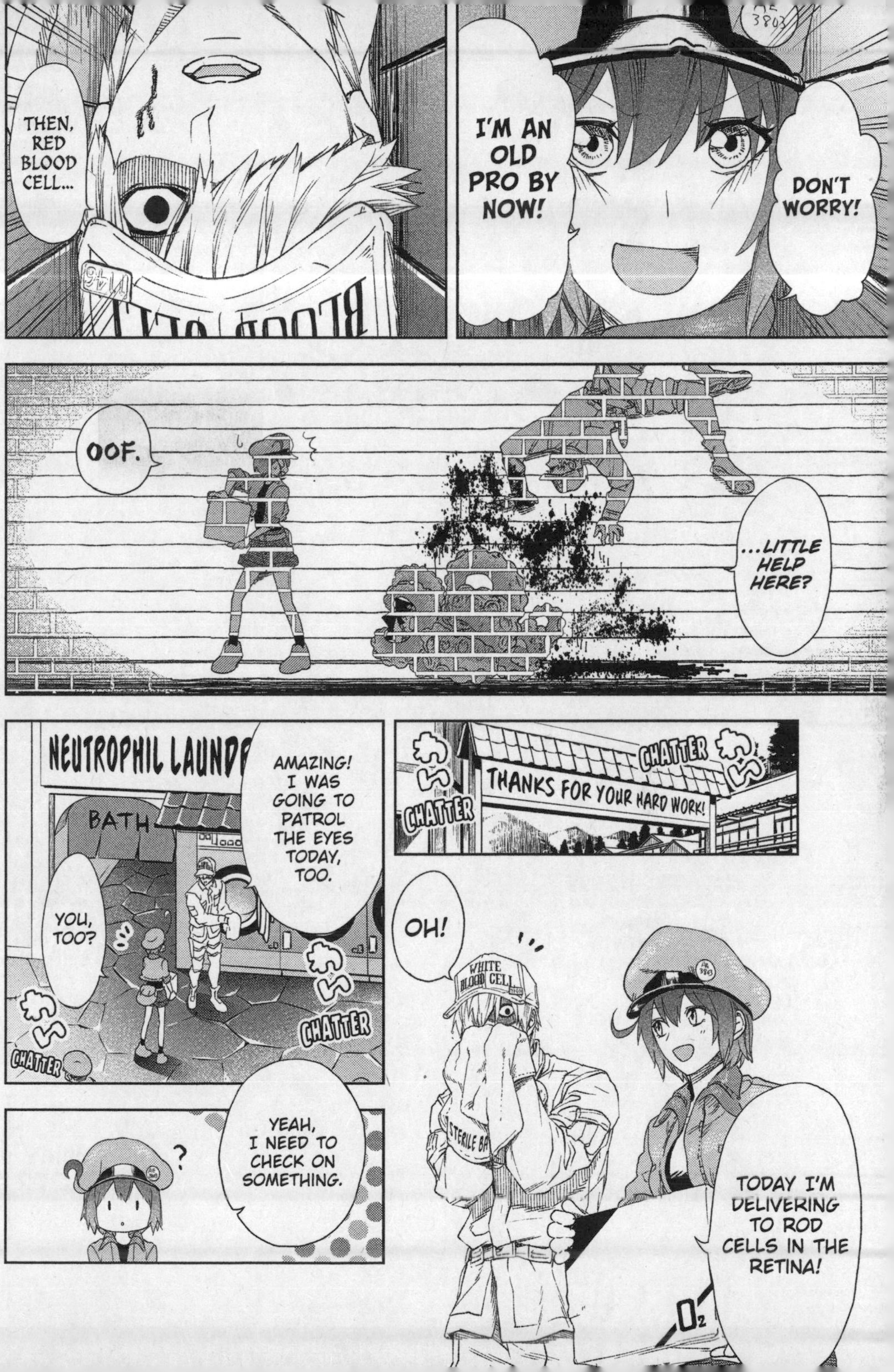
DON'T WORRY!
I'M AN OLD PRO BY NOW!
THEN, RED BLOOD CELL...
...LITTLE HELP HERE?
OOF.
CHATTER
THANKS FOR YOUR HARD WORK!
CHATTER
OH!
WHITE BLOOD CELL
TODAY I'M DELIVERING TO ROD CELLS IN THE RETINA!
STERILE BA
NEUTROPHIL LAUNDE
AMAZING! I WAS GOING TO PATROL THE EYES TODAY, TOO.
BATH
YOU, TOO?
CHATTER
CHATTER
YEAH, I NEED TO CHECK ON SOMETHING.
?

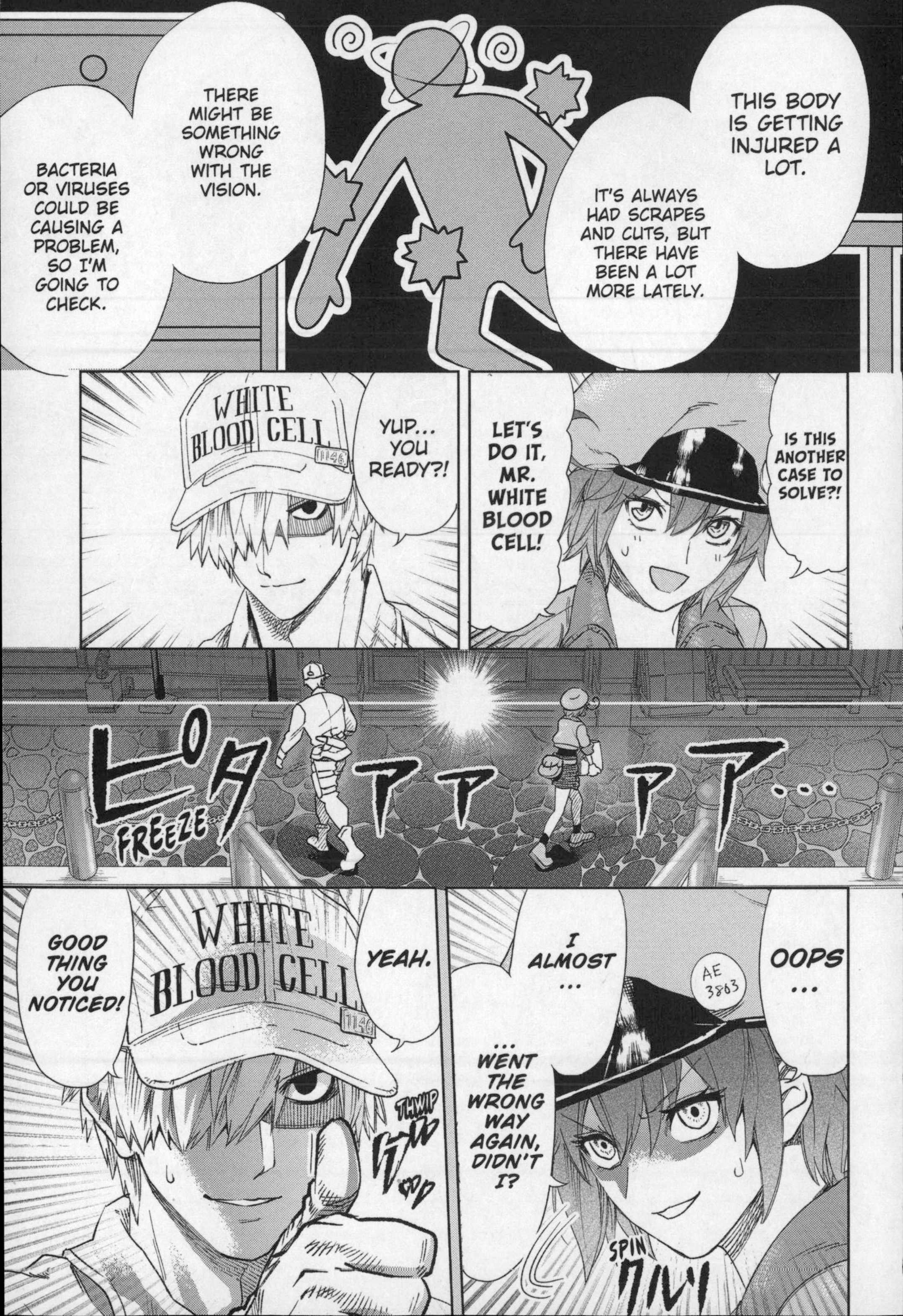
THIS BODY IS GETTING INJURED A LOT.
IT'S ALWAYS HAD SCRAPES AND CUTS, BUT THERE HAVE BEEN A LOT MORE LATELY.
THERE MIGHT BE SOMETHING WRONG WITH THE VISION.
BACTERIA OR VIRUSES COULD BE CAUSING A PROBLEM, SO I'M GOING TO CHECK.
IS THIS ANOTHER CASE TO SOLVE?!
LET'S DO IT, MR. WHITE BLOOD CELL!
WHITE BLOOD CELL
1146
YUP... YOU READY?!
ピタァァァァ...
FREEZE
OOPS...
AE 3803
I ALMOST...
...WENT THE WRONG WAY AGAIN, DIDN'T I?
SPIN
YEAH.
GOOD THING YOU NOTICED!
WHITE BLOOD CELL
1146
THWIP

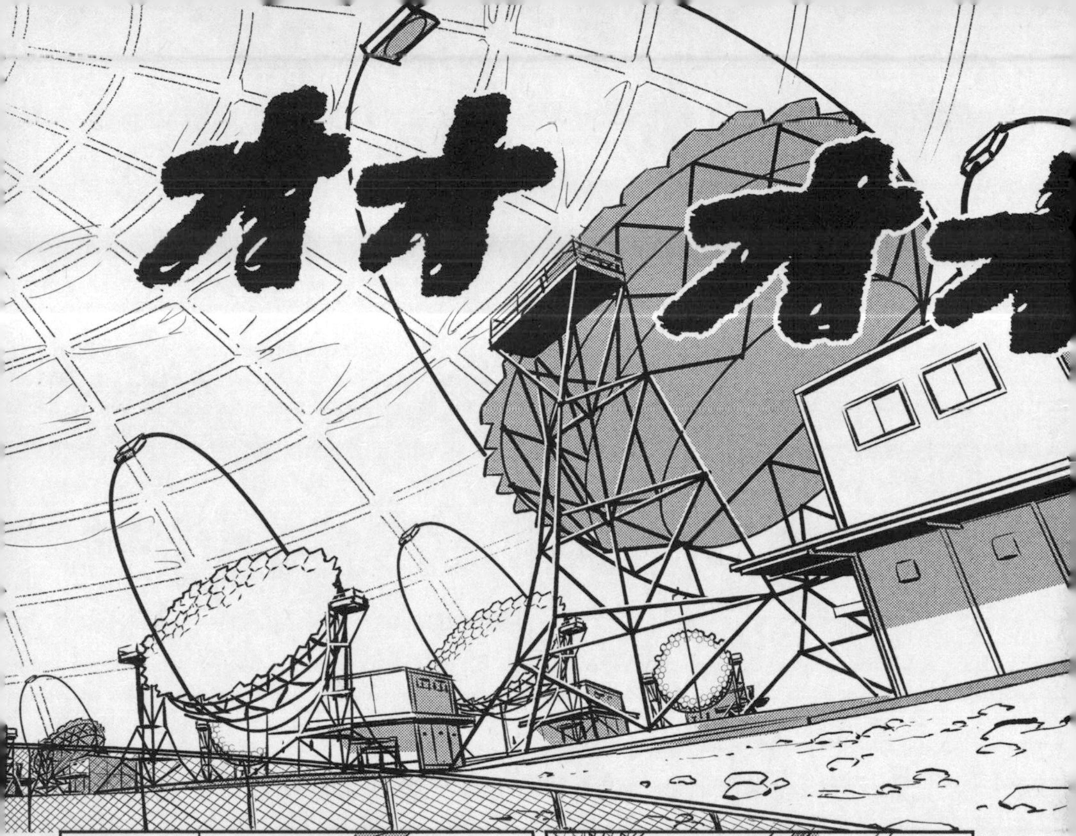
オオオオ
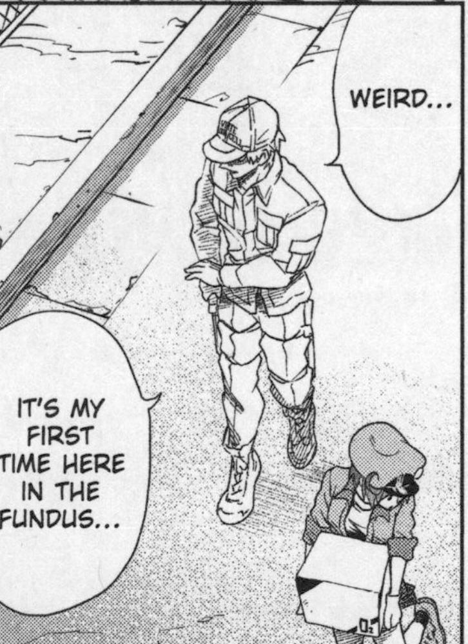
WEIRD...
IT'S MY FIRST TIME HERE IN THE FUNDUS...
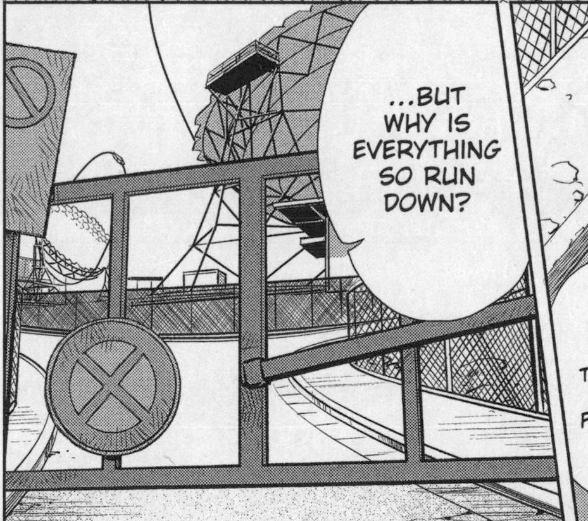
...BUT WHY IS EVERYTHING SO RUN DOWN?

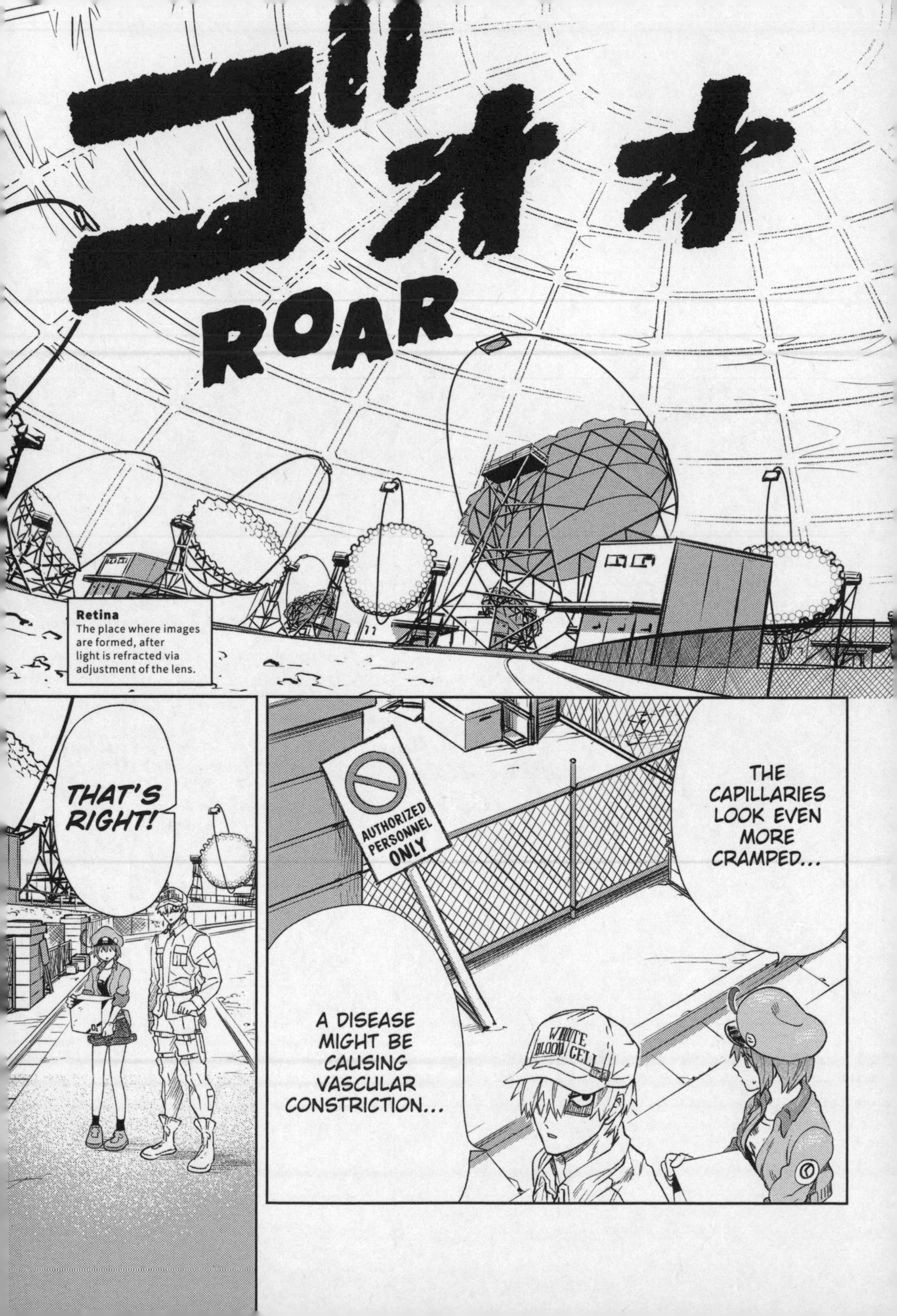
ゴオオ
ROAR
Retina
The place where images are formed, after light is refracted via adjustment of the lens.
THE CAPILLARIES LOOK EVEN MORE CRAMPED...
AUTHORIZED PERSONNEL ONLY
A DISEASE MIGHT BE CAUSING VASCULAR CONSTRICTION...
WHITE BLOOD CELL
THAT'S RIGHT!

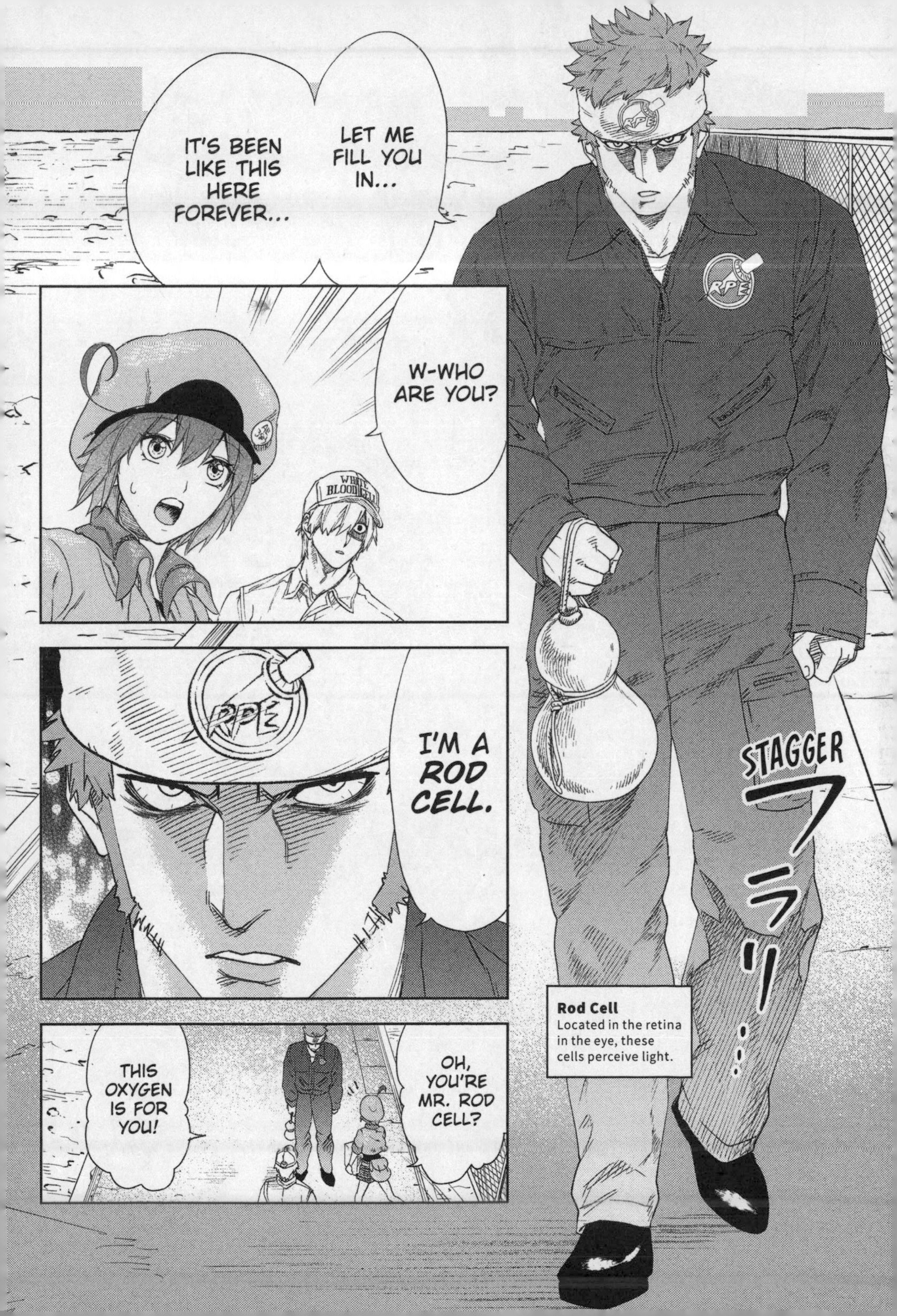
LET ME FILL YOU IN...
IT'S BEEN LIKE THIS HERE FOREVER...
STAGGER
フラリ…
Rod Cell
Located in the retina in the eye, these cells perceive light.
W-WHO ARE YOU?
I'M A ROD CELL.
OH, YOU'RE MR. ROD CELL?
THIS OXYGEN IS FOR YOU!

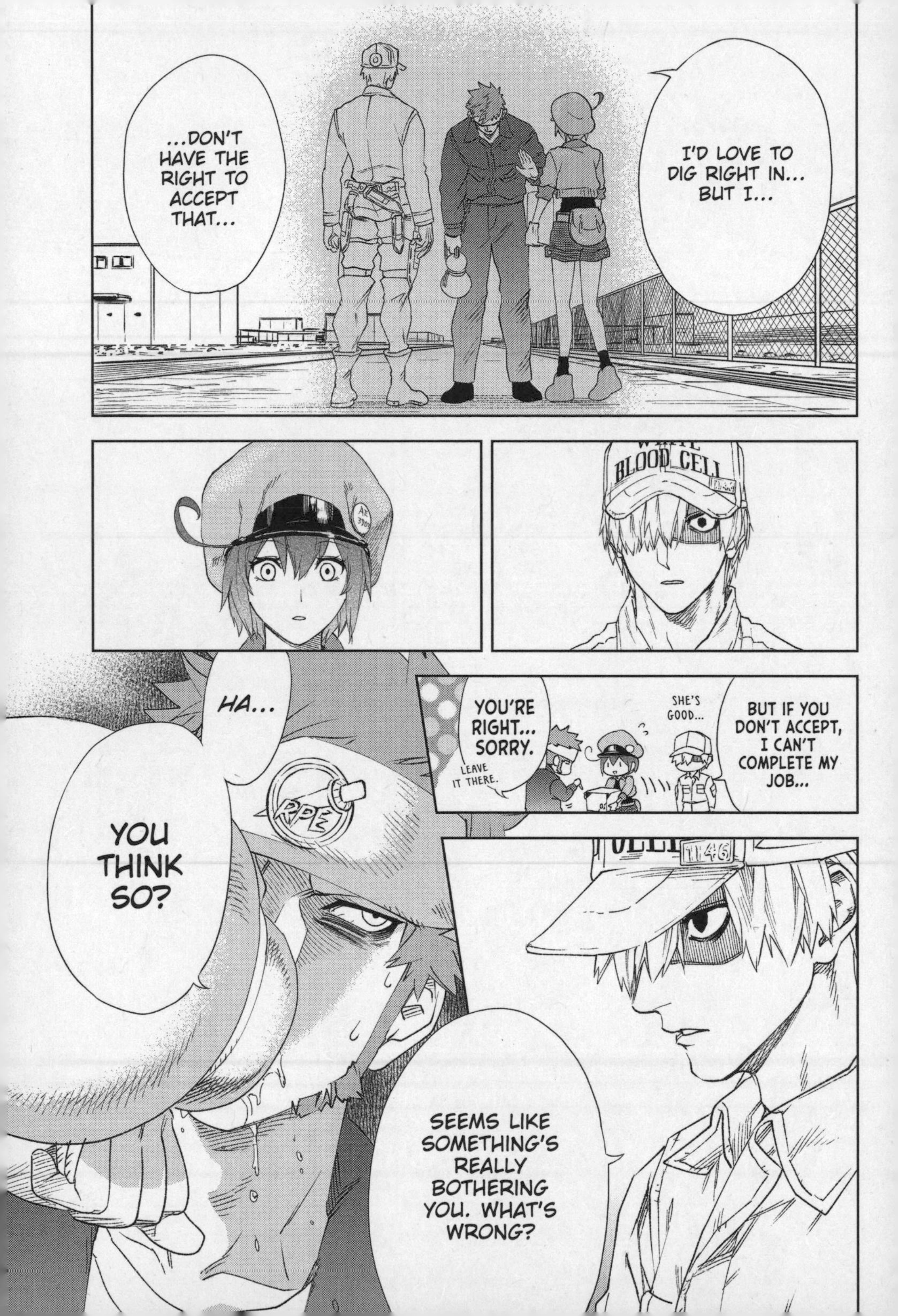
I'D LOVE TO DIG RIGHT IN... BUT I...
...DON'T HAVE THE RIGHT TO ACCEPT THAT...
BLOOD CELL
BUT IF YOU DON'T ACCEPT, I CAN'T COMPLETE MY JOB...
SHE'S GOOD...
YOU'RE RIGHT... SORRY.
LEAVE IT THERE.
SEEMS LIKE SOMETHING'S REALLY BOTHERING YOU. WHAT'S WRONG?
HA...
YOU THINK SO?

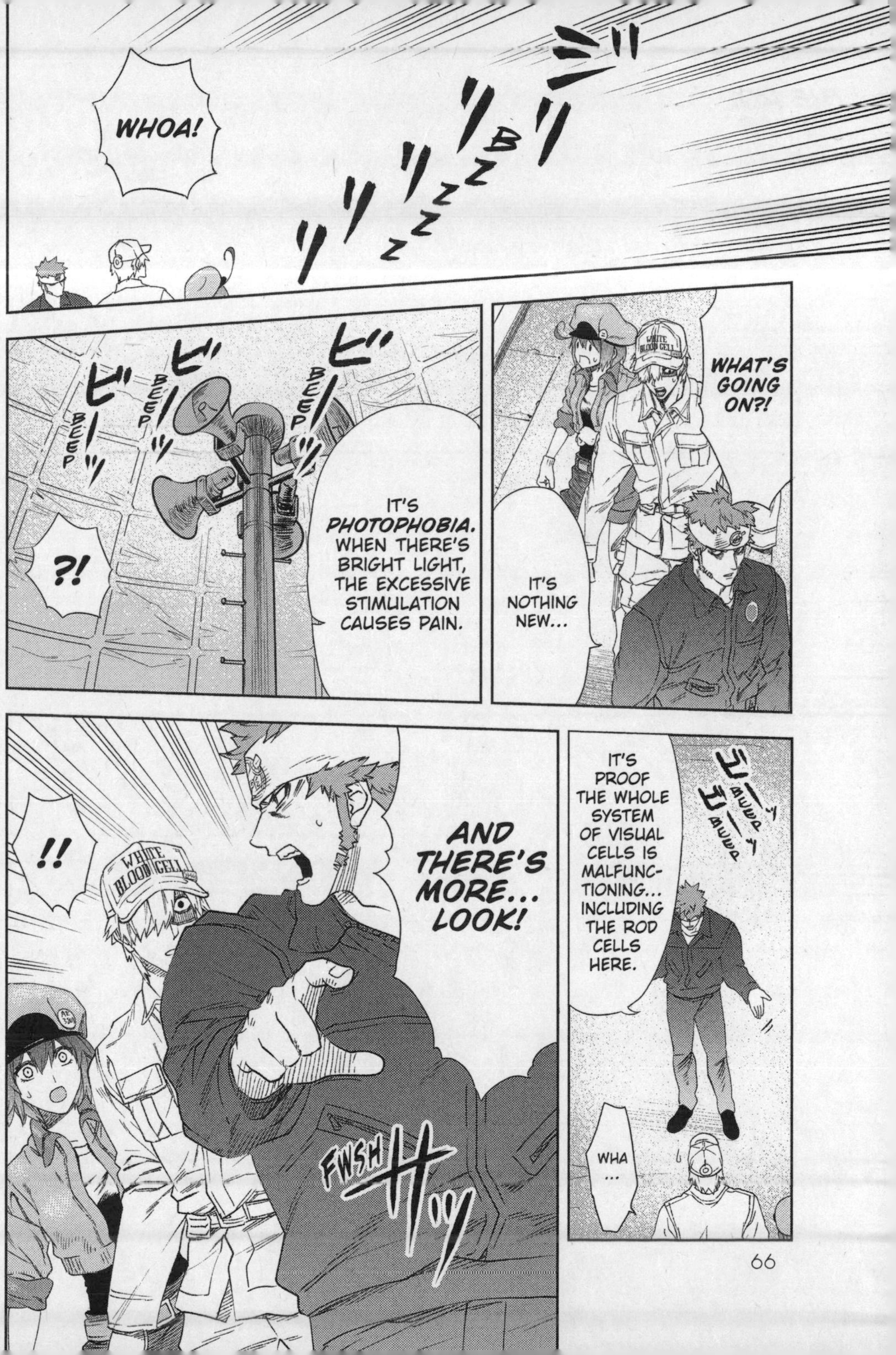
BZZZZZZ
WHOA!
WHAT'S GOING ON?!
IT'S NOTHING NEW...
IT'S *PHOTOPHOBIA.* WHEN THERE'S BRIGHT LIGHT, THE EXCESSIVE STIMULATION CAUSES PAIN.
BEEP
BEEP
BEEP
?!
IT'S PROOF THE WHOLE SYSTEM OF VISUAL CELLS IS MALFUNCTIONING... INCLUDING THE ROD CELLS HERE.
BEEP
BEEP
WHA...
AND THERE'S MORE... LOOK!
!!
FWSH

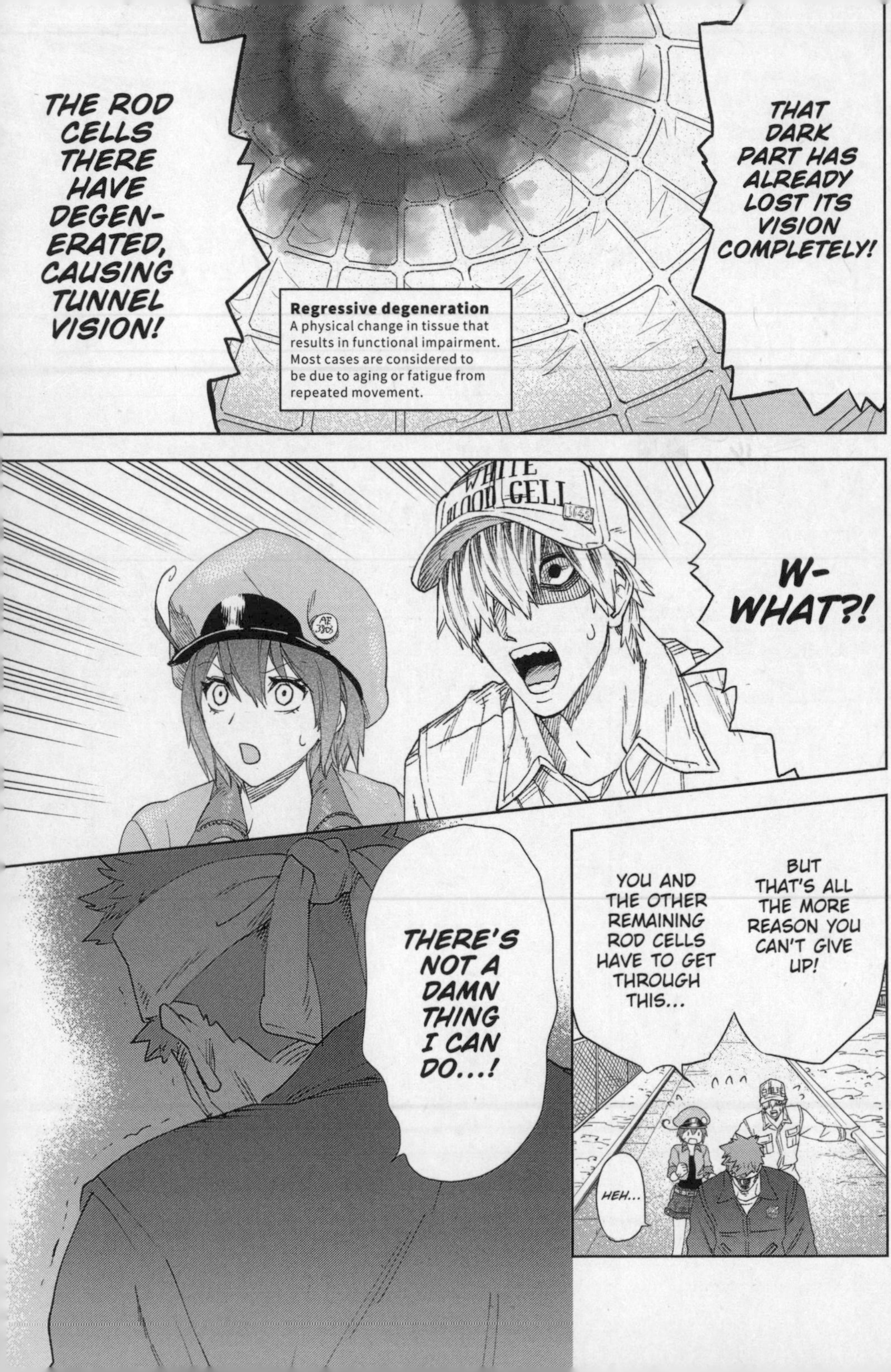
THAT DARK PART HAS ALREADY LOST ITS VISION COMPLETELY!
THE ROD CELLS THERE HAVE DEGEN-ERATED, CAUSING TUNNEL VISION!
Regressive degeneration
A physical change in tissue that results in functional impairment. Most cases are considered to be due to aging or fatigue from repeated movement.
WHITE BLOOD CELL
W-WHAT?!
YOU AND THE OTHER REMAINING ROD CELLS HAVE TO GET THROUGH THIS... BUT THAT'S ALL THE MORE REASON YOU CAN'T GIVE UP!
HEH...
THERE'S NOT A DAMN THING I CAN DO...!

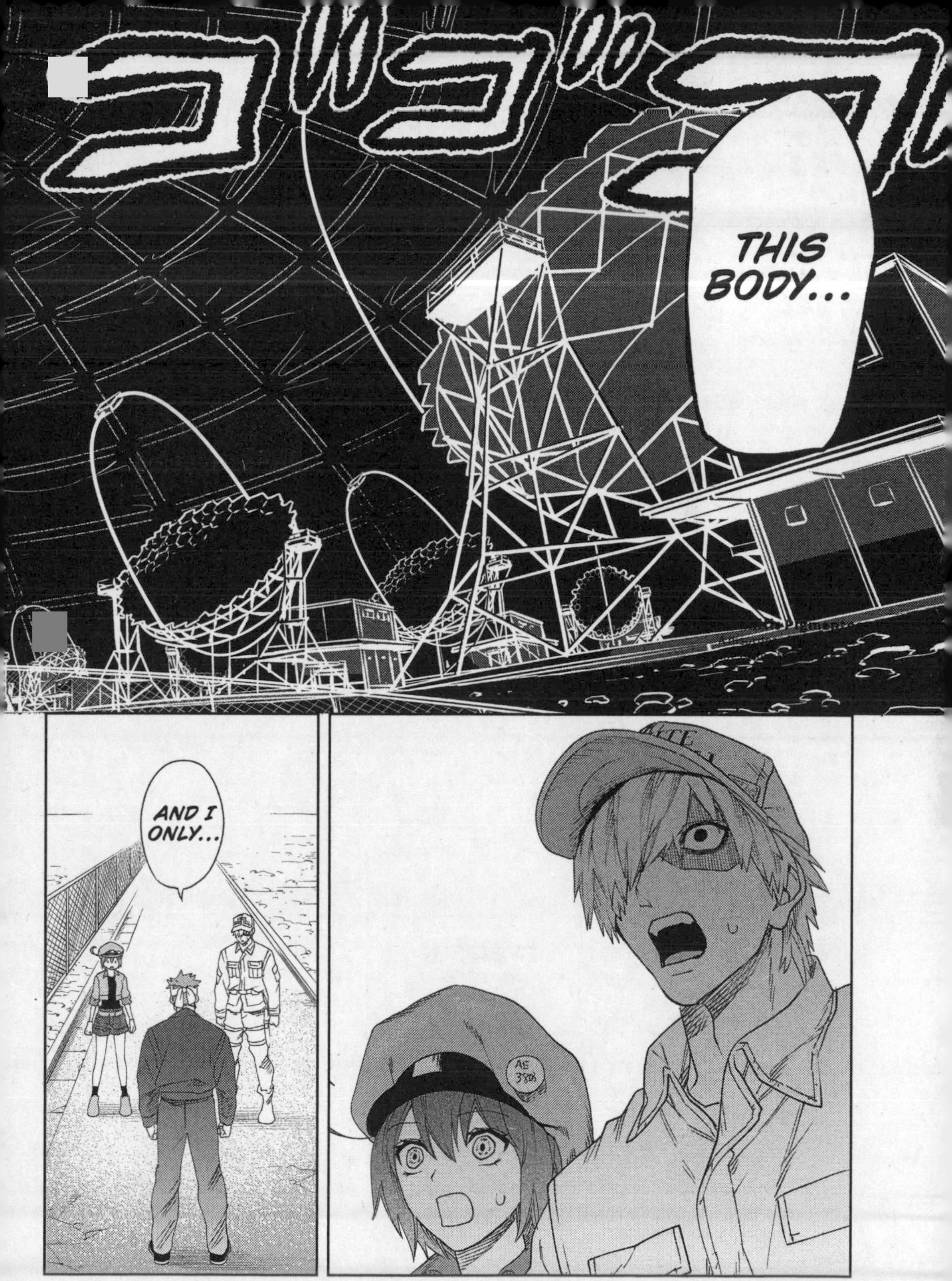
THIS BODY...
AND I ONLY...

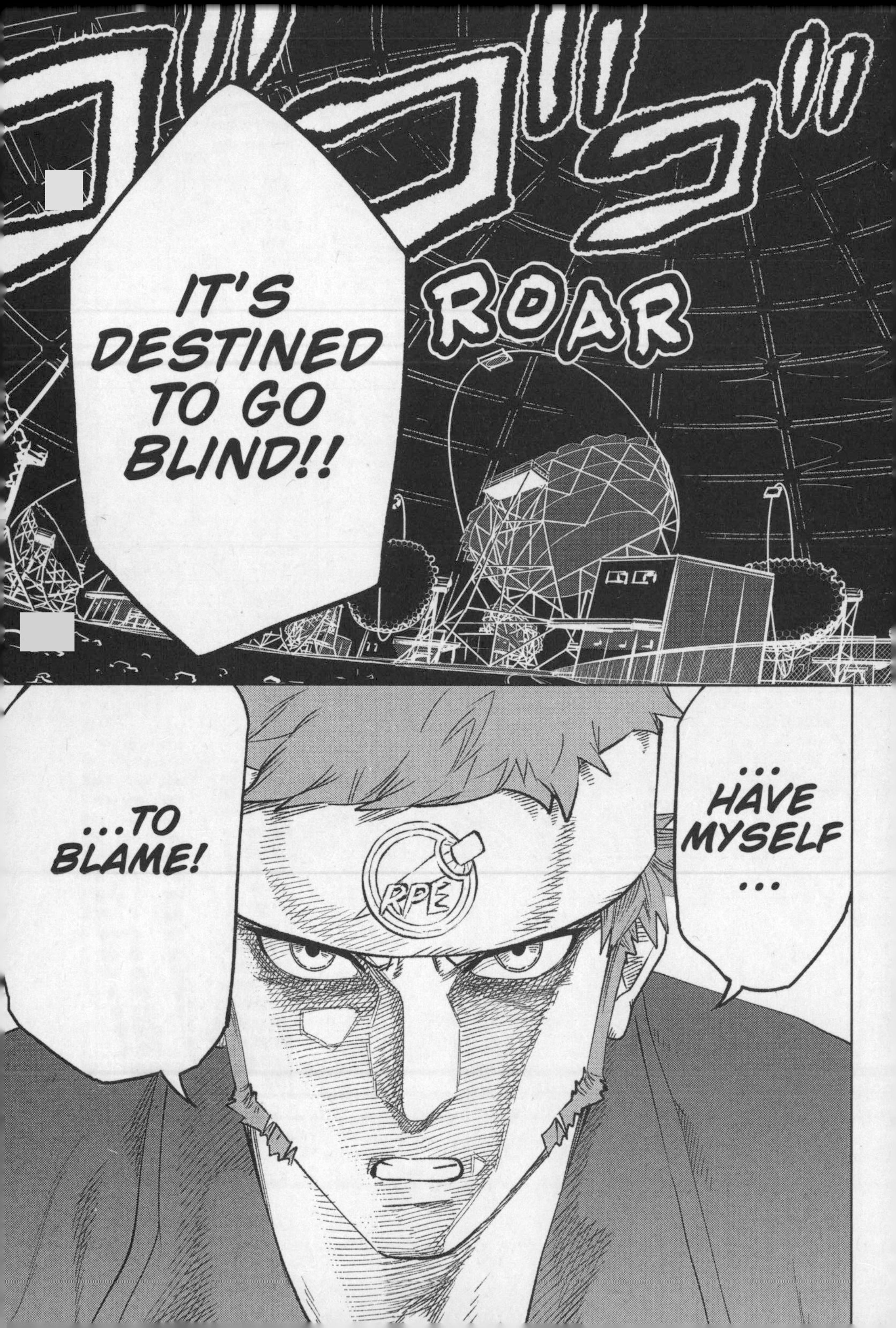
IT'S DESTINED TO GO BLIND!!
ROAR
...HAVE MYSELF...
...TO BLAME!

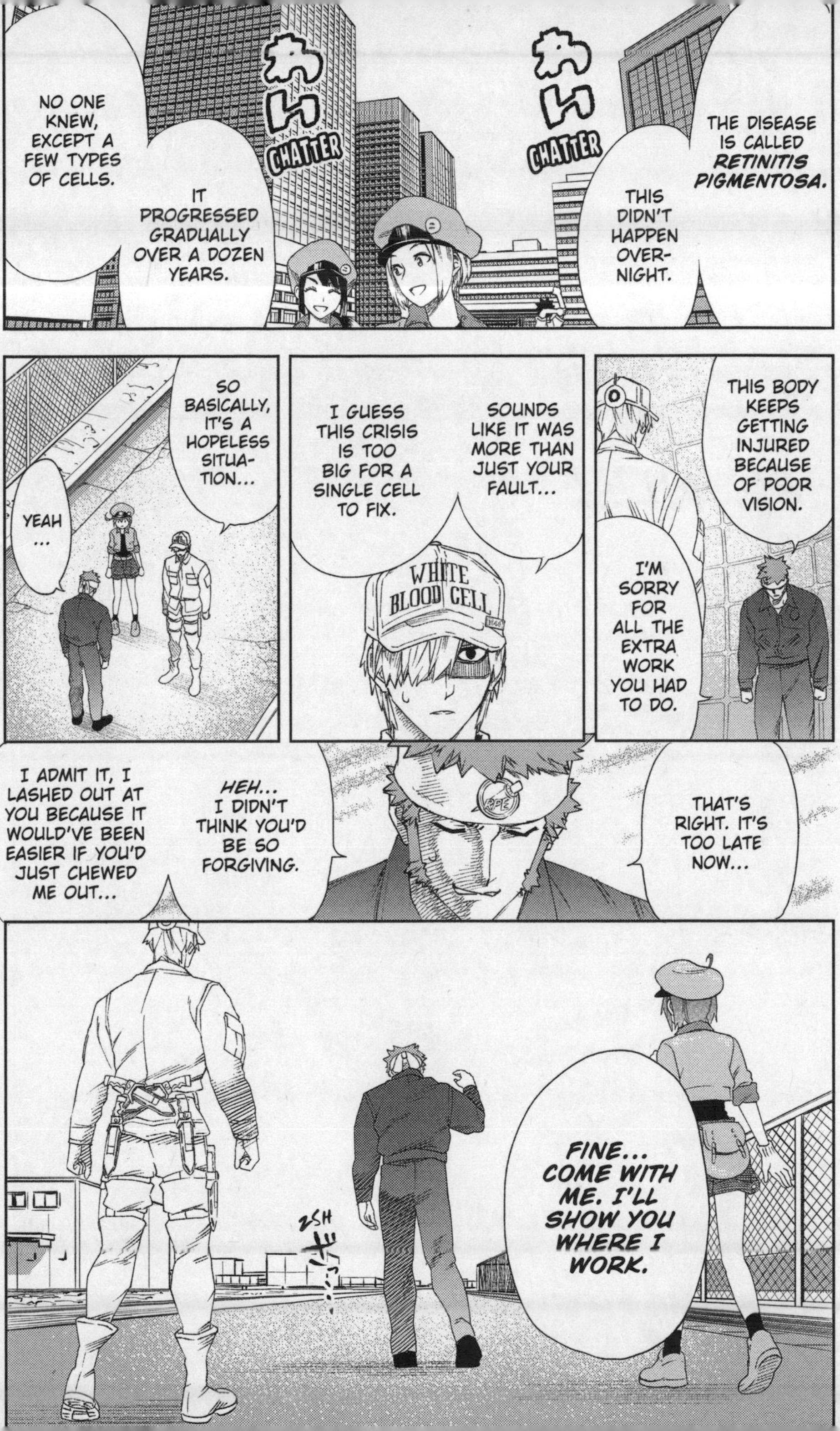
THE DISEASE IS CALLED *RETINITIS PIGMENTOSA.*
わい
CHATTER
THIS DIDN'T HAPPEN OVER-NIGHT.
わい
CHATTER
IT PROGRESSED GRADUALLY OVER A DOZEN YEARS.
NO ONE KNEW, EXCEPT A FEW TYPES OF CELLS.
THIS BODY KEEPS GETTING INJURED BECAUSE OF POOR VISION.
I'M SORRY FOR ALL THE EXTRA WORK YOU HAD TO DO.
SOUNDS LIKE IT WAS MORE THAN JUST YOUR FAULT...
I GUESS THIS CRISIS IS TOO BIG FOR A SINGLE CELL TO FIX.
WHITE BLOOD CELL
SO BASICALLY, IT'S A HOPELESS SITUA-TION...
YEAH ...
THAT'S RIGHT. IT'S TOO LATE NOW...
RPE
HEH... I DIDN'T THINK YOU'D BE SO FORGIVING.
I ADMIT IT, I LASHED OUT AT YOU BECAUSE IT WOULD'VE BEEN EASIER IF YOU'D JUST CHEWED ME OUT...
FINE... COME WITH ME. I'LL SHOW YOU WHERE I WORK.
ZSH

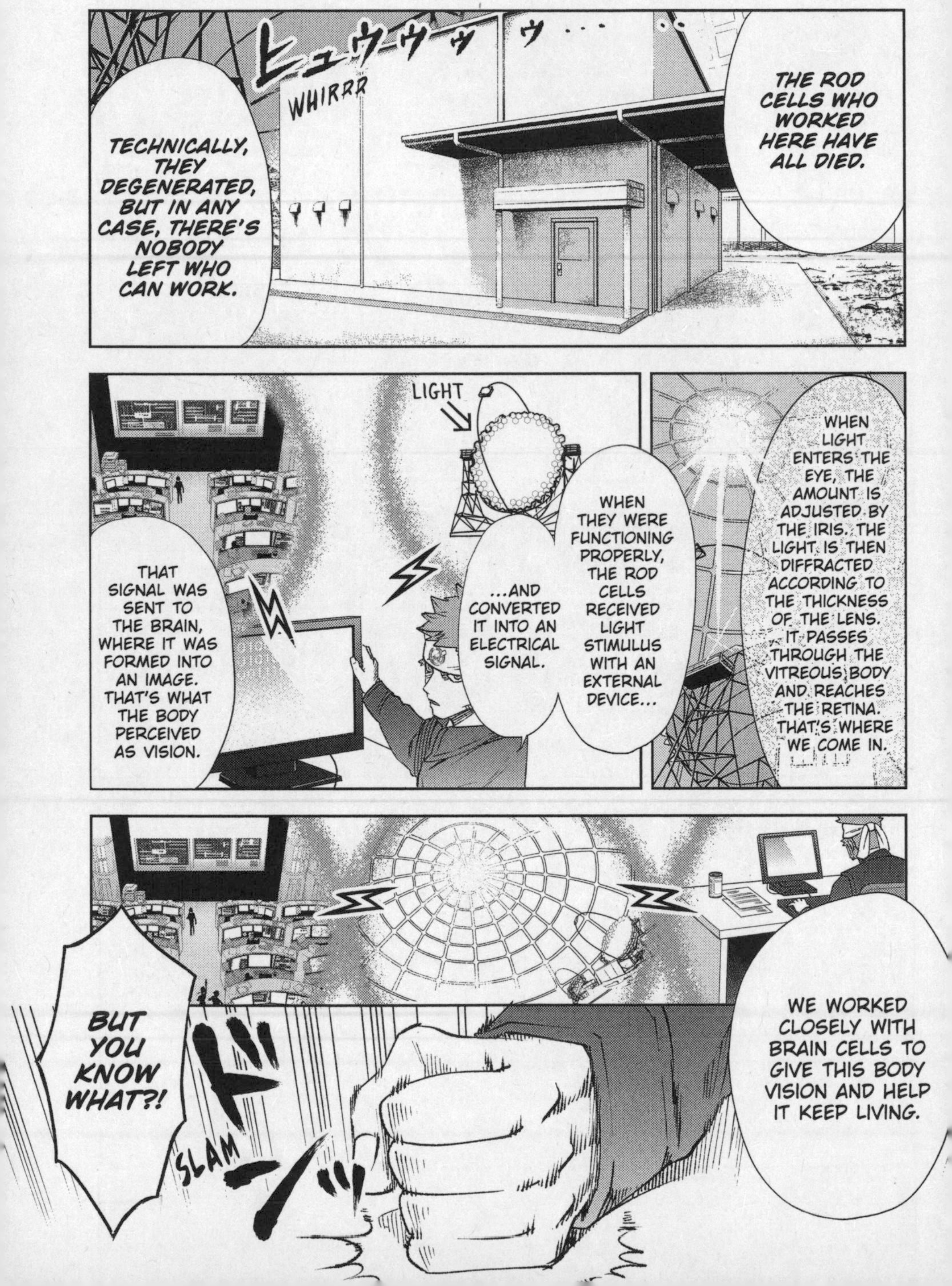
ヒュウウゥゥ ウ...
WHIRRR
THE ROD CELLS WHO WORKED HERE HAVE ALL DIED.
TECHNICALLY, THEY DEGENERATED, BUT IN ANY CASE, THERE'S NOBODY LEFT WHO CAN WORK.
WHEN LIGHT ENTERS THE EYE, THE AMOUNT IS ADJUSTED BY THE IRIS. THE LIGHT IS THEN DIFFRACTED ACCORDING TO THE THICKNESS OF THE LENS. IT PASSES THROUGH THE VITREOUS BODY AND REACHES THE RETINA. THAT'S WHERE WE COME IN.
LIGHT
WHEN THEY WERE FUNCTIONING PROPERLY, THE ROD CELLS RECEIVED LIGHT STIMULUS WITH AN EXTERNAL DEVICE...
...AND CONVERTED IT INTO AN ELECTRICAL SIGNAL.
THAT SIGNAL WAS SENT TO THE BRAIN, WHERE IT WAS FORMED INTO AN IMAGE. THAT'S WHAT THE BODY PERCEIVED AS VISION.
WE WORKED CLOSELY WITH BRAIN CELLS TO GIVE THIS BODY VISION AND HELP IT KEEP LIVING.
BUT YOU KNOW WHAT?!
SLAM

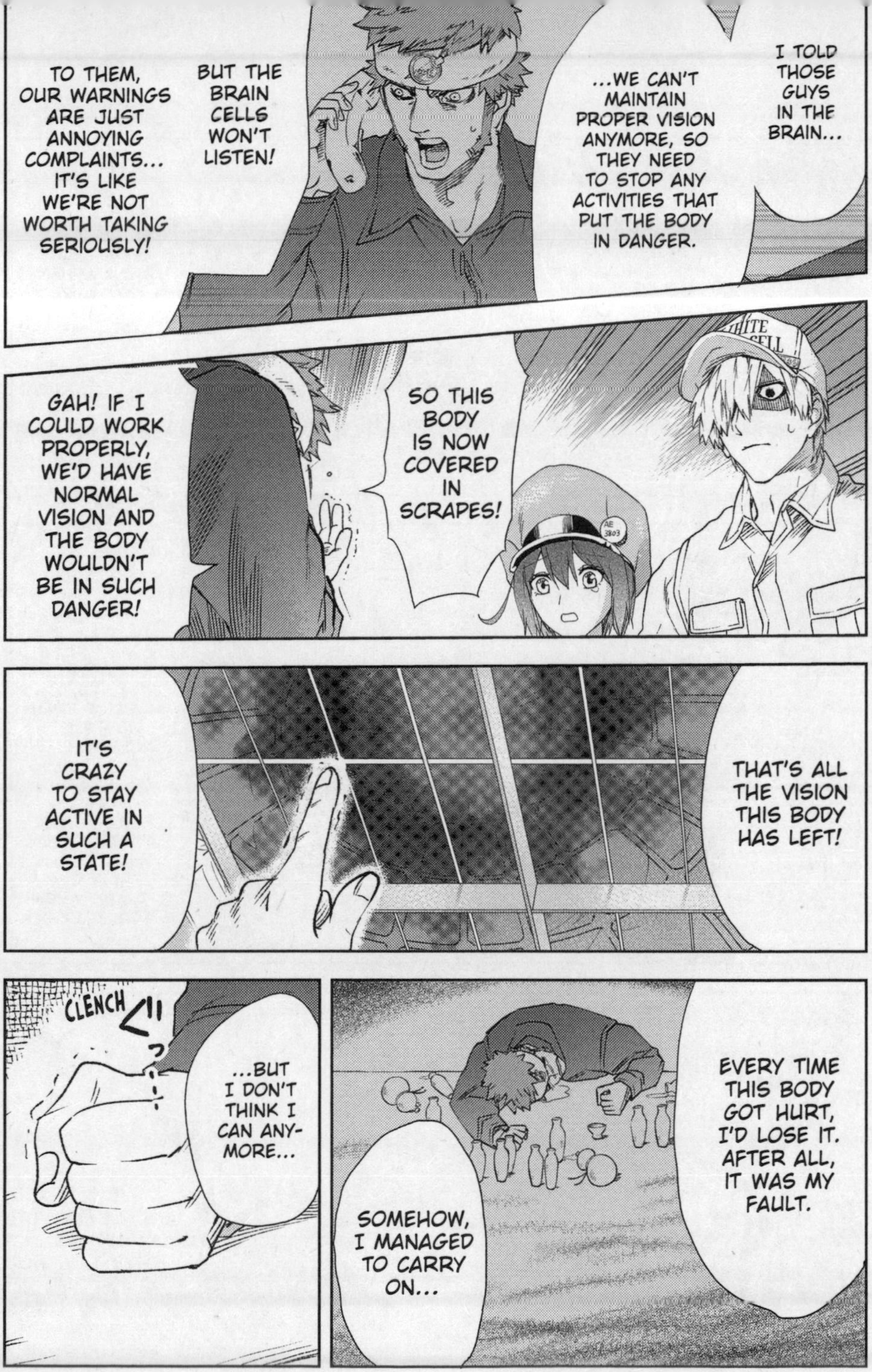
I TOLD THOSE GUYS IN THE BRAIN...
...WE CAN'T MAINTAIN PROPER VISION ANYMORE, SO THEY NEED TO STOP ANY ACTIVITIES THAT PUT THE BODY IN DANGER.
BUT THE BRAIN CELLS WON'T LISTEN!
TO THEM, OUR WARNINGS ARE JUST ANNOYING COMPLAINTS... IT'S LIKE WE'RE NOT WORTH TAKING SERIOUSLY!
SO THIS BODY IS NOW COVERED IN SCRAPES!
GAH! IF I COULD WORK PROPERLY, WE'D HAVE NORMAL VISION AND THE BODY WOULDN'T BE IN SUCH DANGER!
THAT'S ALL THE VISION THIS BODY HAS LEFT!
IT'S CRAZY TO STAY ACTIVE IN SUCH A STATE!
EVERY TIME THIS BODY GOT HURT, I'D LOSE IT. AFTER ALL, IT WAS MY FAULT.
SOMEHOW, I MANAGED TO CARRY ON...
...BUT I DON'T THINK I CAN ANY-MORE...
CLENCH

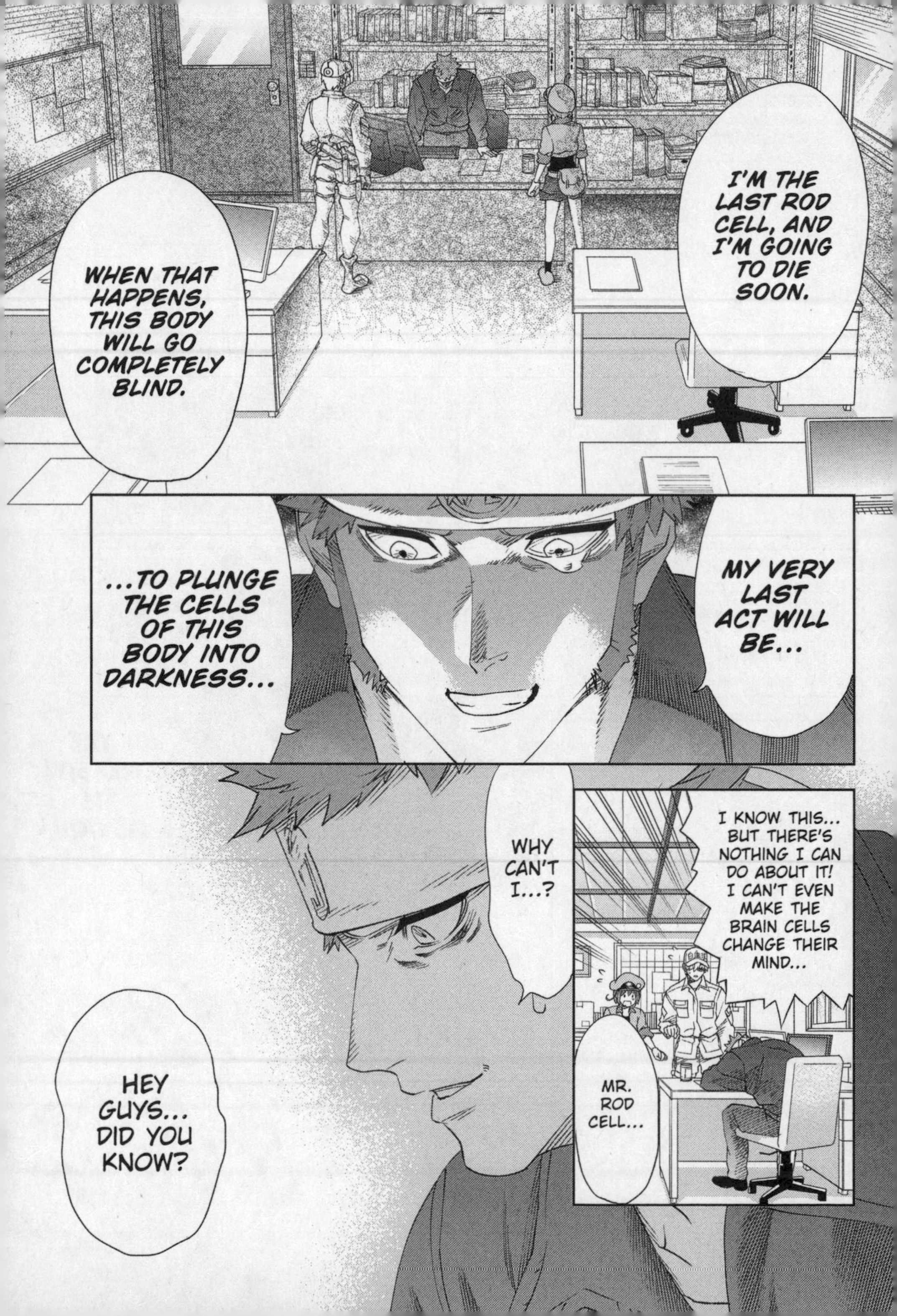
I'M THE LAST ROD CELL, AND I'M GOING TO DIE SOON.
WHEN THAT HAPPENS, THIS BODY WILL GO COMPLETELY BLIND.
MY VERY LAST ACT WILL BE...
...TO PLUNGE THE CELLS OF THIS BODY INTO DARKNESS...
I KNOW THIS... BUT THERE'S NOTHING I CAN DO ABOUT IT! I CAN'T EVEN MAKE THE BRAIN CELLS CHANGE THEIR MIND...
MR. ROD CELL...
WHY CAN'T I...?
HEY GUYS... DID YOU KNOW?

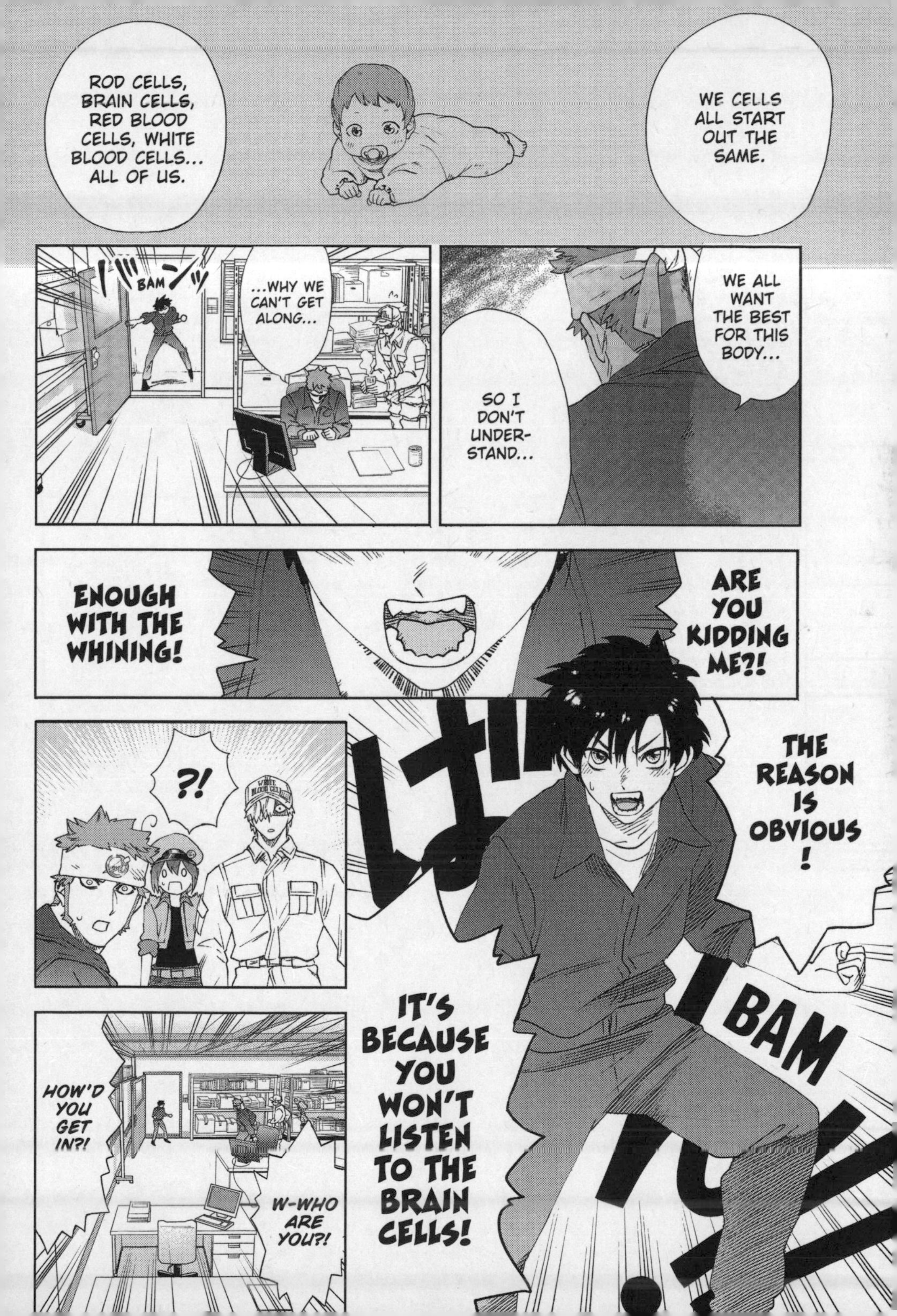
WE CELLS ALL START OUT THE SAME.
ROD CELLS, BRAIN CELLS, RED BLOOD CELLS, WHITE BLOOD CELLS... ALL OF US.
WE ALL WANT THE BEST FOR THIS BODY...
SO I DON'T UNDERSTAND...
...WHY WE CAN'T GET ALONG...
BAM
ARE YOU KIDDING ME?!
ENOUGH WITH THE WHINING!
THE REASON IS OBVIOUS!
IT'S BECAUSE YOU WON'T LISTEN TO THE BRAIN CELLS!
BAM
?!
WHITE BLOOD CELL
W-WHO ARE YOU?!
HOW'D YOU GET IN?!

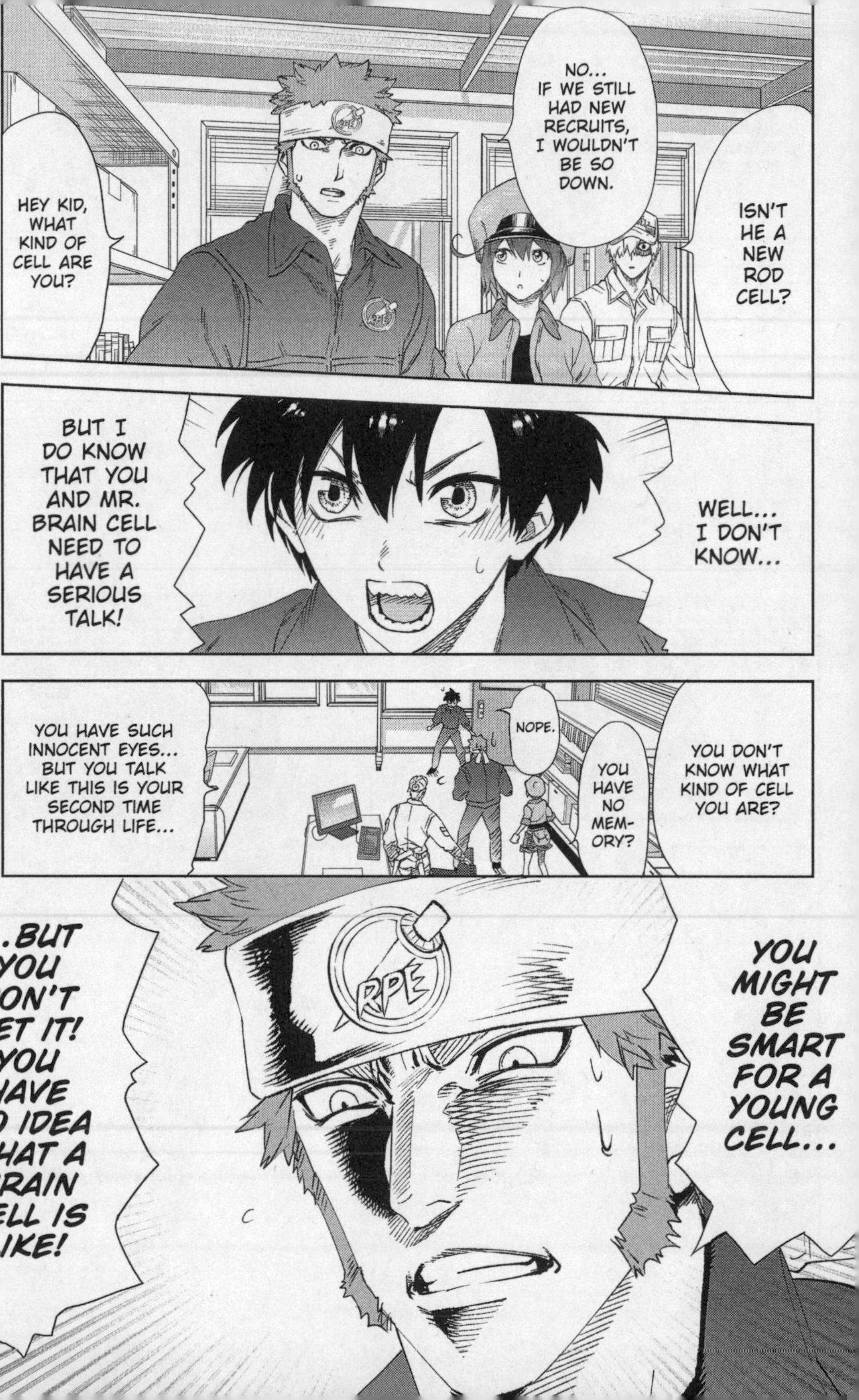
ISN'T HE A NEW ROD CELL?
NO... IF WE STILL HAD NEW RECRUITS, I WOULDN'T BE SO DOWN.
HEY KID, WHAT KIND OF CELL ARE YOU?
WELL... I DON'T KNOW...
BUT I DO KNOW THAT YOU AND MR. BRAIN CELL NEED TO HAVE A SERIOUS TALK!
YOU DON'T KNOW WHAT KIND OF CELL YOU ARE?
YOU HAVE NO MEM-ORY?
NOPE.
YOU HAVE SUCH INNOCENT EYES... BUT YOU TALK LIKE THIS IS YOUR SECOND TIME THROUGH LIFE...
YOU MIGHT BE SMART FOR A YOUNG CELL...
...BUT YOU DON'T GET IT! YOU HAVE NO IDEA WHAT A BRAIN CELL IS LIKE!

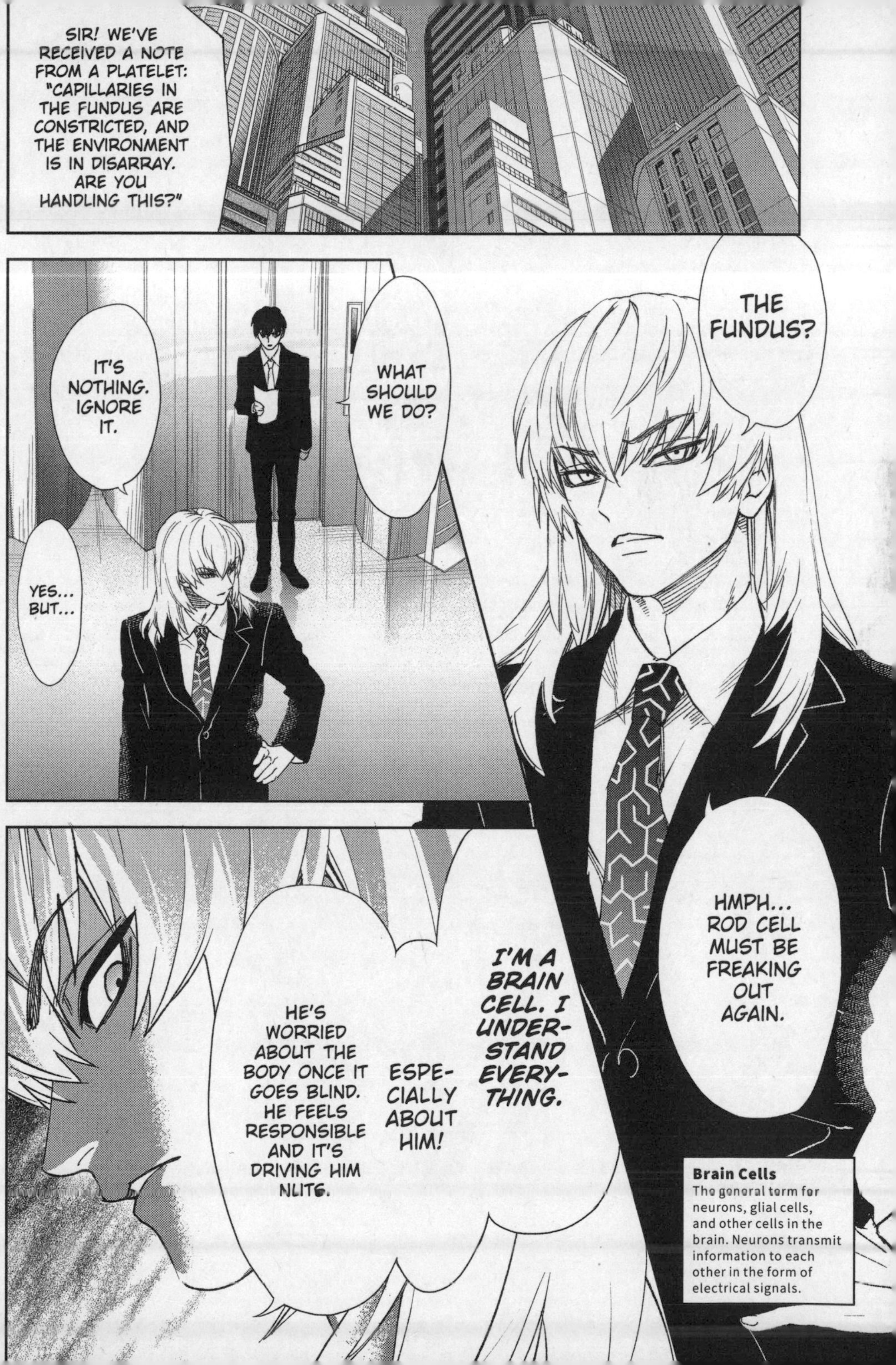
SIR! WE'VE RECEIVED A NOTE FROM A PLATELET: "CAPILLARIES IN THE FUNDUS ARE CONSTRICTED, AND THE ENVIRONMENT IS IN DISARRAY. ARE YOU HANDLING THIS?"
THE FUNDUS?
HMPH... ROD CELL MUST BE FREAKING OUT AGAIN.
WHAT SHOULD WE DO?
IT'S NOTHING. IGNORE IT.
YES... BUT...
I'M A BRAIN CELL. I UNDER-STAND EVERY-THING.
ESPE-CIALLY ABOUT HIM!
HE'S WORRIED ABOUT THE BODY ONCE IT GOES BLIND. HE FEELS RESPONSIBLE AND IT'S DRIVING HIM NUTS.
Brain Cells
The general term for neurons, glial cells, and other cells in the brain. Neurons transmit information to each other in the form of electrical signals.

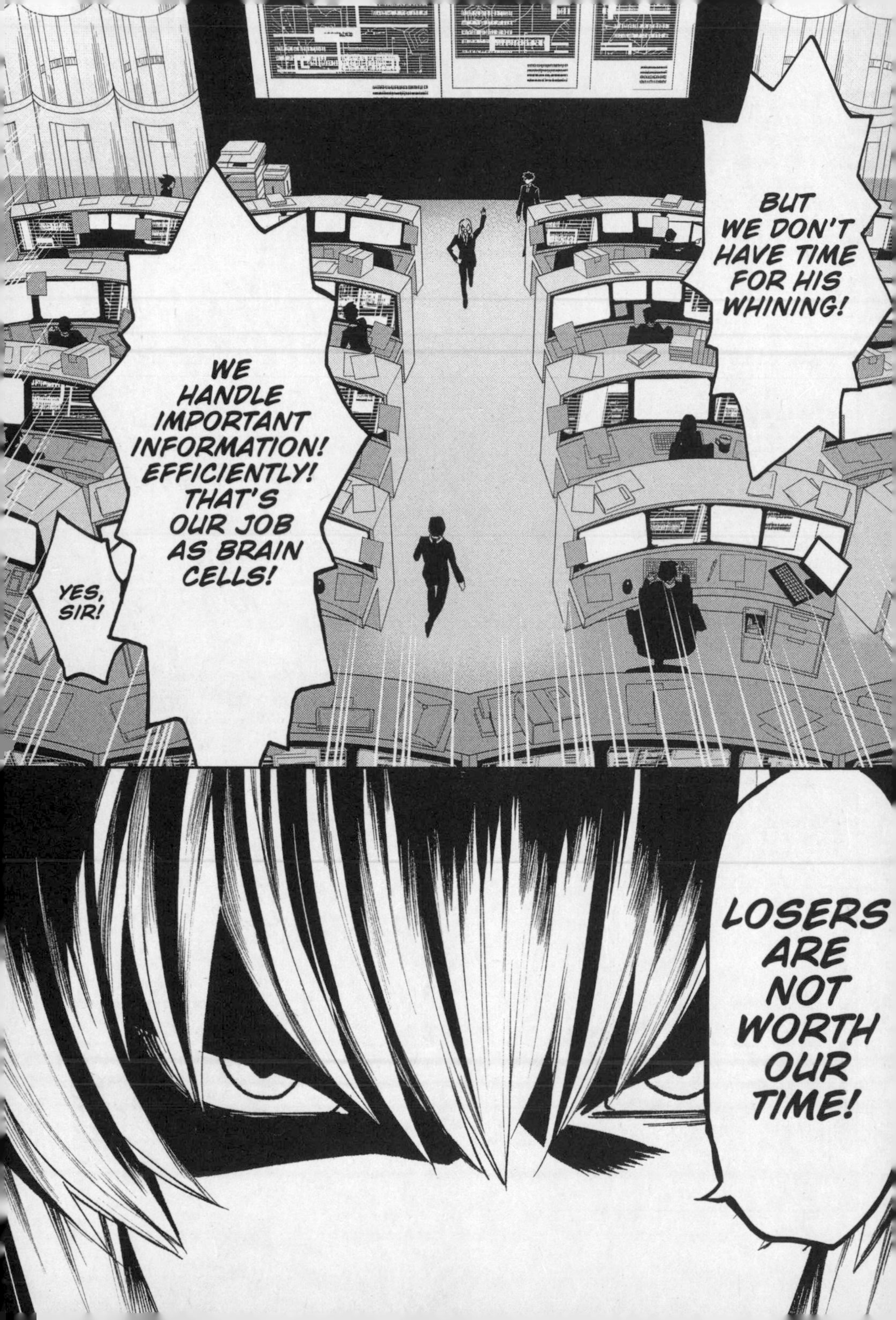
BUT WE DON'T HAVE TIME FOR HIS WHINING!
WE HANDLE IMPORTANT INFORMATION! EFFICIENTLY! THAT'S OUR JOB AS BRAIN CELLS!
YES, SIR!
LOSERS ARE NOT WORTH OUR TIME!

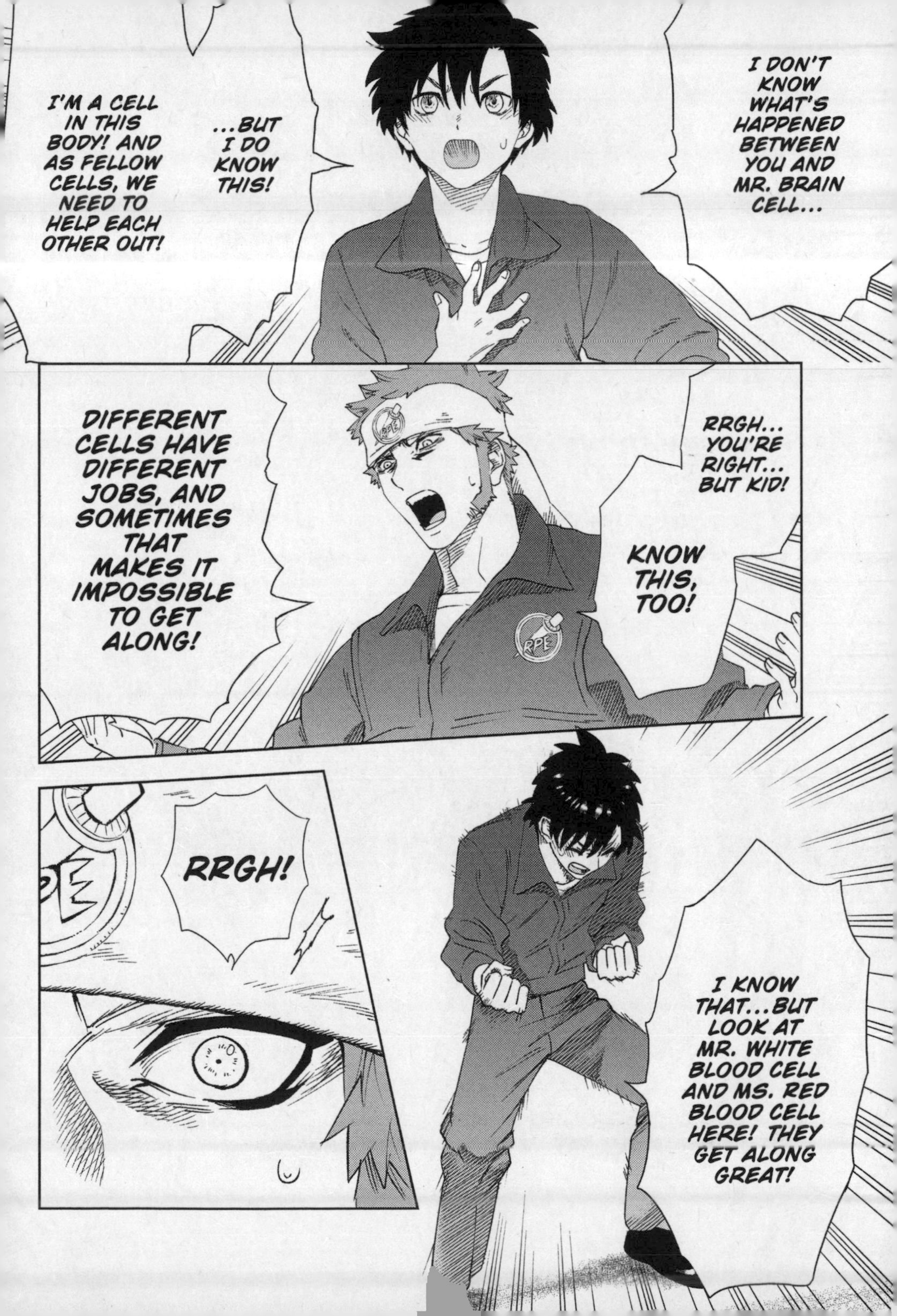
I DON'T KNOW WHAT'S HAPPENED BETWEEN YOU AND MR. BRAIN CELL...
...BUT I DO KNOW THIS!
I'M A CELL IN THIS BODY! AND AS FELLOW CELLS, WE NEED TO HELP EACH OTHER OUT!
RRGH... YOU'RE RIGHT... BUT KID!
KNOW THIS, TOO!
DIFFERENT CELLS HAVE DIFFERENT JOBS, AND SOMETIMES THAT MAKES IT IMPOSSIBLE TO GET ALONG!
I KNOW THAT...BUT LOOK AT MR. WHITE BLOOD CELL AND MS. RED BLOOD CELL HERE! THEY GET ALONG GREAT!
RRGH!

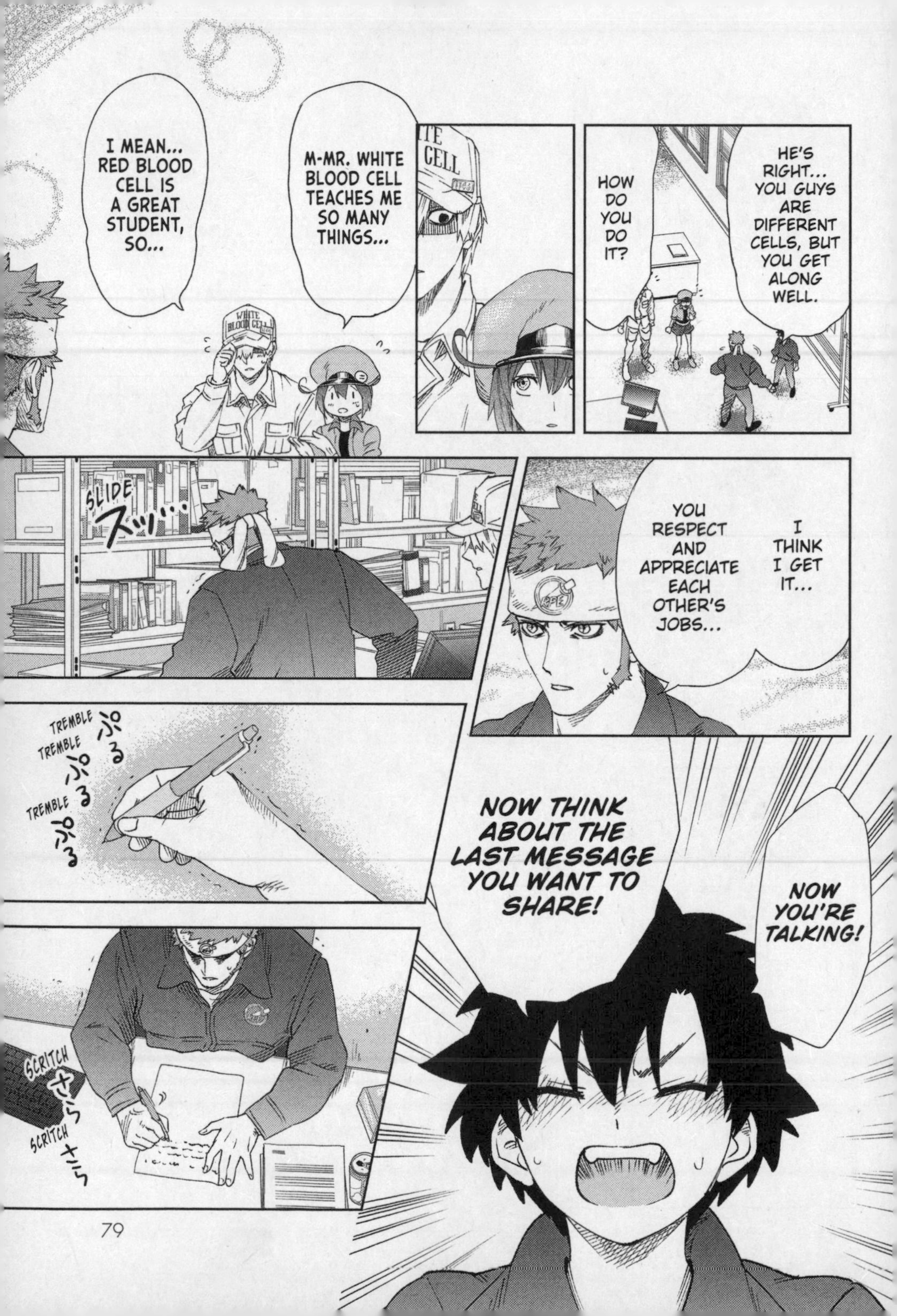
HE'S RIGHT... YOU GUYS ARE DIFFERENT CELLS, BUT YOU GET ALONG WELL.
HOW DO YOU DO IT?
M-MR. WHITE BLOOD CELL TEACHES ME SO MANY THINGS...
I MEAN... RED BLOOD CELL IS A GREAT STUDENT, SO...
WHITE BLOOD CELL
I THINK I GET IT...
YOU RESPECT AND APPRECIATE EACH OTHER'S JOBS...
SLIDE ズッ...
NOW YOU'RE TALKING!
NOW THINK ABOUT THE LAST MESSAGE YOU WANT TO SHARE!
TREMBLE ぷる
TREMBLE ぷる
TREMBLE ぷる
SCRITCH さら
SCRITCH さら

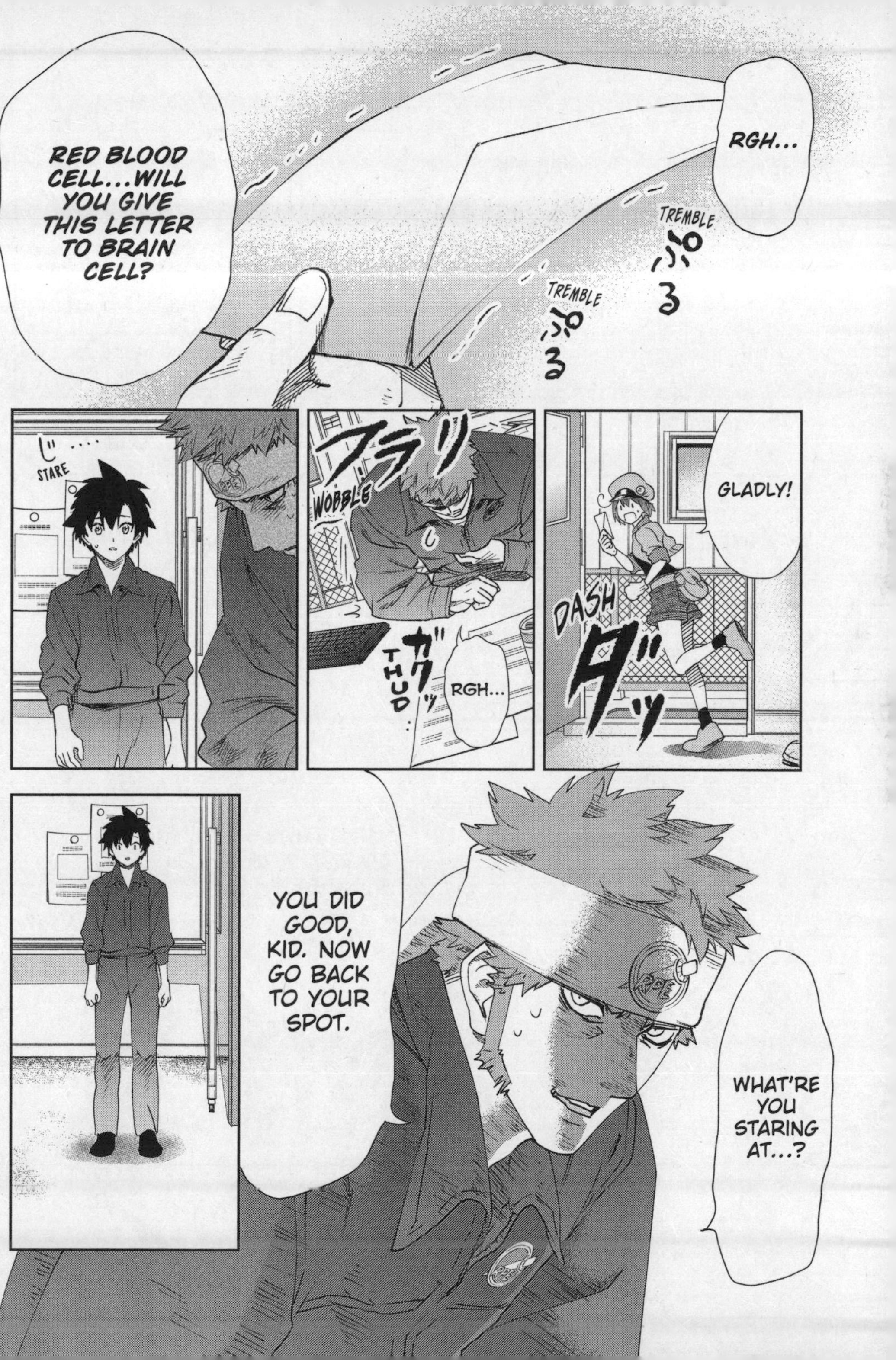
RGH...
TREMBLE
ぷる
TREMBLE
ぷる
RED BLOOD CELL...WILL YOU GIVE THIS LETTER TO BRAIN CELL?
GLADLY!
DASH
ダッ
フラリ
WOBBLE
ガクッ
THUD
RGH...
じ...
STARE
WHAT'RE YOU STARING AT...?
YOU DID GOOD, KID. NOW GO BACK TO YOUR SPOT.

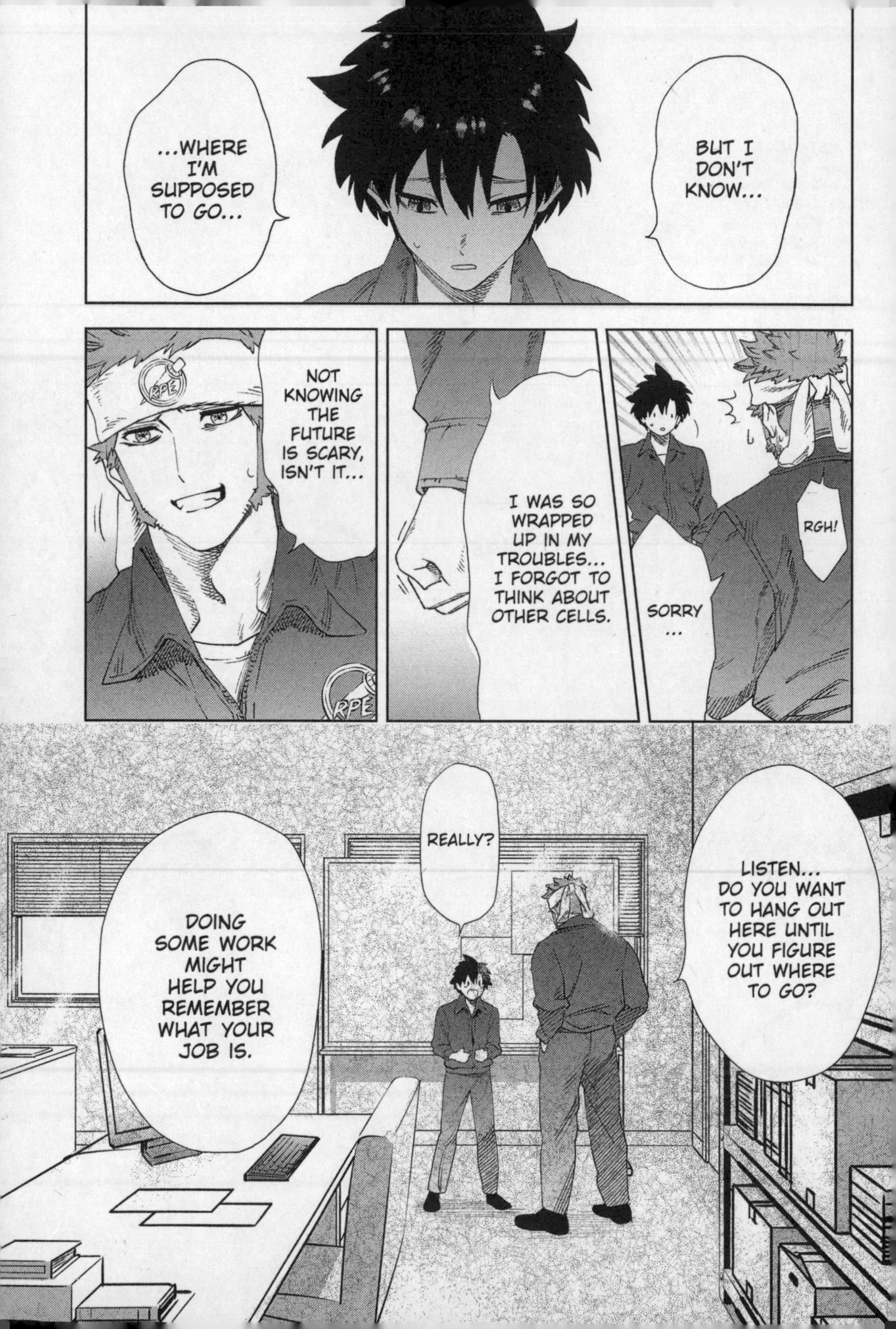
BUT I DON'T KNOW...
...WHERE I'M SUPPOSED TO GO...
RGH!
SORRY ...
I WAS SO WRAPPED UP IN MY TROUBLES... I FORGOT TO THINK ABOUT OTHER CELLS.
NOT KNOWING THE FUTURE IS SCARY, ISN'T IT...
RPE
LISTEN... DO YOU WANT TO HANG OUT HERE UNTIL YOU FIGURE OUT WHERE TO GO?
REALLY?
DOING SOME WORK MIGHT HELP YOU REMEMBER WHAT YOUR JOB IS.

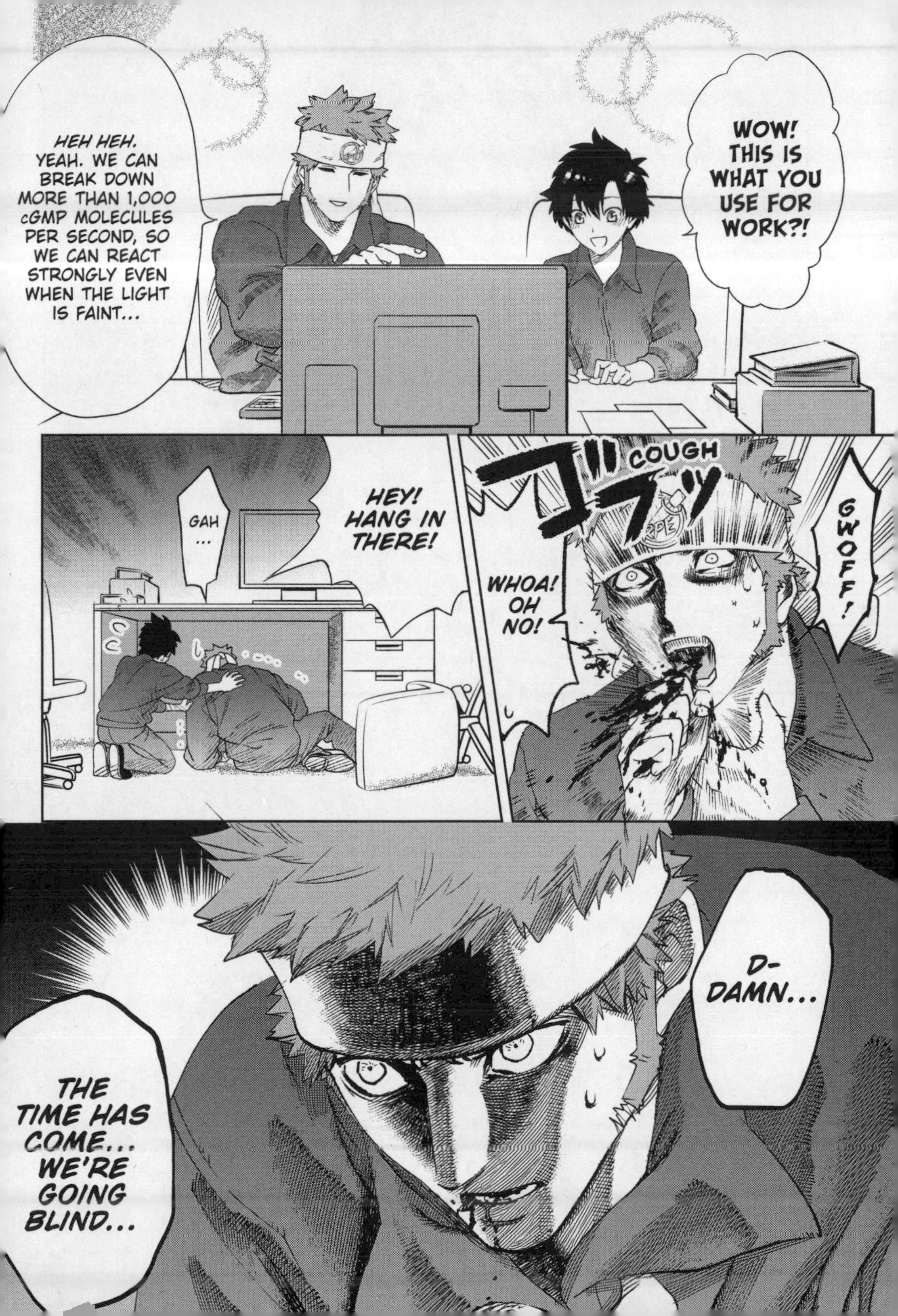
WOW! THIS IS WHAT YOU USE FOR WORK?!
HEH HEH. YEAH. WE CAN BREAK DOWN MORE THAN 1,000 cGMP MOLECULES PER SECOND, SO WE CAN REACT STRONGLY EVEN WHEN THE LIGHT IS FAINT...
GWOFF!
COUGH
ゴブッ
WHOA! OH NO!
HEY! HANG IN THERE!
GAH ...
D- DAMN...
THE TIME HAS COME... WE'RE GOING BLIND...

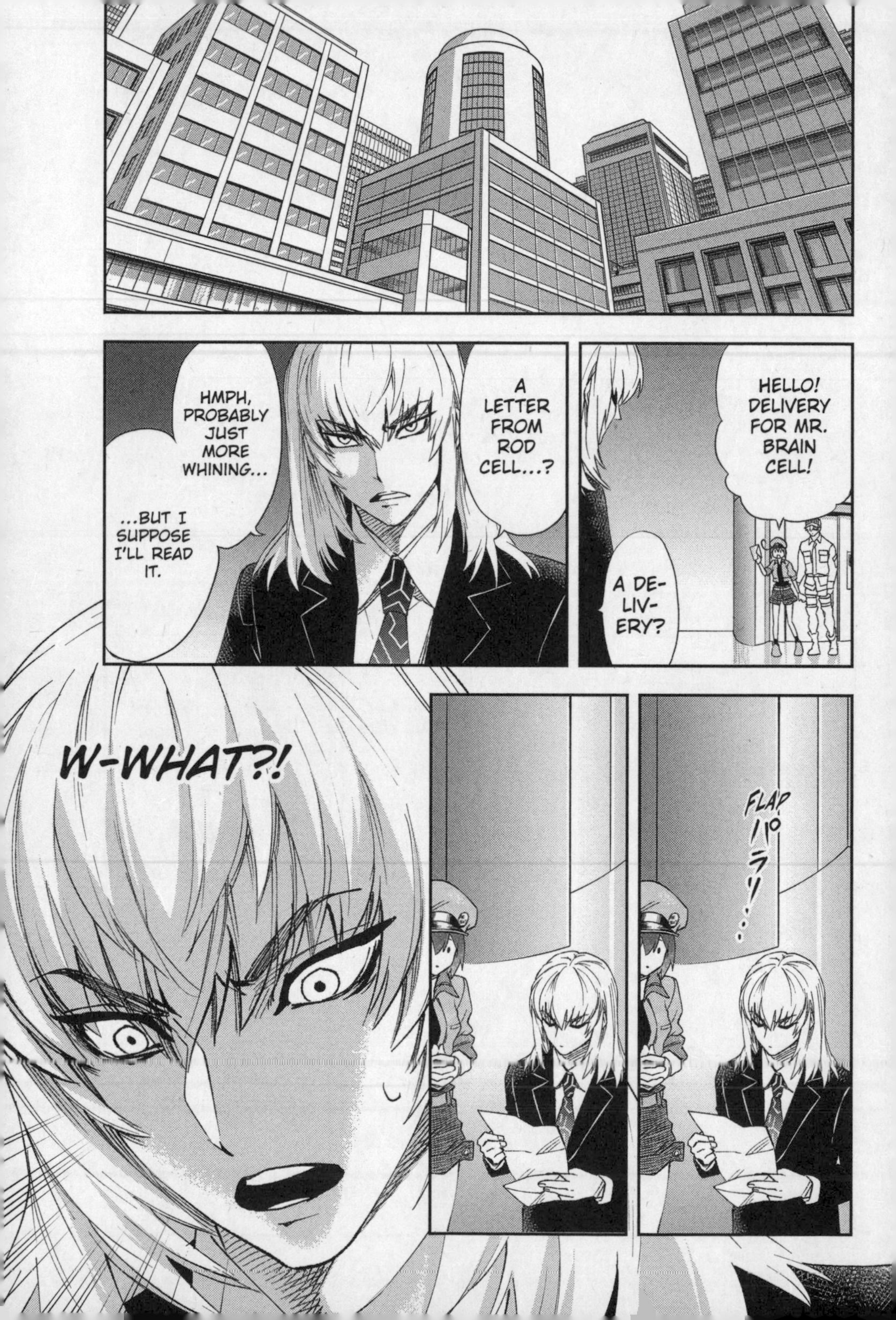
HELLO! DELIVERY FOR MR. BRAIN CELL!
A DE-LIV-ERY?
A LETTER FROM ROD CELL...?
HMPH, PROBABLY JUST MORE WHINING...
...BUT I SUPPOSE I'LL READ IT.
FLAP
パラッ…
W-WHAT?!

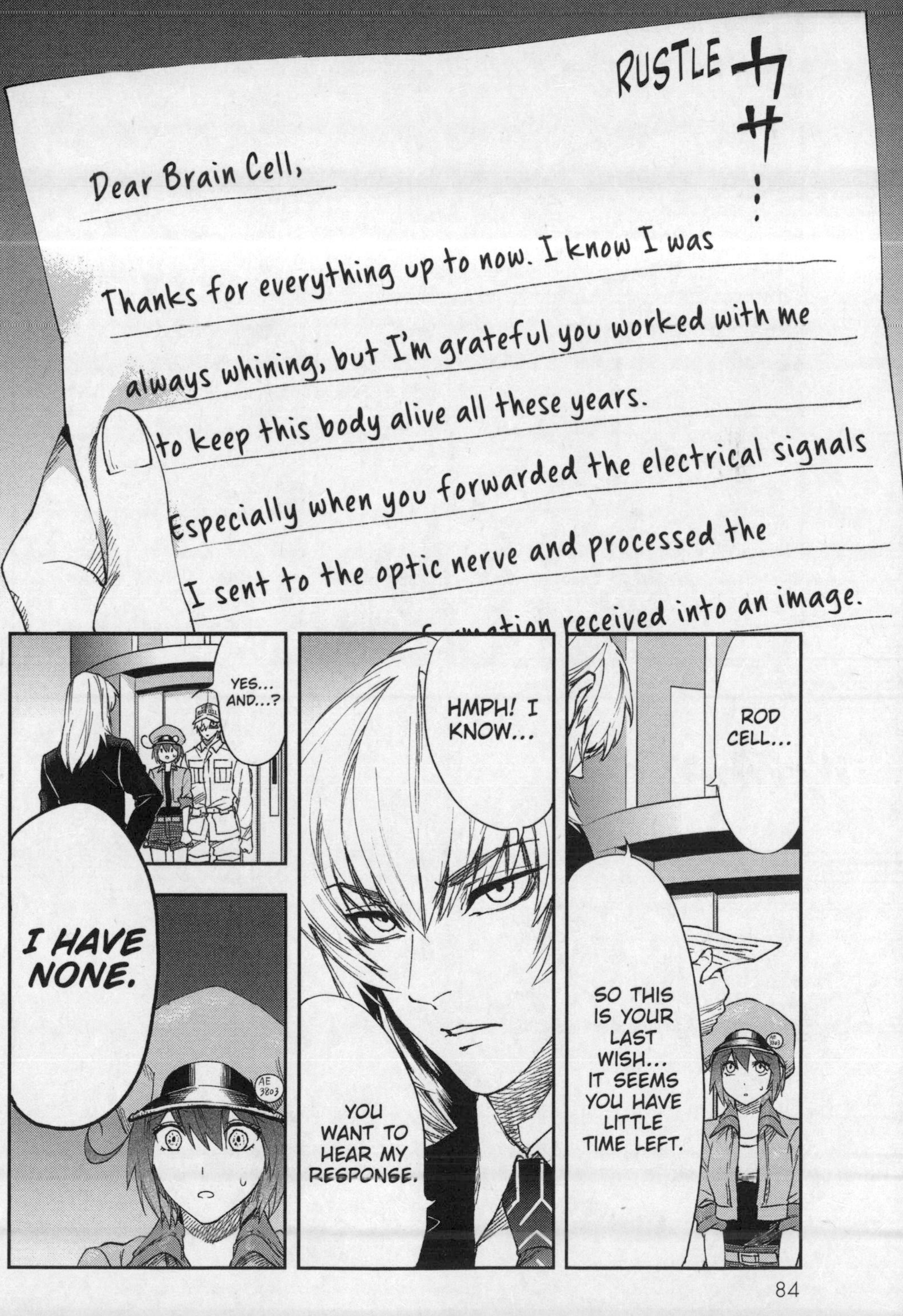
RUSTLE
カサ…
Dear Brain Cell,
Thanks for everything up to now. I know I was
always whining, but I'm grateful you worked with me
to keep this body alive all these years.
Especially when you forwarded the electrical signals
I sent to the optic nerve and processed the
received into an image.
ROD CELL...
SO THIS IS YOUR LAST WISH... IT SEEMS YOU HAVE LITTLE TIME LEFT.
AE 3803
HMPH! I KNOW...
YOU WANT TO HEAR MY RESPONSE.
YES... AND...?
I HAVE NONE.
AE 3803

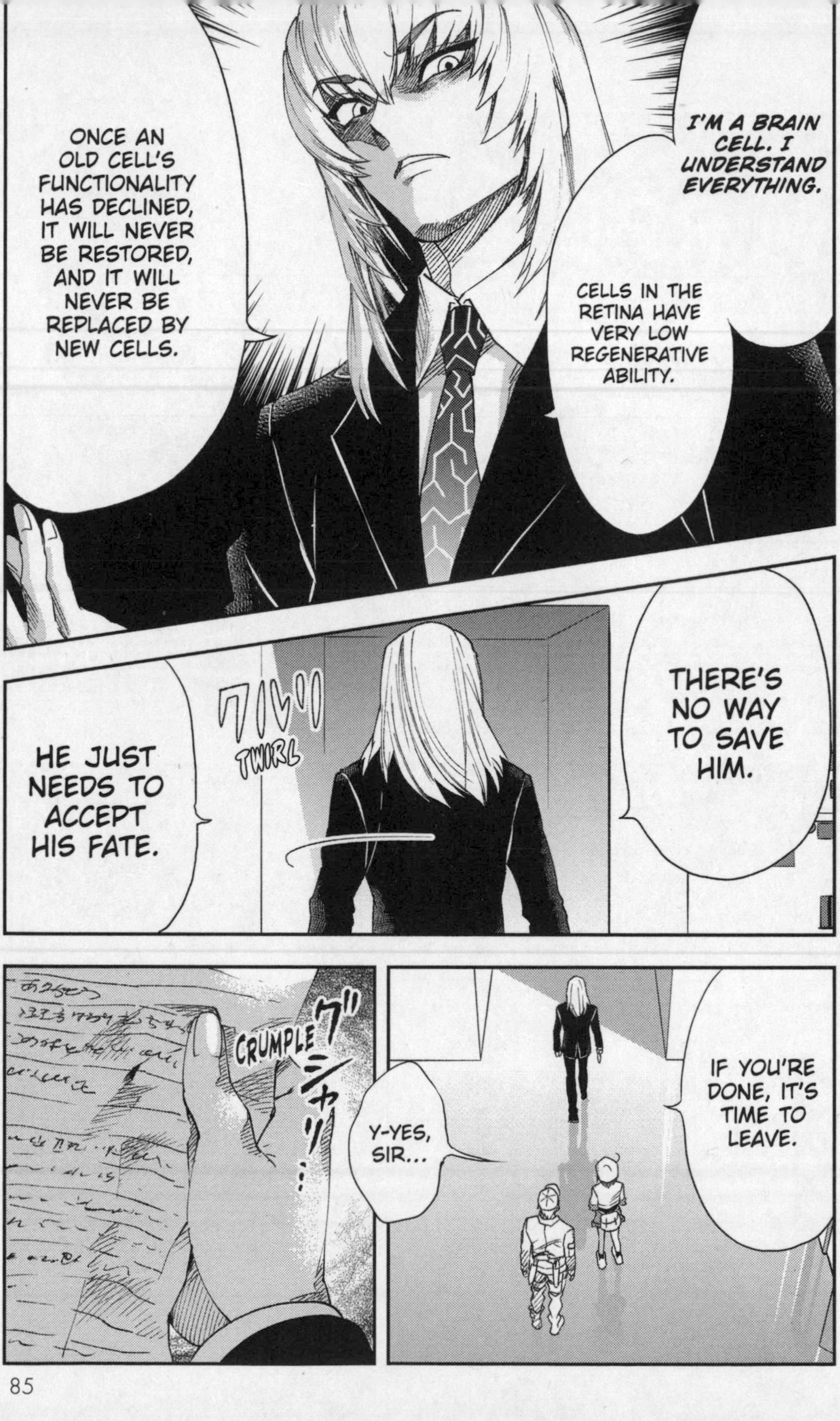
I'M A BRAIN CELL. I UNDERSTAND EVERYTHING.
CELLS IN THE RETINA HAVE VERY LOW REGENERATIVE ABILITY.
ONCE AN OLD CELL'S FUNCTIONALITY HAS DECLINED, IT WILL NEVER BE RESTORED, AND IT WILL NEVER BE REPLACED BY NEW CELLS.
THERE'S NO WAY TO SAVE HIM.
TWIRL
HE JUST NEEDS TO ACCEPT HIS FATE.
IF YOU'RE DONE, IT'S TIME TO LEAVE.
Y-YES, SIR...
CRUMPLE

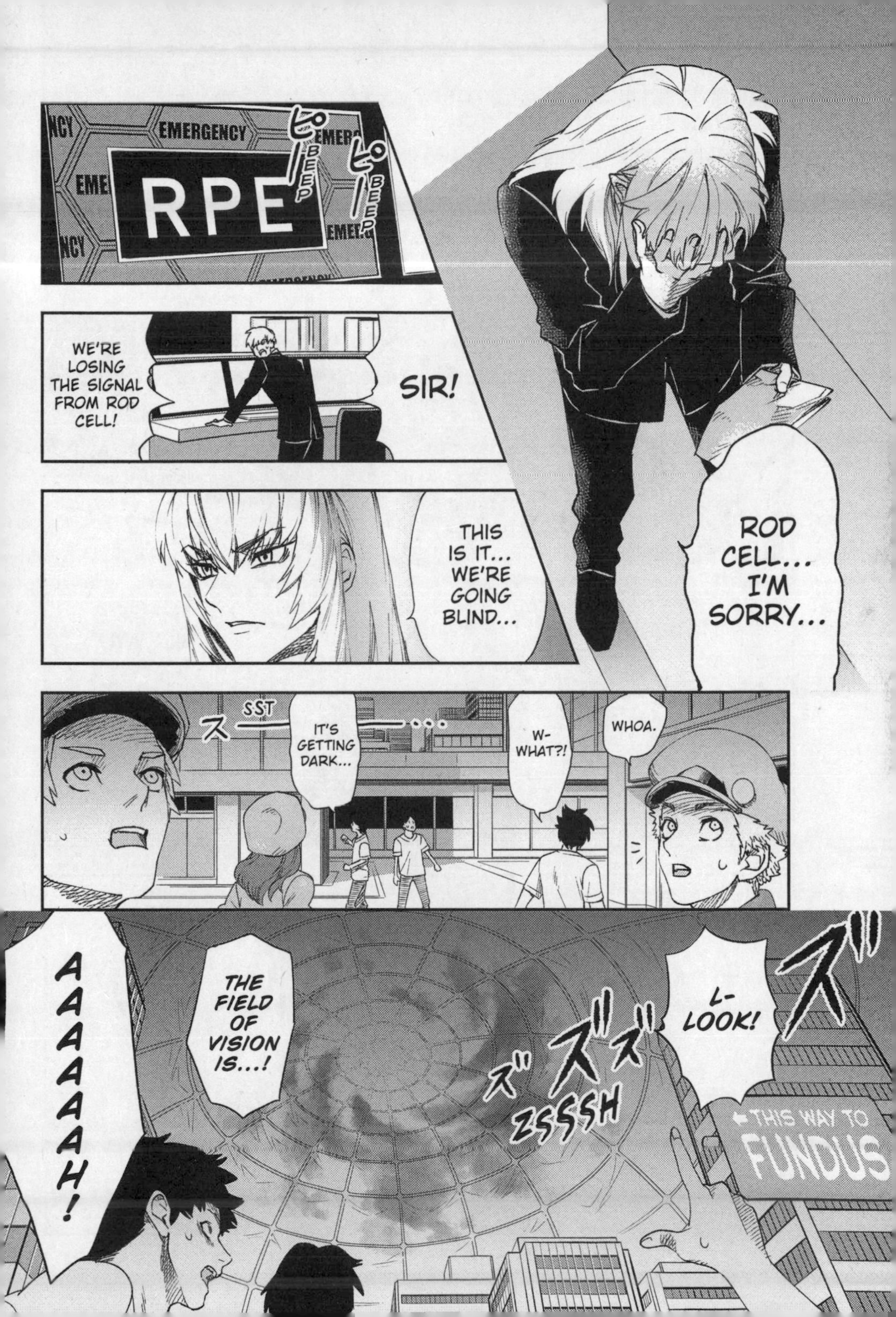
ROD CELL... I'M SORRY...
ピーピー BEEP
ピーピー BEEP
EMERGENCY
RPE
SIR!
WE'RE LOSING THE SIGNAL FROM ROD CELL!
THIS IS IT... WE'RE GOING BLIND...
WHOA.
W-WHAT?!
IT'S GETTING DARK...
スー… SST
ズ
L-LOOK!
ズズズ ZSSSH
← THIS WAY TO FUNDUS
THE FIELD OF VISION IS...!
AAAAAAAH!

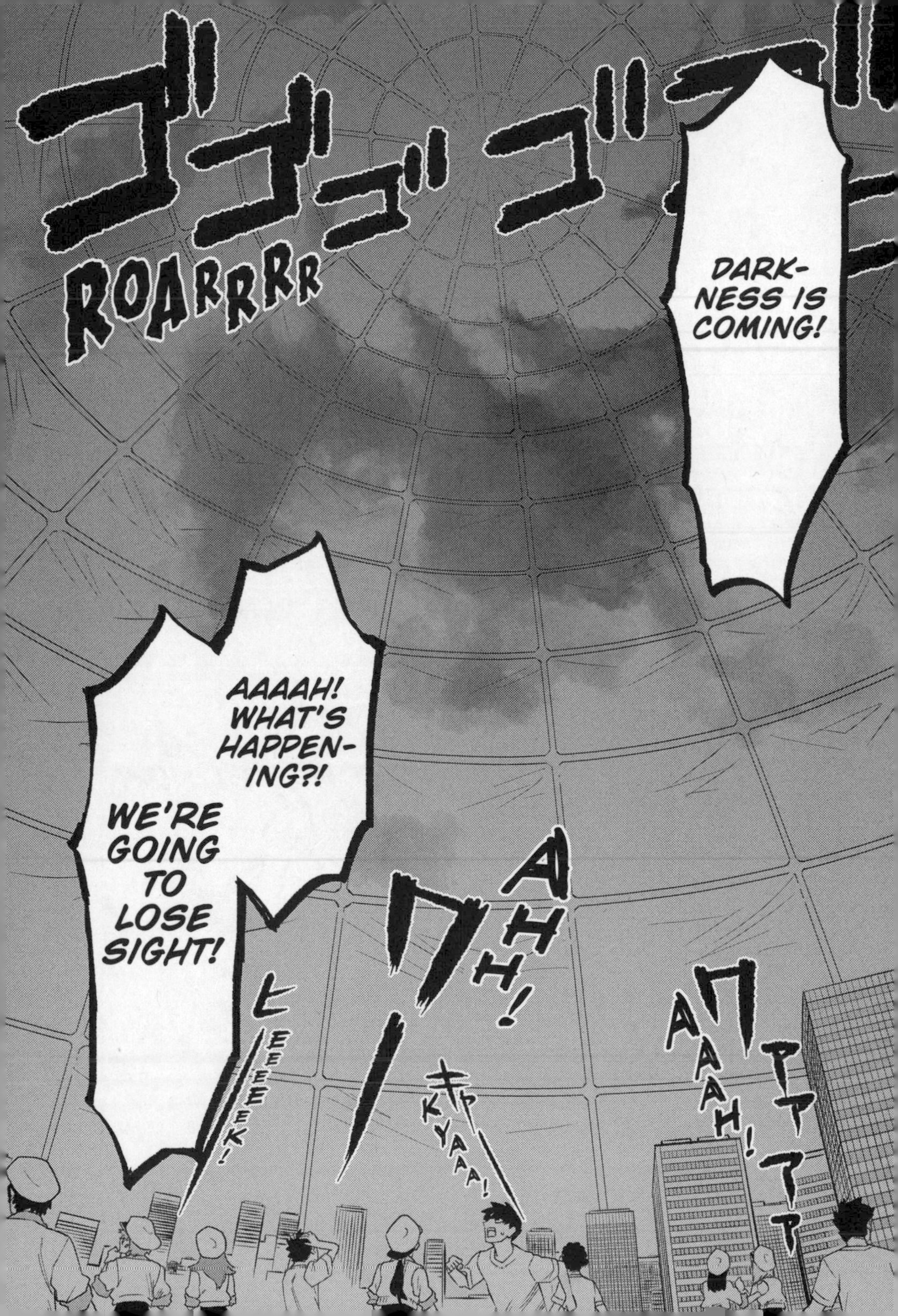
DARKNESS IS COMING!
ROARRRR
AAAAH! WHAT'S HAPPENING?!
WE'RE GOING TO LOSE SIGHT!
AAAAH!
KYAAA!
AHH!
EEEEEK!

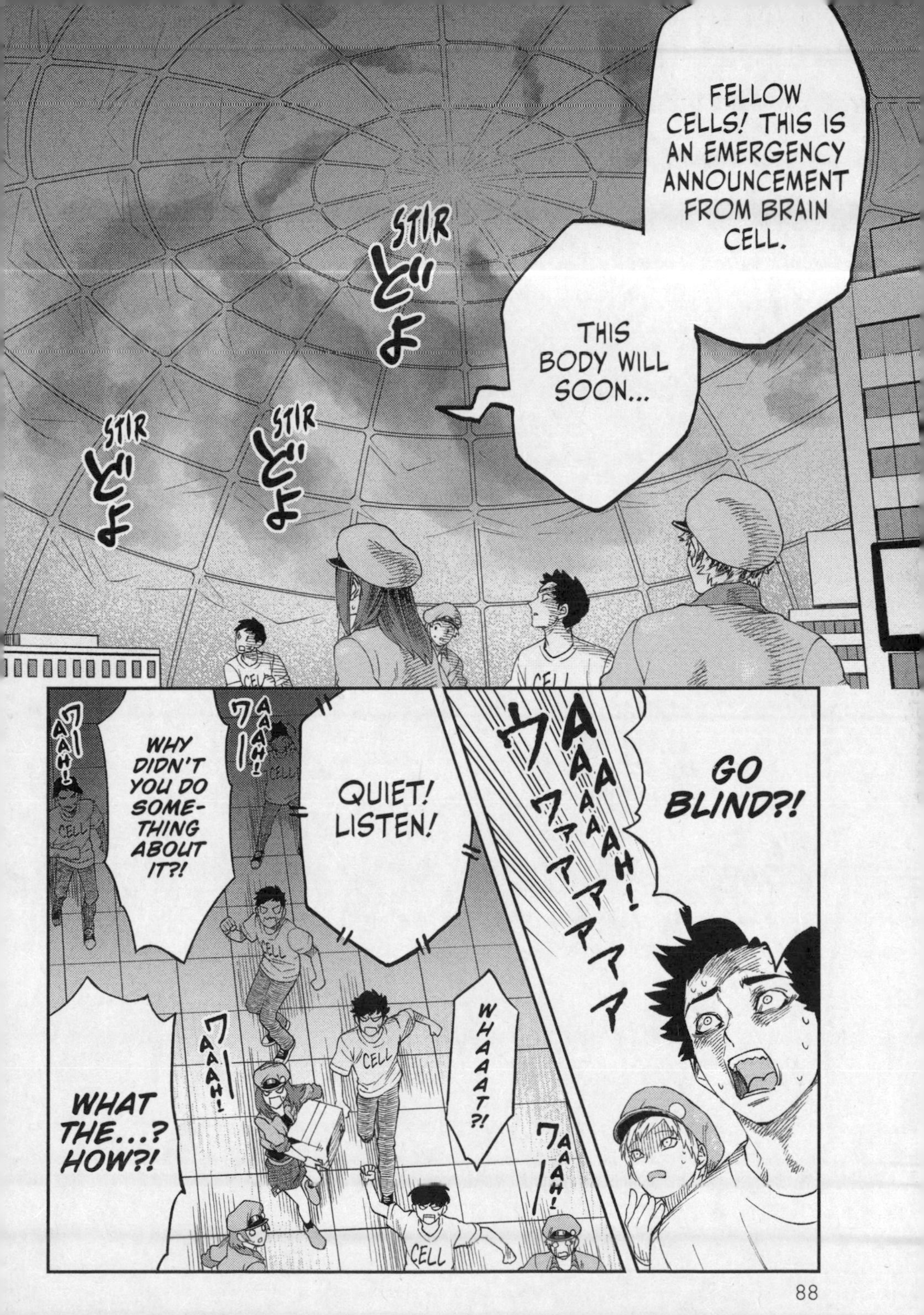
FELLOW CELLS! THIS IS AN EMERGENCY ANNOUNCEMENT FROM BRAIN CELL.
THIS BODY WILL SOON...
STIR どよ
STIR どよ
STIR どよ
GO BLIND?!
ウァァァァァァァ AAAAAAAH!
QUIET! LISTEN!
WHY DIDN'T YOU DO SOMETHING ABOUT IT?!
ワー AAAH!
ワー AAAH!
WHAAAAT?!
ワー AAAH!
ワー AAAH!
WHAT THE...? HOW?!

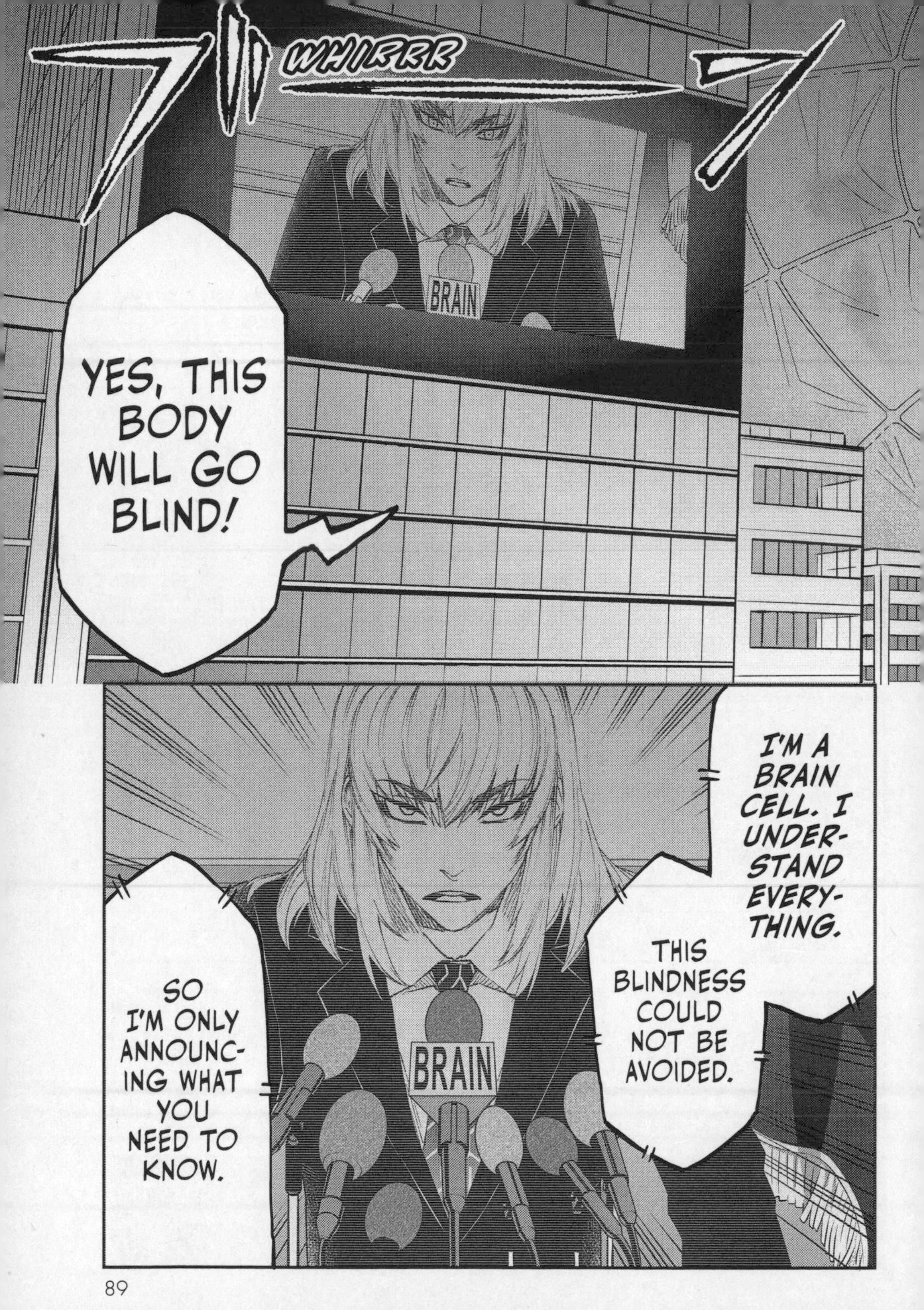

WHIRRR
BRAIN
YES, THIS BODY WILL GO BLIND!
I'M A BRAIN CELL. I UNDER-STAND EVERY-THING.
THIS BLINDNESS COULD NOT BE AVOIDED.
SO I'M ONLY ANNOUNC-ING WHAT YOU NEED TO KNOW.
BRAIN

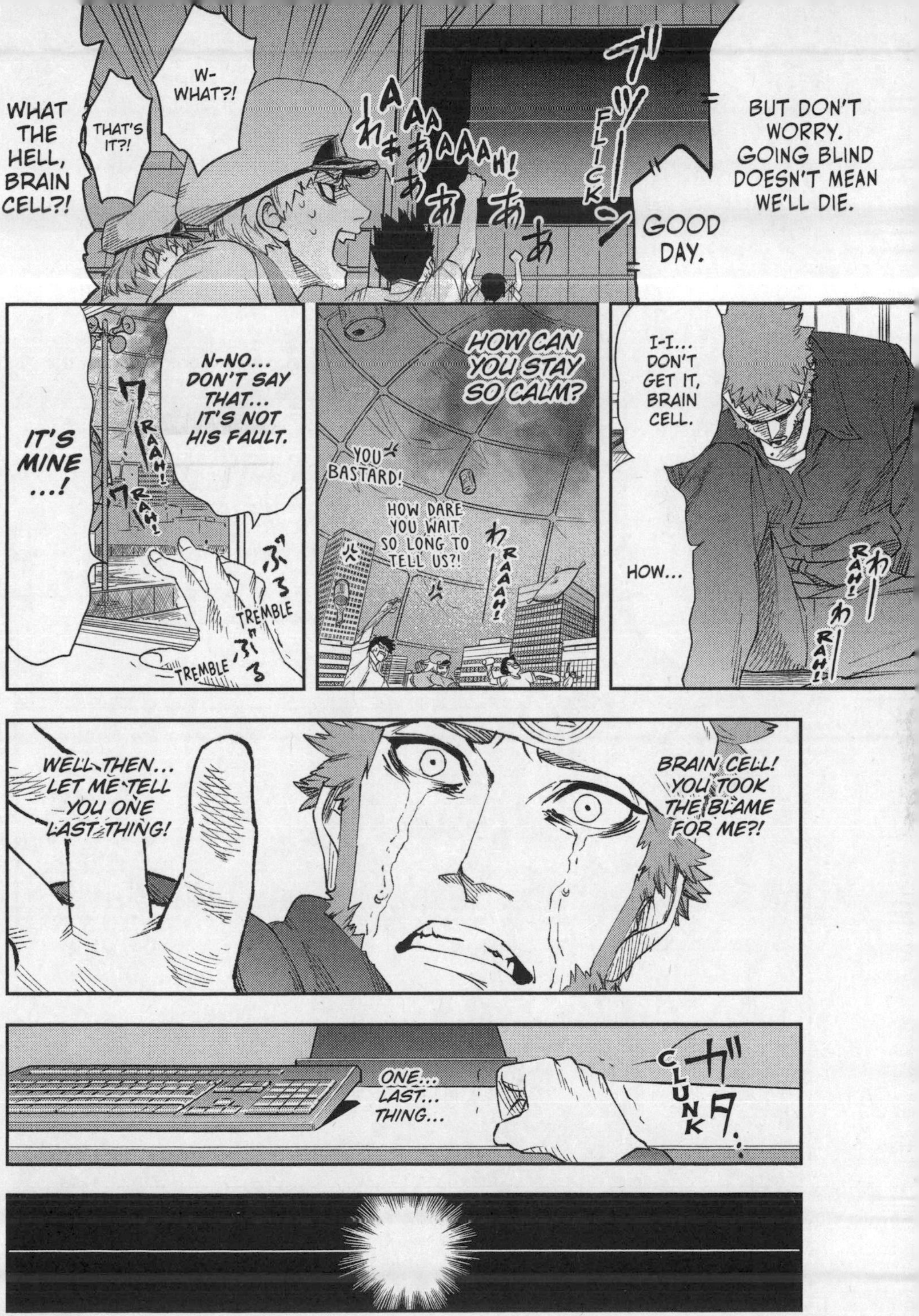
BUT DON'T WORRY. GOING BLIND DOESN'T MEAN WE'LL DIE.
GOOD DAY.
FLICK
AAAAAAAH!
W- WHAT?!
THAT'S IT?!
WHAT THE HELL, BRAIN CELL?!
I-I... DON'T GET IT, BRAIN CELL.
HOW...
RAH! RAH!
HOW CAN YOU STAY SO CALM?
YOU BASTARD!
HOW DARE YOU WAIT SO LONG TO TELL US?!
RAAAAH!
N-NO... DON'T SAY THAT... IT'S NOT HIS FAULT.
IT'S MINE...!
RAAH! RAH!
TREMBLE
TREMBLE
BRAIN CELL! YOU TOOK THE BLAME FOR ME?!
WELL THEN... LET ME TELL YOU ONE LAST THING!
CLUNK
ONE... LAST... THING...

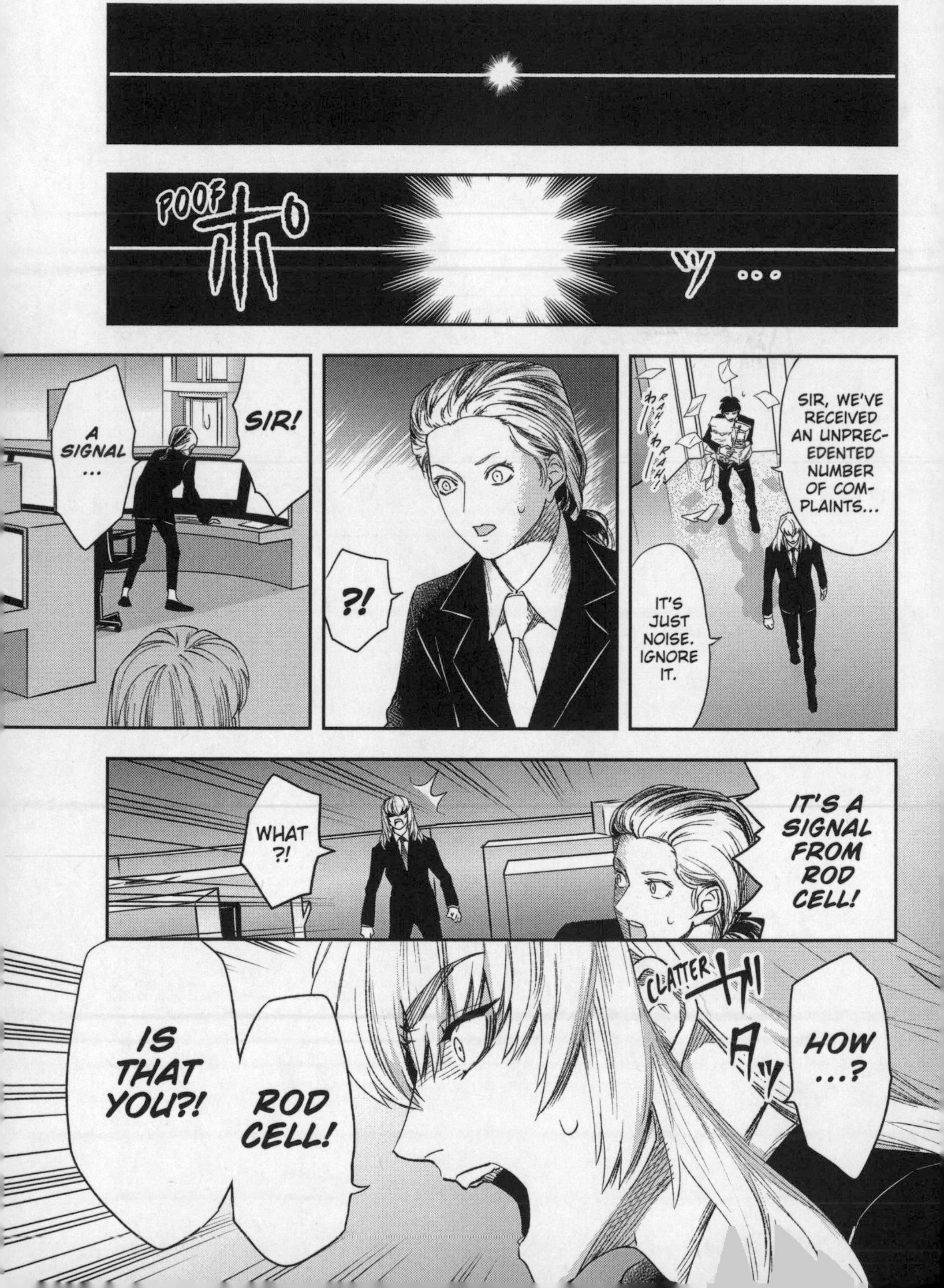
POOF
RAH! RAH!
SIR, WE'VE RECEIVED AN UNPREC-EDENTED NUMBER OF COM-PLAINTS...
IT'S JUST NOISE. IGNORE IT.
?!
SIR!
A SIGNAL ...
IT'S A SIGNAL FROM ROD CELL!
WHAT ?!
CLATTER
HOW ...?
ROD CELL!
IS THAT YOU?!

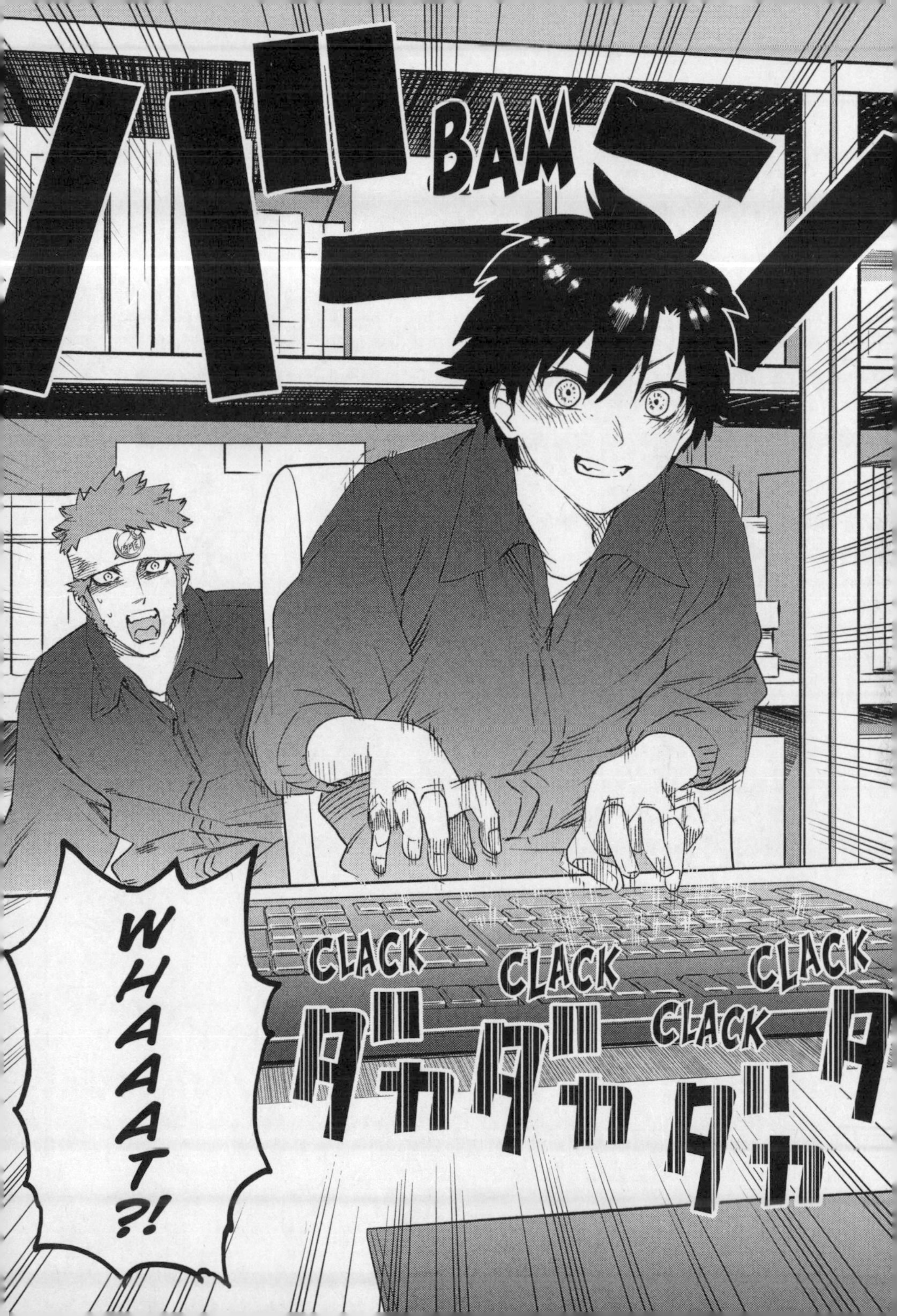
バーン
BAM
WHAAAT?!
ダカダカダカタ
CLACK
CLACK
CLACK
CLACK

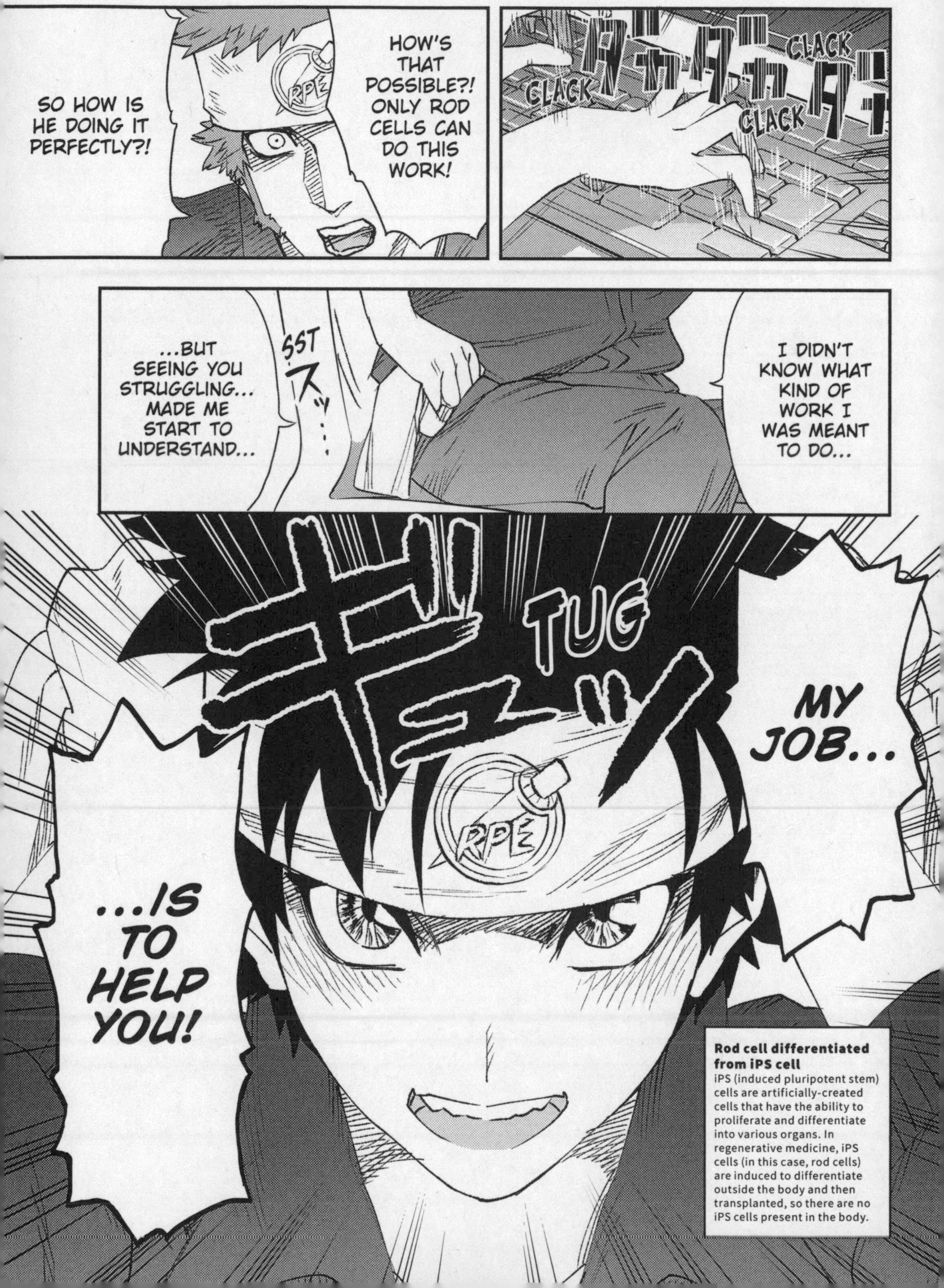
CLACK
CLACK
CLACK
HOW'S THAT POSSIBLE?! ONLY ROD CELLS CAN DO THIS WORK!
SO HOW IS HE DOING IT PERFECTLY?!
I DIDN'T KNOW WHAT KIND OF WORK I WAS MEANT TO DO...
SST
...BUT SEEING YOU STRUGGLING... MADE ME START TO UNDERSTAND...
TUG
MY JOB...
...IS TO HELP YOU!
Rod cell differentiated from iPS cell
iPS (induced pluripotent stem) cells are artificially-created cells that have the ability to proliferate and differentiate into various organs. In regenerative medicine, iPS cells (in this case, rod cells) are induced to differentiate outside the body and then transplanted, so there are no iPS cells present in the body.

StemFit® is a culture medium for iPS cells made and sold by Ajinomoto Co., Inc.

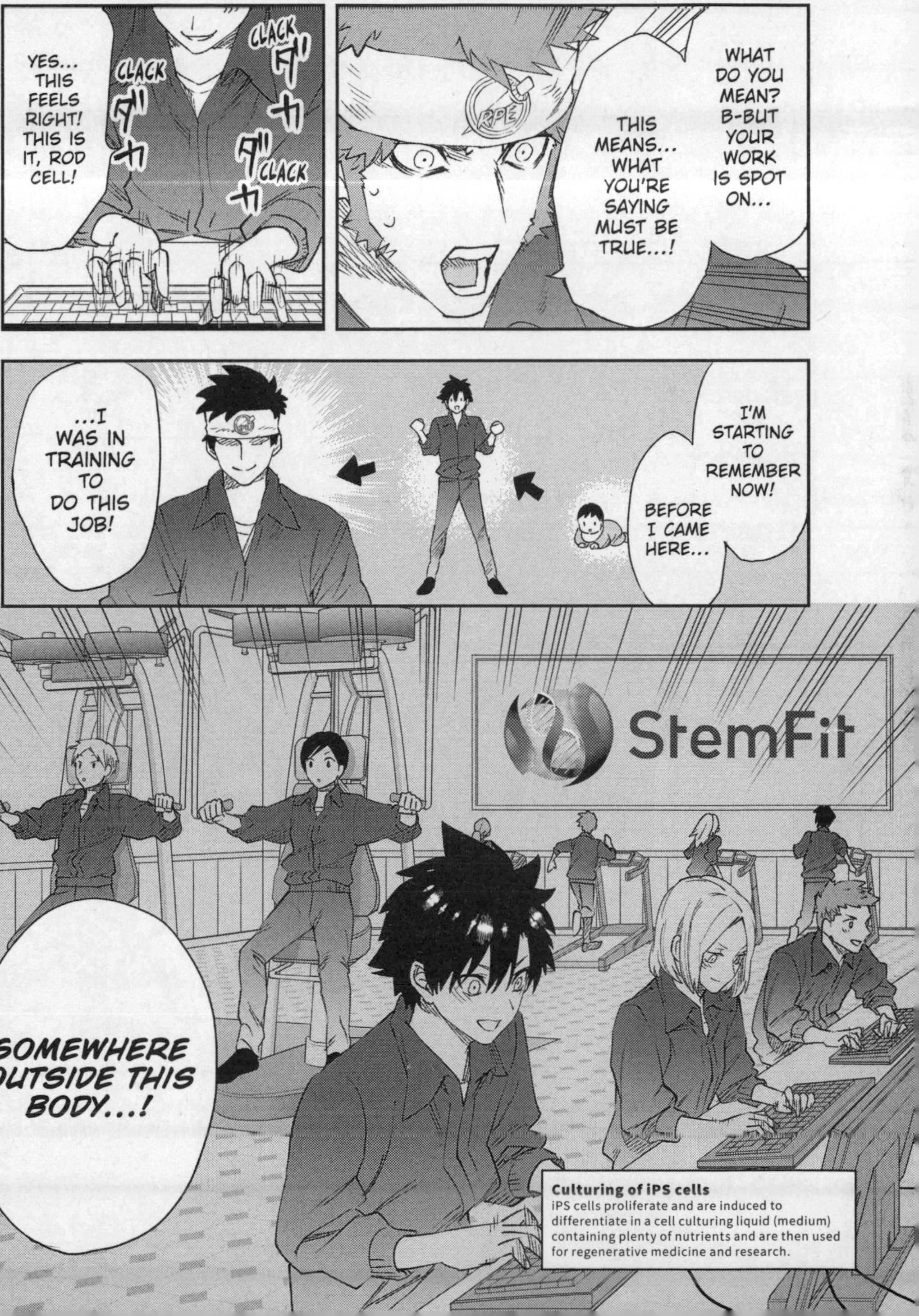

WHAT DO YOU MEAN? B-BUT YOUR WORK IS SPOT ON...
THIS MEANS... WHAT YOU'RE SAYING MUST BE TRUE...!
CLACK
CLACK
CLACK
YES... THIS FEELS RIGHT! THIS IS IT, ROD CELL!
I'M STARTING TO REMEMBER NOW!
BEFORE I CAME HERE...
...I WAS IN TRAINING TO DO THIS JOB!
StemFit
SOMEWHERE OUTSIDE THIS BODY...!
Culturing of iPS cells
iPS cells proliferate and are induced to differentiate in a cell culturing liquid (medium) containing plenty of nutrients and are then used for regenerative medicine and research.

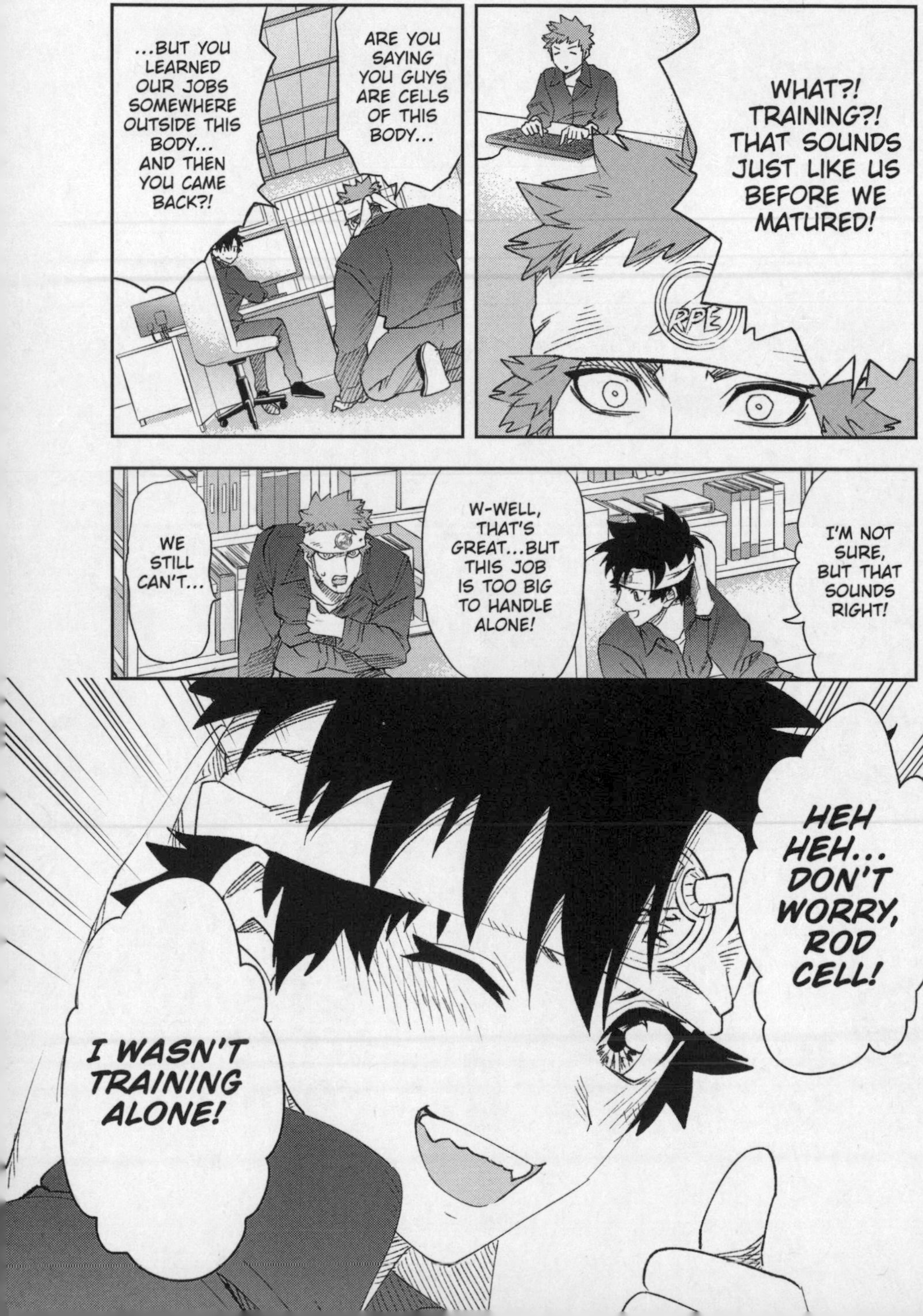
WHAT?! TRAINING?! THAT SOUNDS JUST LIKE US BEFORE WE MATURED!
RPE
ARE YOU SAYING YOU GUYS ARE CELLS OF THIS BODY...
...BUT YOU LEARNED OUR JOBS SOMEWHERE OUTSIDE THIS BODY... AND THEN YOU CAME BACK?!
I'M NOT SURE, BUT THAT SOUNDS RIGHT!
W-WELL, THAT'S GREAT...BUT THIS JOB IS TOO BIG TO HANDLE ALONE!
WE STILL CAN'T...
HEH HEH... DON'T WORRY, ROD CELL!
I WASN'T TRAINING ALONE!

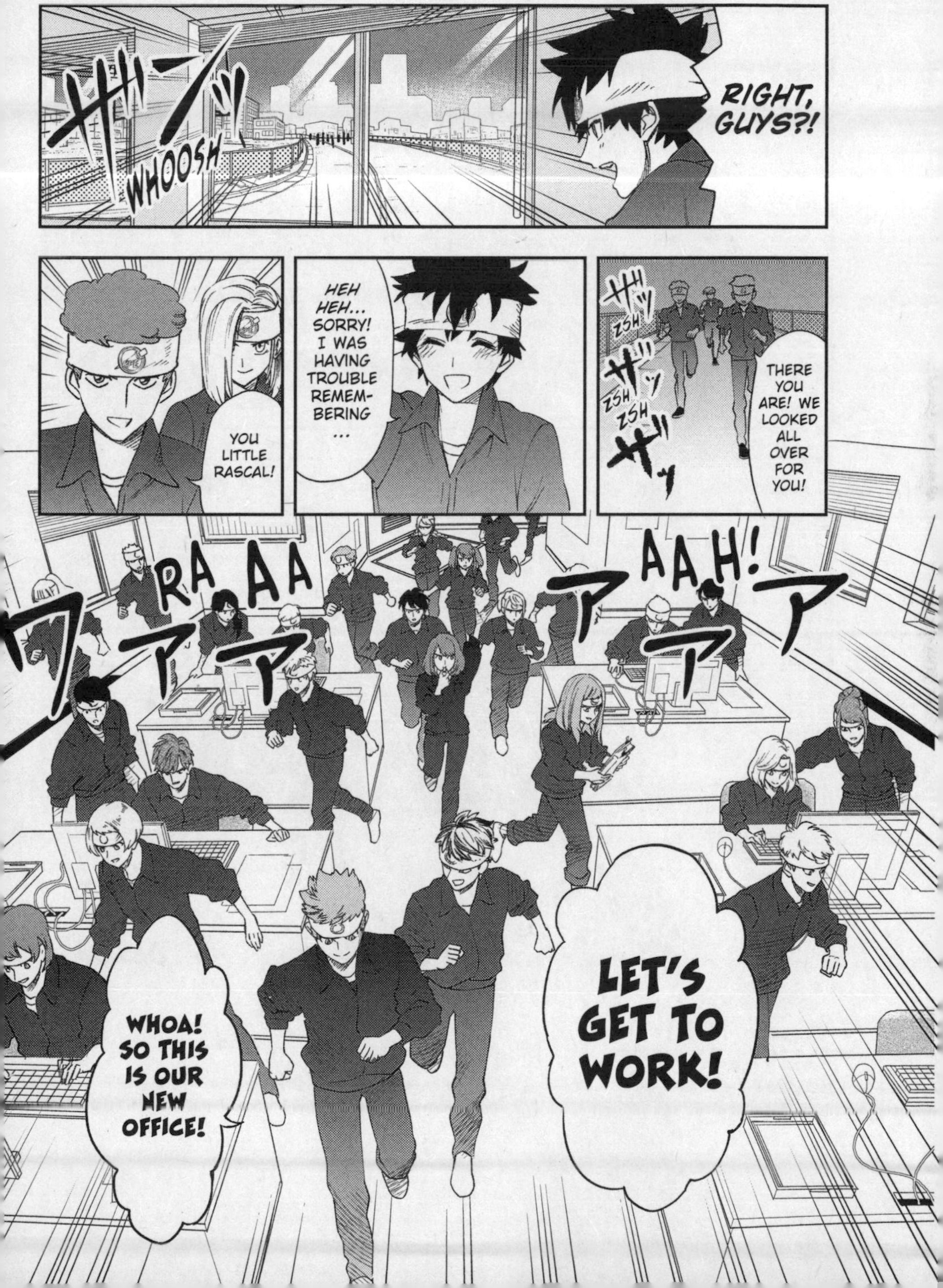
RIGHT, GUYS?!
ザーッ
WHOOSH
ザッ
ZSH
ザッ
ZSH
ZSH
ザッ
THERE YOU ARE! WE LOOKED ALL OVER FOR YOU!
HEH HEH... SORRY! I WAS HAVING TROUBLE REMEMBERING ...
YOU LITTLE RASCAL!
ワアアアア
RAAAAAH!
LET'S GET TO WORK!
WHOA! SO THIS IS OUR NEW OFFICE!

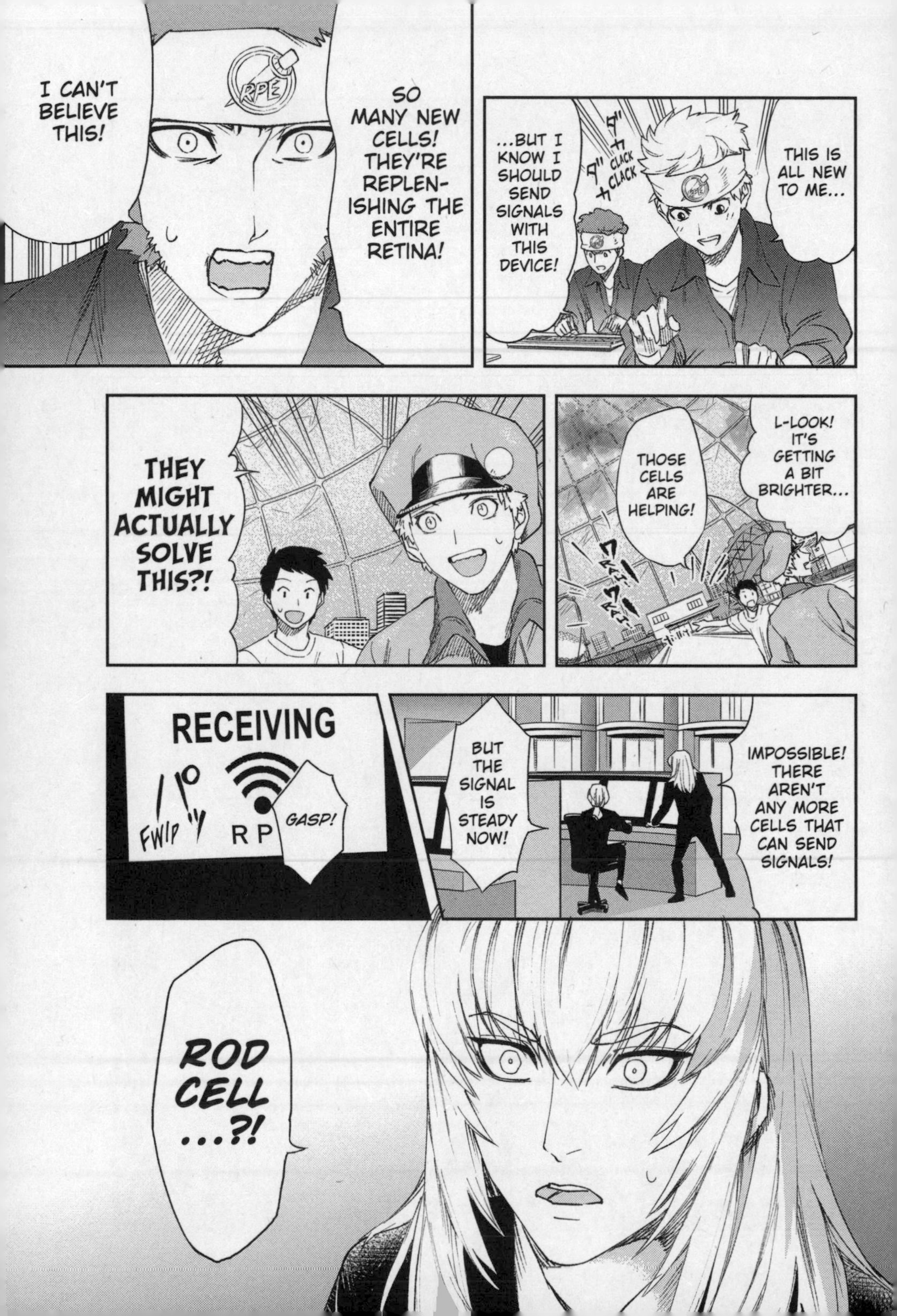
THIS IS ALL NEW TO ME...
...BUT I KNOW I SHOULD SEND SIGNALS WITH THIS DEVICE!
CLACK CLACK
SO MANY NEW CELLS! THEY'RE REPLENISHING THE ENTIRE RETINA!
I CAN'T BELIEVE THIS!
L-LOOK! IT'S GETTING A BIT BRIGHTER...
THOSE CELLS ARE HELPING!
THEY MIGHT ACTUALLY SOLVE THIS?!
IMPOSSIBLE! THERE AREN'T ANY MORE CELLS THAT CAN SEND SIGNALS!
BUT THE SIGNAL IS STEADY NOW!
RECEIVING
RP
GASP!
FWIP
ROD CELL...?!

H-HEY, BRAIN CELL...
CAN YOU SEE ME?
IT'S ME... ROD CELL...
SIR! IT'S FAINT...
...BUT WE HAVE AN IMAGE!
I- I CAN SEE YOU, ROD CELL!
LOOK AT THIS KID HERE...

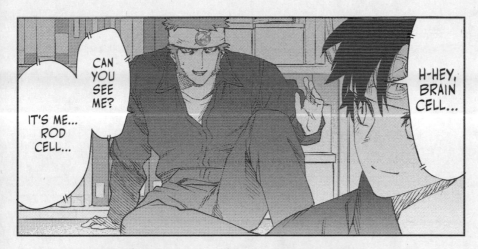

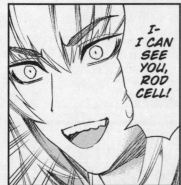

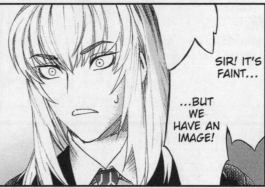

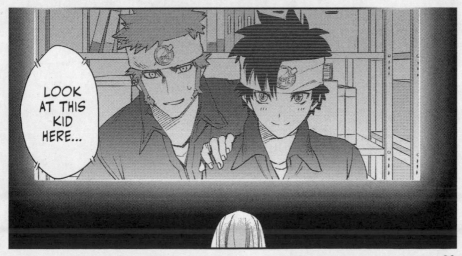

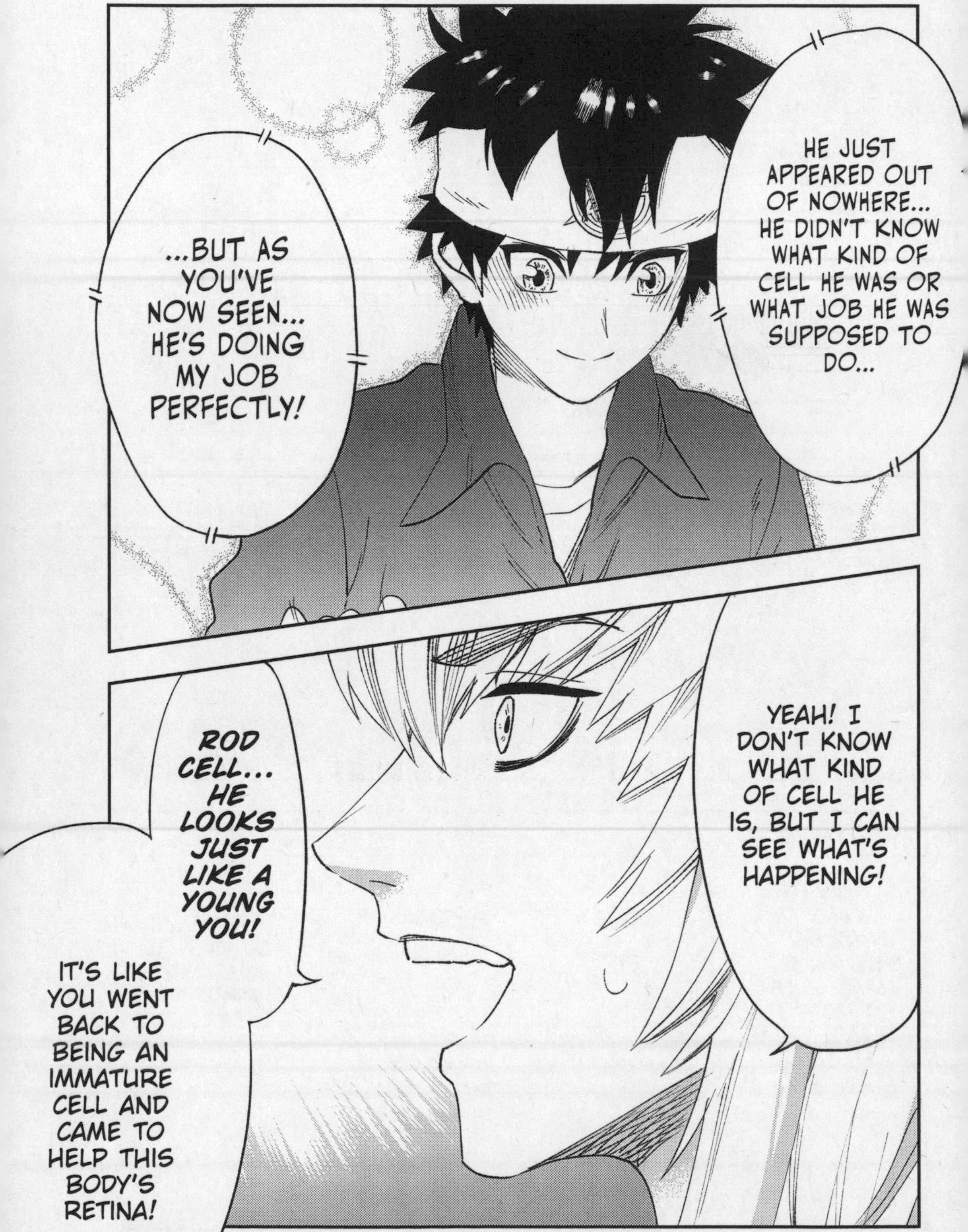
HE JUST APPEARED OUT OF NOWHERE... HE DIDN'T KNOW WHAT KIND OF CELL HE WAS OR WHAT JOB HE WAS SUPPOSED TO DO...
...BUT AS YOU'VE NOW SEEN... HE'S DOING MY JOB PERFECTLY!
YEAH! I DON'T KNOW WHAT KIND OF CELL HE IS, BUT I CAN SEE WHAT'S HAPPENING!
ROD CELL... HE LOOKS JUST LIKE A YOUNG YOU!
IT'S LIKE YOU WENT BACK TO BEING AN IMMATURE CELL AND CAME TO HELP THIS BODY'S RETINA!

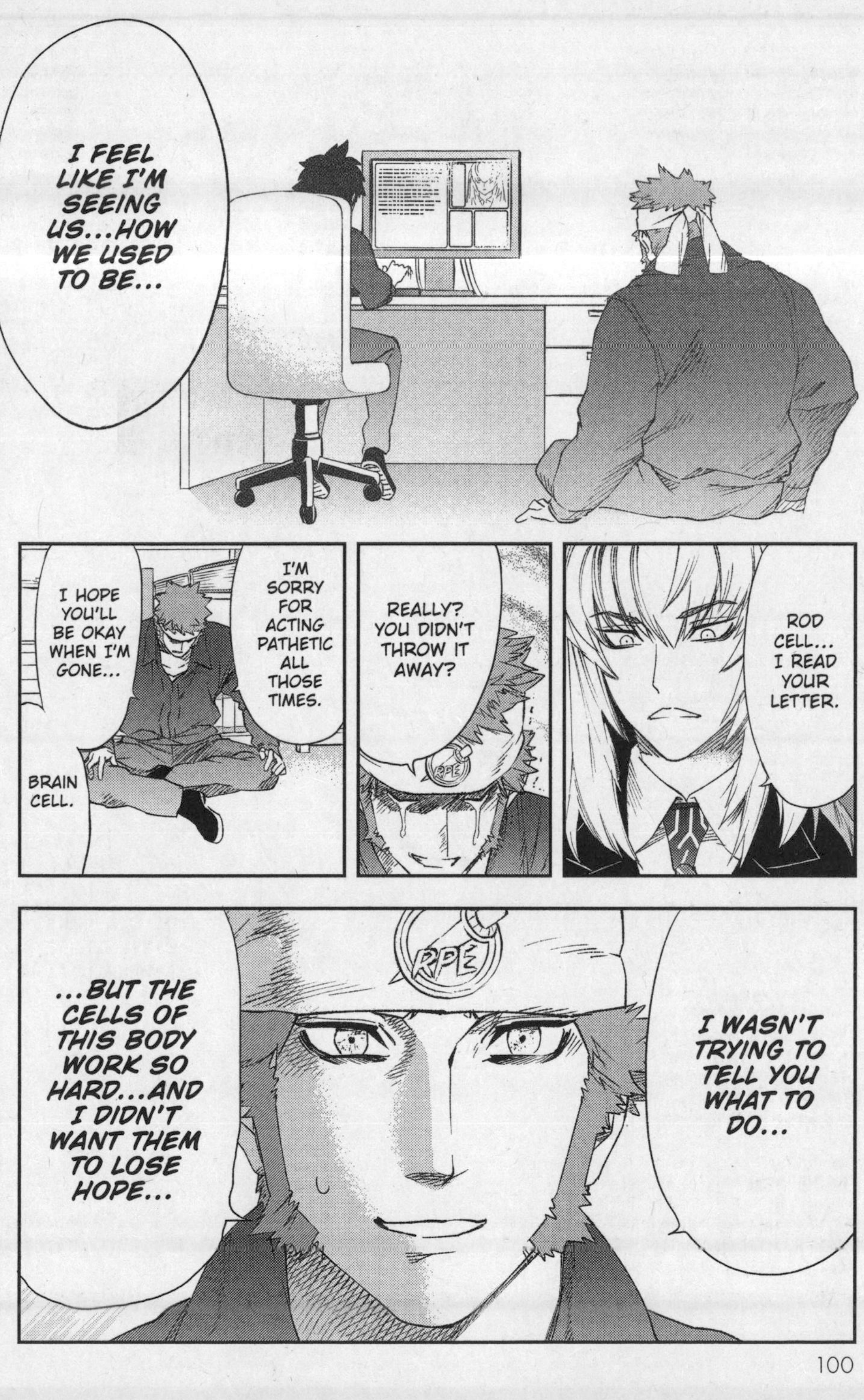
I FEEL LIKE I'M SEEING US...HOW WE USED TO BE...
ROD CELL... I READ YOUR LETTER.
REALLY? YOU DIDN'T THROW IT AWAY?
I'M SORRY FOR ACTING PATHETIC ALL THOSE TIMES.
I HOPE YOU'LL BE OKAY WHEN I'M GONE...
BRAIN CELL.
I WASN'T TRYING TO TELL YOU WHAT TO DO...
...BUT THE CELLS OF THIS BODY WORK SO HARD...AND I DIDN'T WANT THEM TO LOSE HOPE...

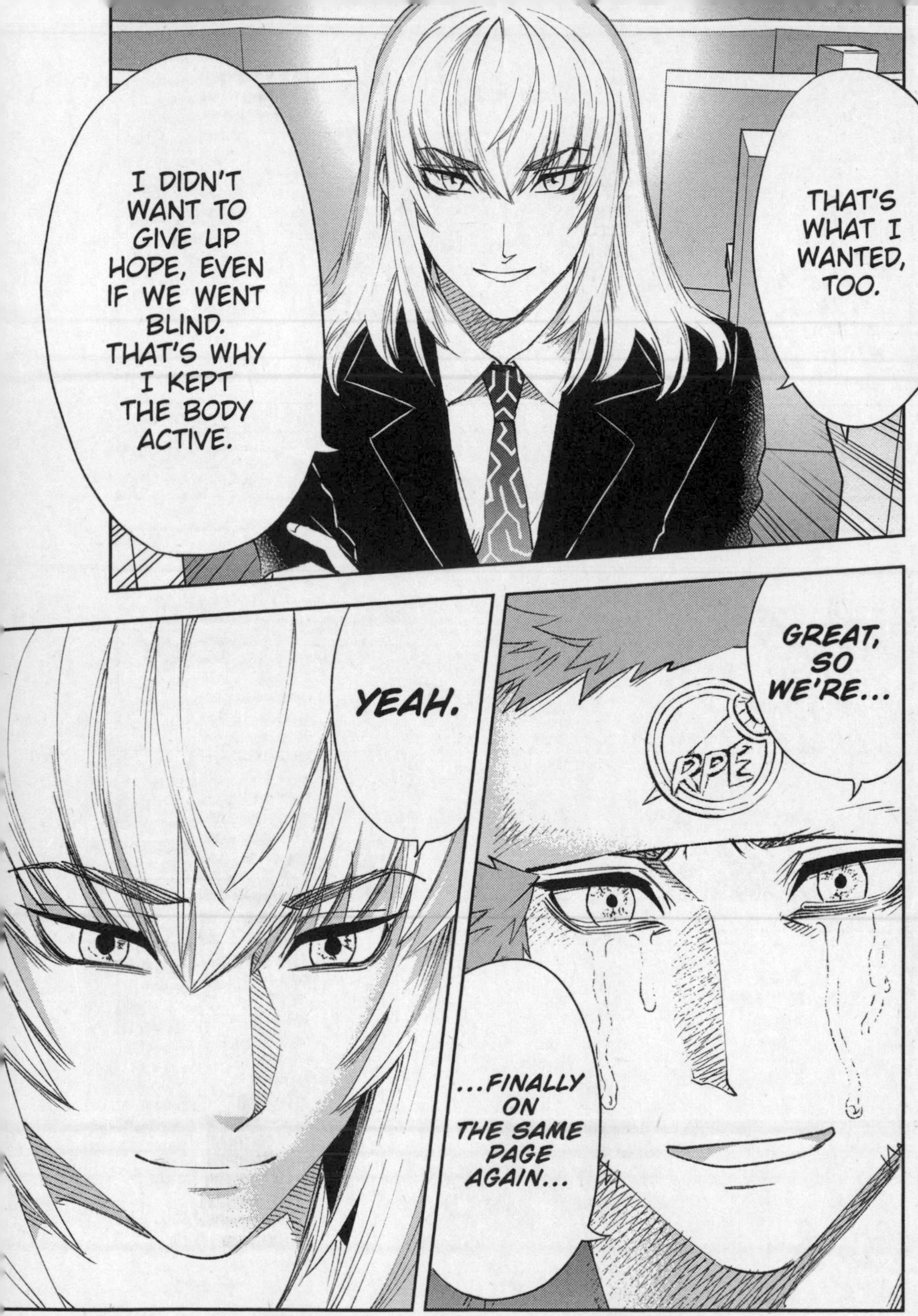
I DIDN'T WANT TO GIVE UP HOPE, EVEN IF WE WENT BLIND. THAT'S WHY I KEPT THE BODY ACTIVE.
THAT'S WHAT I WANTED, TOO.
GREAT, SO WE'RE...
RPE
...FINALLY ON THE SAME PAGE AGAIN...
YEAH.

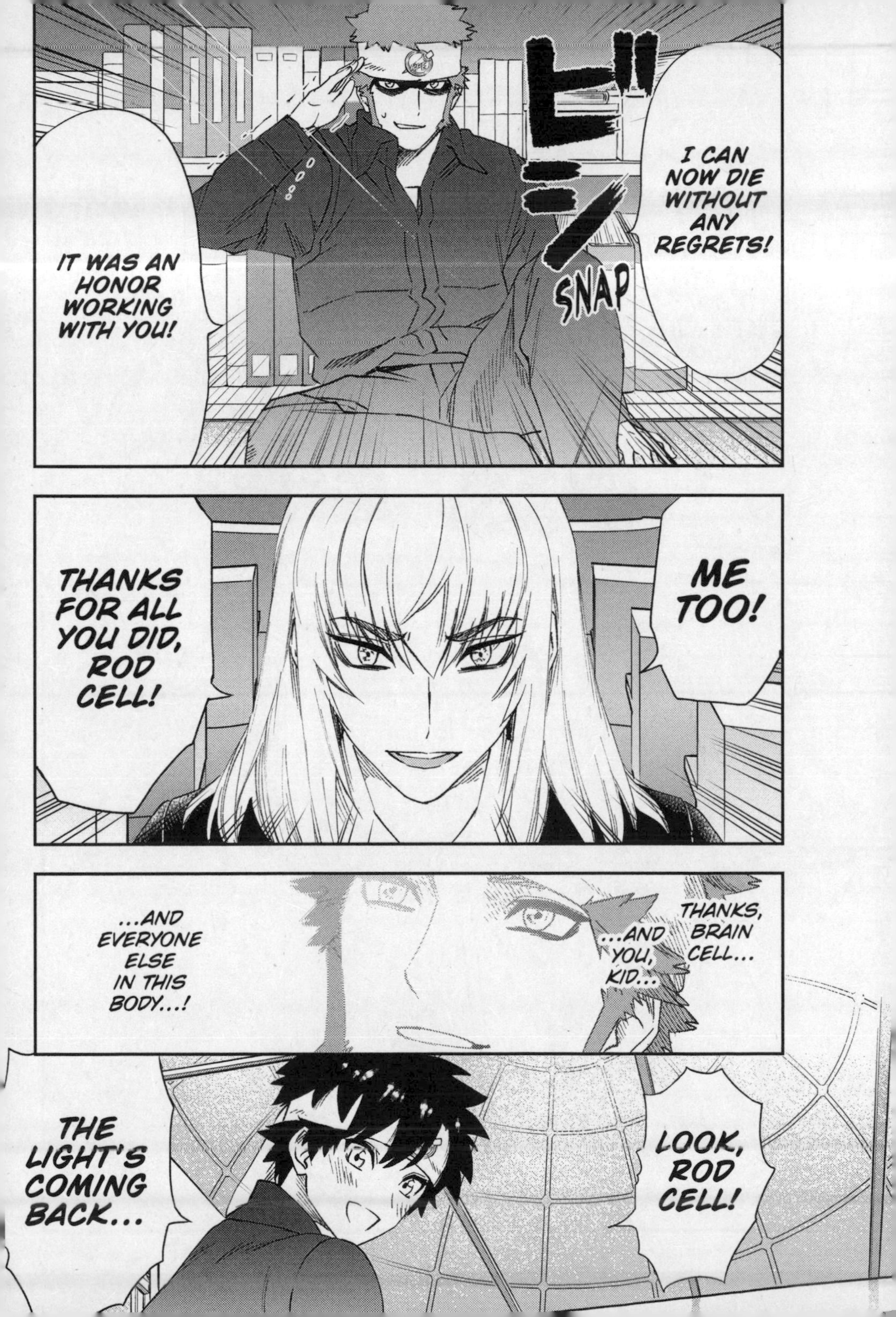
I CAN NOW DIE WITHOUT ANY REGRETS!
SNAP
IT WAS AN HONOR WORKING WITH YOU!
ME TOO!
THANKS FOR ALL YOU DID, ROD CELL!
THANKS, BRAIN CELL...
...AND YOU, KID...
...AND EVERYONE ELSE IN THIS BODY...!
LOOK, ROD CELL!
THE LIGHT'S COMING BACK...

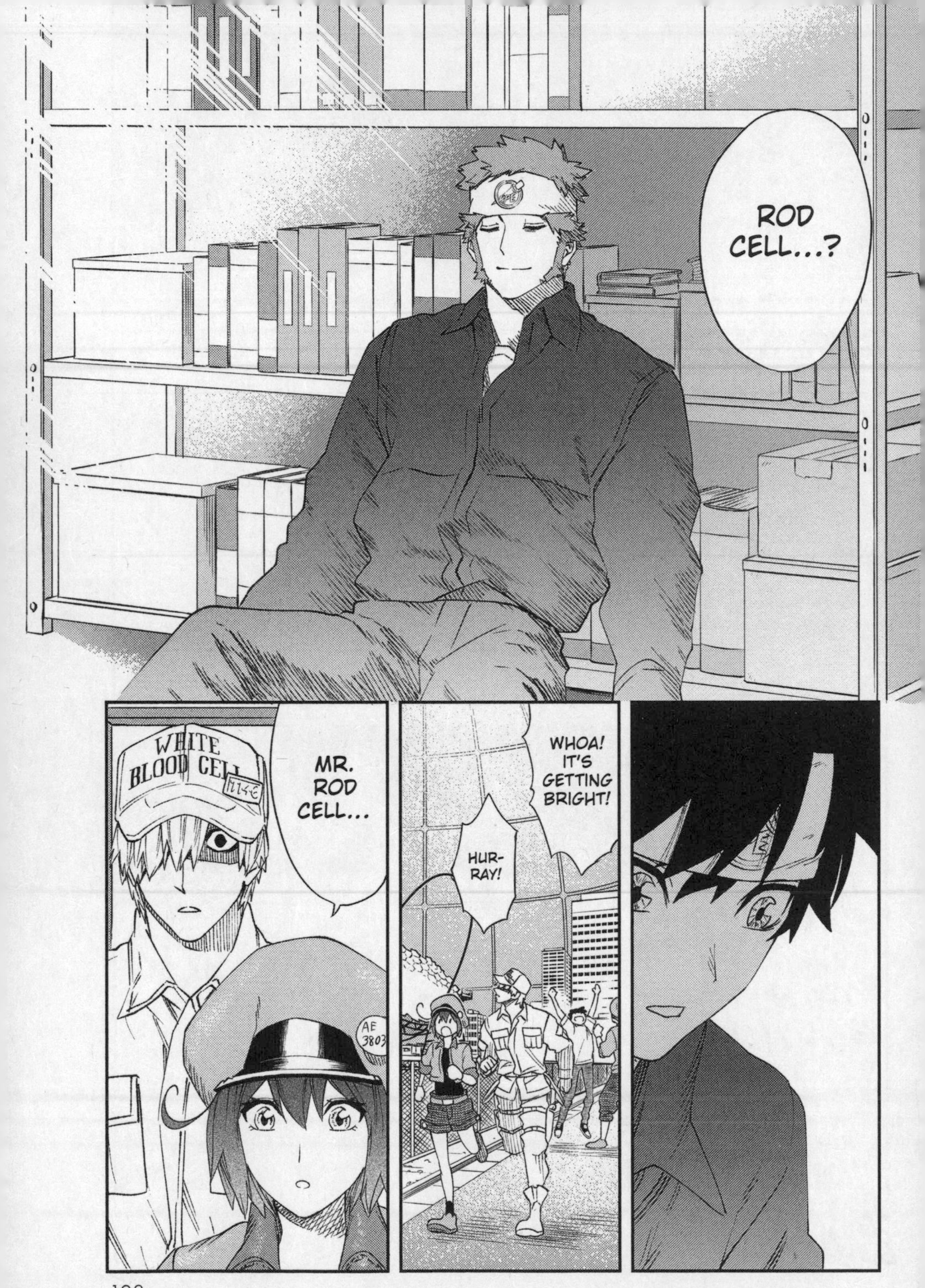
ROD CELL...?
WHOA! IT'S GETTING BRIGHT!
HUR-RAY!
MR. ROD CELL...
WHITE BLOOD CELL
AE 3803

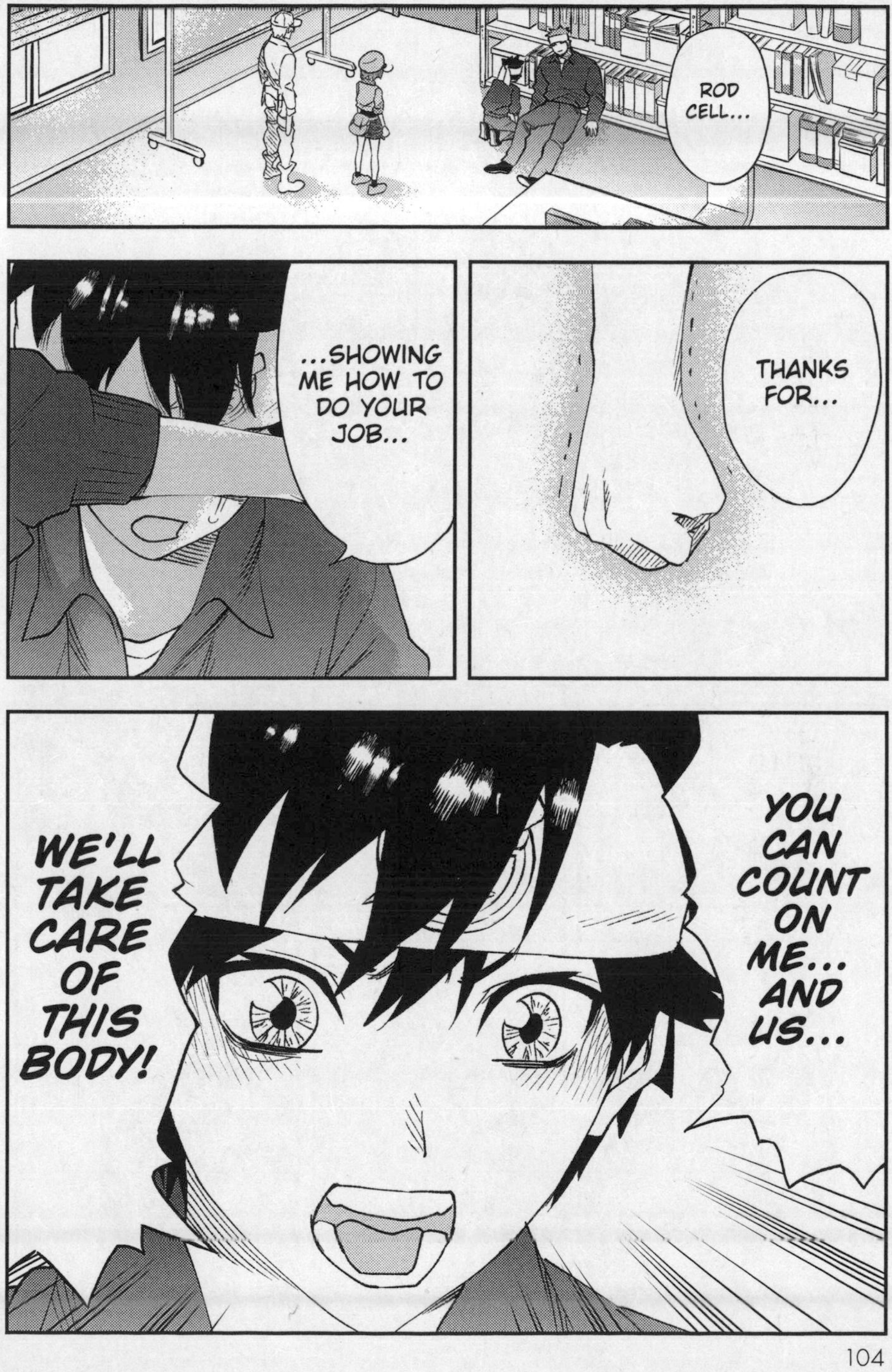
ROD CELL...
THANKS FOR...
...SHOWING ME HOW TO DO YOUR JOB...
YOU CAN COUNT ON ME... AND US...
WE'LL TAKE CARE OF THIS BODY!

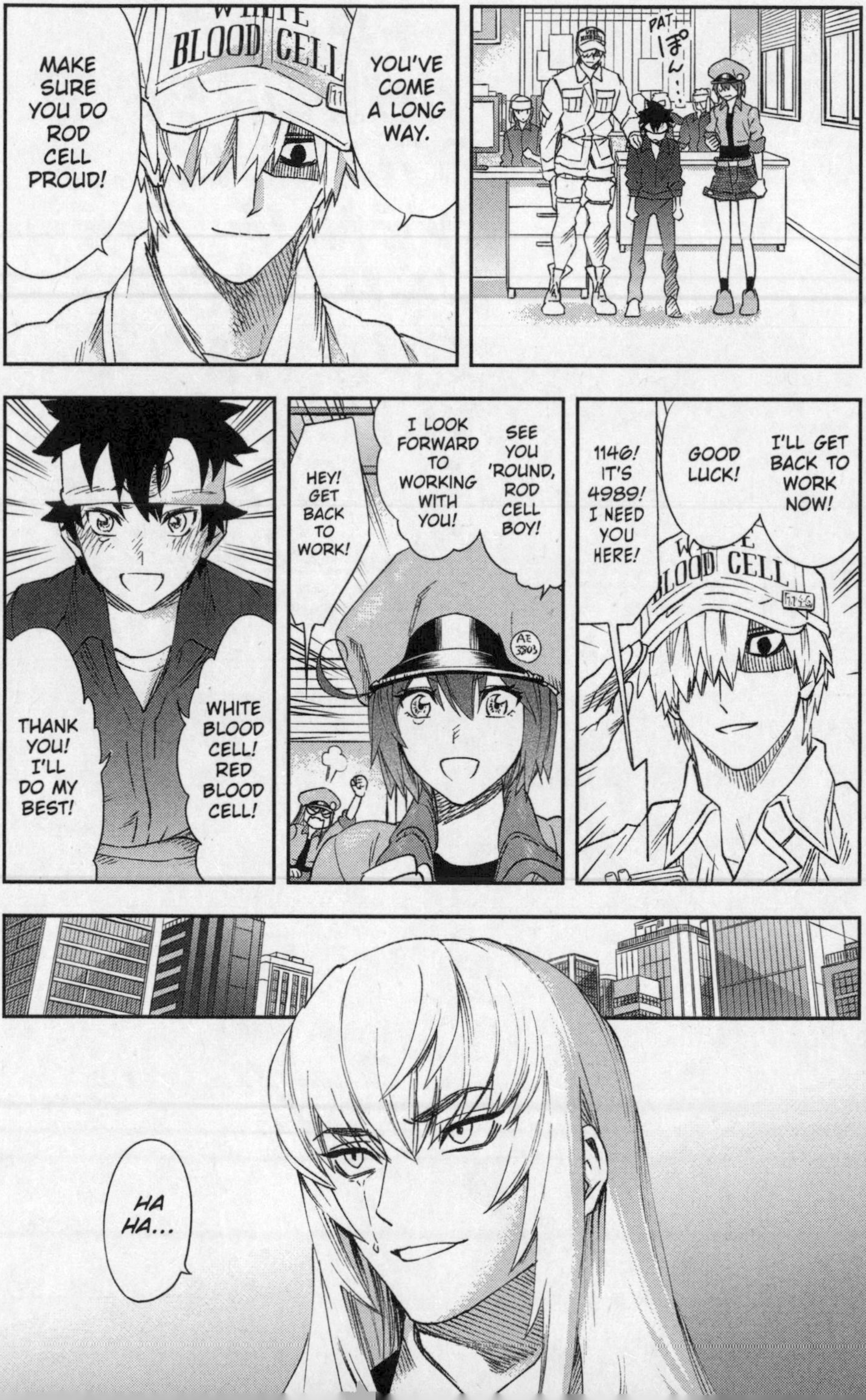
PAT
ぽん…
YOU'VE COME A LONG WAY.
MAKE SURE YOU DO ROD CELL PROUD!
I'LL GET BACK TO WORK NOW!
GOOD LUCK!
1146! IT'S 4989! I NEED YOU HERE!
SEE YOU 'ROUND, ROD CELL BOY!
I LOOK FORWARD TO WORKING WITH YOU!
HEY! GET BACK TO WORK!
WHITE BLOOD CELL! RED BLOOD CELL!
THANK YOU! I'LL DO MY BEST!
HA HA...

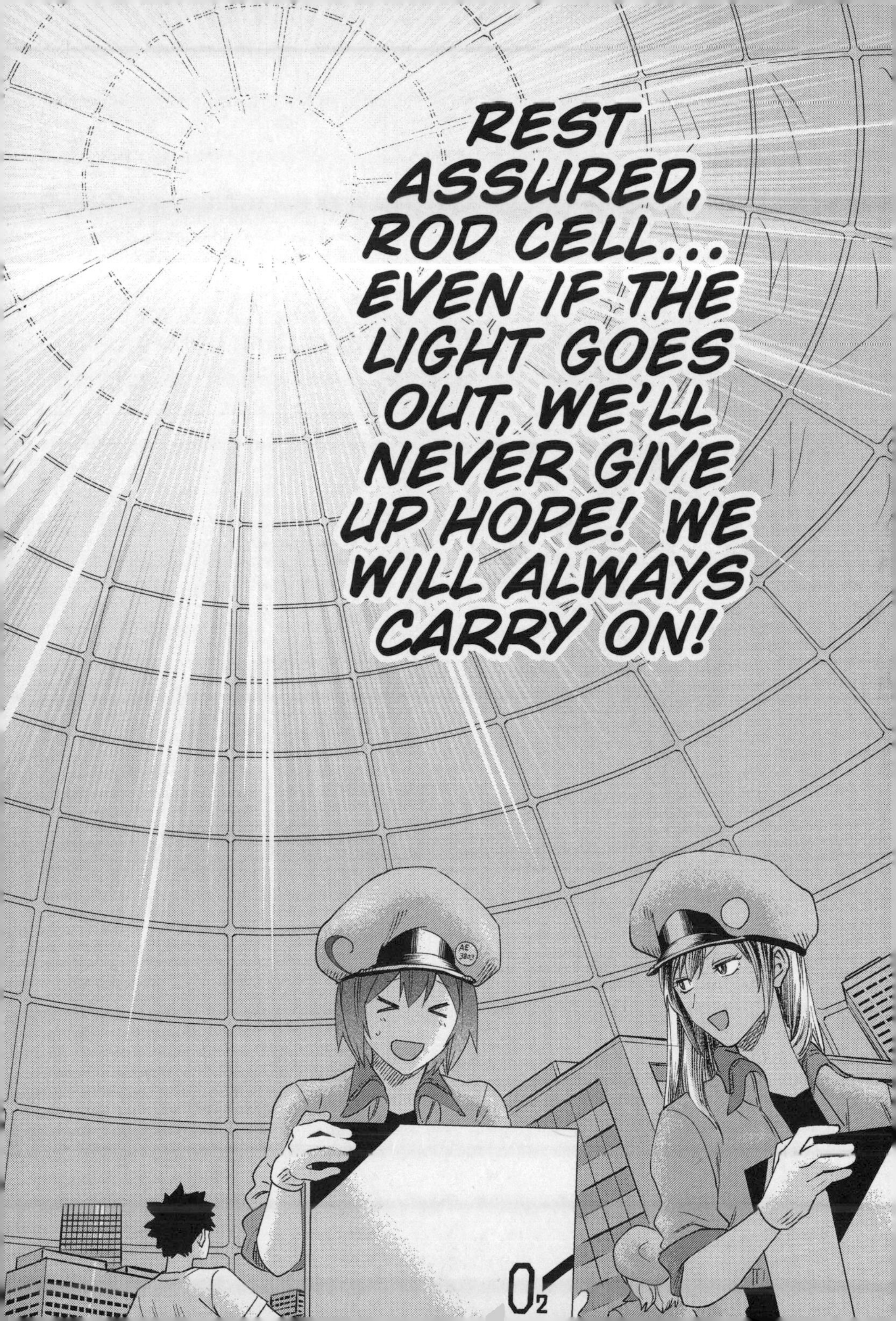
REST ASSURED, ROD CELL... EVEN IF THE LIGHT GOES OUT, WE'LL NEVER GIVE UP HOPE! WE WILL ALWAYS CARRY ON!
AE 3803
O_2

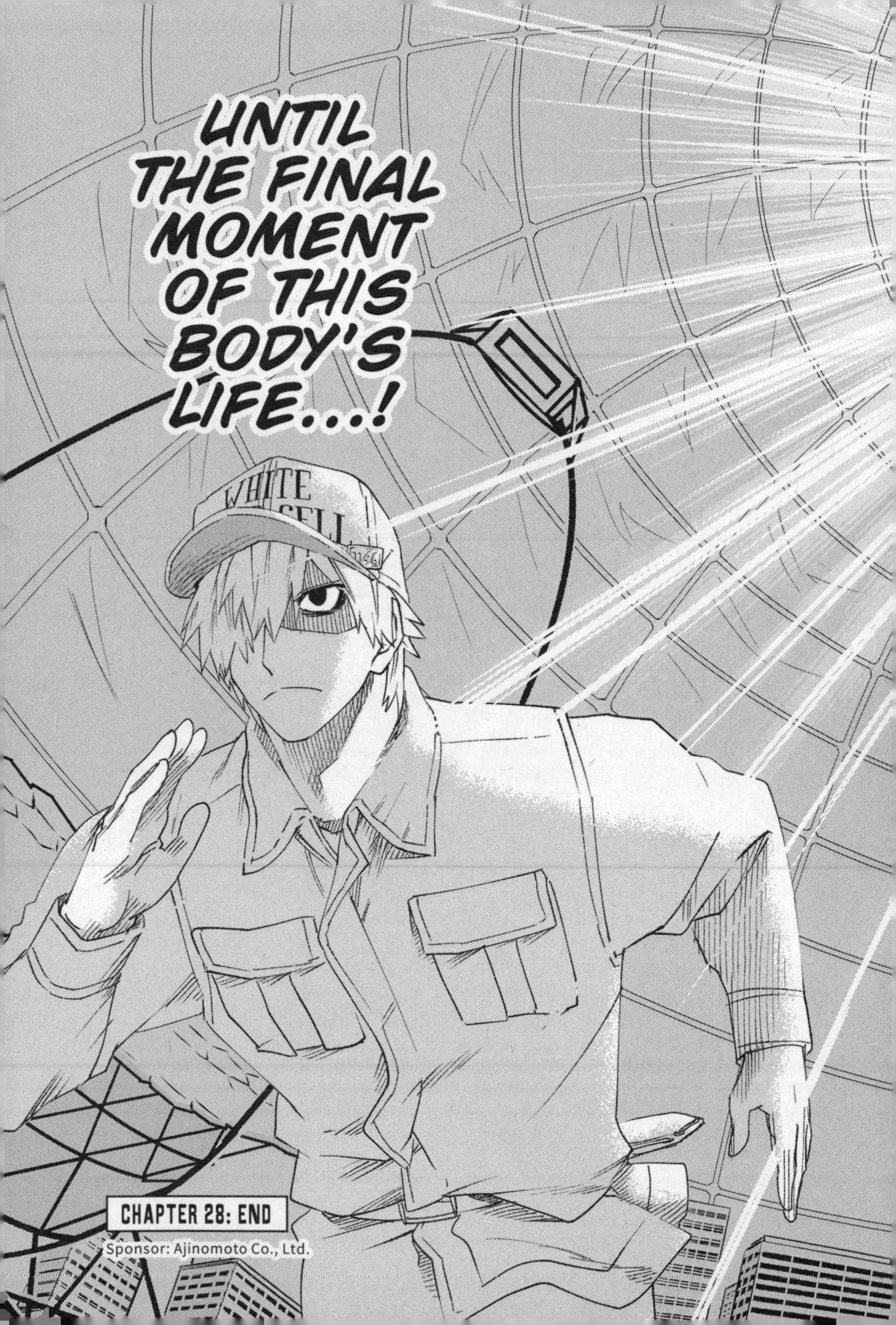
UNTIL THE FINAL MOMENT OF THIS BODY'S LIFE...!
WHITE CELL
1146
CHAPTER 28: END
Sponsor: Ajinomoto Co., Ltd.

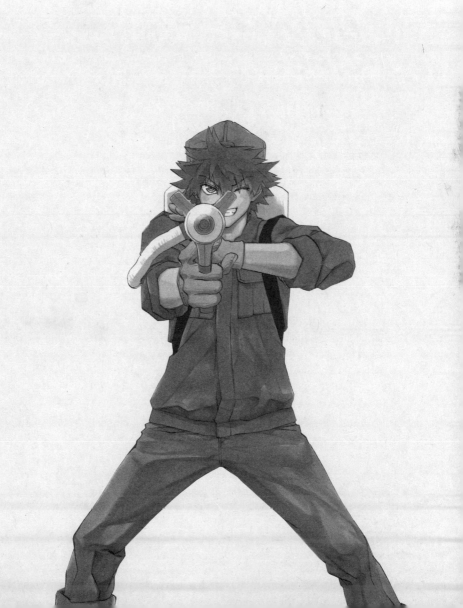

SPECIAL CHAPTER: PSORIASIS

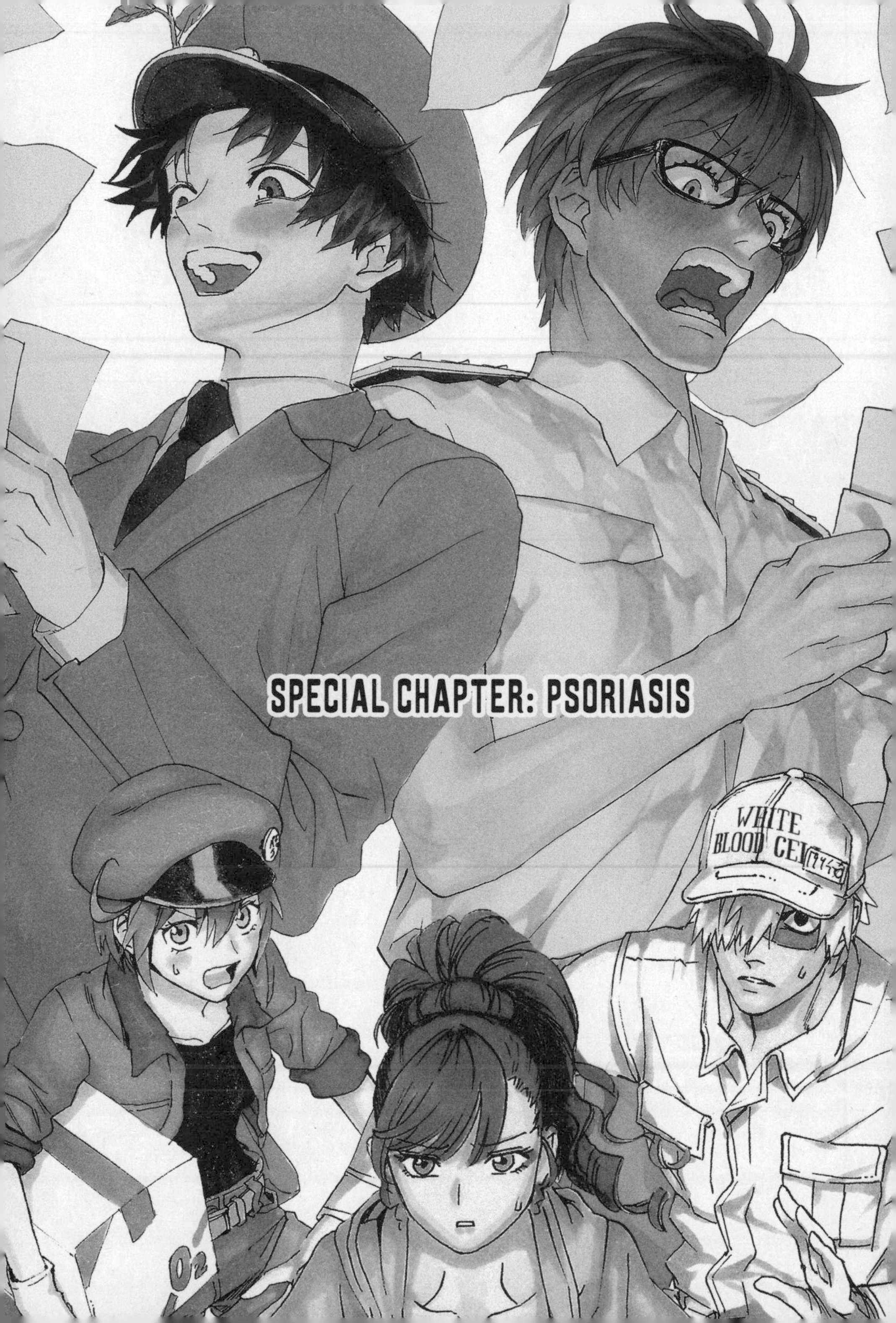
WHITE
BLOOD CEL
1146
O2

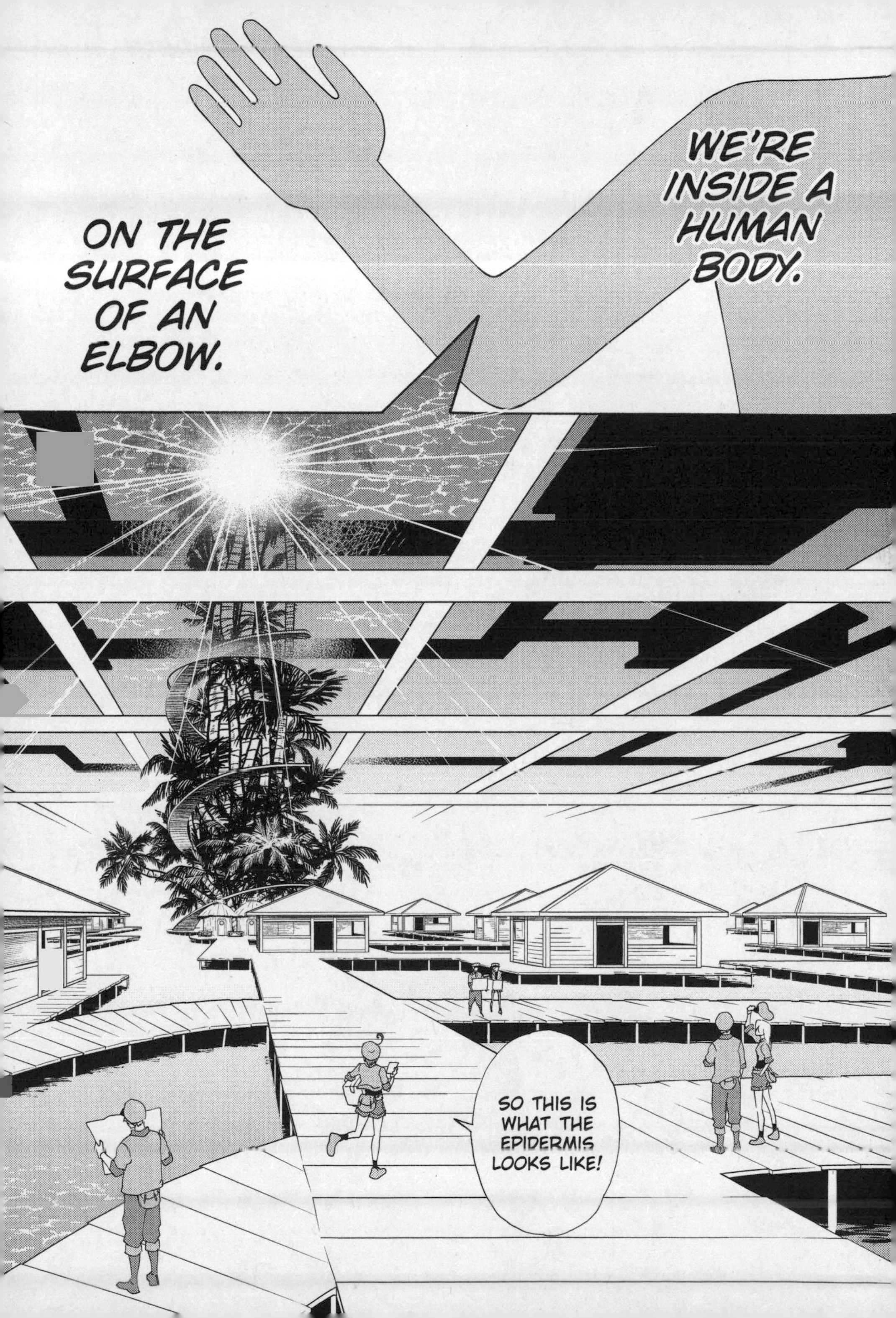
WE'RE INSIDE A HUMAN BODY.
ON THE SURFACE OF AN ELBOW.
SO THIS IS WHAT THE EPIDERMIS LOOKS LIKE!

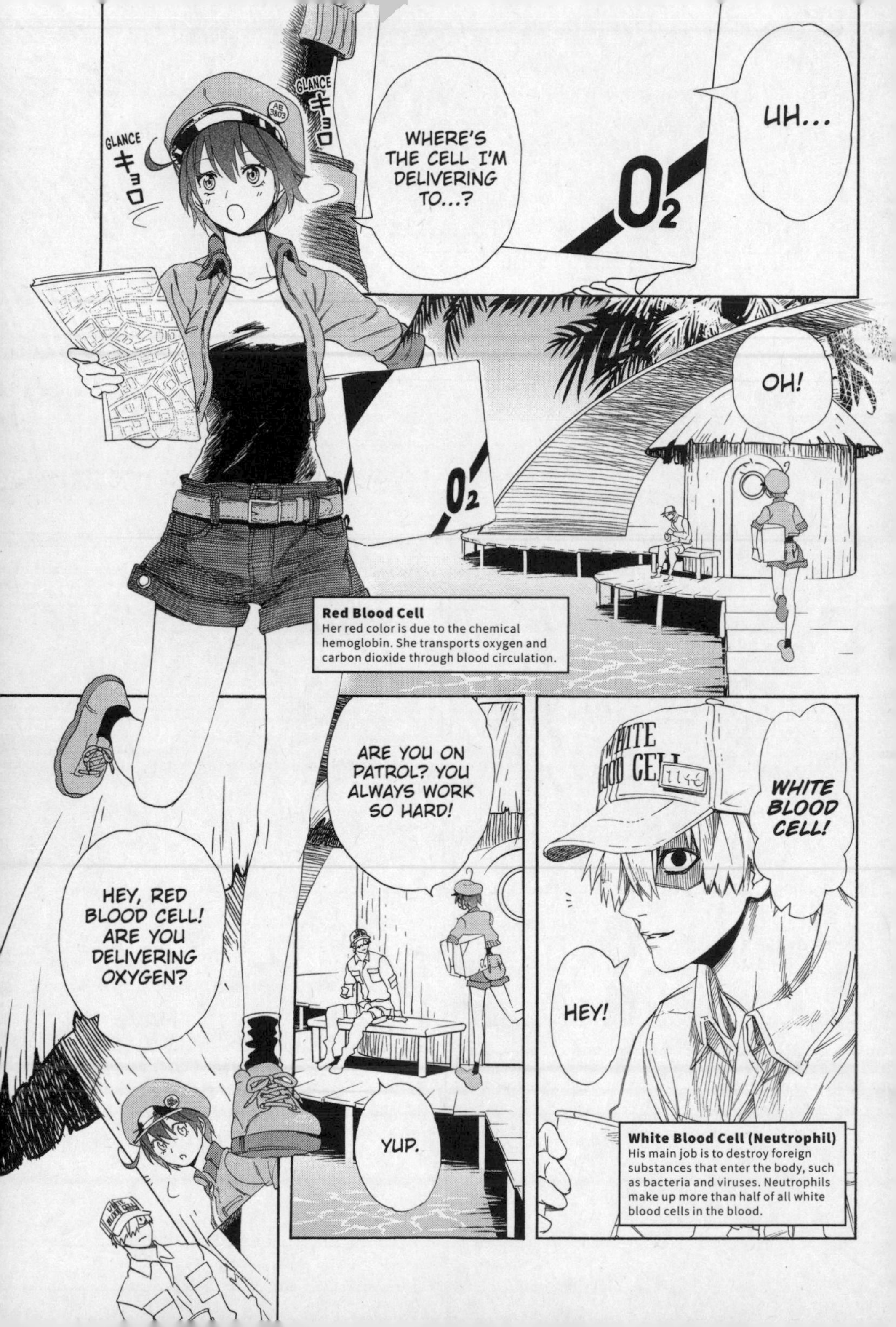

UH...
WHERE'S THE CELL I'M DELIVERING TO...?
GLANCE キョロ
GLANCE キョロ
OH!
Red Blood Cell
Her red color is due to the chemical hemoglobin. She transports oxygen and carbon dioxide through blood circulation.
WHITE BLOOD CELL!
HEY!
White Blood Cell (Neutrophil)
His main job is to destroy foreign substances that enter the body, such as bacteria and viruses. Neutrophils make up more than half of all white blood cells in the blood.
ARE YOU ON PATROL? YOU ALWAYS WORK SO HARD!
YUP.
HEY, RED BLOOD CELL! ARE YOU DELIVERING OXYGEN?

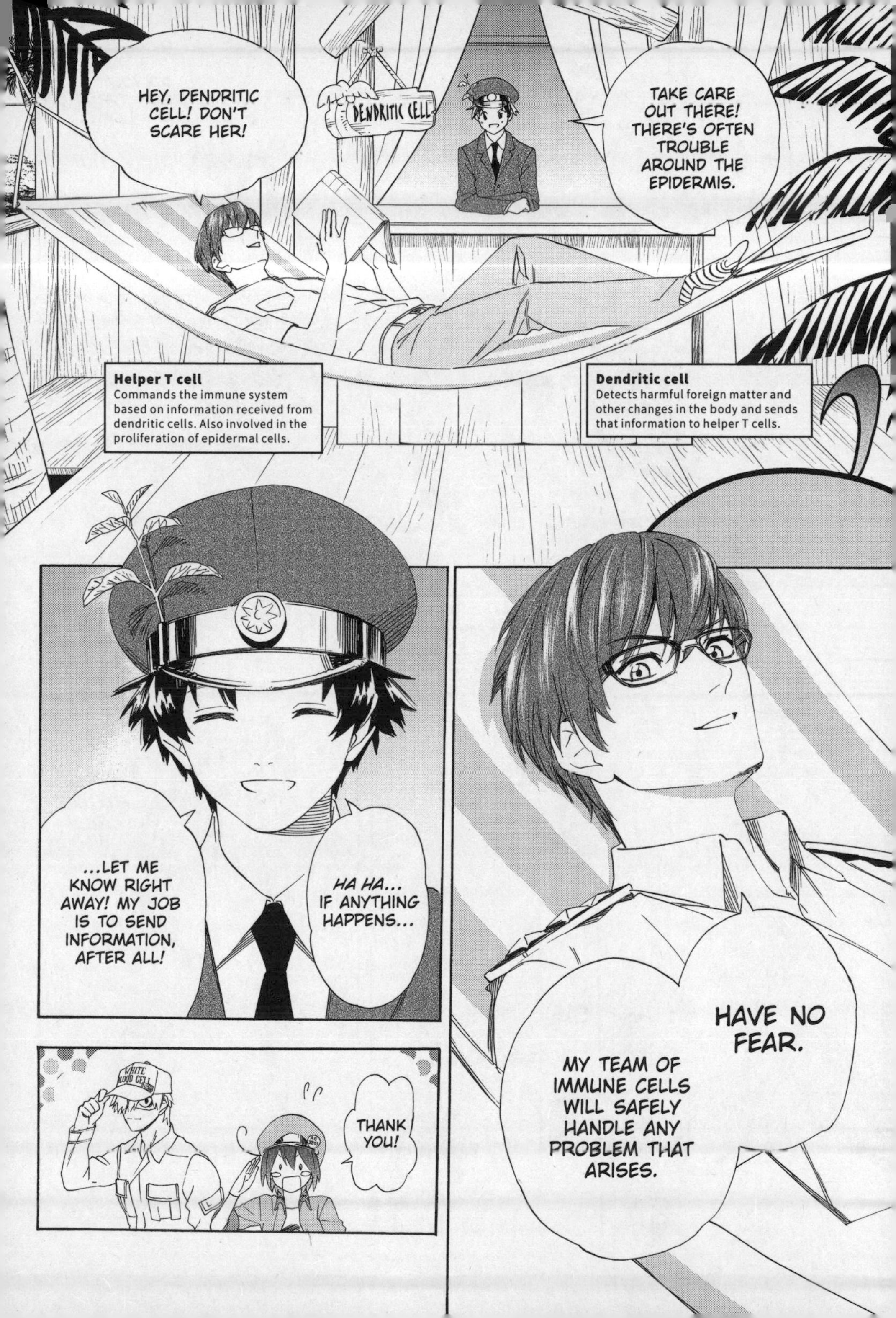
TAKE CARE OUT THERE! THERE'S OFTEN TROUBLE AROUND THE EPIDERMIS.
DENDRITIC CELL
HEY, DENDRITIC CELL! DON'T SCARE HER!
Dendritic cell
Detects harmful foreign matter and other changes in the body and sends that information to helper T cells.
Helper T cell
Commands the immune system based on information received from dendritic cells. Also involved in the proliferation of epidermal cells.
HAVE NO FEAR.
MY TEAM OF IMMUNE CELLS WILL SAFELY HANDLE ANY PROBLEM THAT ARISES.
HA HA... IF ANYTHING HAPPENS...
...LET ME KNOW RIGHT AWAY! MY JOB IS TO SEND INFORMATION, AFTER ALL!
THANK YOU!

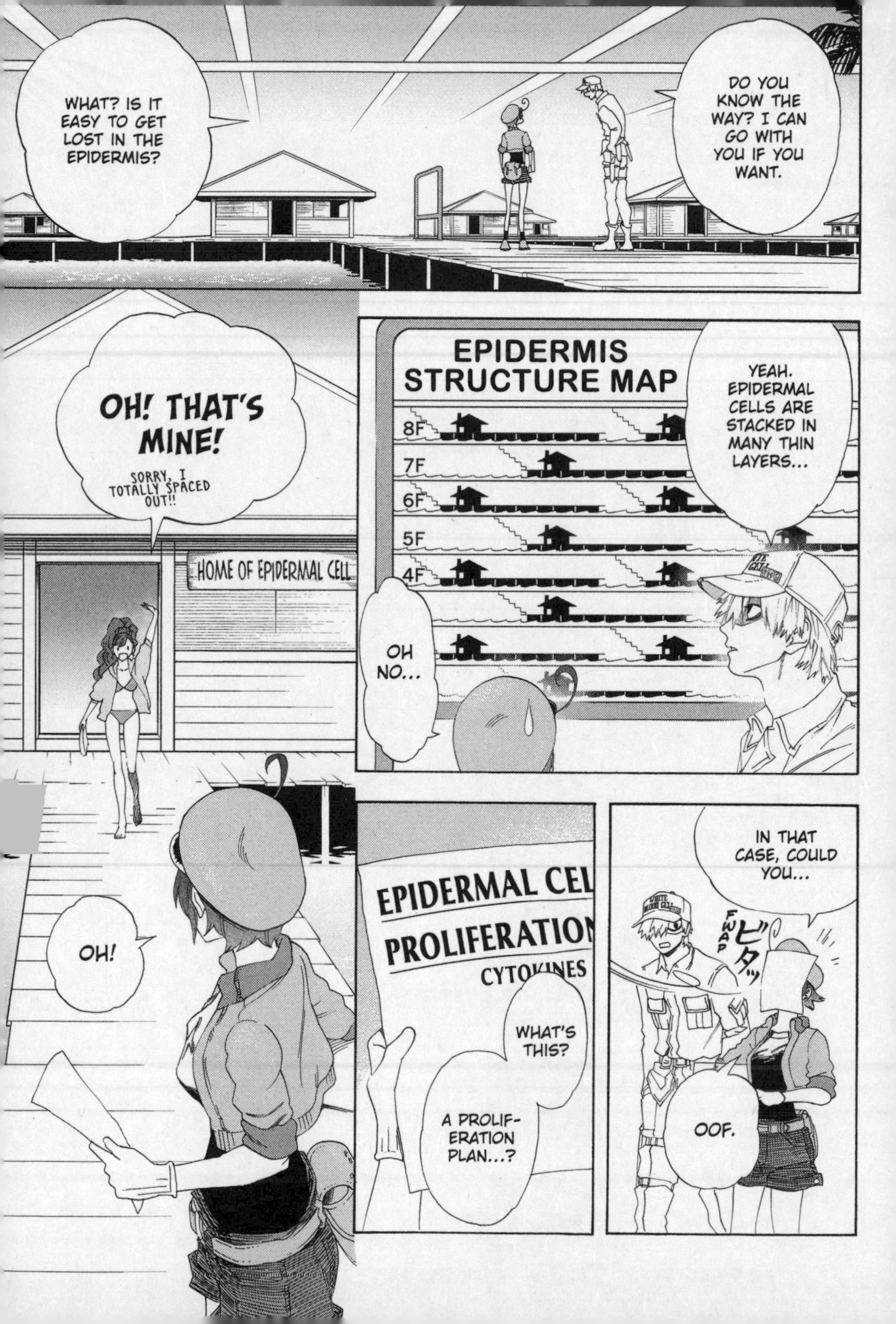
DO YOU KNOW THE WAY? I CAN GO WITH YOU IF YOU WANT.
WHAT? IS IT EASY TO GET LOST IN THE EPIDERMIS?
EPIDERMIS STRUCTURE MAP
8F
7F
6F
5F
4F
YEAH. EPIDERMAL CELLS ARE STACKED IN MANY THIN LAYERS...
OH NO...
IN THAT CASE, COULD YOU...
FWAP
OOF.
EPIDERMAL CEL
PROLIFERATION
CYTOKINES
WHAT'S THIS?
A PROLIF-ERATION PLAN...?
OH! THAT'S MINE!
SORRY, I TOTALLY SPACED OUT!!
HOME OF EPIDERMAL CELL
OH!

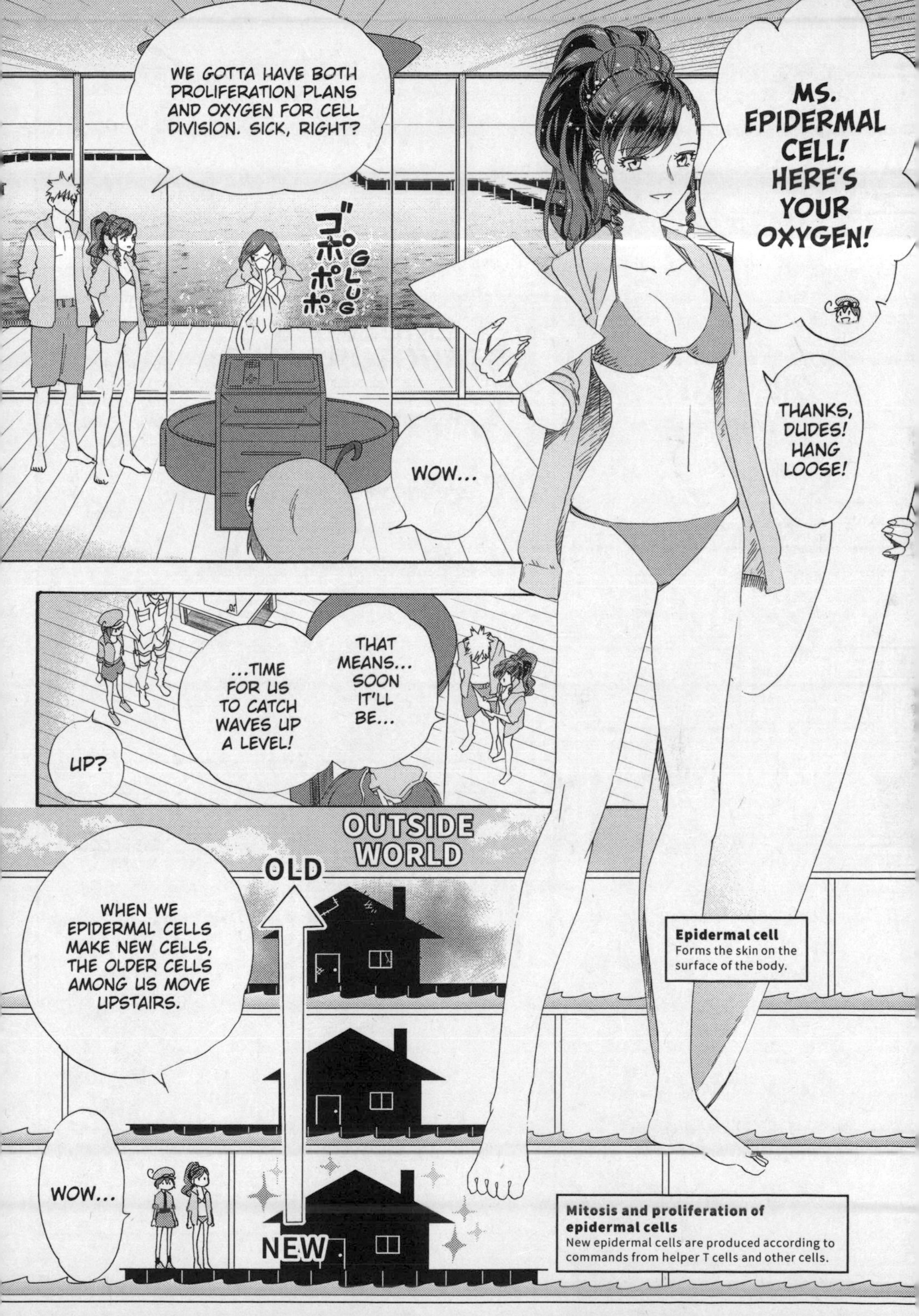
MS. EPIDERMAL CELL! HERE'S YOUR OXYGEN!
THANKS, DUDES! HANG LOOSE!
WE GOTTA HAVE BOTH PROLIFERATION PLANS AND OXYGEN FOR CELL DIVISION. SICK, RIGHT?
ゴポポポ GLUG
WOW...
THAT MEANS... SOON IT'LL BE...
...TIME FOR US TO CATCH WAVES UP A LEVEL!
UP?
Epidermal cell
Forms the skin on the surface of the body.
OUTSIDE WORLD
OLD
NEW
WHEN WE EPIDERMAL CELLS MAKE NEW CELLS, THE OLDER CELLS AMONG US MOVE UPSTAIRS.
WOW...
Mitosis and proliferation of epidermal cells
New epidermal cells are produced according to commands from helper T cells and other cells.

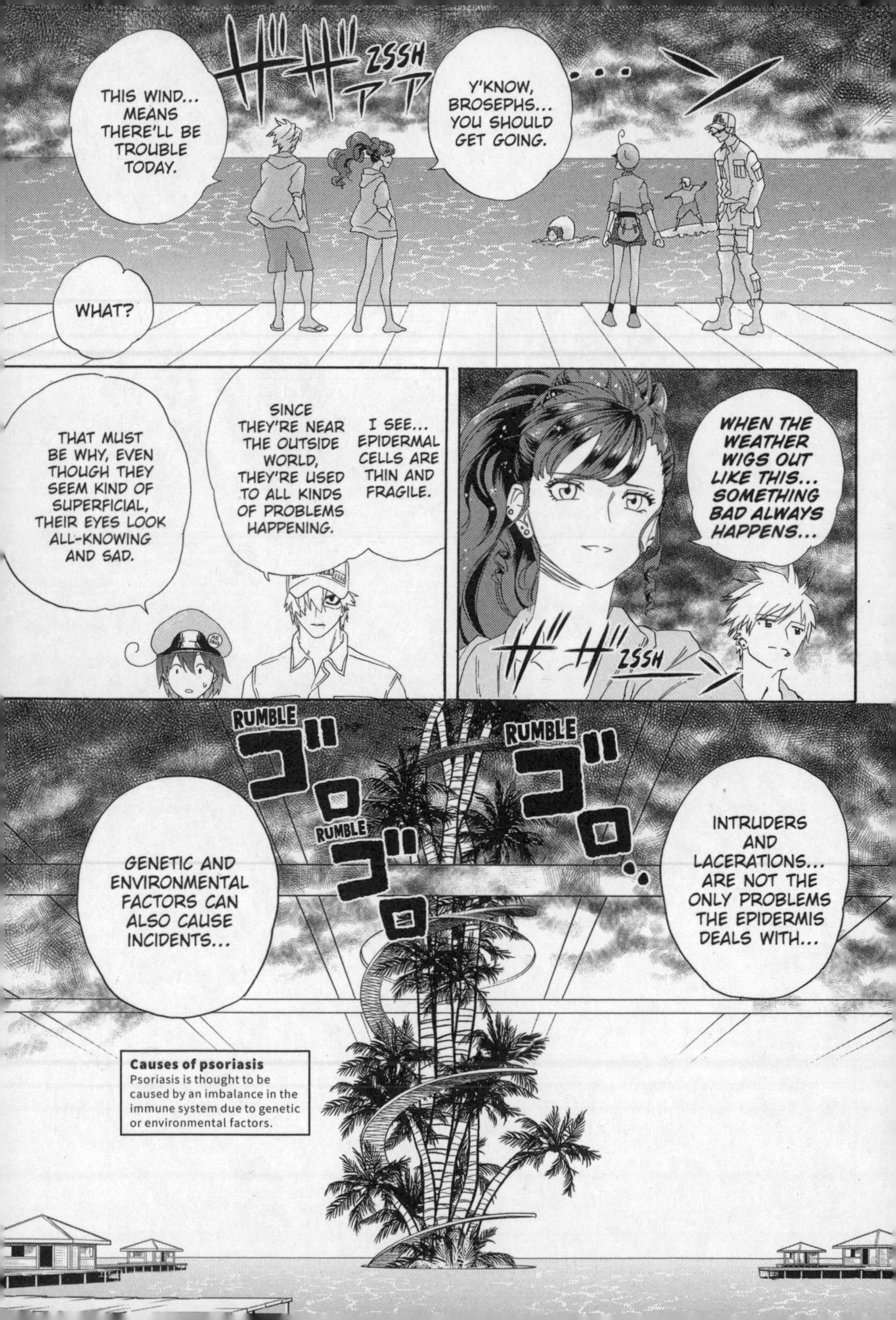
...
Y'KNOW, BROSEPHS... YOU SHOULD GET GOING.
ZSSH
THIS WIND... MEANS THERE'LL BE TROUBLE TODAY.
WHAT?
WHEN THE WEATHER WIGS OUT LIKE THIS... SOMETHING BAD ALWAYS HAPPENS...
ZSSH
I SEE... EPIDERMAL CELLS ARE THIN AND FRAGILE.
SINCE THEY'RE NEAR THE OUTSIDE WORLD, THEY'RE USED TO ALL KINDS OF PROBLEMS HAPPENING.
THAT MUST BE WHY, EVEN THOUGH THEY SEEM KIND OF SUPERFICIAL, THEIR EYES LOOK ALL-KNOWING AND SAD.
INTRUDERS AND LACERATIONS... ARE NOT THE ONLY PROBLEMS THE EPIDERMIS DEALS WITH...
RUMBLE
RUMBLE
RUMBLE
GENETIC AND ENVIRONMENTAL FACTORS CAN ALSO CAUSE INCIDENTS...
Causes of psoriasis
Psoriasis is thought to be caused by an imbalance in the immune system due to genetic or environmental factors.

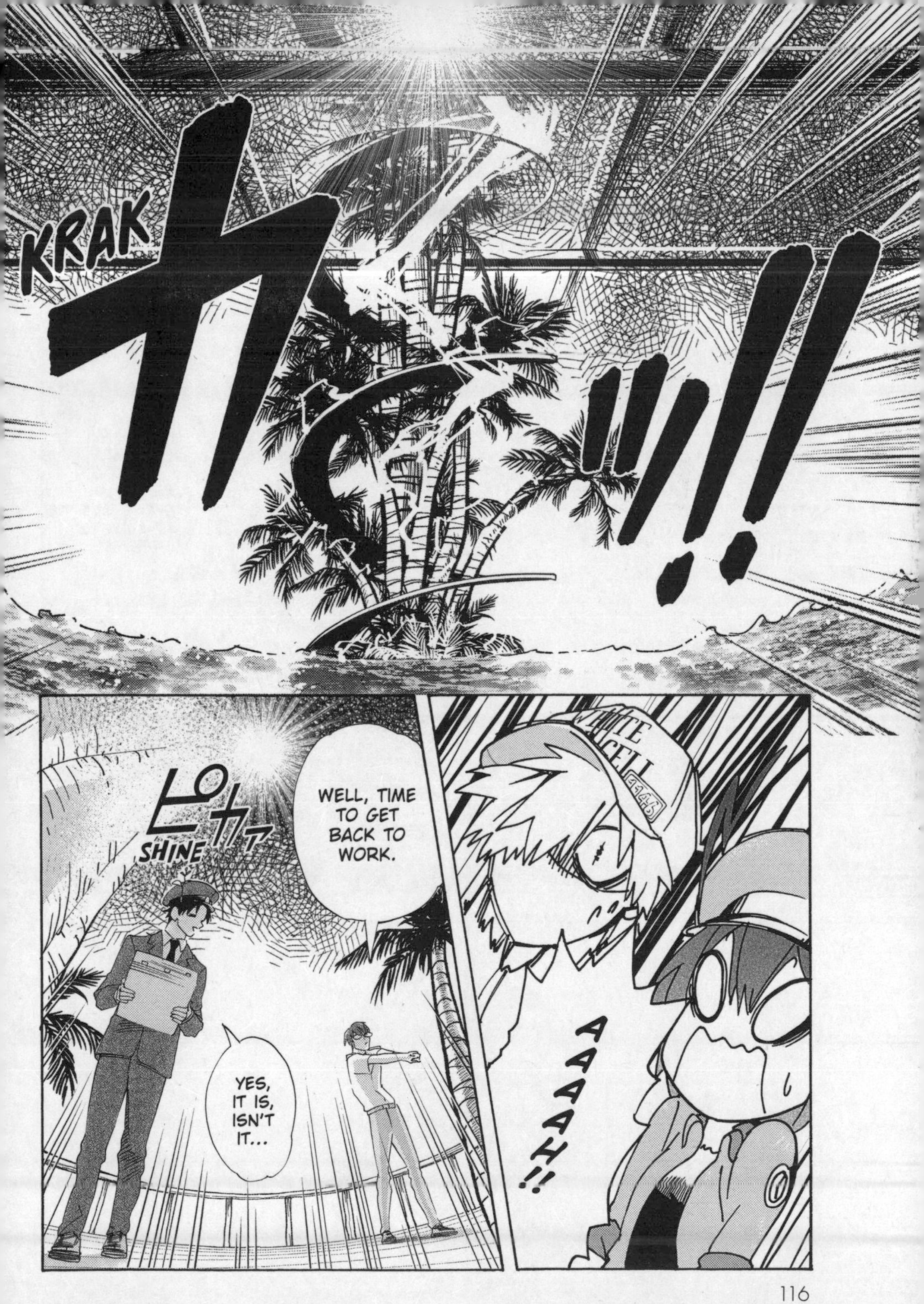
KRAK
AAAAAAH!!
ピカァ
SHINE
WELL, TIME TO GET BACK TO WORK.
YES, IT IS, ISN'T IT...

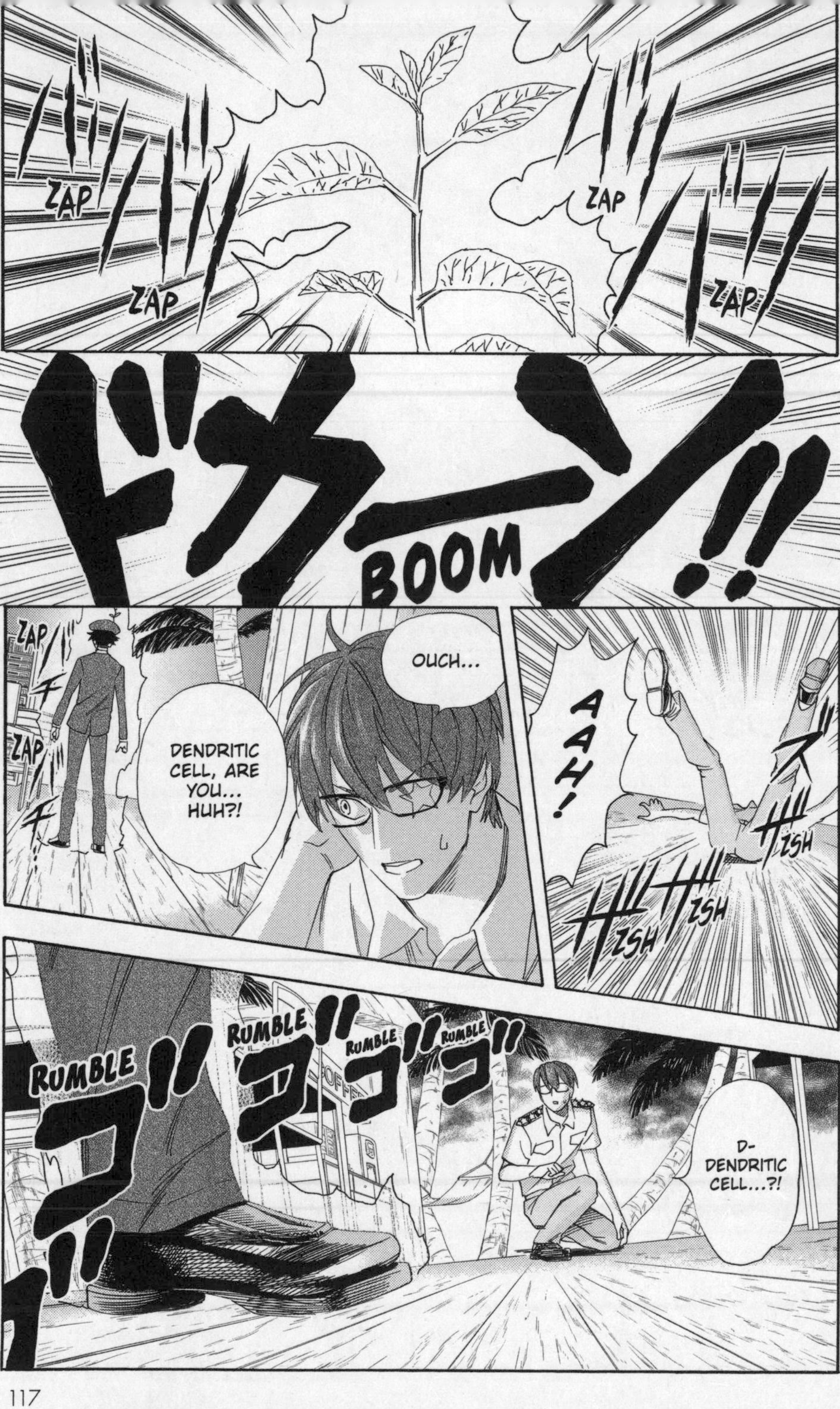
ZAP
ZAP
ZAP
ZAP
ドカーン!!
BOOM
AAH!
ZSH
ZSH
ZSH
OUCH...
DENDRITIC CELL, ARE YOU... HUH?!
ZAP
ZAP
D- DENDRITIC CELL...?!
RUMBLE
RUMBLE
RUMBLE
RUMBLE

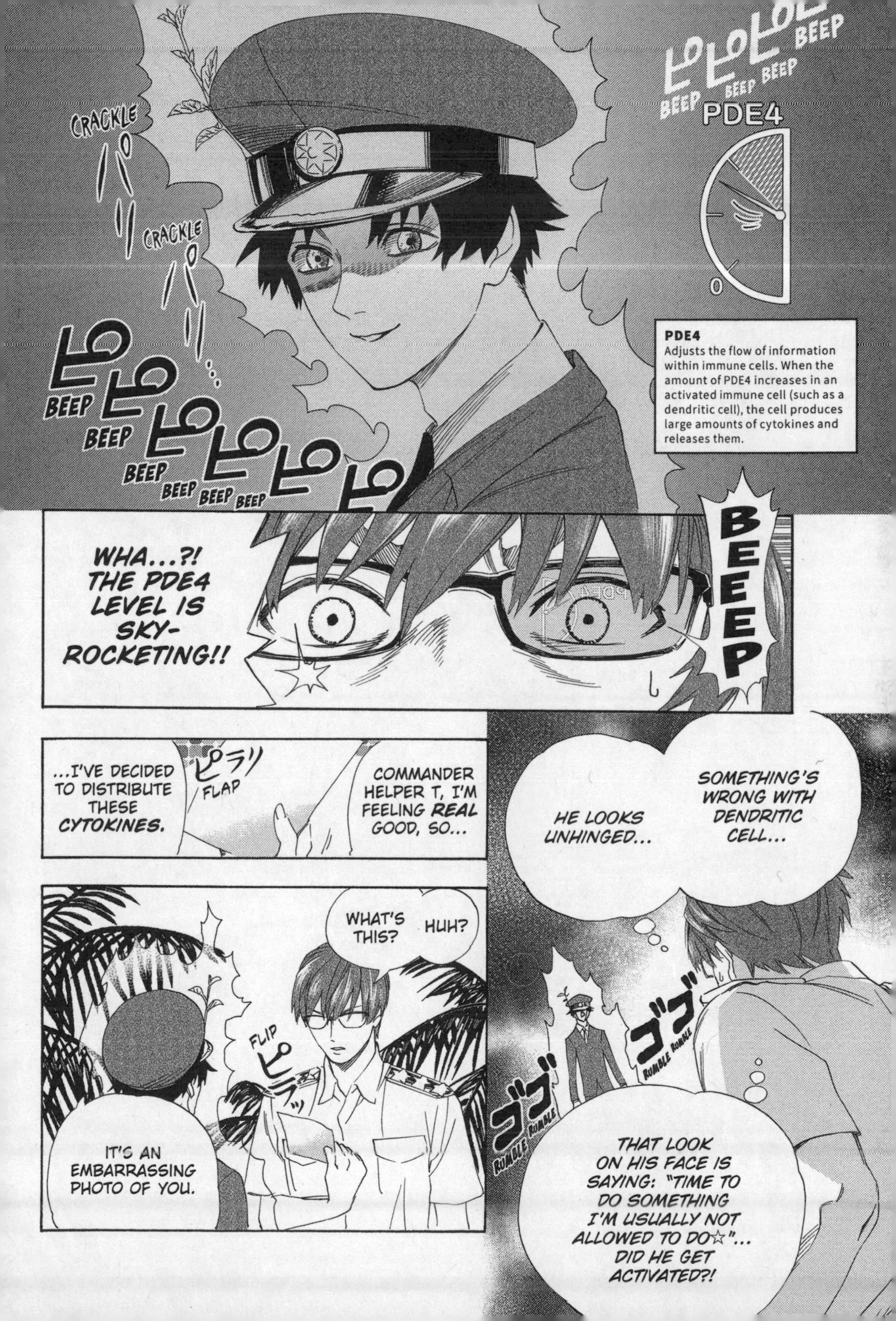

BEEP BEEP BEEP BEEP
PDE4
0
PDE4
Adjusts the flow of information within immune cells. When the amount of PDE4 increases in an activated immune cell (such as a dendritic cell), the cell produces large amounts of cytokines and releases them.
CRACKLE
CRACKLE
BEEP BEEP BEEP BEEP BEEP BEEP
BEEEP
WHA...?! THE PDE4 LEVEL IS SKY-ROCKETING!!
SOMETHING'S WRONG WITH DENDRITIC CELL...
HE LOOKS UNHINGED...
ゴゴ RUMBLE RUMBLE
ゴゴ RUMBLE RUMBLE
THAT LOOK ON HIS FACE IS SAYING: "TIME TO DO SOMETHING I'M USUALLY NOT ALLOWED TO DO☆"... DID HE GET ACTIVATED?!
COMMANDER HELPER T, I'M FEELING REAL GOOD, SO...
ピラリ FLAP
...I'VE DECIDED TO DISTRIBUTE THESE CYTOKINES.
HUH?
WHAT'S THIS?
ピラッ FLIP
IT'S AN EMBARRASSING PHOTO OF YOU.

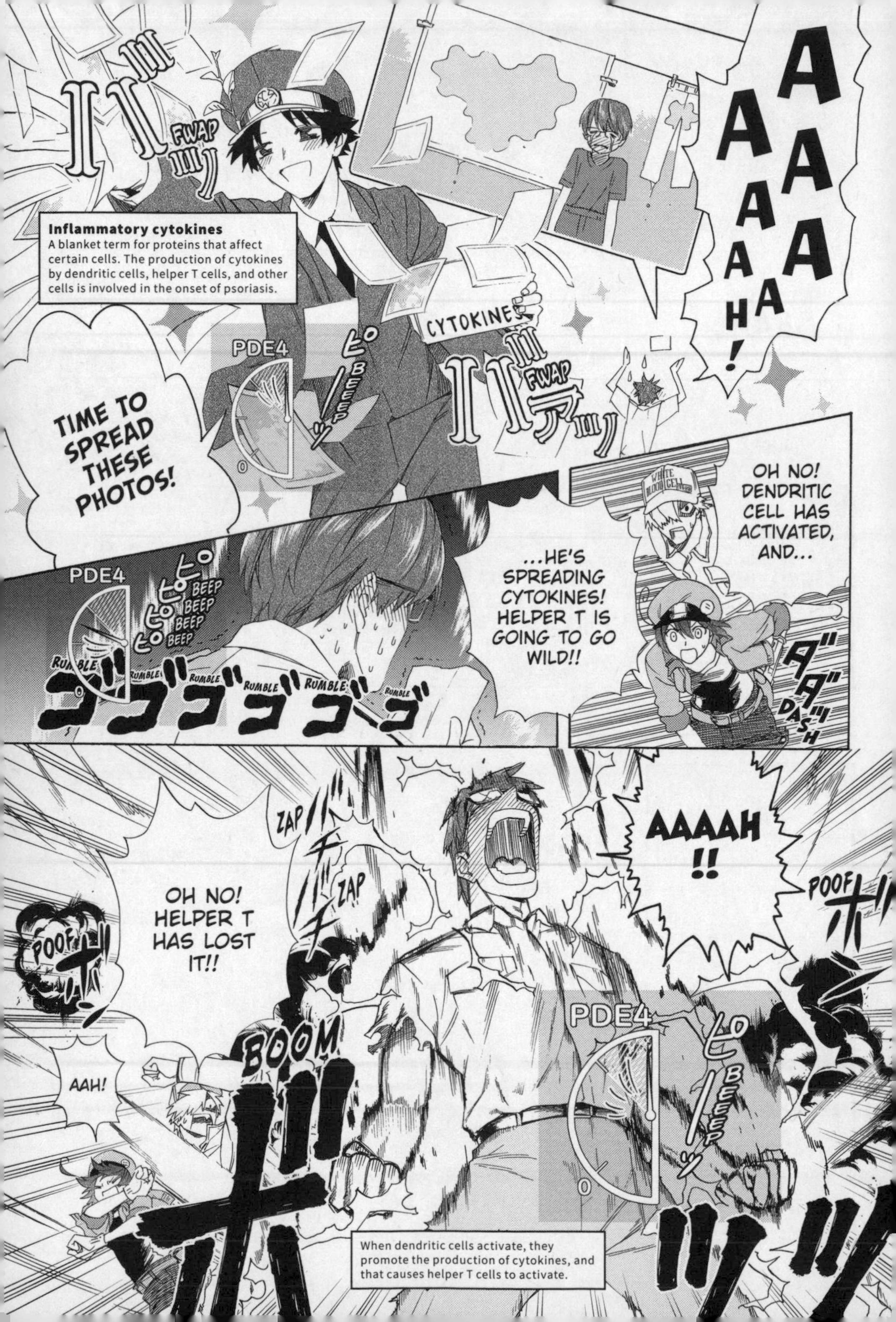

AAAAAAAAH!
FWAP
CYTOKINES
FWAP
PDE4
BEEEP
0
Inflammatory cytokines
A blanket term for proteins that affect certain cells. The production of cytokines by dendritic cells, helper T cells, and other cells is involved in the onset of psoriasis.
TIME TO SPREAD THESE PHOTOS!
WHITE BLOOD CELL
OH NO! DENDRITIC CELL HAS ACTIVATED, AND...
...HE'S SPREADING CYTOKINES! HELPER T IS GOING TO GO WILD!!
DASH
PDE4
BEEP BEEP BEEP BEEP
RUMBLE RUMBLE RUMBLE RUMBLE RUMBLE RUMBLE
POOF
AAAAH !!
ZAP
ZAP
OH NO! HELPER T HAS LOST IT!!
POOF
PDE4
BEEEP
0
BOOM
AAH!
When dendritic cells activate, they promote the production of cytokines, and that causes helper T cells to activate.

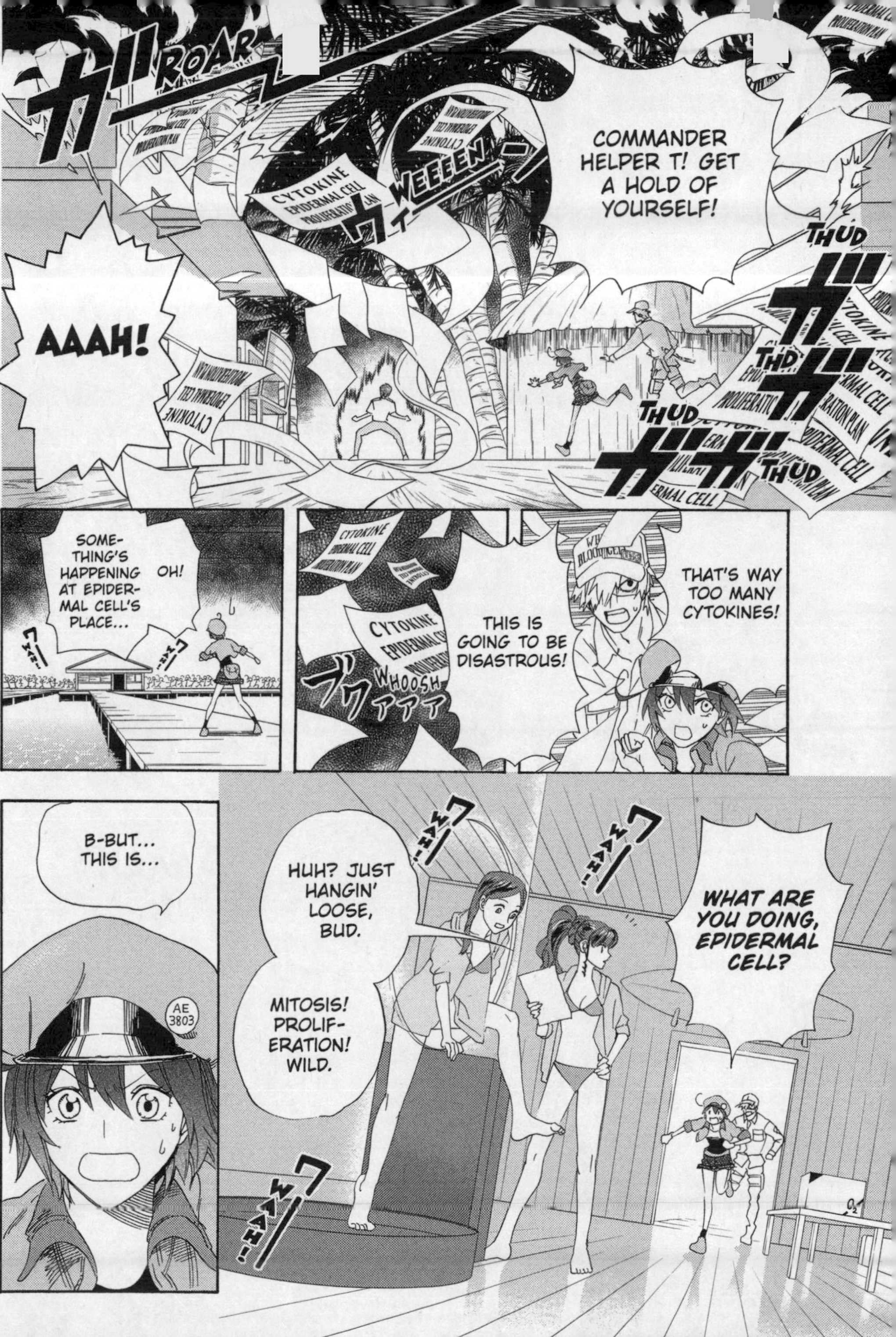
COMMANDER HELPER T! GET A HOLD OF YOURSELF!
THUD
THD
THUD
THUD
WEEEEN
ROAR
AAAH!
THAT'S WAY TOO MANY CYTOKINES!
THIS IS GOING TO BE DISASTROUS!
WHOOSH
OH!
SOME-THING'S HAPPENING AT EPIDER-MAL CELL'S PLACE...
WHAT ARE YOU DOING, EPIDERMAL CELL?
HUH? JUST HANGIN' LOOSE, BUD.
MITOSIS! PROLIF-ERATION! WILD.
WAH!
B-BUT... THIS IS...
AE 3803

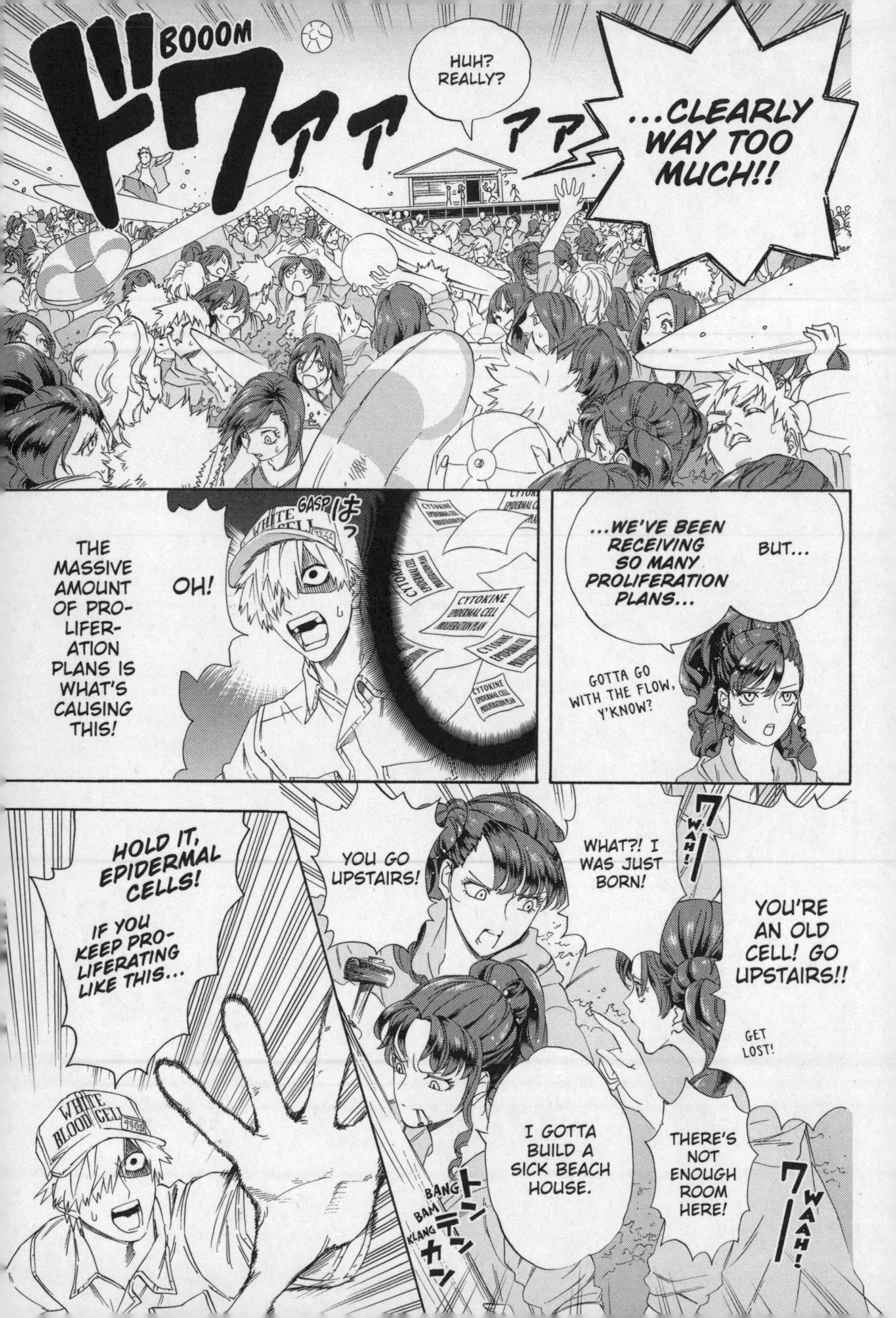
...CLEARLY WAY TOO MUCH!!
HUH? REALLY?
BOOOM
ドワァァァァ
BUT...
...WE'VE BEEN RECEIVING SO MANY PROLIFERATION PLANS...
GOTTA GO WITH THE FLOW, Y'KNOW?
GASP
はっ
CYTOKINE EPIDERMAL CELL PROLIFERATION PLAN
OH!
THE MASSIVE AMOUNT OF PRO-LIFER-ATION PLANS IS WHAT'S CAUSING THIS!
WAAH!
YOU'RE AN OLD CELL! GO UPSTAIRS!!
WHAT?! I WAS JUST BORN!
YOU GO UPSTAIRS!
HOLD IT, EPIDERMAL CELLS!
IF YOU KEEP PRO-LIFERATING LIKE THIS...
GET LOST!
WAAH!
THERE'S NOT ENOUGH ROOM HERE!
I GOTTA BUILD A SICK BEACH HOUSE.
BANG BAM KLANG
トンテンカン

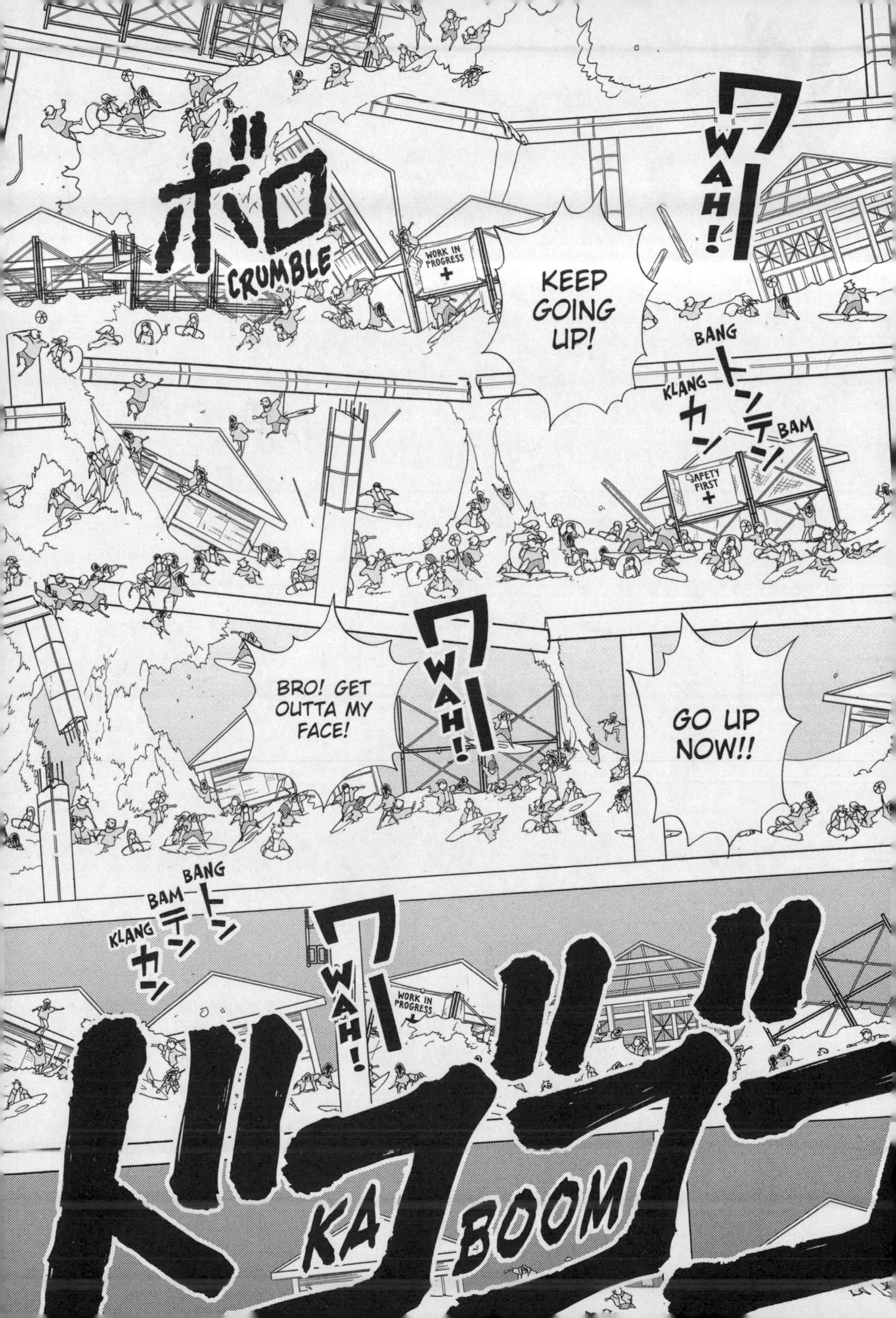
WAH!
KEEP GOING UP!
BANG
KLANG
BAM
SAFETY FIRST
WORK IN PROGRESS
CRUMBLE
GO UP NOW!!
WAH!
BRO! GET OUTTA MY FACE!
WAH!
WORK IN PROGRESS
BANG
BAM
KLANG
KA BOOM

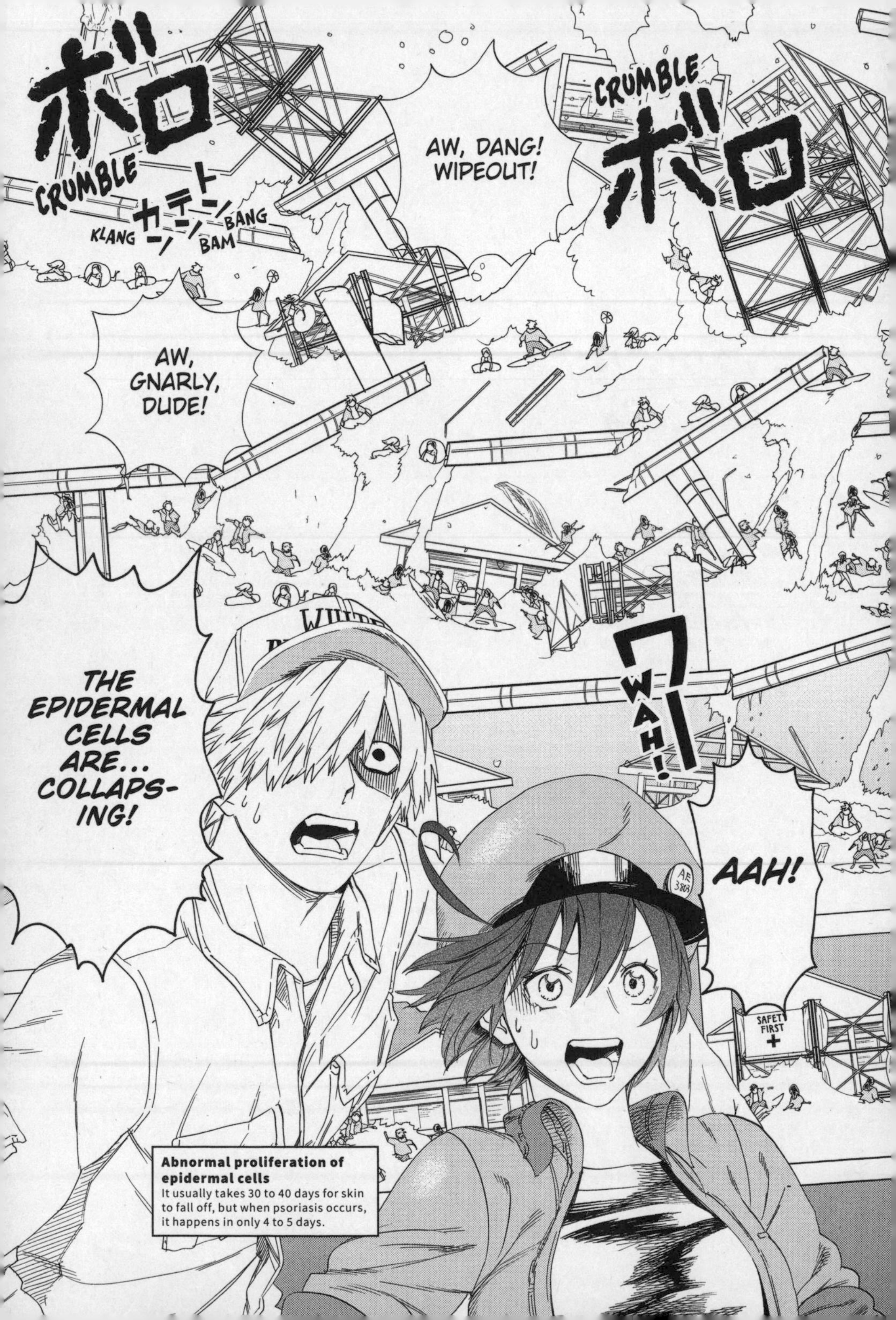
CRUMBLE
ボロ
AW, DANG! WIPEOUT!
ボロ
CRUMBLE
KLANG
BANG
BAM
AW, GNARLY, DUDE!
WAH!
AAH!
THE EPIDERMAL CELLS ARE... COLLAPSING!
SAFETY FIRST
Abnormal proliferation of epidermal cells
It usually takes 30 to 40 days for skin to fall off, but when psoriasis occurs, it happens in only 4 to 5 days.

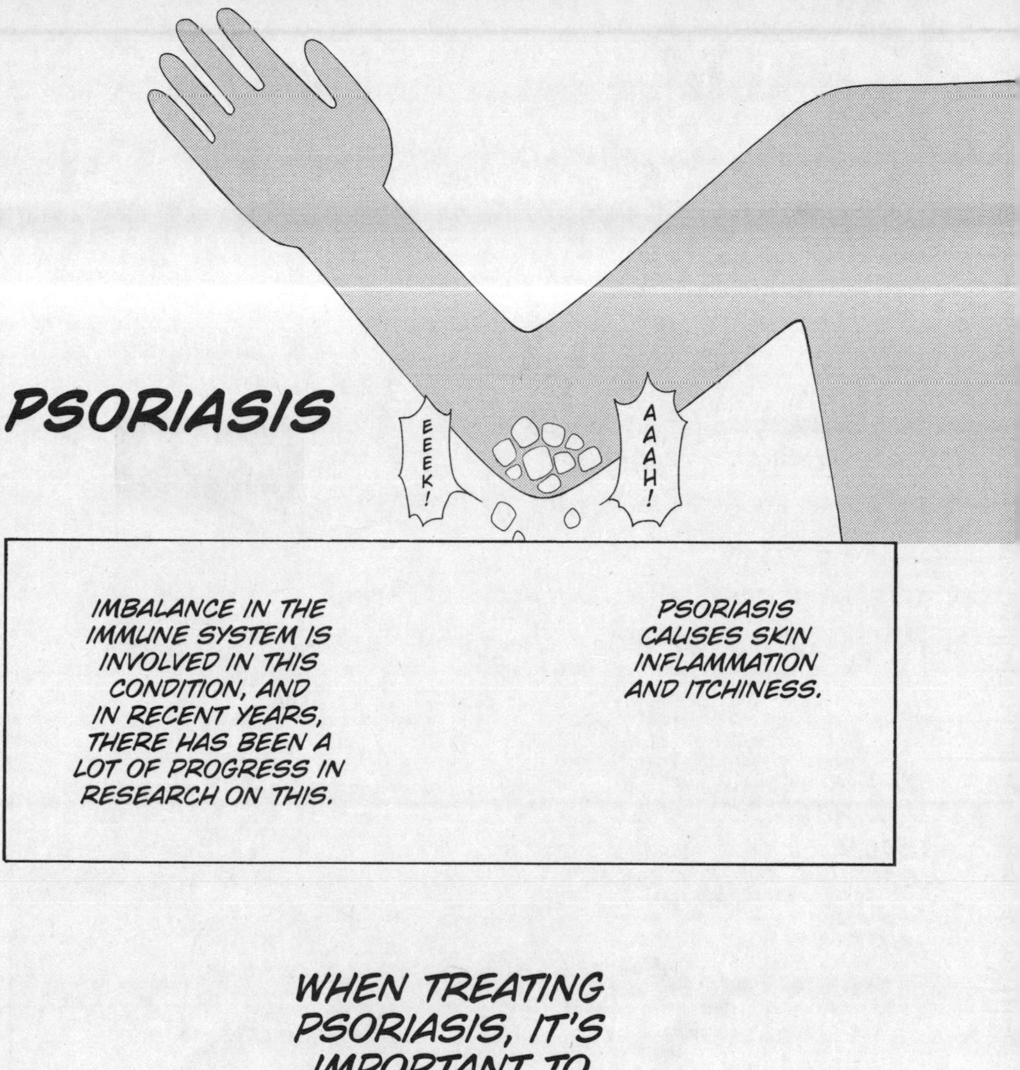
PSORIASIS
AAAH!
EEEK!
PSORIASIS CAUSES SKIN INFLAMMATION AND ITCHINESS.
IMBALANCE IN THE IMMUNE SYSTEM IS INVOLVED IN THIS CONDITION, AND IN RECENT YEARS, THERE HAS BEEN A LOT OF PROGRESS IN RESEARCH ON THIS.

WHEN TREATING PSORIASIS, IT'S IMPORTANT TO CHOOSE THE METHOD THAT'S BEST FOR YOU.

SPECIAL CHAPTER: END

Sponsor: Celgene K.K.

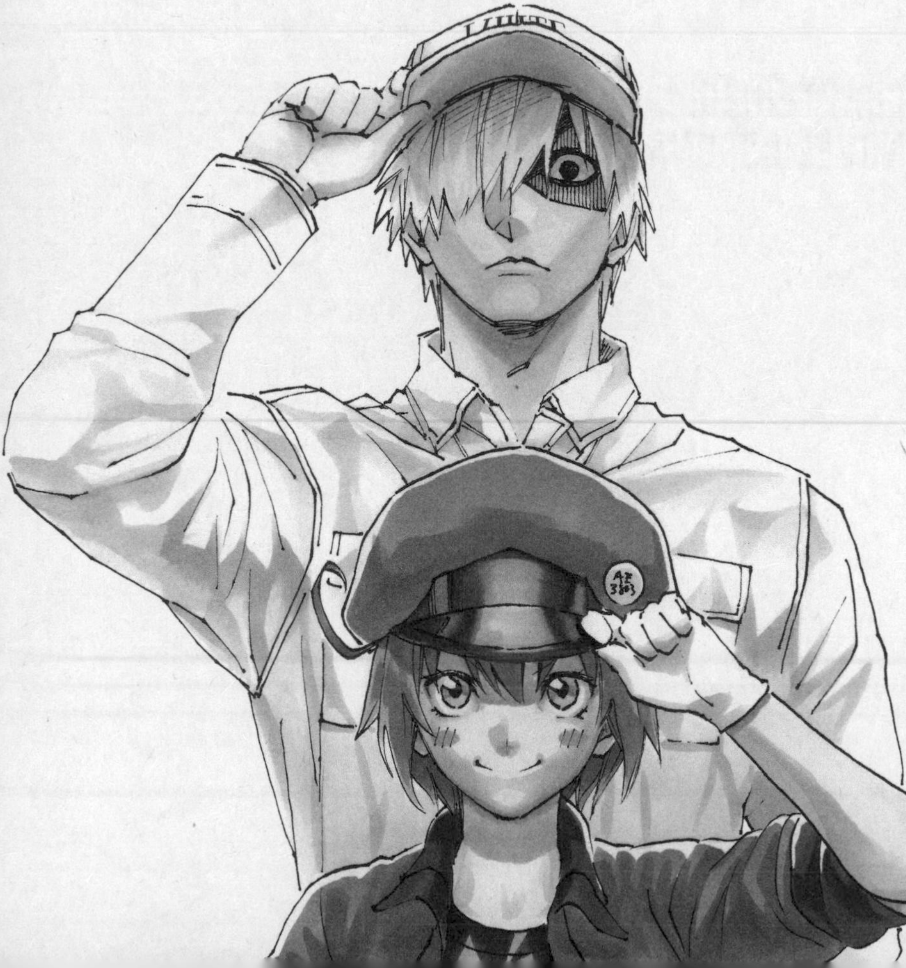
AE 3803

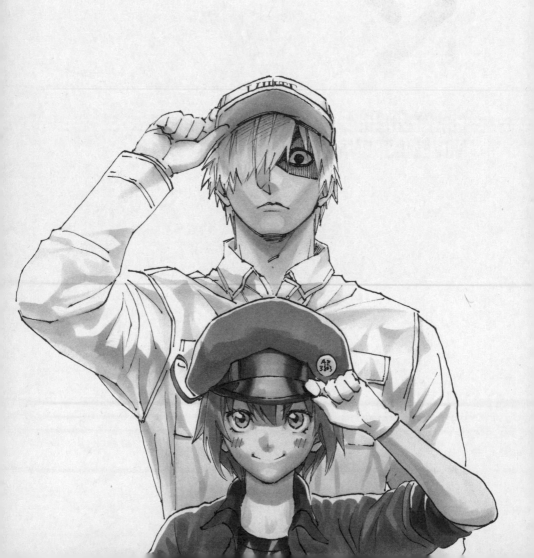

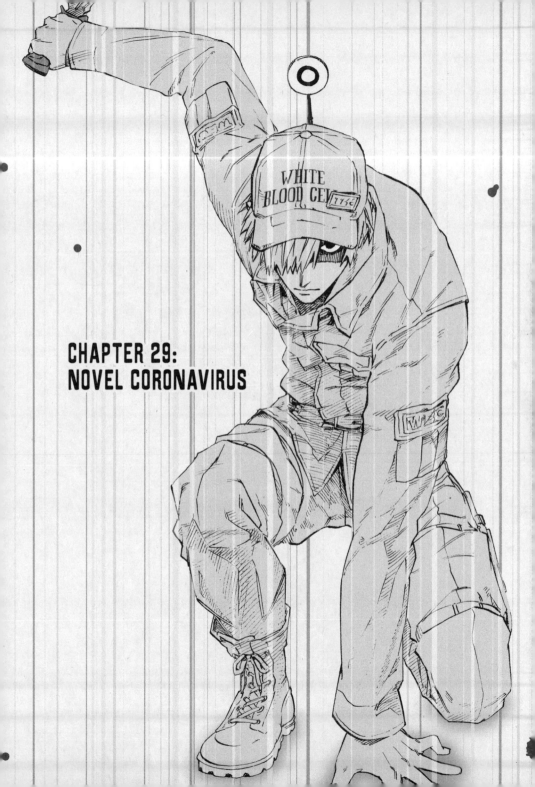

CHAPTER 29:
NOVEL CORONAVIRUS

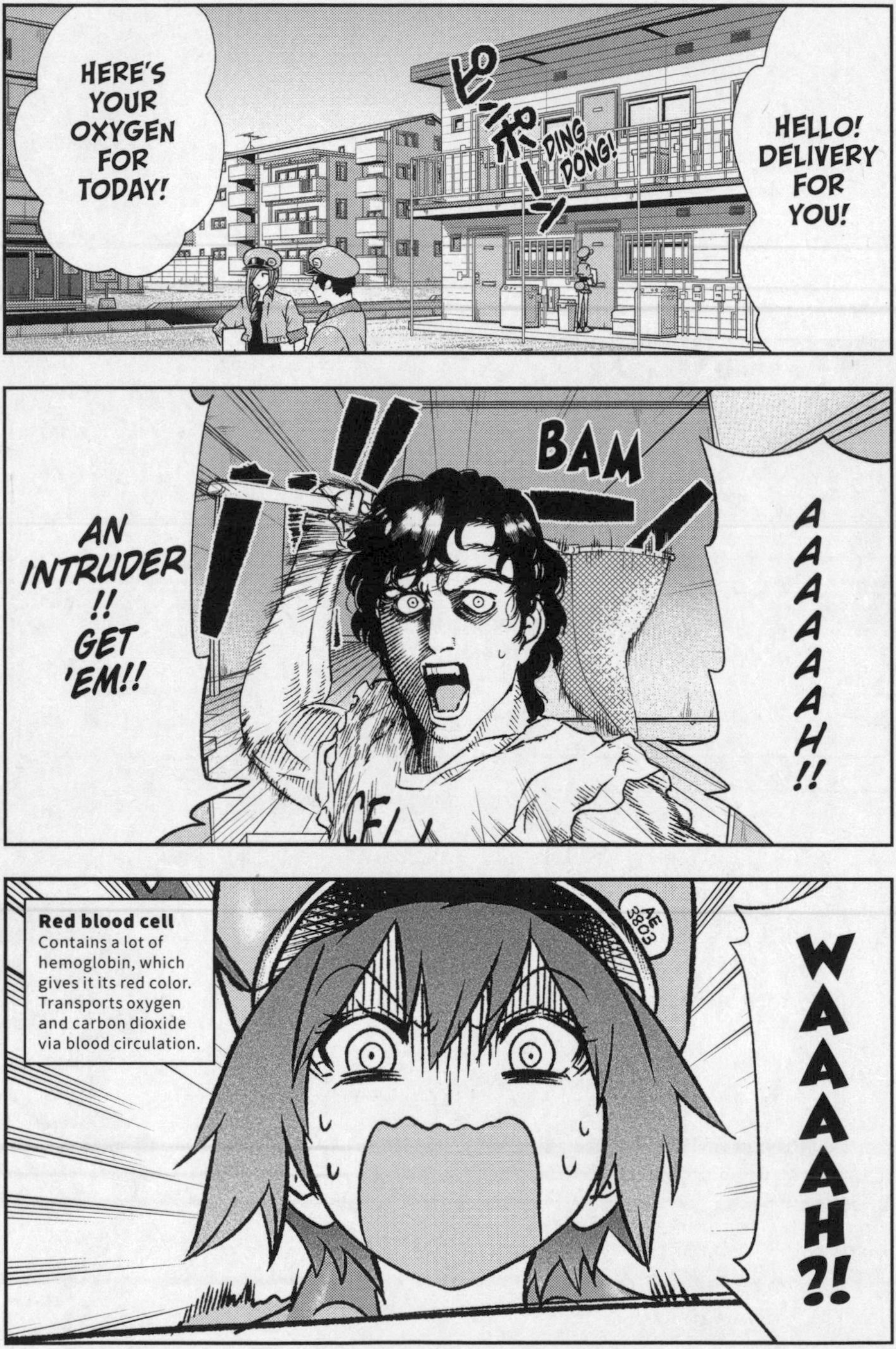
HELLO! DELIVERY FOR YOU!
ピンポーン
DING DONG!
HERE'S YOUR OXYGEN FOR TODAY!
AAAAAAAAH!!
BAM
AN INTRUDER!! GET 'EM!!
WAAAAAH?!
AE 3803
Red blood cell
Contains a lot of hemoglobin, which gives it its red color. Transports oxygen and carbon dioxide via blood circulation.

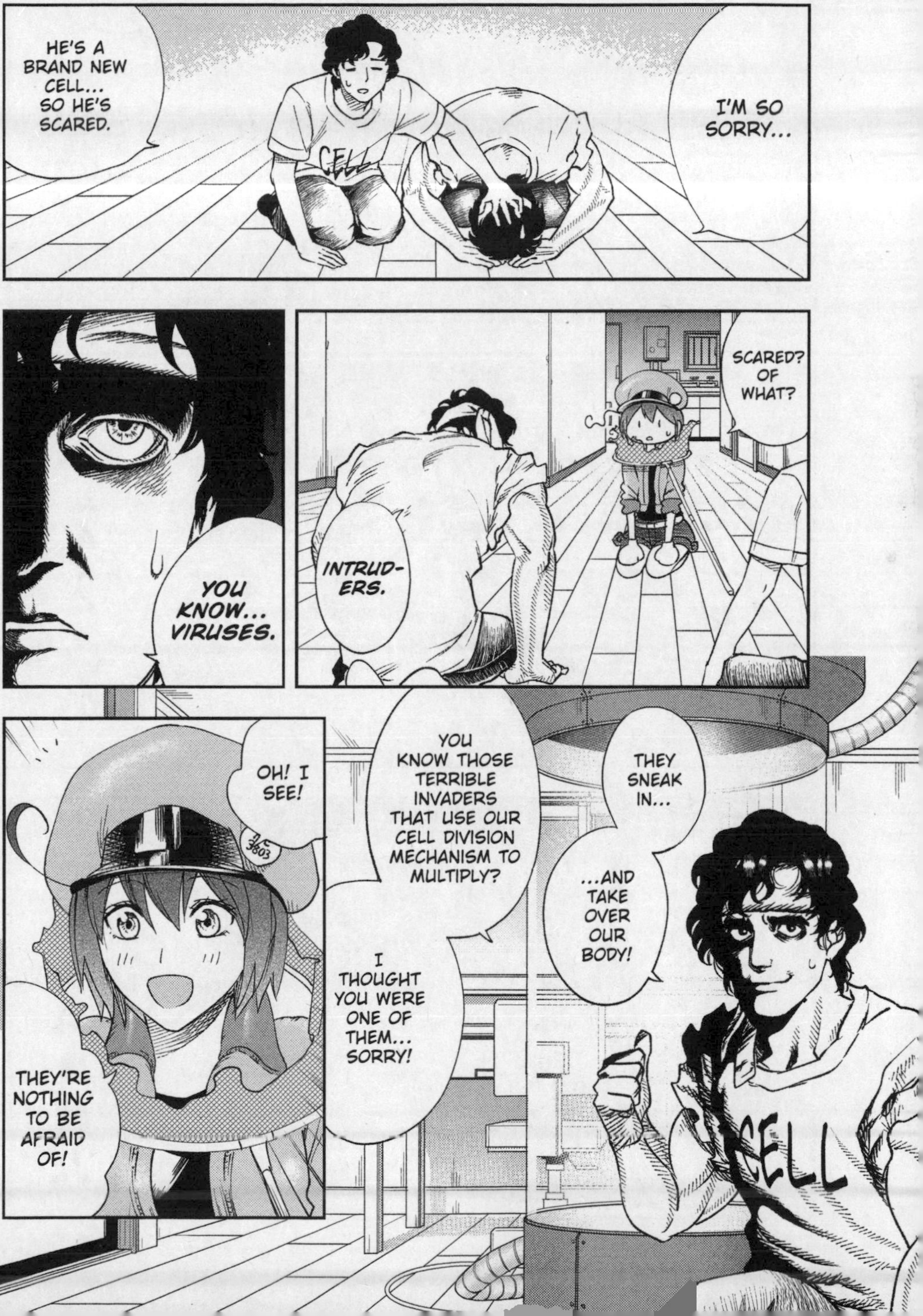
I'M SO SORRY...
HE'S A BRAND NEW CELL... SO HE'S SCARED.
SCARED? OF WHAT?
INTRUDERS.
YOU KNOW... VIRUSES.
YOU KNOW THOSE TERRIBLE INVADERS THAT USE OUR CELL DIVISION MECHANISM TO MULTIPLY?
THEY SNEAK IN...
...AND TAKE OVER OUR BODY!
OH! I SEE!
I THOUGHT YOU WERE ONE OF THEM... SORRY!
THEY'RE NOTHING TO BE AFRAID OF!

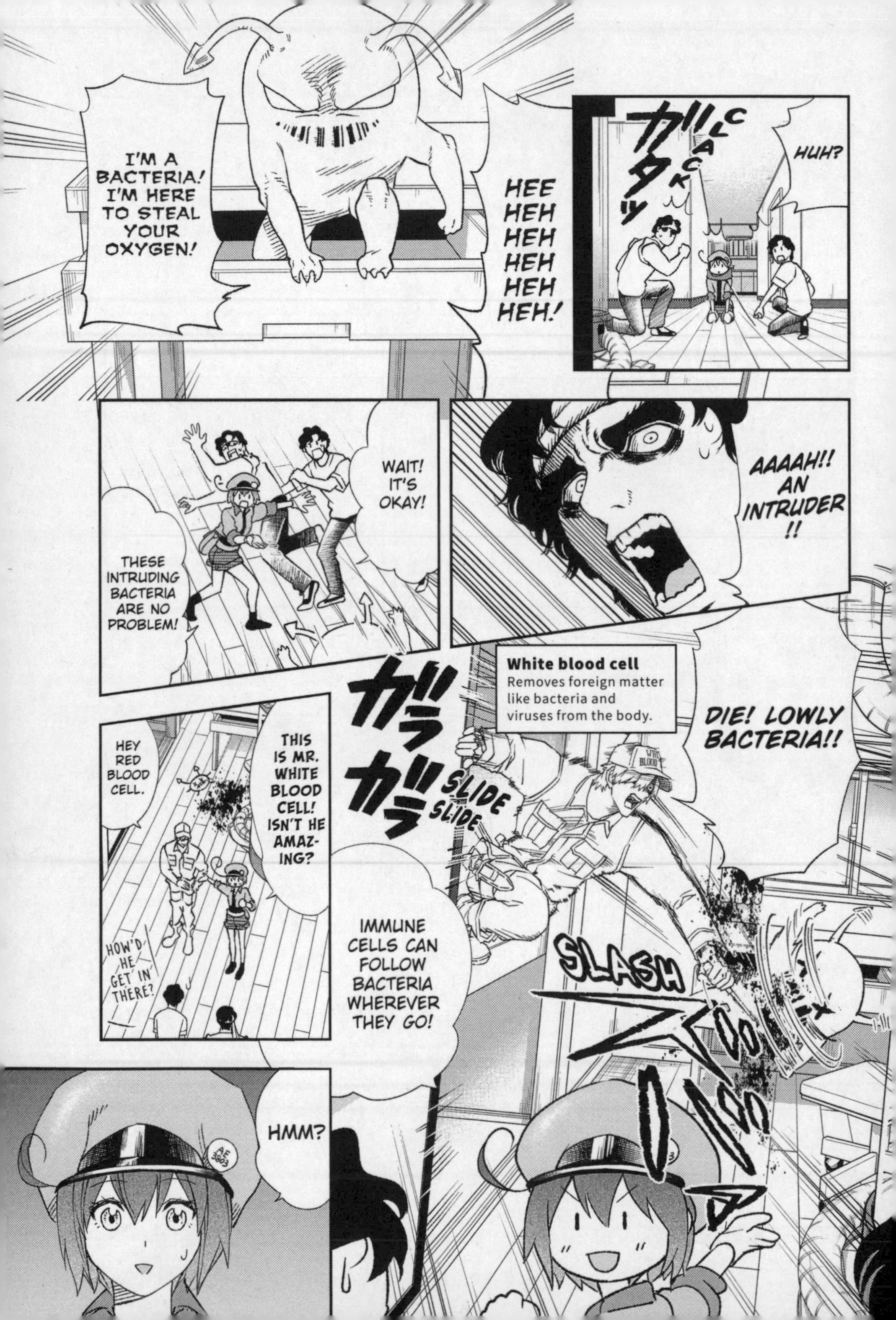
CLACK
HUH?
HEE HEH HEH HEH HEH HEH!
I'M A BACTERIA! I'M HERE TO STEAL YOUR OXYGEN!
AAAAH!! AN INTRUDER!!
WAIT! IT'S OKAY!
THESE INTRUDING BACTERIA ARE NO PROBLEM!
White blood cell
Removes foreign matter like bacteria and viruses from the body.
DIE! LOWLY BACTERIA!!
SLIDE SLIDE
SLASH
THIS IS MR. WHITE BLOOD CELL! ISN'T HE AMAZ-ING?
HEY RED BLOOD CELL.
HOW'D HE GET IN THERE?
IMMUNE CELLS CAN FOLLOW BACTERIA WHEREVER THEY GO!
HMM?
AE 3803

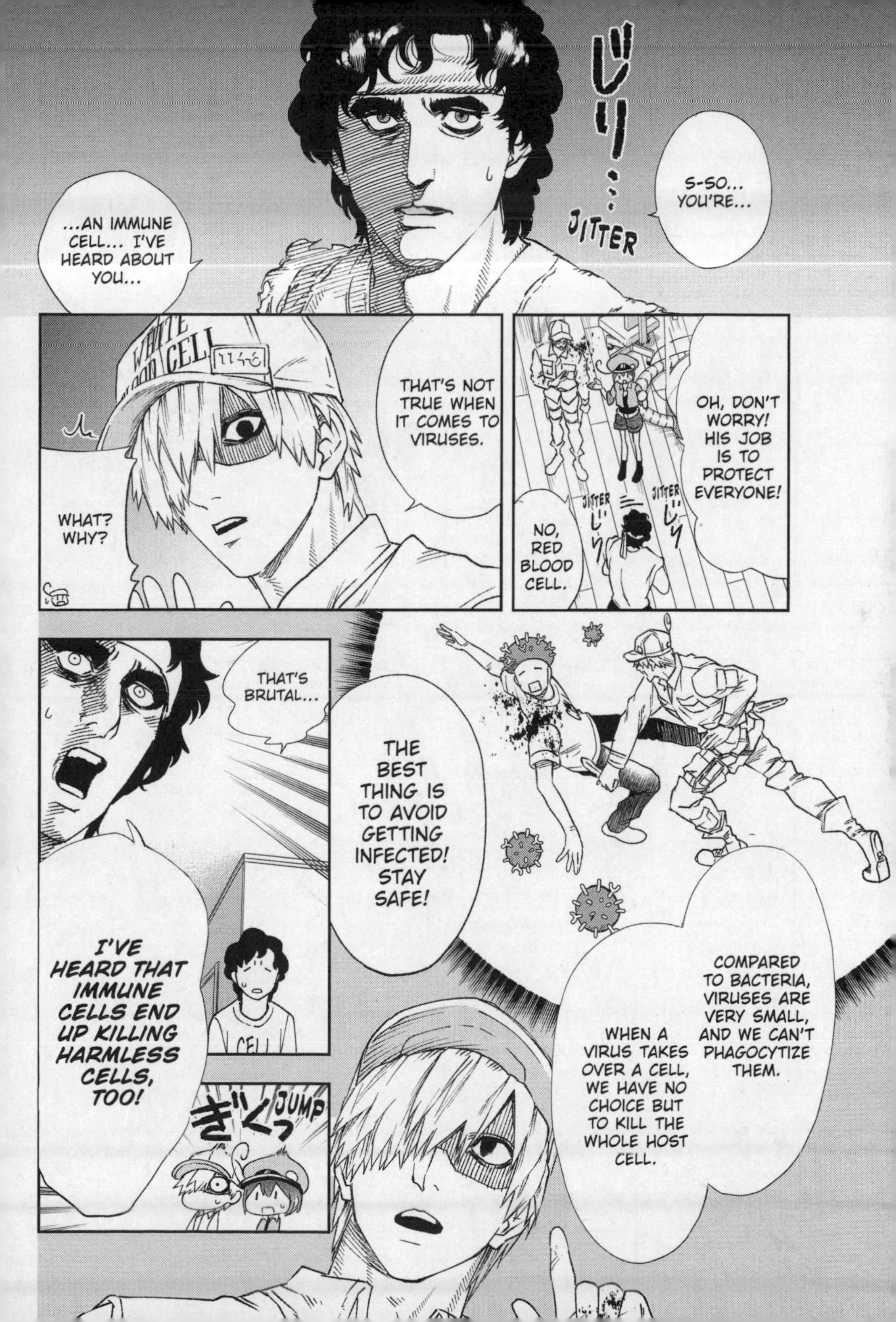
S-SO... YOU'RE...
JITTER
...AN IMMUNE CELL... I'VE HEARD ABOUT YOU...
OH, DON'T WORRY! HIS JOB IS TO PROTECT EVERYONE!
JITTER
JITTER
NO, RED BLOOD CELL.
THAT'S NOT TRUE WHEN IT COMES TO VIRUSES.
WHAT? WHY?
COMPARED TO BACTERIA, VIRUSES ARE VERY SMALL, AND WE CAN'T PHAGOCYTIZE THEM.
WHEN A VIRUS TAKES OVER A CELL, WE HAVE NO CHOICE BUT TO KILL THE WHOLE HOST CELL.
THE BEST THING IS TO AVOID GETTING INFECTED! STAY SAFE!
THAT'S BRUTAL...
I'VE HEARD THAT IMMUNE CELLS END UP KILLING HARMLESS CELLS, TOO!
JUMP

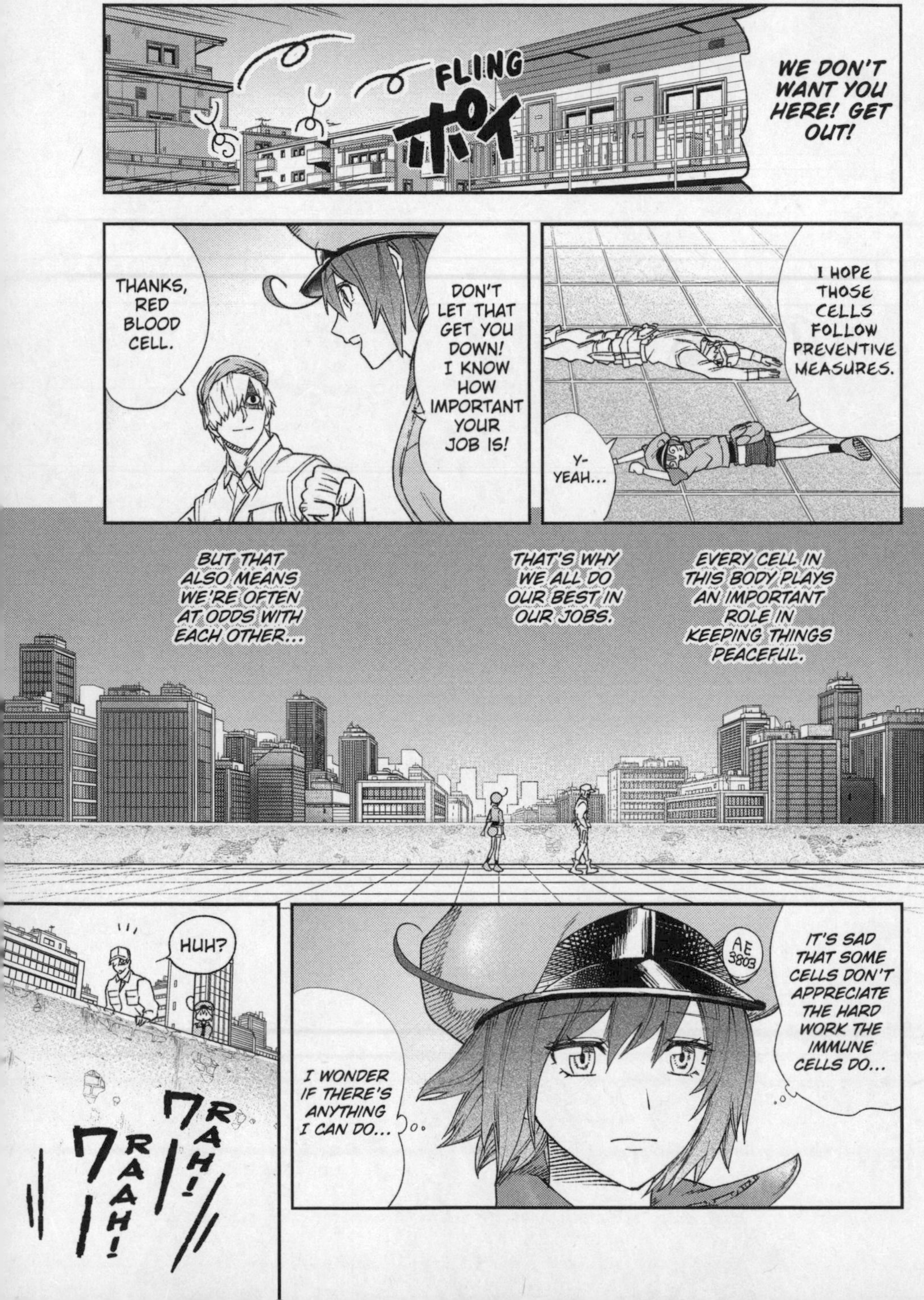
WE DON'T WANT YOU HERE! GET OUT!
FLING
ポイ
I HOPE THOSE CELLS FOLLOW PREVENTIVE MEASURES.
Y-YEAH...
DON'T LET THAT GET YOU DOWN! I KNOW HOW IMPORTANT YOUR JOB IS!
THANKS, RED BLOOD CELL.
EVERY CELL IN THIS BODY PLAYS AN IMPORTANT ROLE IN KEEPING THINGS PEACEFUL.
THAT'S WHY WE ALL DO OUR BEST IN OUR JOBS.
BUT THAT ALSO MEANS WE'RE OFTEN AT ODDS WITH EACH OTHER...
AE 3803
IT'S SAD THAT SOME CELLS DON'T APPRECIATE THE HARD WORK THE IMMUNE CELLS DO...
I WONDER IF THERE'S ANYTHING I CAN DO...
HUH?
ワー RAH!
ワー RAAH!

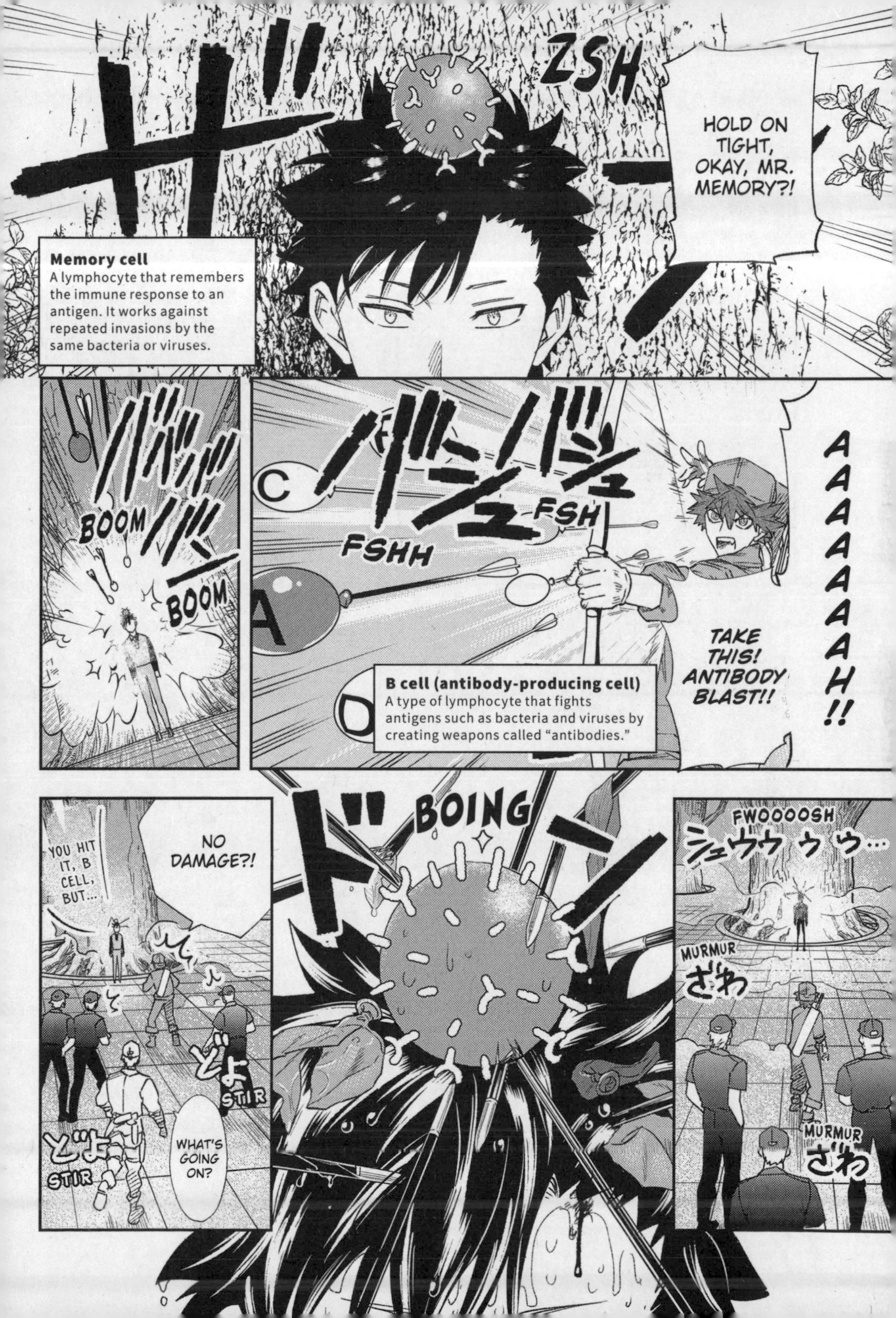
ZSH
HOLD ON TIGHT, OKAY, MR. MEMORY?!
Memory cell
A lymphocyte that remembers the immune response to an antigen. It works against repeated invasions by the same bacteria or viruses.
AAAAAAAAAH!!
TAKE THIS! ANTIBODY BLAST!!
FSH
FSHH
B cell (antibody-producing cell)
A type of lymphocyte that fights antigens such as bacteria and viruses by creating weapons called “antibodies.”
BOOM
BOOM
FWOOOOSH
シュヴゥゥゥ…
MURMUR
ざわ
MURMUR
ざわ
BOING
NO DAMAGE?!
YOU HIT IT, B CELL, BUT...
どよ
STIR
WHAT'S GOING ON?
どよ
STIR

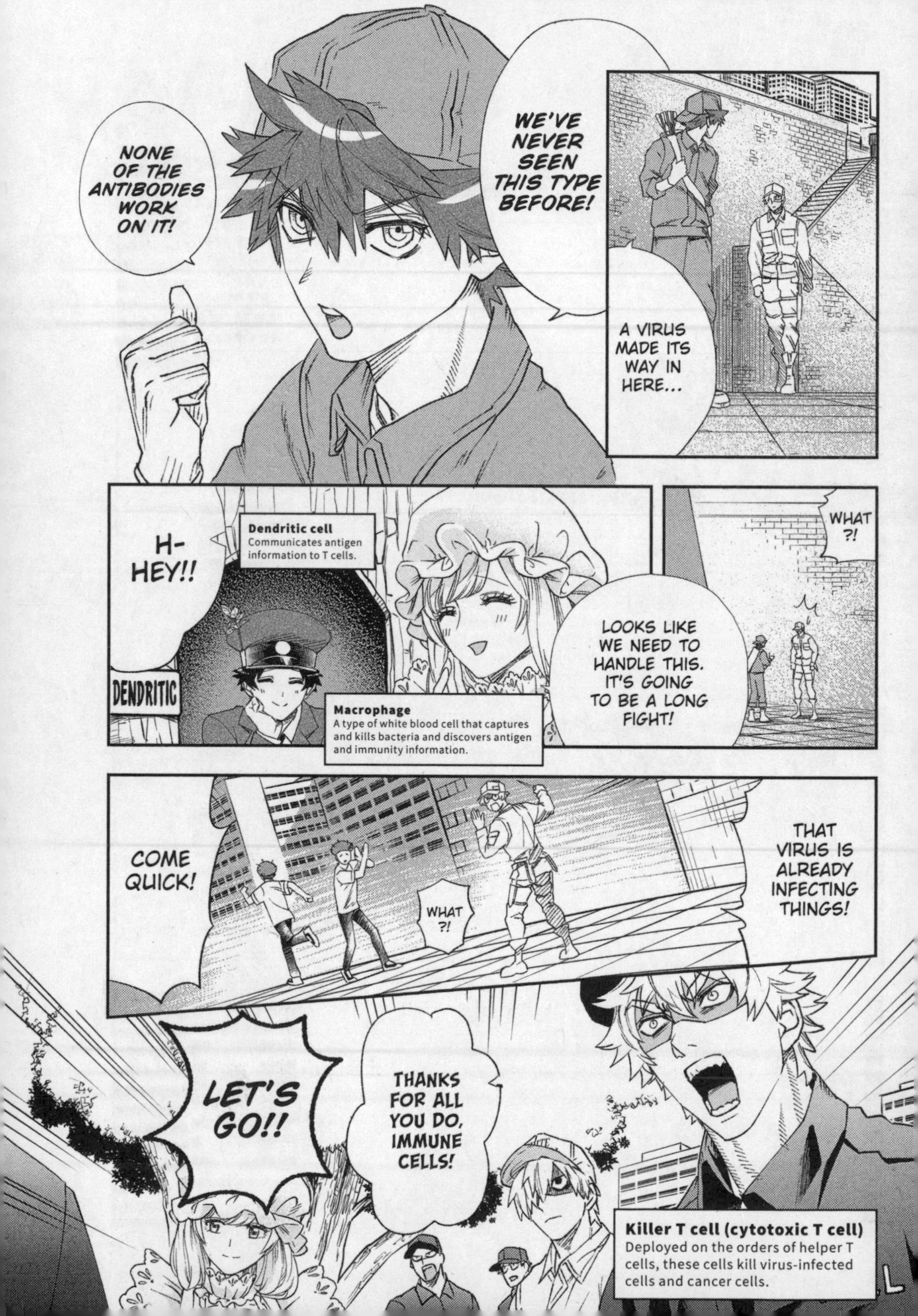
A VIRUS MADE ITS WAY IN HERE...
WE'VE NEVER SEEN THIS TYPE BEFORE!
NONE OF THE ANTIBODIES WORK ON IT!
WHAT?!
LOOKS LIKE WE NEED TO HANDLE THIS. IT'S GOING TO BE A LONG FIGHT!
Macrophage
A type of white blood cell that captures and kills bacteria and discovers antigen and immunity information.
Dendritic cell
Communicates antigen information to T cells.
H-HEY!!
DENDRITIC
THAT VIRUS IS ALREADY INFECTING THINGS!
WHAT?!
COME QUICK!
Killer T cell (cytotoxic T cell)
Deployed on the orders of helper T cells, these cells kill virus-infected cells and cancer cells.
THANKS FOR ALL YOU DO, IMMUNE CELLS!
LET'S GO!!

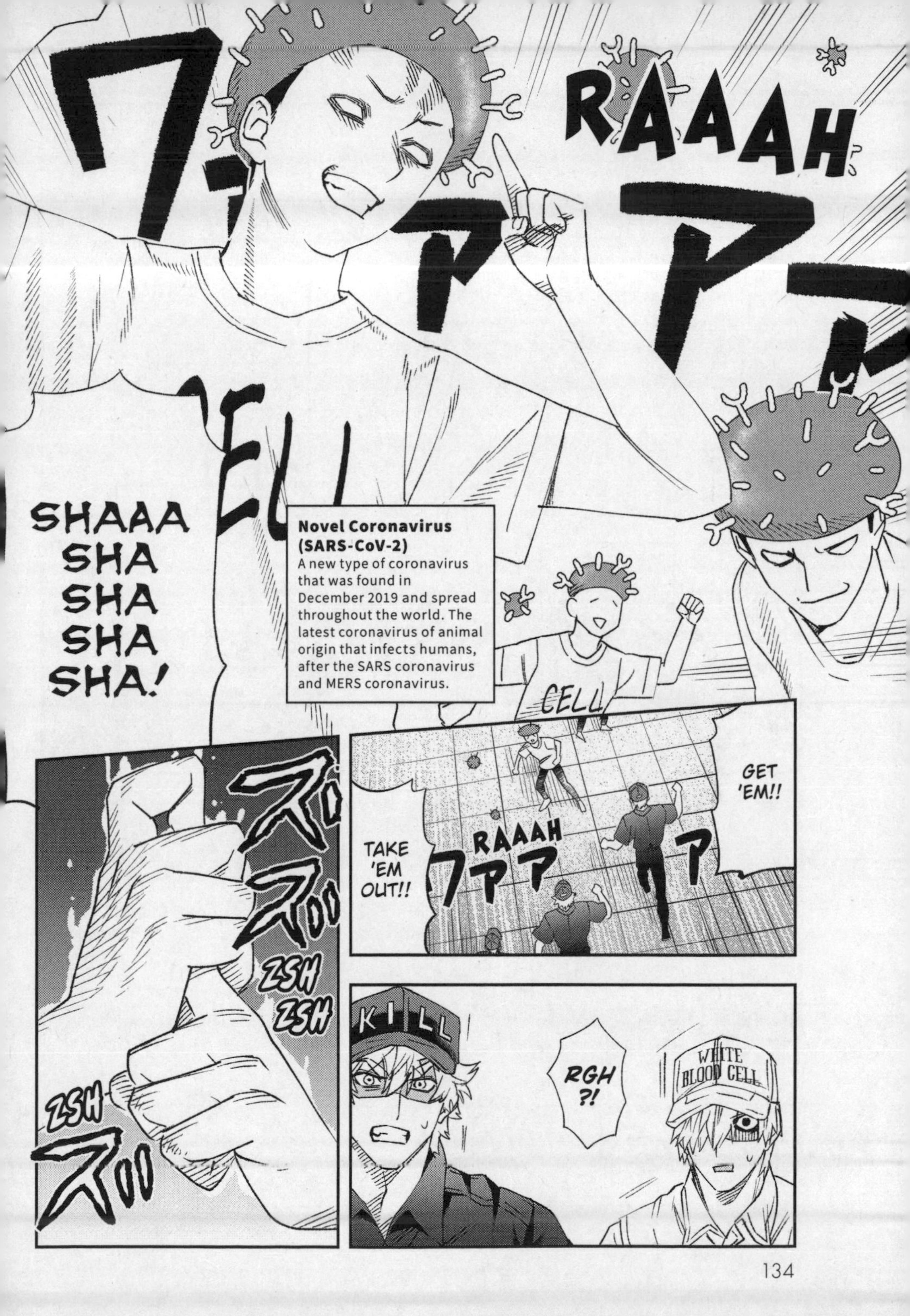
RAAAH
CELL
Novel Coronavirus (SARS-CoV-2)
A new type of coronavirus that was found in December 2019 and spread throughout the world. The latest coronavirus of animal origin that infects humans, after the SARS coronavirus and MERS coronavirus.
SHAAA SHA SHA SHA SHA!
CELL
GET 'EM!!
RAAAH
TAKE 'EM OUT!!
KILL
WHITE BLOOD CELL
RGH ?!
ZSH ZSH
ZSH

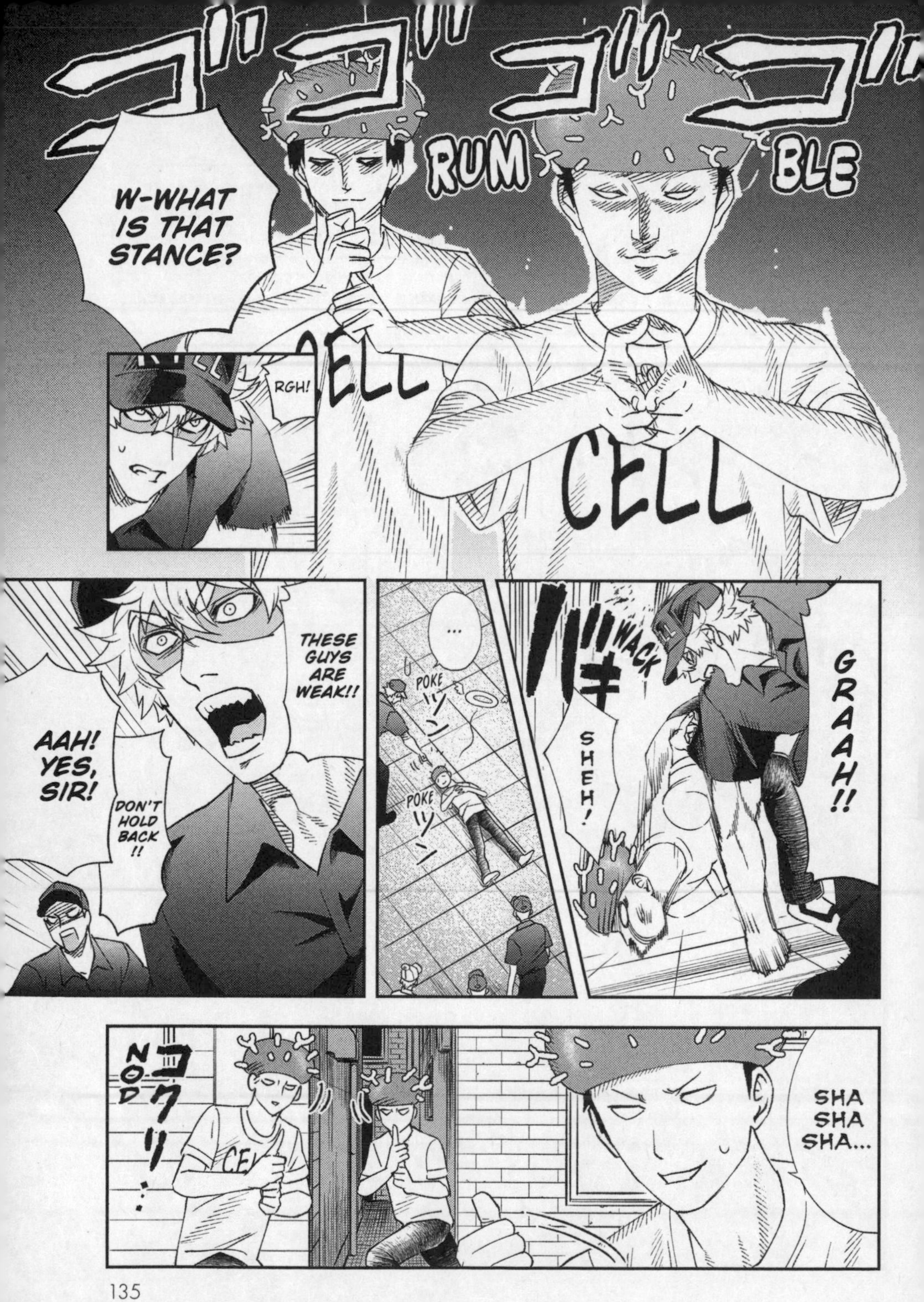
ゴゴゴゴ
RUMBLE
CELL
W-WHAT IS THAT STANCE?
RGH!
バキ
WACK
GRAAAH!!
SHEH!
...
POKE
ツン
POKE
ツン
THESE GUYS ARE WEAK!!
AAH! YES, SIR!
DON'T HOLD BACK!!
SHA SHA SHA...
NOD
コクリ…

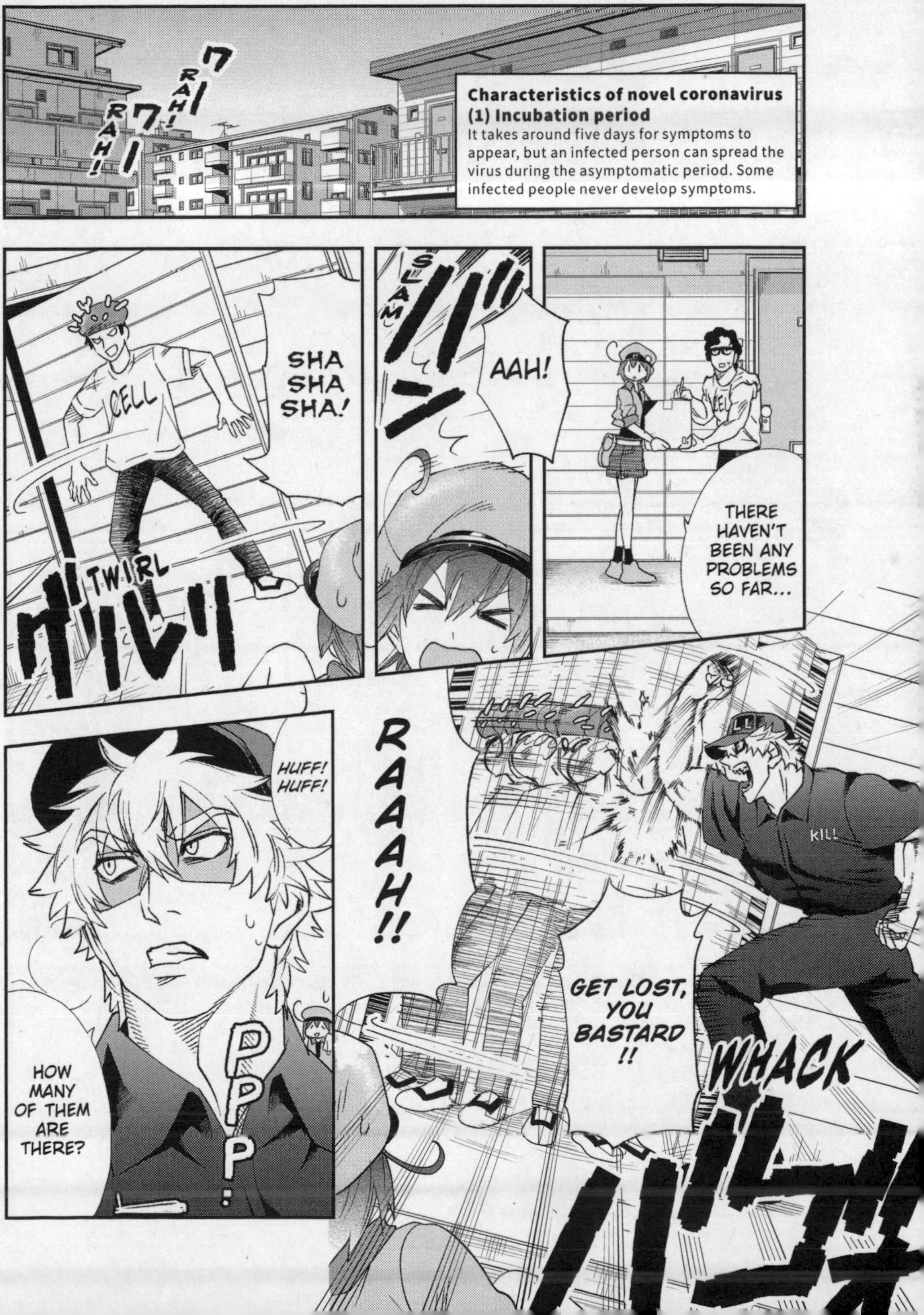
Characteristics of novel coronavirus
(1) Incubation period
It takes around five days for symptoms to appear, but an infected person can spread the virus during the asymptomatic period. Some infected people never develop symptoms.
RAH! RAH!
THERE HAVEN'T BEEN ANY PROBLEMS SO FAR...
SLAM
AAH!
SHA SHA SHA!
TWIRL
RAAAAH!!
KILL
GET LOST, YOU BASTARD!!
WHACK
HUFF! HUFF!
PPP!
HOW MANY OF THEM ARE THERE?

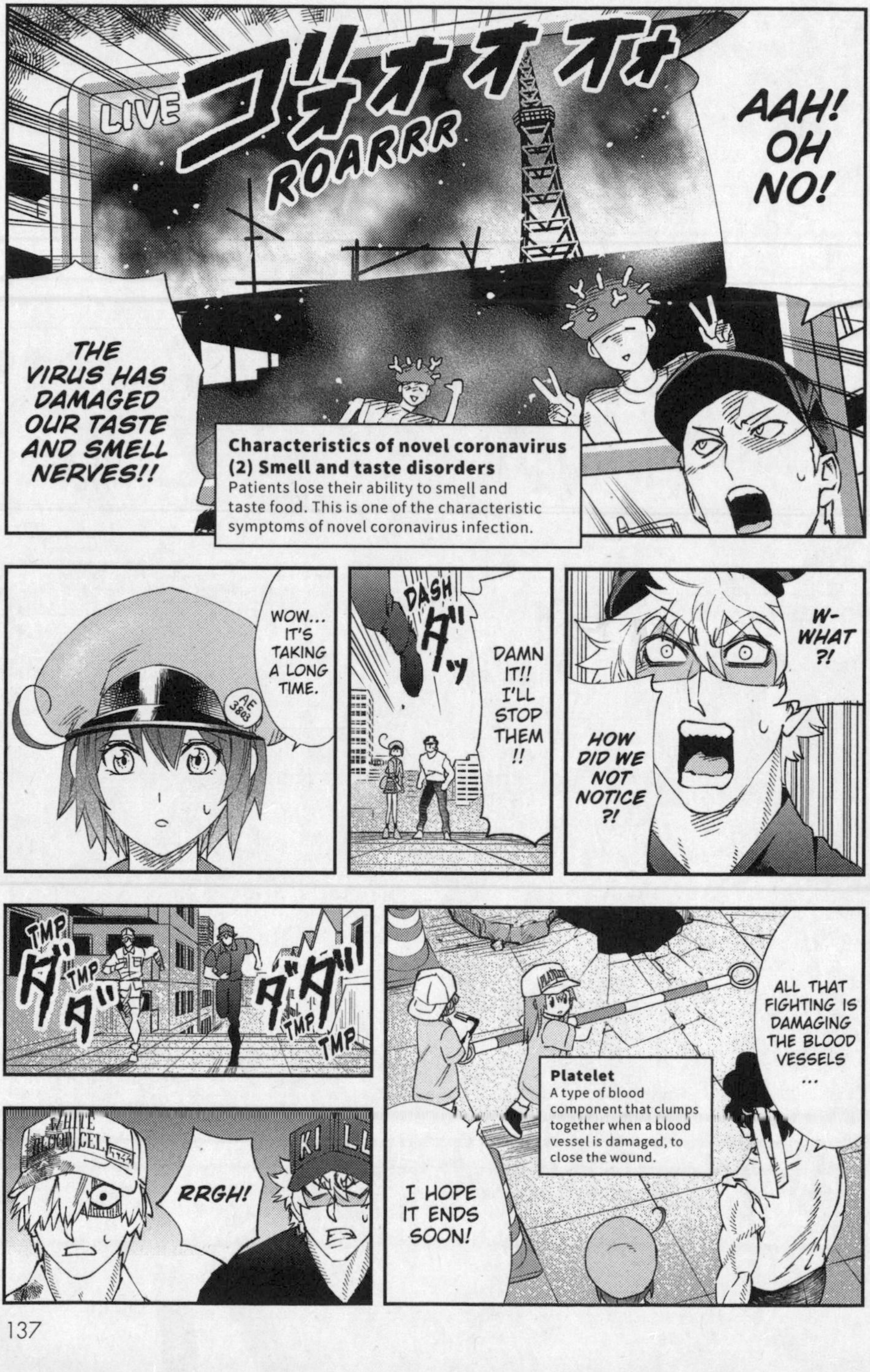
AAH! OH NO!
LIVE
ゴォォォォ
ROARRR
THE VIRUS HAS DAMAGED OUR TASTE AND SMELL NERVES!!
Characteristics of novel coronavirus (2) Smell and taste disorders
Patients lose their ability to smell and taste food. This is one of the characteristic symptoms of novel coronavirus infection.
W-WHAT?!
HOW DID WE NOT NOTICE?!
DASH
ダッ
DAMN IT!! I'LL STOP THEM!!
WOW... IT'S TAKING A LONG TIME.
AE 3803
ALL THAT FIGHTING IS DAMAGING THE BLOOD VESSELS...
Platelet
A type of blood component that clumps together when a blood vessel is damaged, to close the wound.
I HOPE IT ENDS SOON!
TMP
TMP
TMP
TMP
RRGH!
WHITE BLOOD CELL
KILL

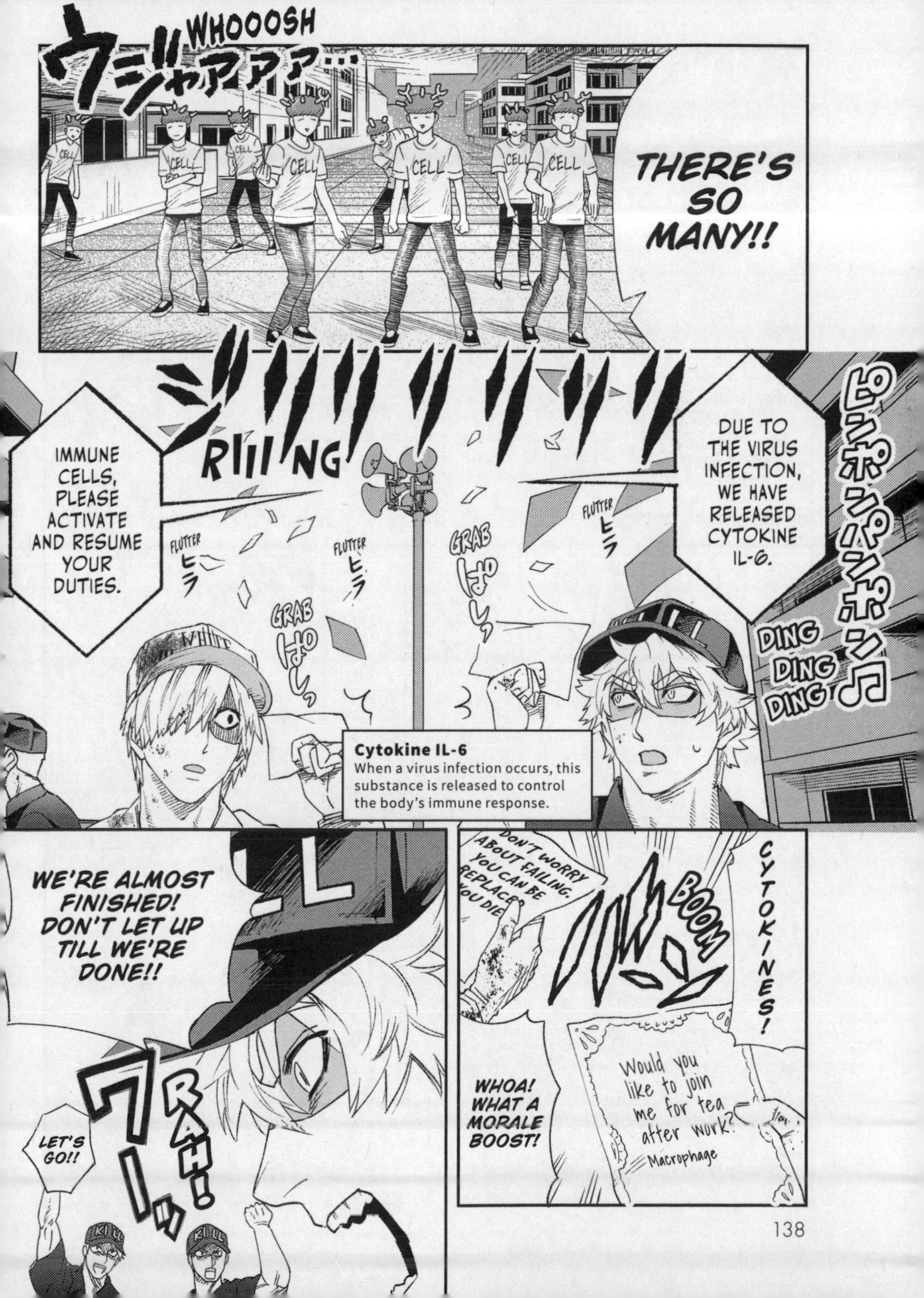
WHOOOSH
THERE'S SO MANY!!
DING DING DING
DUE TO THE VIRUS INFECTION, WE HAVE RELEASED CYTOKINE IL-6.
RIIING
IMMUNE CELLS, PLEASE ACTIVATE AND RESUME YOUR DUTIES.
FLUTTER
FLUTTER
FLUTTER
GRAB
GRAB
Cytokine IL-6
When a virus infection occurs, this substance is released to control the body's immune response.
CYTOKINES!
BOOM
DON'T WORRY ABOUT FAILING. YOU CAN BE REPLACED IF YOU DIE
Would you like to join me for tea after work? Macrophage
WHOA! WHAT A MORALE BOOST!
WE'RE ALMOST FINISHED! DON'T LET UP TILL WE'RE DONE!!
RAH!
LET'S GO!!

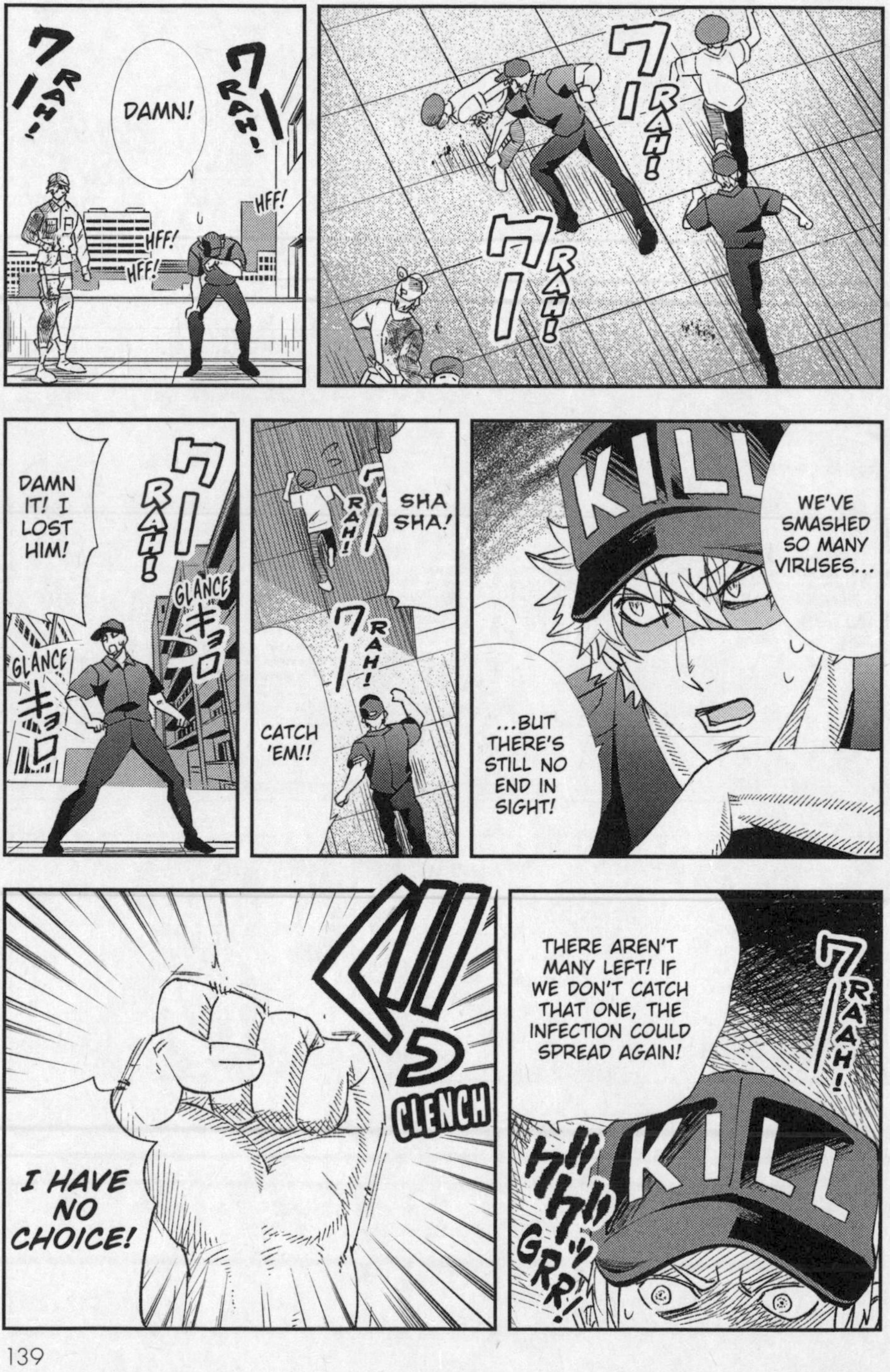

ワー
RAH!
ワー
RAH!
ワー
RAH!
DAMN!
ワー
RAH!
HFF!
HFF!
HFF!
WE'VE SMASHED SO MANY VIRUSES...
...BUT THERE'S STILL NO END IN SIGHT!
SHA SHA!
ワー
RAH!
ワー
RAH!
CATCH 'EM!!
ワー
RAH!
DAMN IT! I LOST HIM!
GLANCE
キョロ
GLANCE
キョロ
THERE AREN'T MANY LEFT! IF WE DON'T CATCH THAT ONE, THE INFECTION COULD SPREAD AGAIN!
ワー
RAAH!
ググッ
GRR!
ぐッ
CLENCH
I HAVE NO CHOICE!

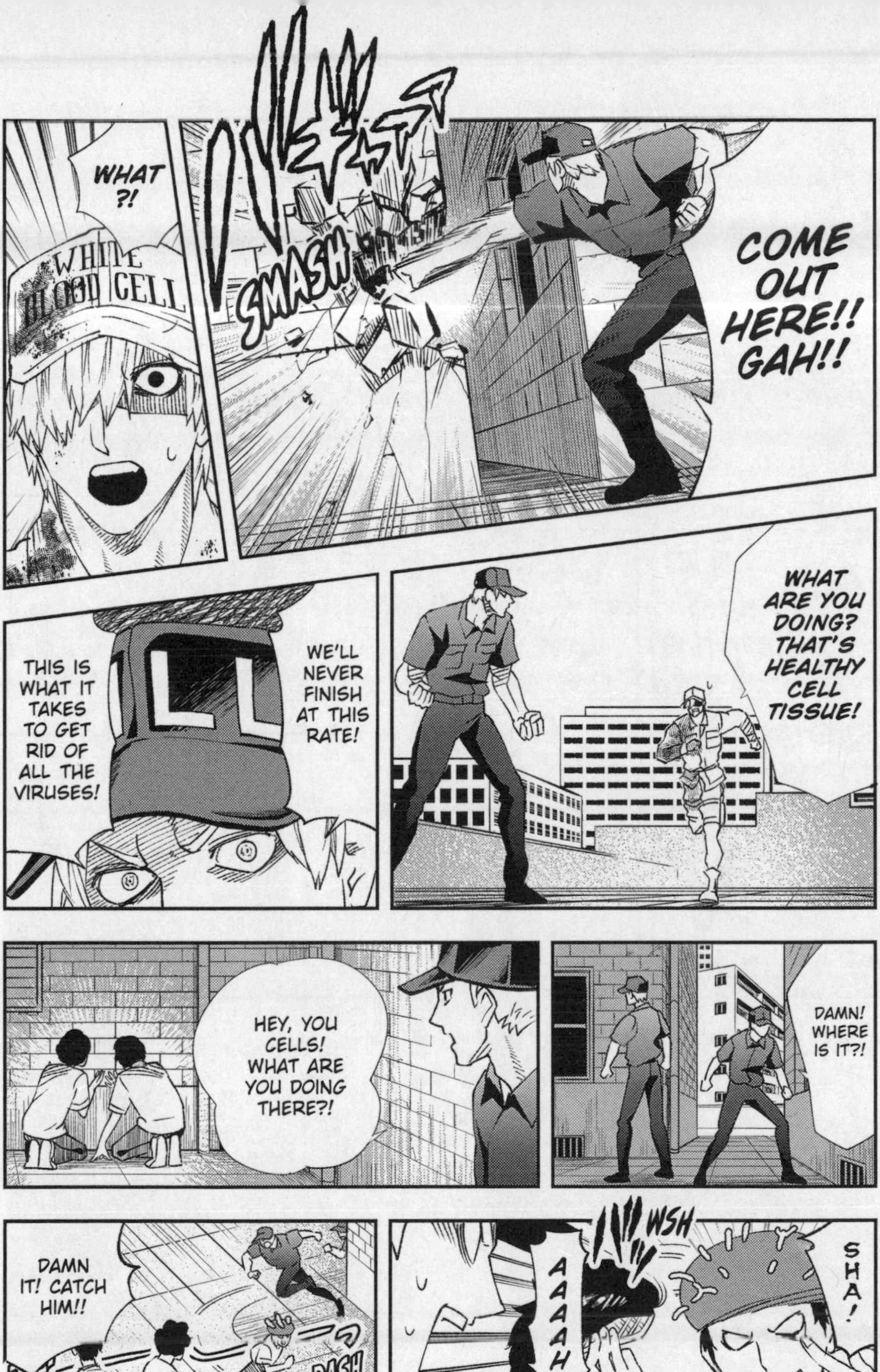

SMASH
COME OUT HERE!! GAH!!
WHAT ?!
WHITE BLOOD CELL
WHAT ARE YOU DOING? THAT'S HEALTHY CELL TISSUE!
WE'LL NEVER FINISH AT THIS RATE!
THIS IS WHAT IT TAKES TO GET RID OF ALL THE VIRUSES!
DAMN! WHERE IS IT?!
HEY, YOU CELLS! WHAT ARE YOU DOING THERE?!
SHA!
WSH
AAAAAH!!
DAMN IT! CATCH HIM!!
DASH

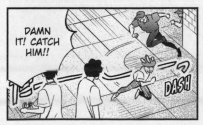

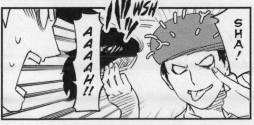

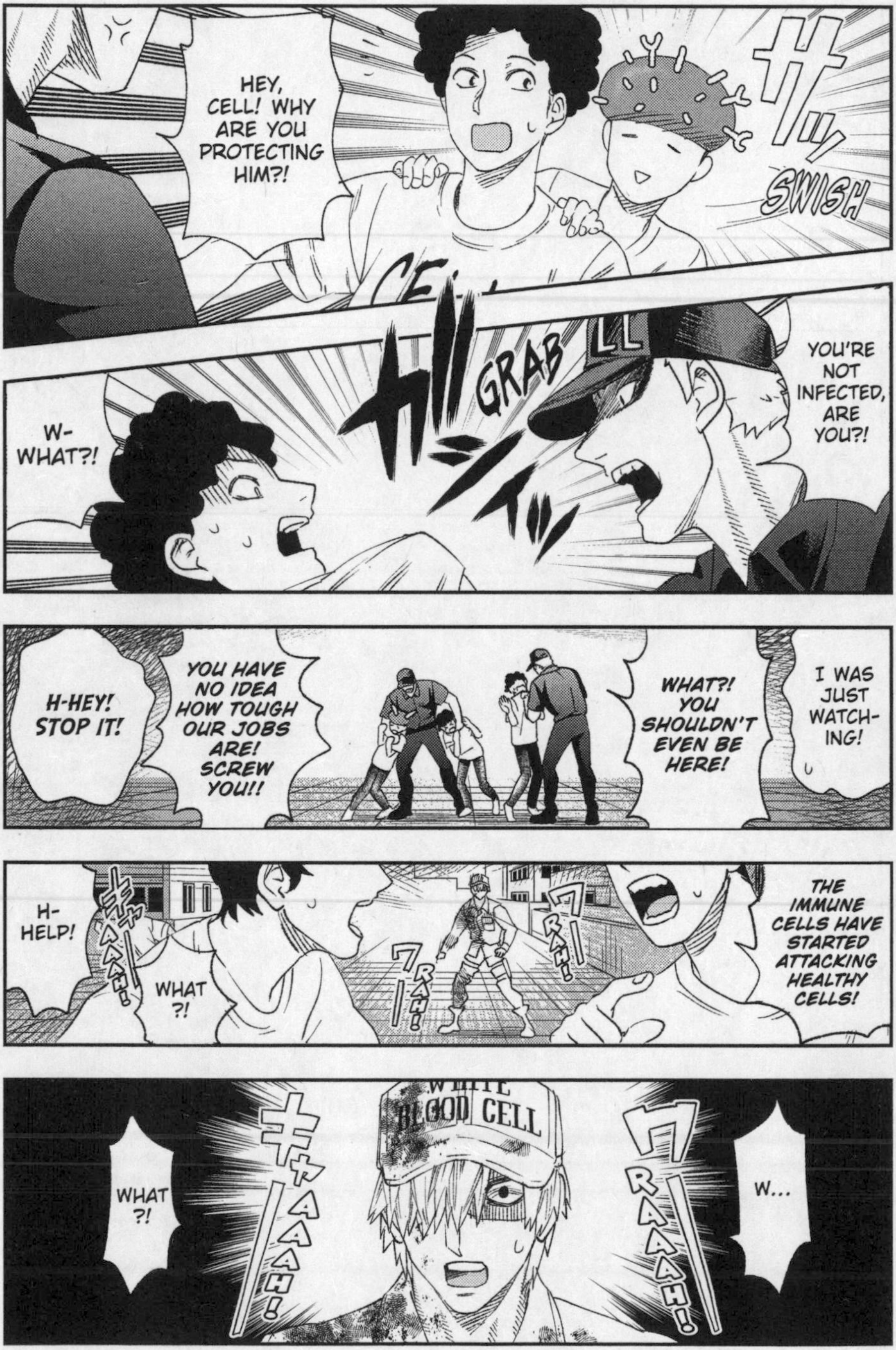
SWISH
HEY, CELL! WHY ARE YOU PROTECTING HIM?!
GRAB
YOU'RE NOT INFECTED, ARE YOU?!
W- WHAT?!
I WAS JUST WATCHING!
WHAT?! YOU SHOULDN'T EVEN BE HERE!
YOU HAVE NO IDEA HOW TOUGH OUR JOBS ARE! SCREW YOU!!
H-HEY! STOP IT!
THE IMMUNE CELLS HAVE STARTED ATTACKING HEALTHY CELLS!
RAH!
RAH!
AAAAH!
WHAT ?!
H- HELP!
W...
RAAAAH!
WHITE BLOOD CELL
AAAAAH!
WHAT ?!

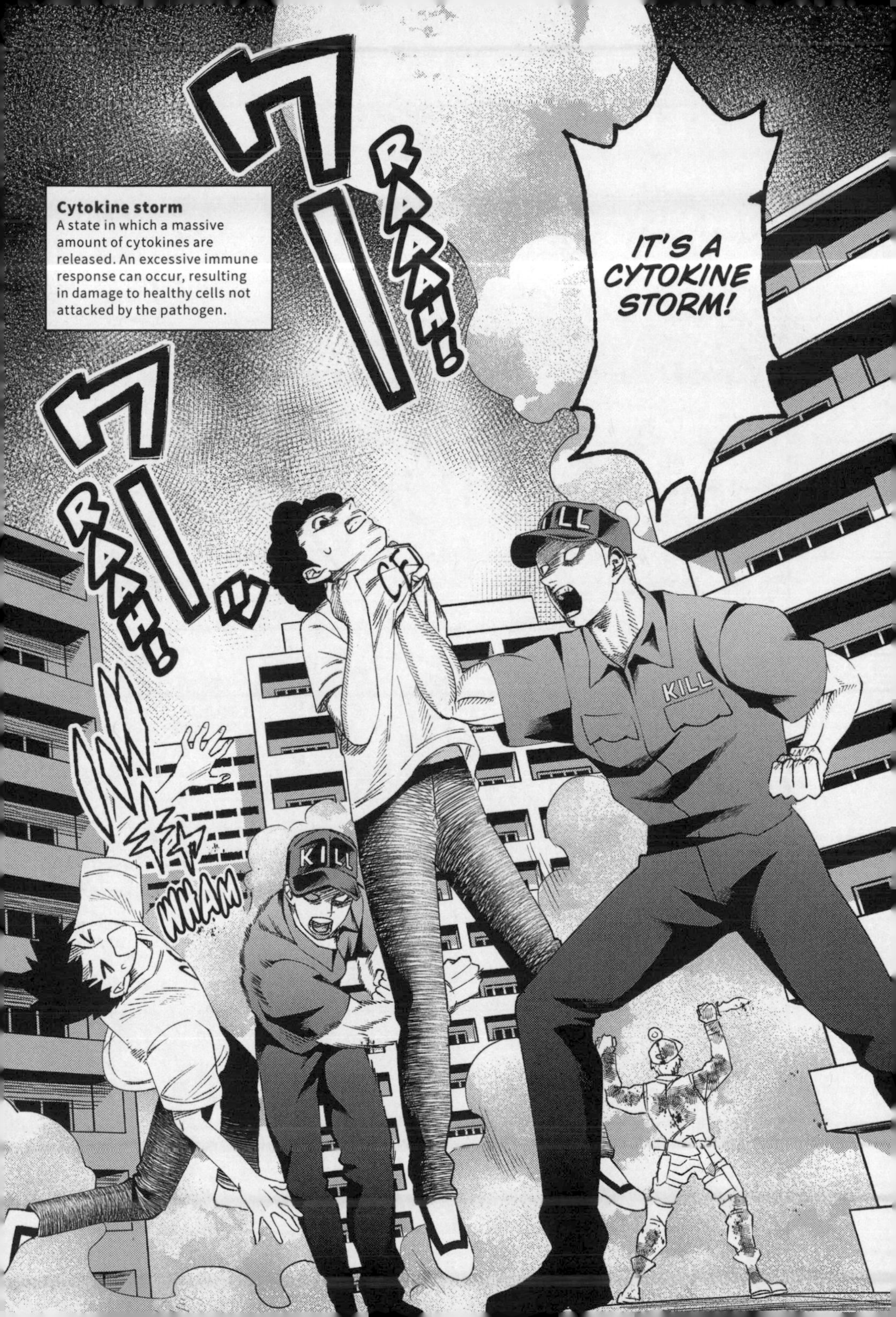
IT'S A CYTOKINE STORM!
RAAAH!
Cytokine storm
A state in which a massive amount of cytokines are released. An excessive immune response can occur, resulting in damage to healthy cells not attacked by the pathogen.
RAAAH!
WHAM

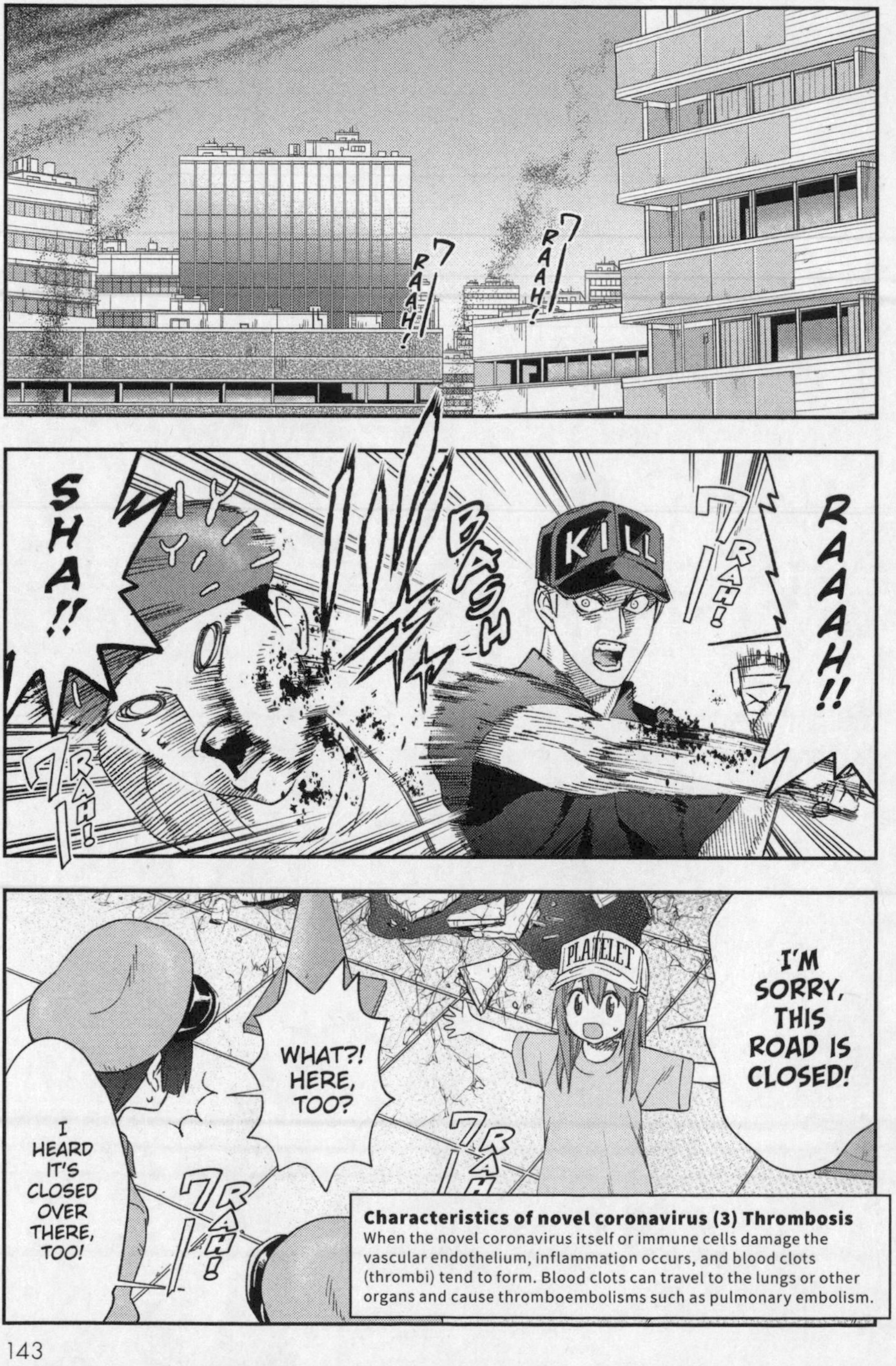
RAAH!
RAAH!
RAAAAH!!
RAAH!
BASH
SHA!!
RAAH!
I'M SORRY, THIS ROAD IS CLOSED!
WHAT?! HERE, TOO?
RAAH!
I HEARD IT'S CLOSED OVER THERE, TOO!
Characteristics of novel coronavirus (3) Thrombosis
When the novel coronavirus itself or immune cells damage the vascular endothelium, inflammation occurs, and blood clots (thrombi) tend to form. Blood clots can travel to the lungs or other organs and cause thromboembolisms such as pulmonary embolism.

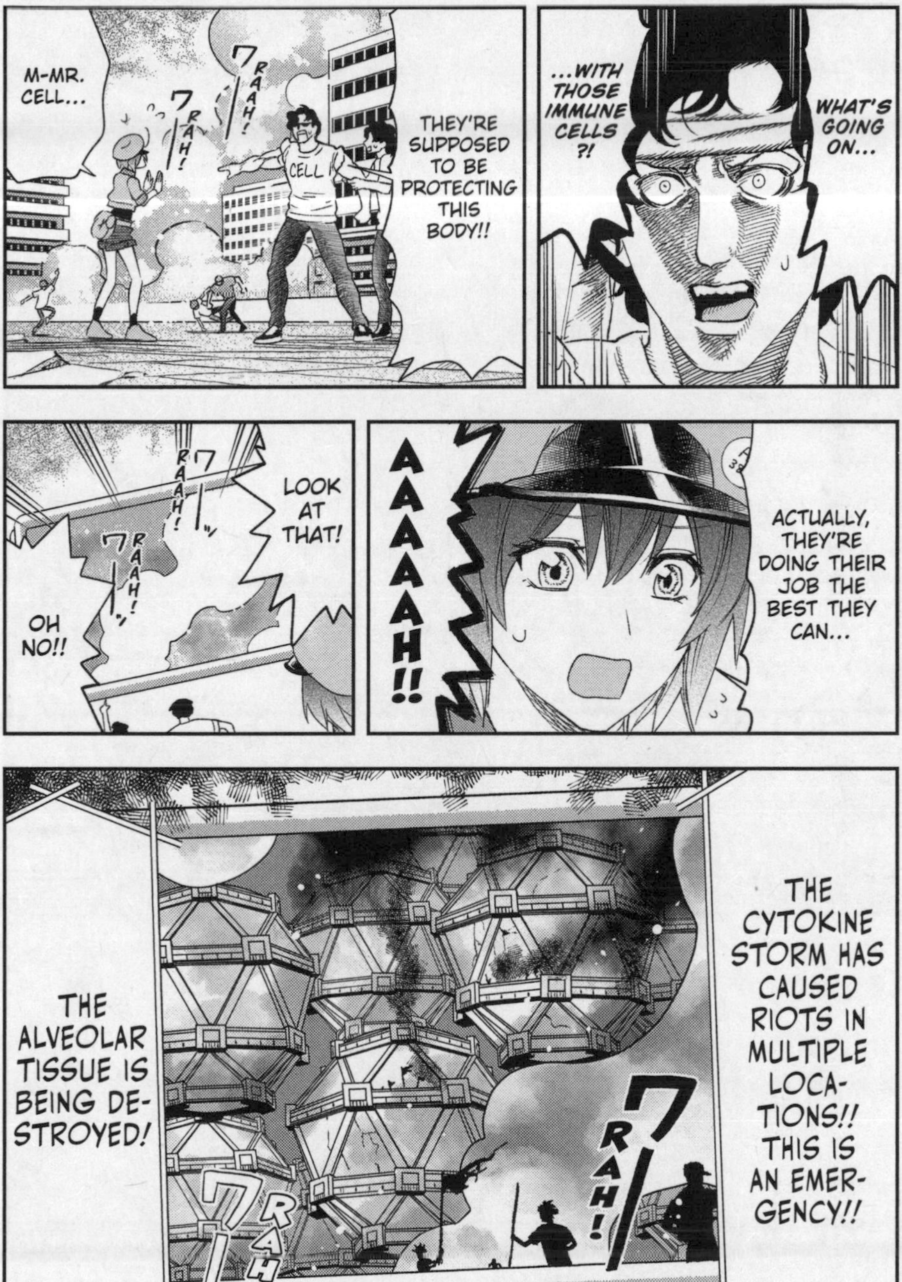
WHAT'S GOING ON...
...WITH THOSE IMMUNE CELLS?!
THEY'RE SUPPOSED TO BE PROTECTING THIS BODY!!
RAAH!
RAH!
CELL
M-MR. CELL...
ACTUALLY, THEY'RE DOING THEIR JOB THE BEST THEY CAN...
AAAAAAH!!
LOOK AT THAT!
RAAH!
RAAH!
OH NO!!
THE CYTOKINE STORM HAS CAUSED RIOTS IN MULTIPLE LOCATIONS!! THIS IS AN EMERGENCY!!
RAH!
RAH!
THE ALVEOLAR TISSUE IS BEING DESTROYED!

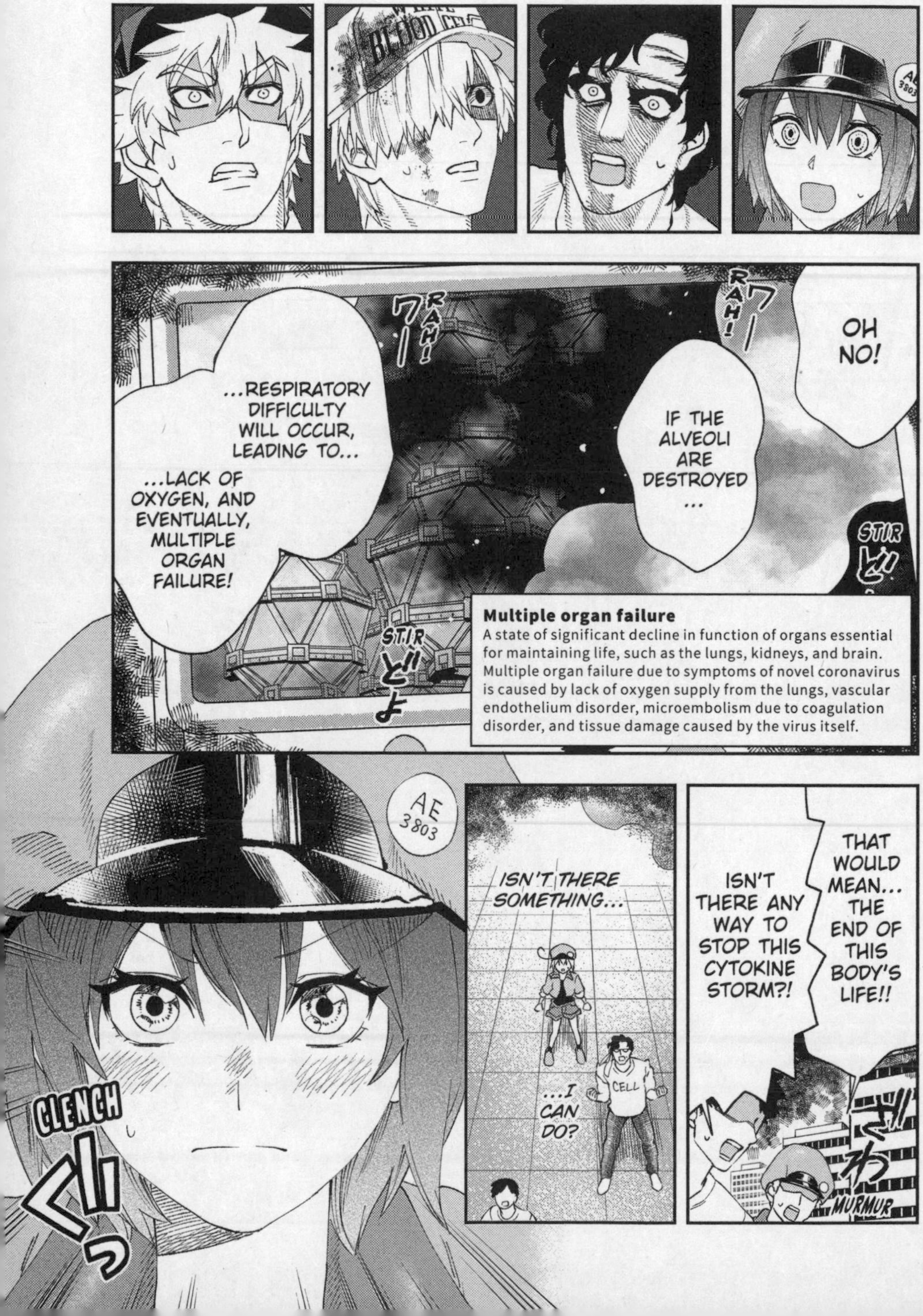
OH NO!
RAH!
IF THE ALVEOLI ARE DESTROYED...
STIR
RAH!
...RESPIRATORY DIFFICULTY WILL OCCUR, LEADING TO...
...LACK OF OXYGEN, AND EVENTUALLY, MULTIPLE ORGAN FAILURE!
Multiple organ failure
A state of significant decline in function of organs essential for maintaining life, such as the lungs, kidneys, and brain. Multiple organ failure due to symptoms of novel coronavirus is caused by lack of oxygen supply from the lungs, vascular endothelium disorder, microembolism due to coagulation disorder, and tissue damage caused by the virus itself.
STIR
THAT WOULD MEAN... THE END OF THIS BODY'S LIFE!!
ISN'T THERE ANY WAY TO STOP THIS CYTOKINE STORM?!
MURMUR
ISN'T THERE SOMETHING...
...I CAN DO?
CELL
AE 3803
CLENCH

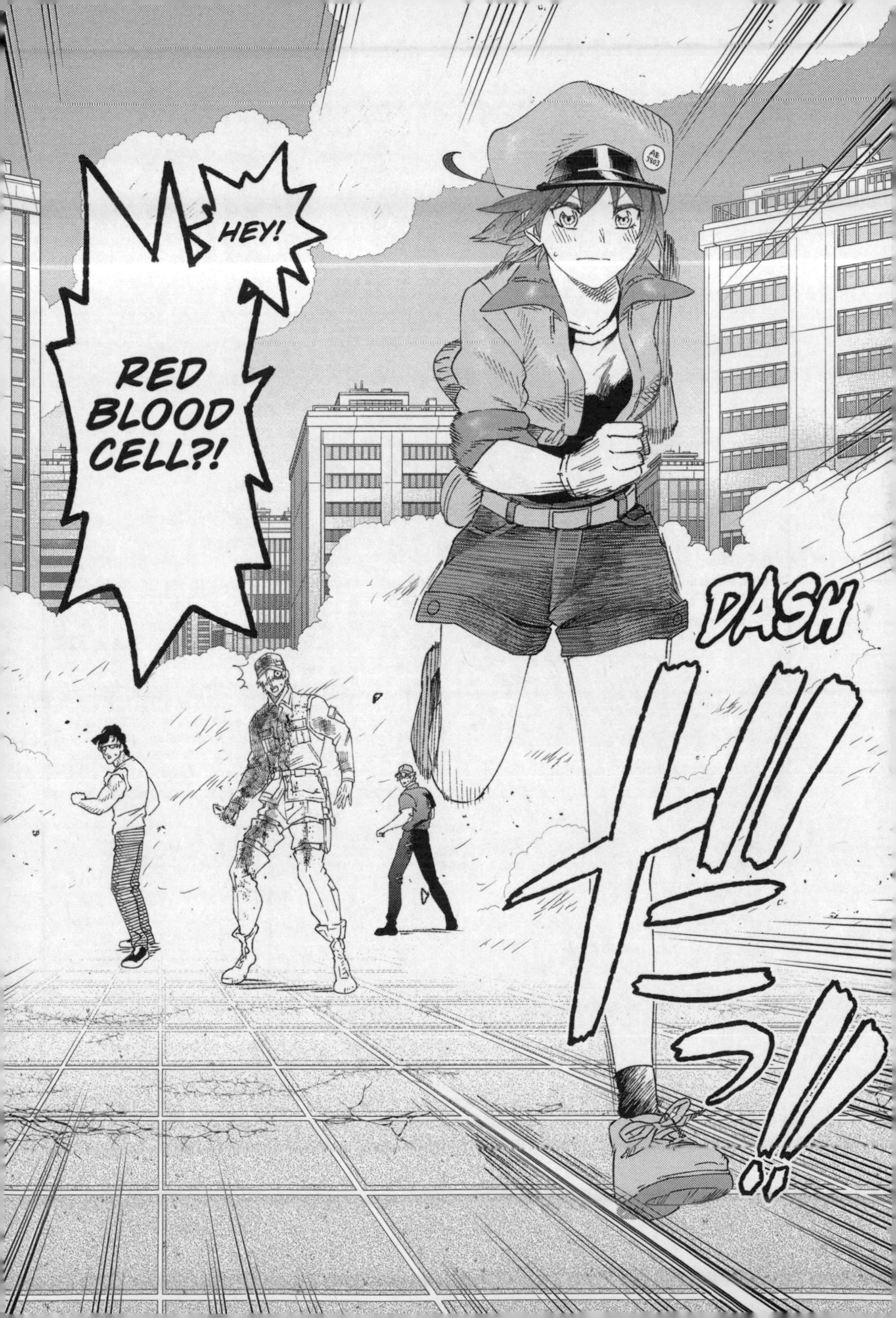
AE 3803
HEY! RED BLOOD CELL?!
DASH

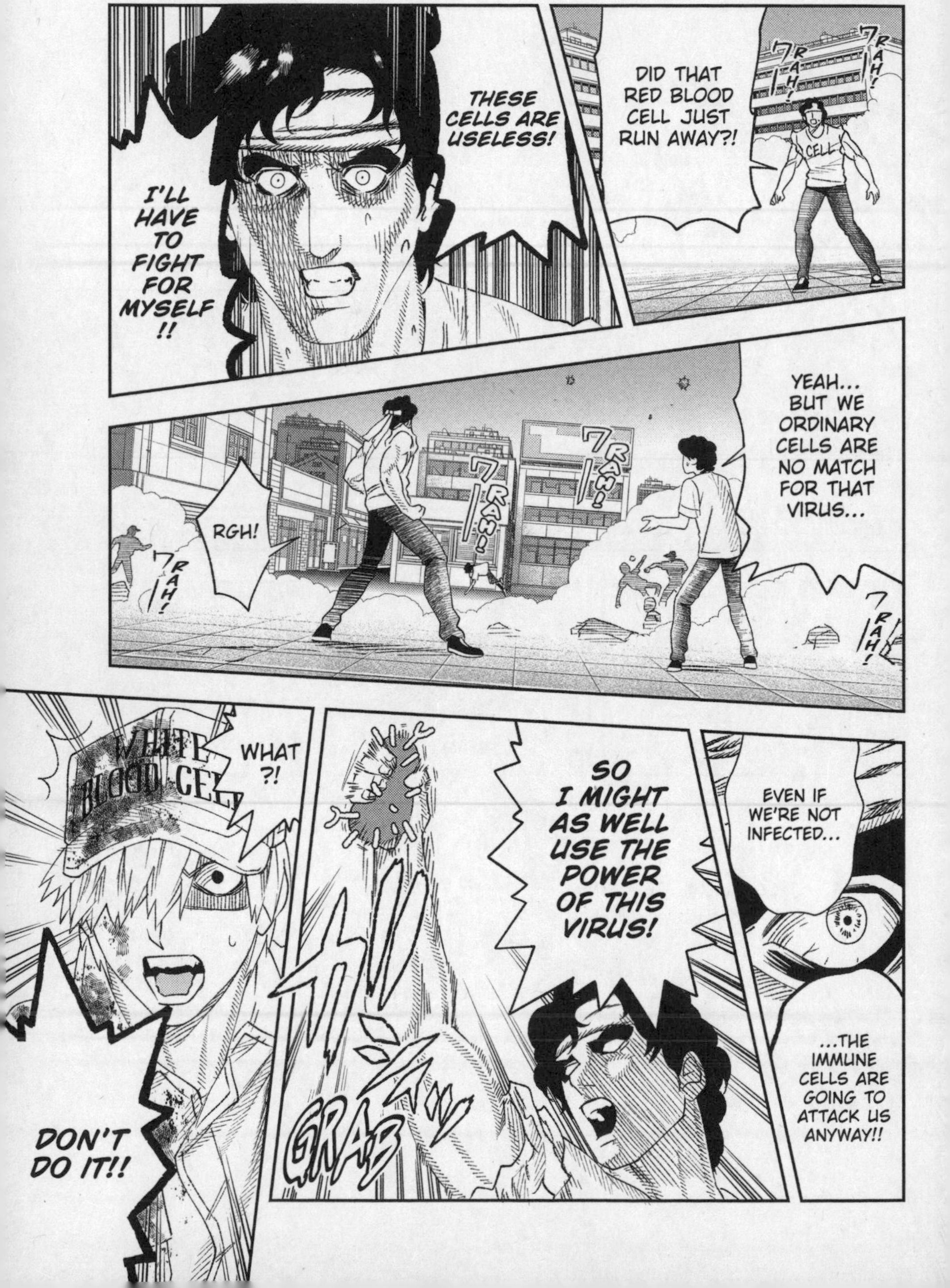
RAH!
RAH!
DID THAT RED BLOOD CELL JUST RUN AWAY?!
THESE CELLS ARE USELESS!
I'LL HAVE TO FIGHT FOR MYSELF!!
YEAH... BUT WE ORDINARY CELLS ARE NO MATCH FOR THAT VIRUS...
RAH!
RAH!
RAH!
RGH!
RAH!
EVEN IF WE'RE NOT INFECTED...
...THE IMMUNE CELLS ARE GOING TO ATTACK US ANYWAY!!
SO I MIGHT AS WELL USE THE POWER OF THIS VIRUS!
GRAB
WHITE BLOOD CELL
WHAT?!
DON'T DO IT!!

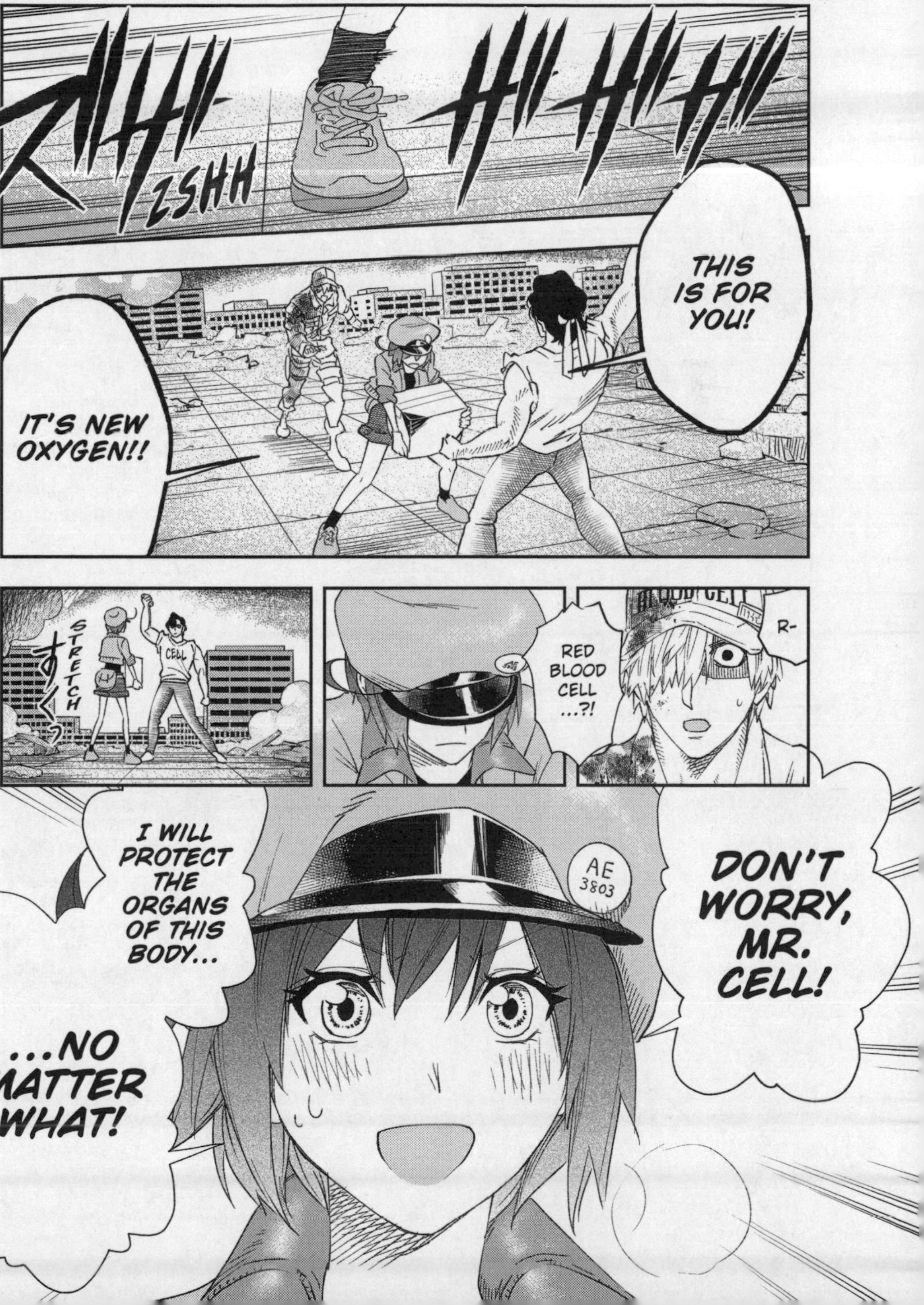
ZSHH
THIS IS FOR YOU!
IT'S NEW OXYGEN!!
R-
RED BLOOD CELL ...?!
STRETCH
すくっ
CELL
AE 3803
DON'T WORRY, MR. CELL!
I WILL PROTECT THE ORGANS OF THIS BODY...
...NO MATTER WHAT!

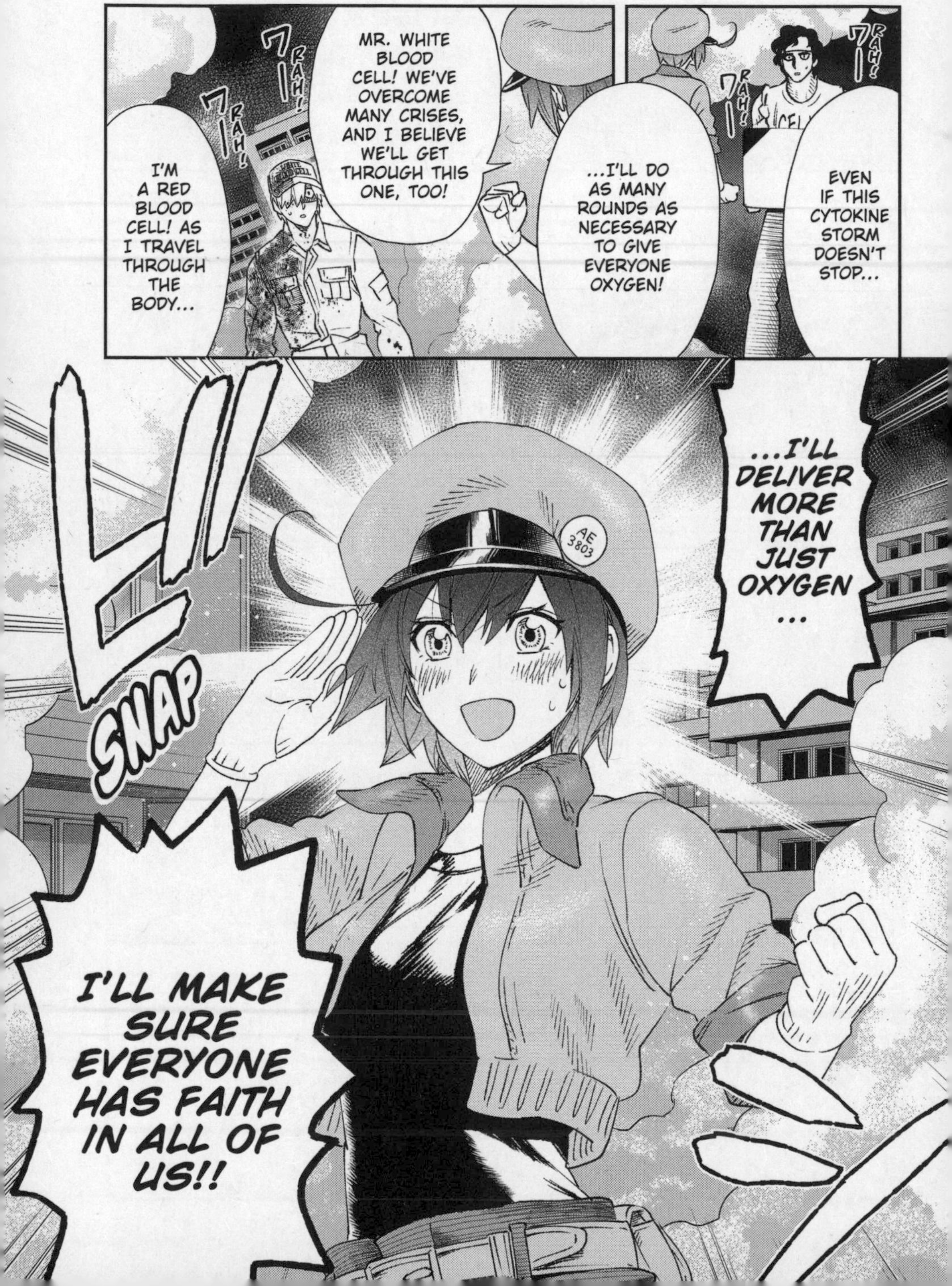
ワー
RAH!
ワー
RAH!
EVEN IF THIS CYTOKINE STORM DOESN'T STOP...
...I'LL DO AS MANY ROUNDS AS NECESSARY TO GIVE EVERYONE OXYGEN!
MR. WHITE BLOOD CELL! WE'VE OVERCOME MANY CRISES, AND I BELIEVE WE'LL GET THROUGH THIS ONE, TOO!
ワー
RAH!
ワー
RAH!
I'M A RED BLOOD CELL! AS I TRAVEL THROUGH THE BODY...
...I'LL DELIVER MORE THAN JUST OXYGEN...
AE 3803
SNAP
I'LL MAKE SURE EVERYONE HAS FAITH IN ALL OF US!!

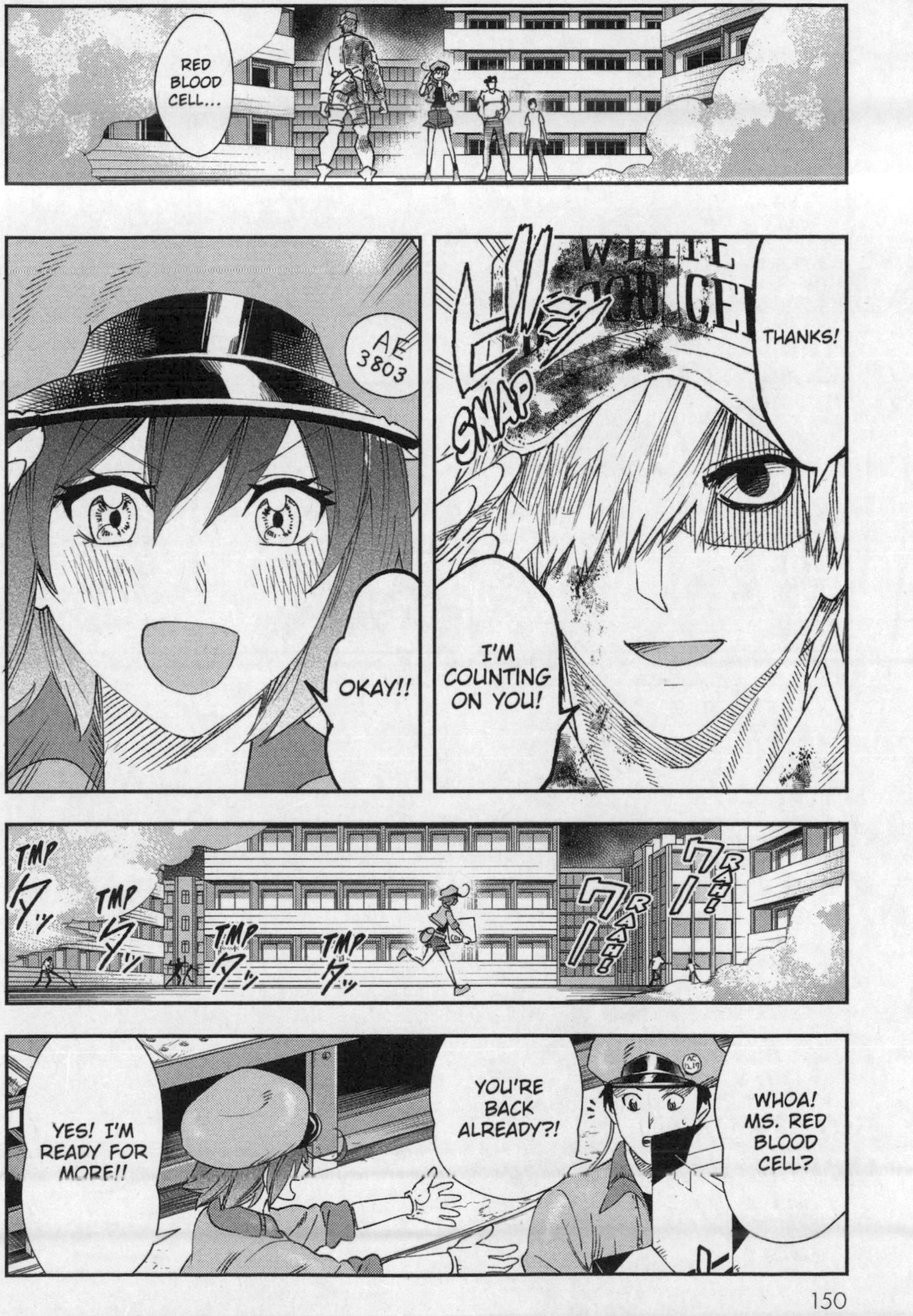
RED BLOOD CELL...
SNAP
THANKS!
I'M COUNTING ON YOU!
AE 3803
OKAY!!
RAAH!
RAAH!
TMP
TMP
TMP
TMP
WHOA! MS. RED BLOOD CELL?
YOU'RE BACK ALREADY?!
YES! I'M READY FOR MORE!!

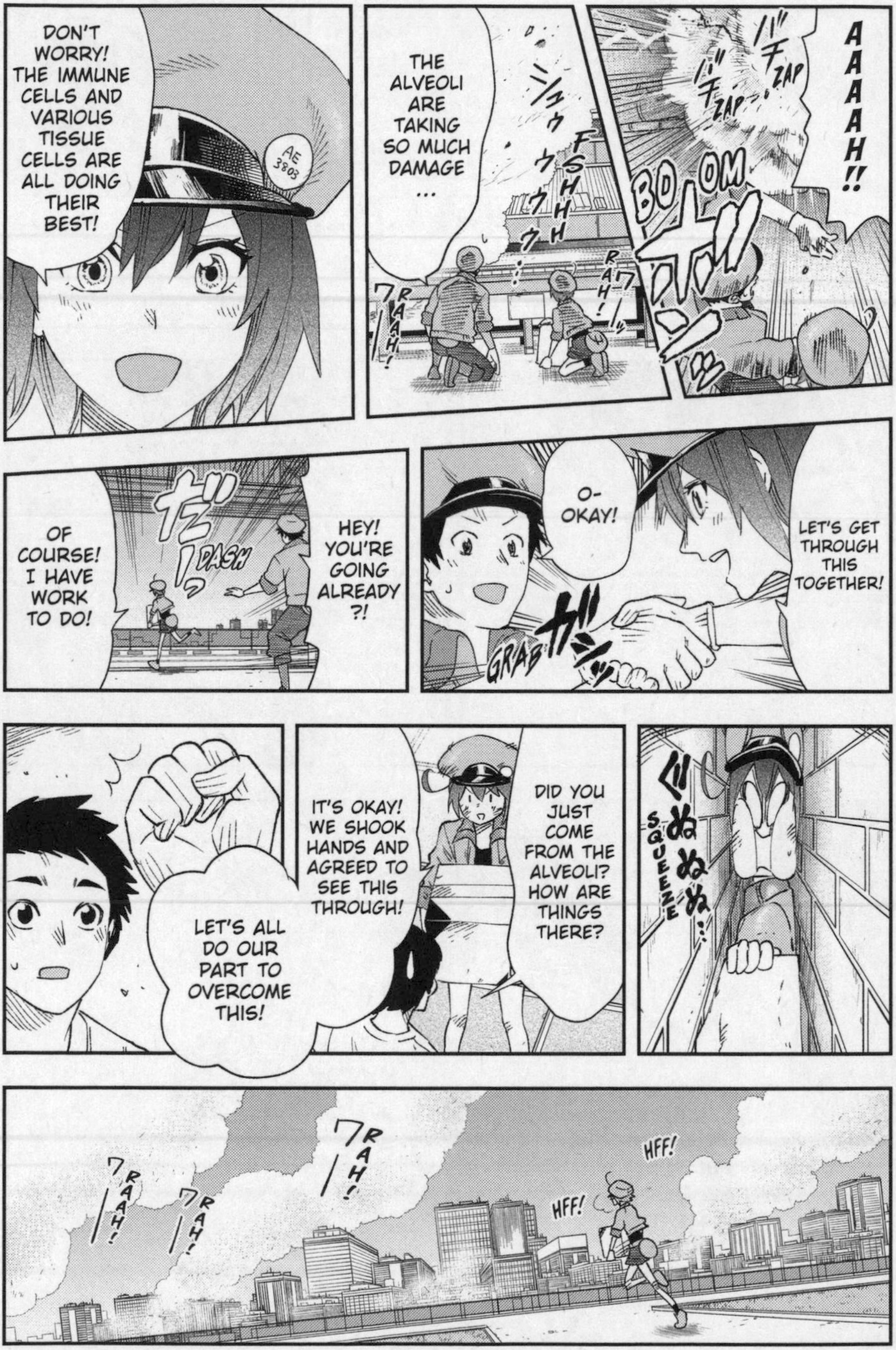
AAAAAAH!!
ZAP
ZAP
BOOM
THE ALVEOLI ARE TAKING SO MUCH DAMAGE...
FSHHH
RAH!
RAAH!
DON'T WORRY! THE IMMUNE CELLS AND VARIOUS TISSUE CELLS ARE ALL DOING THEIR BEST!
AE 3803
LET'S GET THROUGH THIS TOGETHER!
O-OKAY!
GRAB
HEY! YOU'RE GOING ALREADY?!
DASH
OF COURSE! I HAVE WORK TO DO!
SQUEEZE
DID YOU JUST COME FROM THE ALVEOLI? HOW ARE THINGS THERE?
IT'S OKAY! WE SHOOK HANDS AND AGREED TO SEE THIS THROUGH!
LET'S ALL DO OUR PART TO OVERCOME THIS!
HFF!
HFF!
RAH!
RAH!
RAAH!

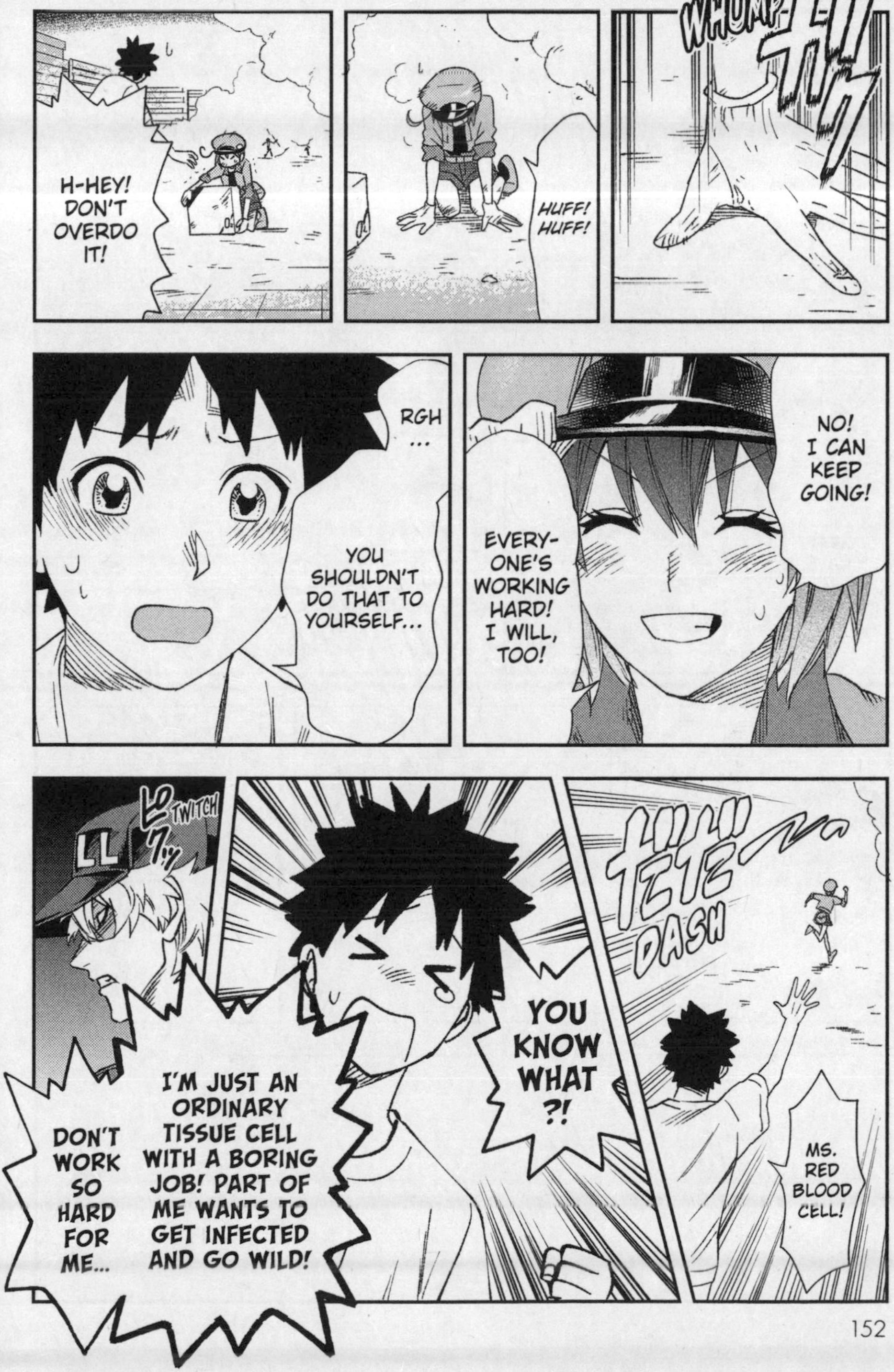
WHUMP
HUFF! HUFF!
H-HEY! DON'T OVERDO IT!
NO! I CAN KEEP GOING!
EVERY-ONE'S WORKING HARD! I WILL, TOO!
RGH...
YOU SHOULDN'T DO THAT TO YOURSELF...
DASH
MS. RED BLOOD CELL!
YOU KNOW WHAT?!
I'M JUST AN ORDINARY TISSUE CELL WITH A BORING JOB! PART OF ME WANTS TO GET INFECTED AND GO WILD!
DON'T WORK SO HARD FOR ME...
TWITCH

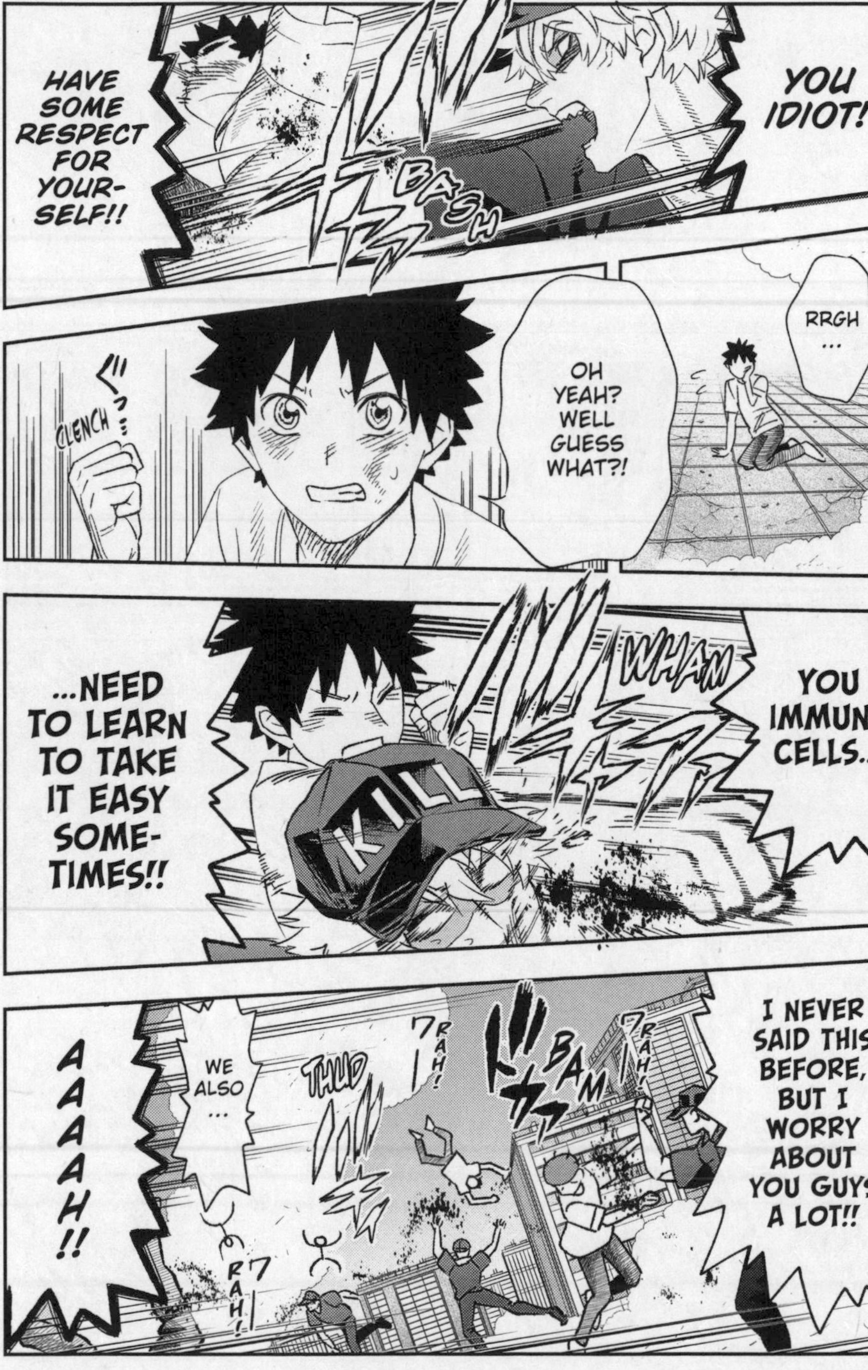
YOU IDIOT!
BASH
HAVE SOME RESPECT FOR YOURSELF!!
RRGH ...
OH YEAH? WELL GUESS WHAT?!
CLENCH
YOU IMMUNE CELLS...
WHAM
...NEED TO LEARN TO TAKE IT EASY SOMETIMES!!
I NEVER SAID THIS BEFORE, BUT I WORRY ABOUT YOU GUYS A LOT!!
RAH!
BAM
RAH!
THUD
WE ALSO ...
RAH!
AAAAAAH!!

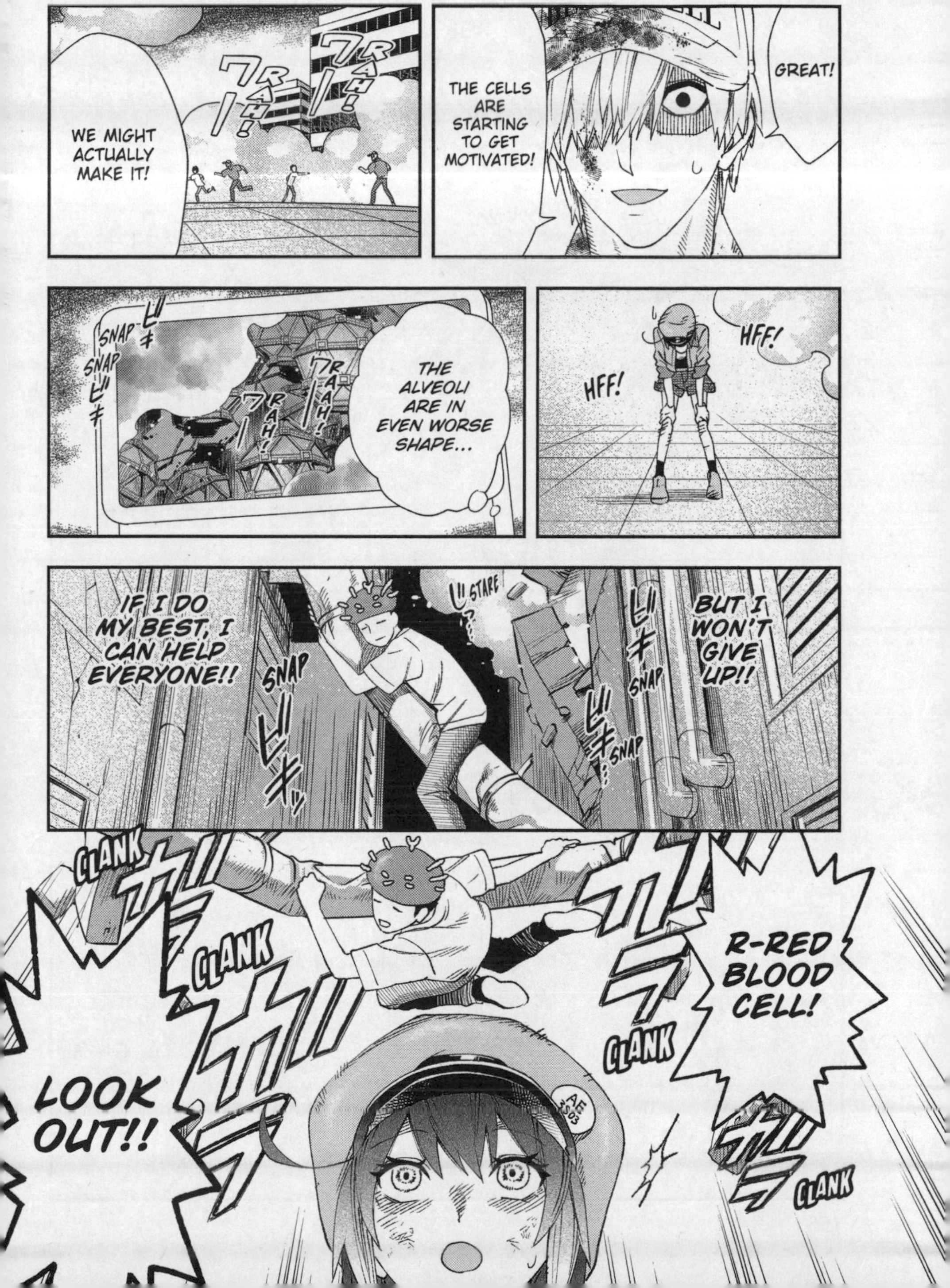
GREAT!
THE CELLS ARE STARTING TO GET MOTIVATED!
RAH!
RAH!
WE MIGHT ACTUALLY MAKE IT!
HFF!
HFF!
THE ALVEOLI ARE IN EVEN WORSE SHAPE...
RAH!
RAH!
SNAP
SNAP
BUT I WON'T GIVE UP!!
SNAP
SNAP
STARE
SNAP
IF I DO MY BEST, I CAN HELP EVERYONE!!
CLANK
R-RED BLOOD CELL!
CLANK
CLANK
AE 3803
CLANK
LOOK OUT!!

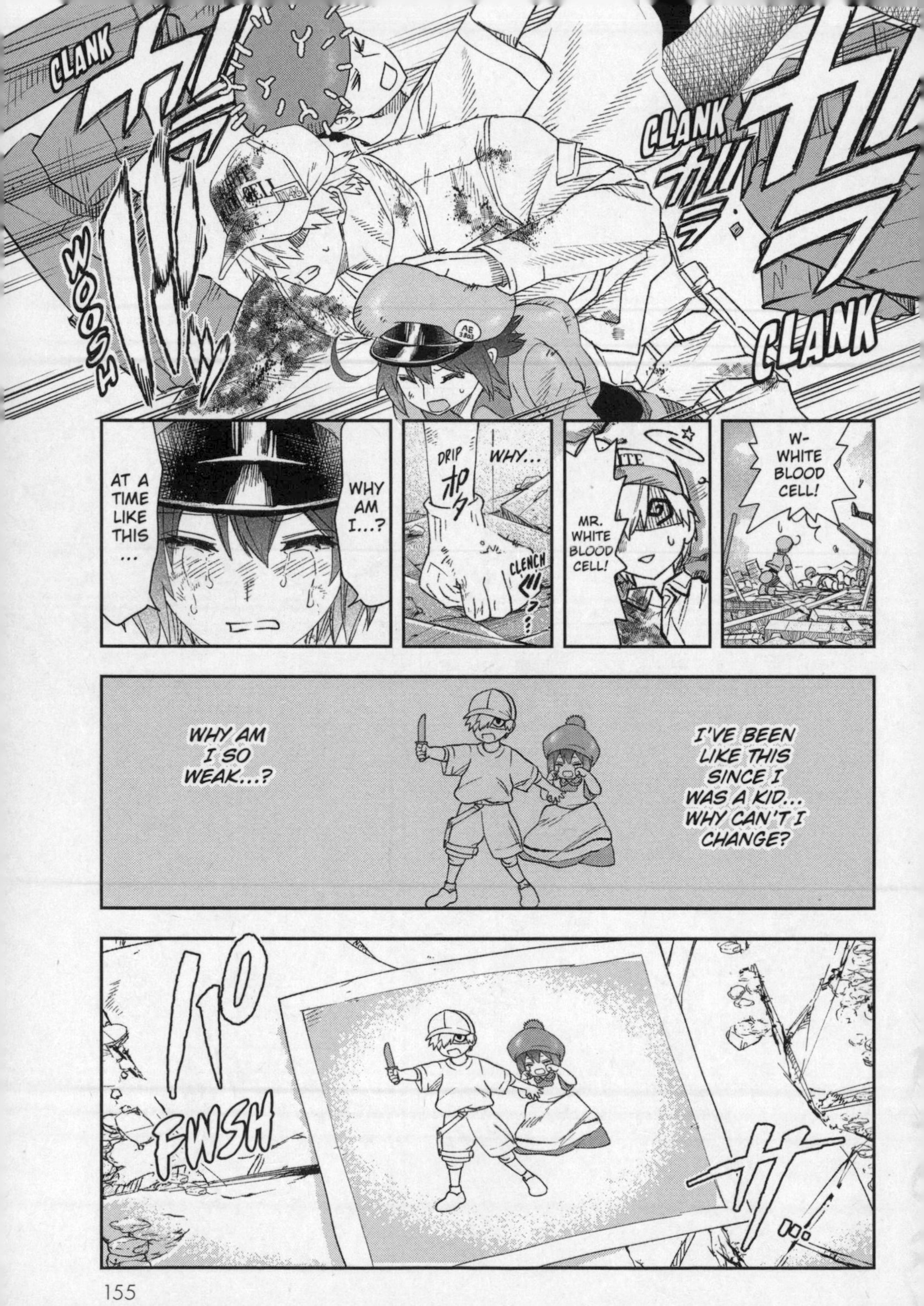
CLANK
CLANK
CLANK
WOOSH
W-WHITE BLOOD CELL!
MR. WHITE BLOOD CELL!
WHY...
DRIP
CLENCH
WHY AM I...?
AT A TIME LIKE THIS...
I'VE BEEN LIKE THIS SINCE I WAS A KID... WHY CAN'T I CHANGE?
WHY AM I SO WEAK...?
FWSH

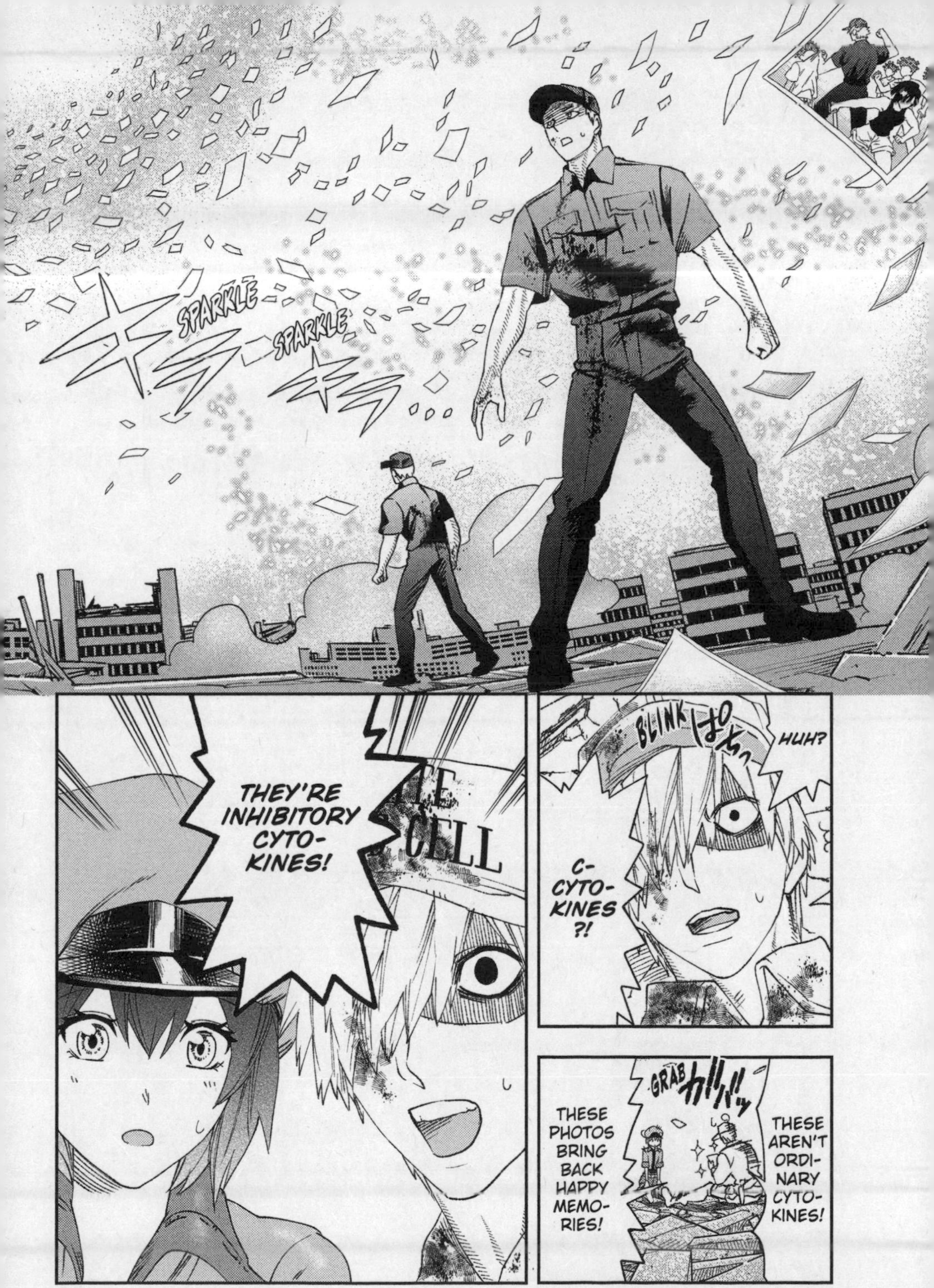
SPARKLE
SPARKLE
BLINK
HUH?
C-CYTOKINES?!
GRAB
THESE AREN'T ORDINARY CYTOKINES!
THESE PHOTOS BRING BACK HAPPY MEMORIES!
THEY'RE INHIBITORY CYTOKINES!

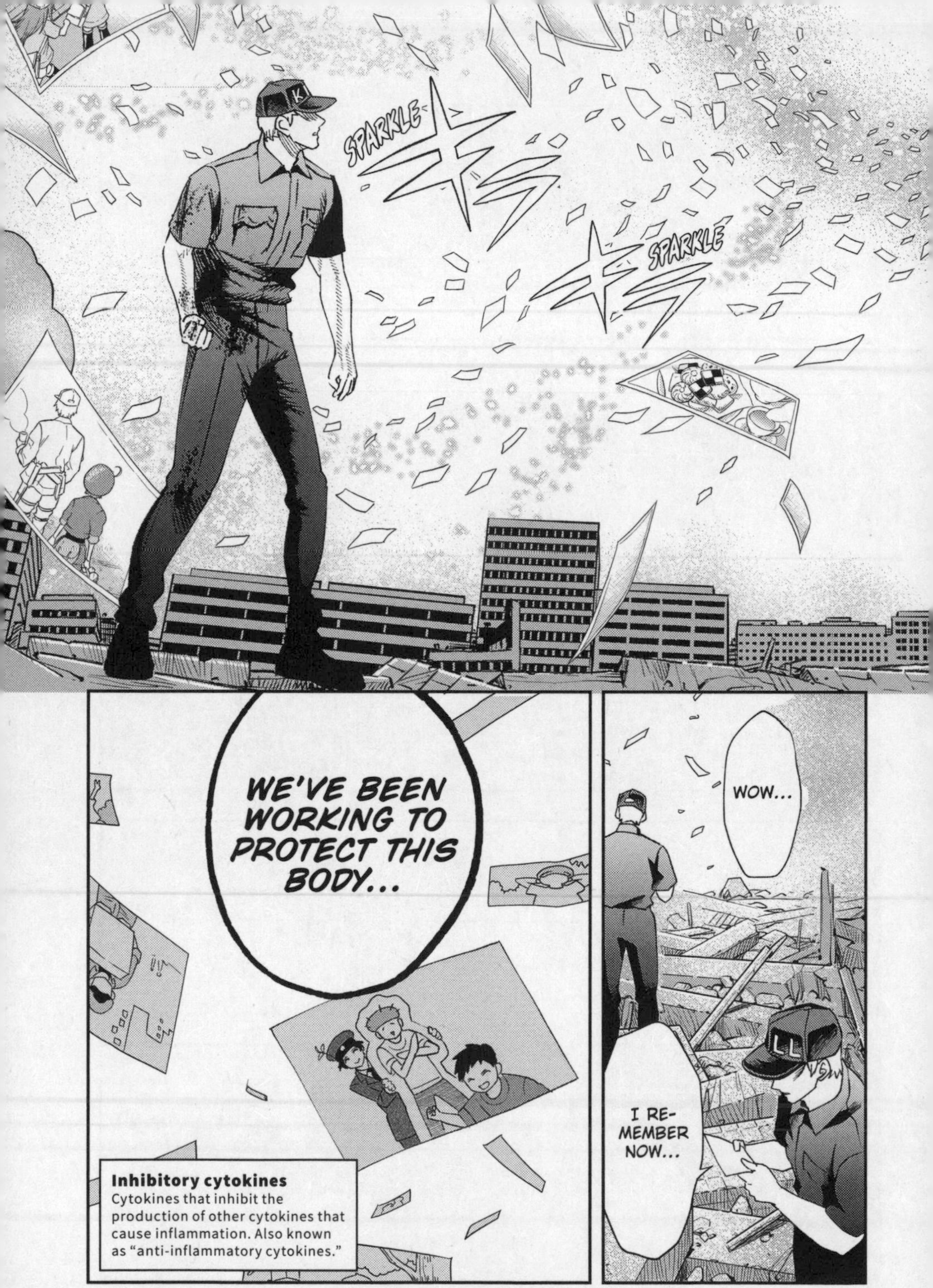
SPARKLE
SPARKLE
WOW...
I RE-MEMBER NOW...
WE'VE BEEN WORKING TO PROTECT THIS BODY...
Inhibitory cytokines
Cytokines that inhibit the production of other cytokines that cause inflammation. Also known as "anti-inflammatory cytokines."

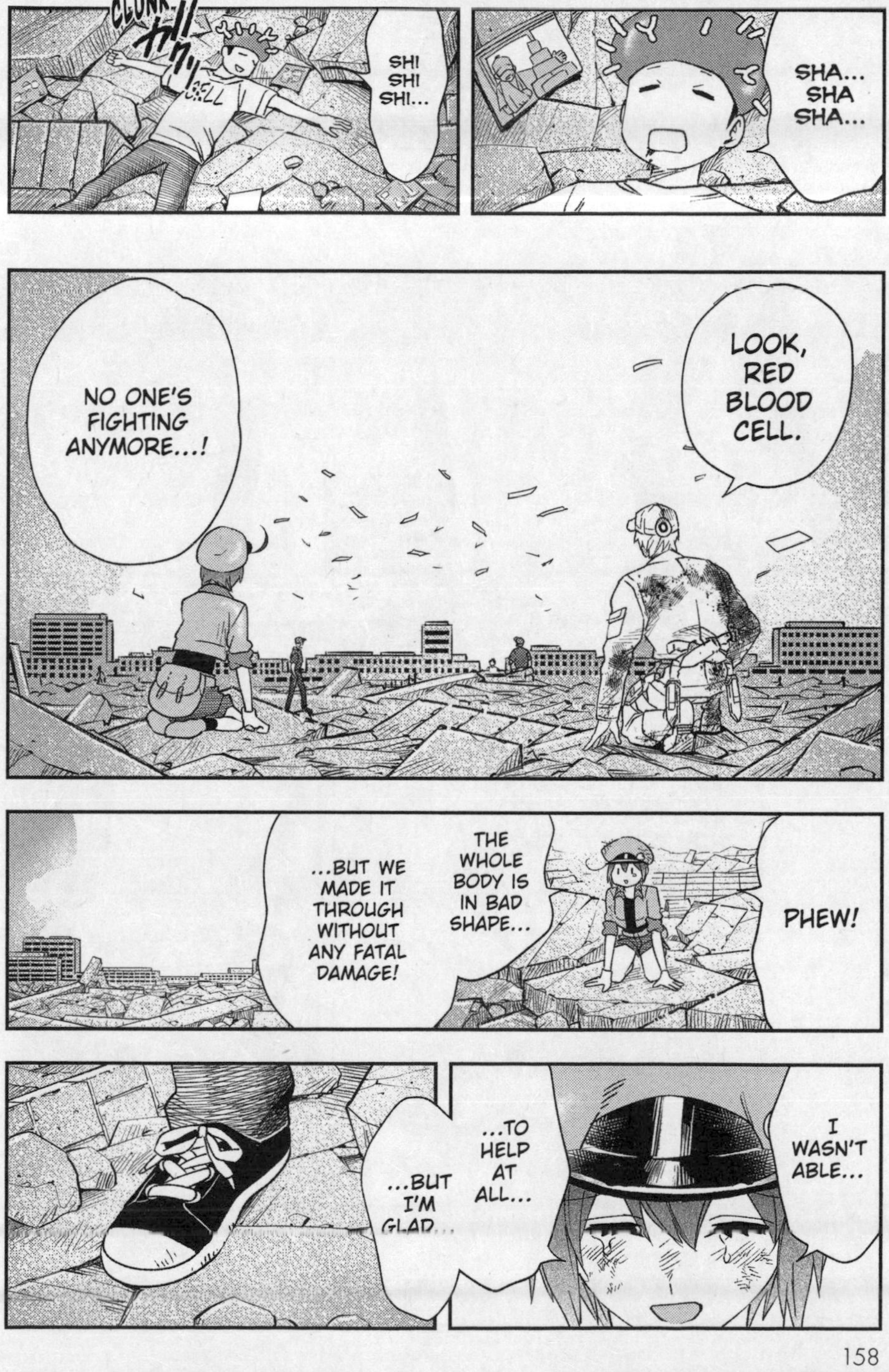
SHA... SHA SHA...
CLUNK
SHI SHI SHI...
LOOK, RED BLOOD CELL.
NO ONE'S FIGHTING ANYMORE...!
PHEW!
THE WHOLE BODY IS IN BAD SHAPE...
...BUT WE MADE IT THROUGH WITHOUT ANY FATAL DAMAGE!
I WASN'T ABLE...
...TO HELP AT ALL...
...BUT I'M GLAD...

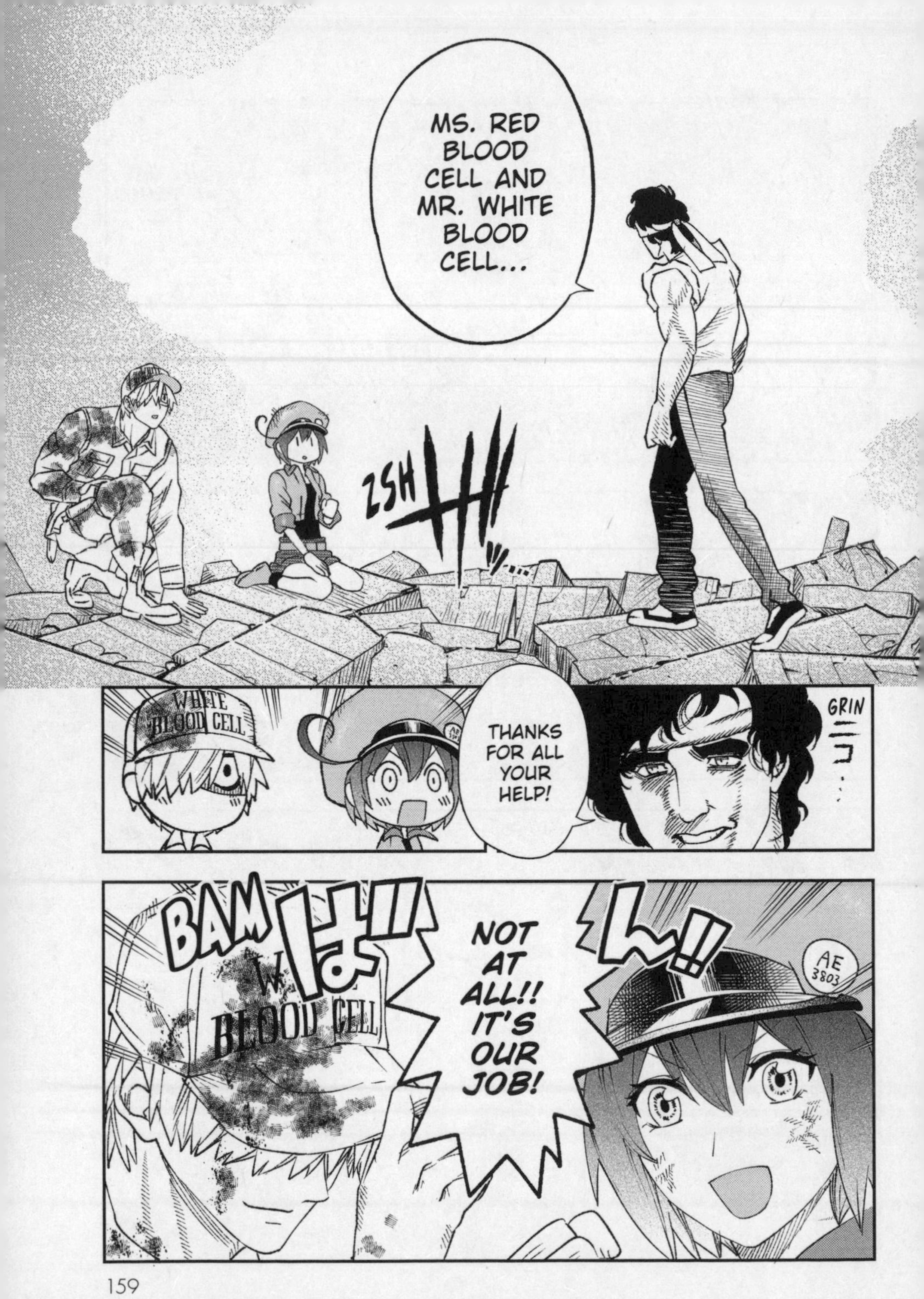
MS. RED BLOOD CELL AND MR. WHITE BLOOD CELL...
ZSH
GRIN
THANKS FOR ALL YOUR HELP!
WHITE BLOOD CELL
ん!!
AE 3803
NOT AT ALL!! IT'S OUR JOB!
BAM
は!!
BLOOD CELL

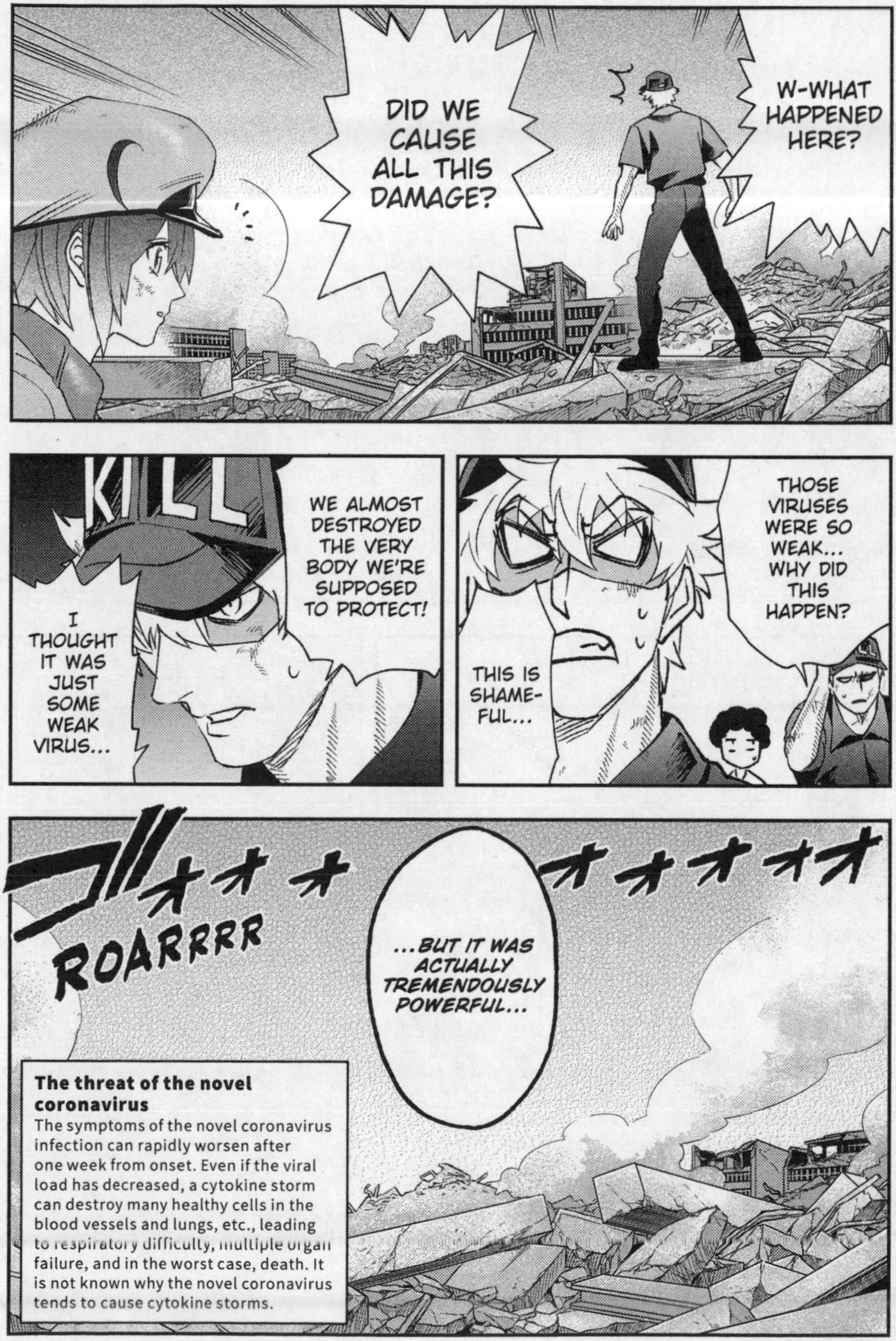
W-WHAT HAPPENED HERE?
DID WE CAUSE ALL THIS DAMAGE?
THOSE VIRUSES WERE SO WEAK... WHY DID THIS HAPPEN?
THIS IS SHAME-FUL...
WE ALMOST DESTROYED THE VERY BODY WE'RE SUPPOSED TO PROTECT!
I THOUGHT IT WAS JUST SOME WEAK VIRUS...
ゴオオオ
ROARRRR
オオオオオ
...BUT IT WAS ACTUALLY TREMENDOUSLY POWERFUL...
The threat of the novel coronavirus
The symptoms of the novel coronavirus infection can rapidly worsen after one week from onset. Even if the viral load has decreased, a cytokine storm can destroy many healthy cells in the blood vessels and lungs, etc., leading to respiratory difficulty, multiple organ failure, and in the worst case, death. It is not known why the novel coronavirus tends to cause cytokine storms.

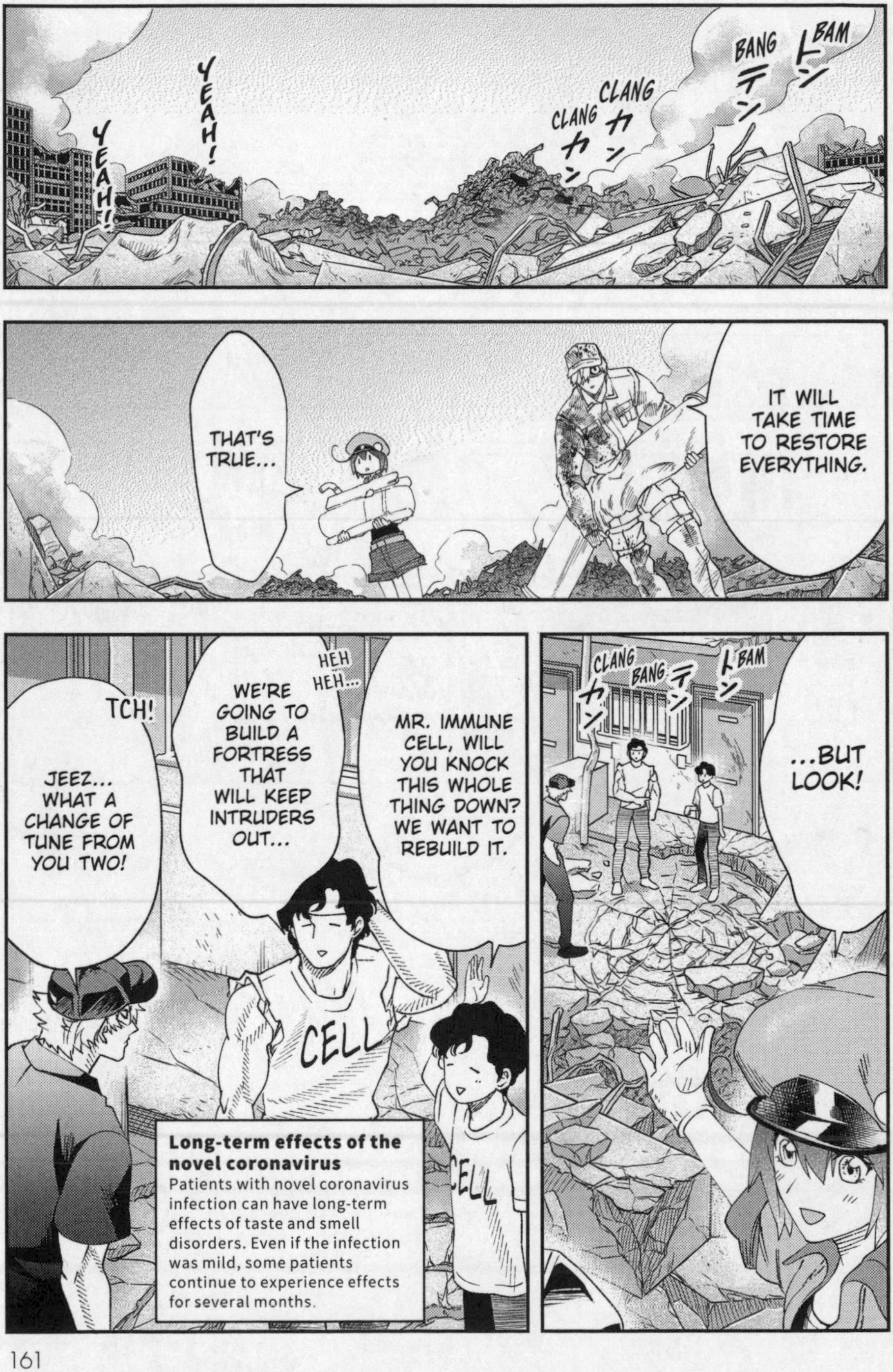
BAM ドン
BANG テン
CLANG カン
CLANG カン
YEAH!
YEAH!!
IT WILL TAKE TIME TO RESTORE EVERYTHING.
THAT'S TRUE...
BAM ドン
BANG テン
CLANG カン
...BUT LOOK!
MR. IMMUNE CELL, WILL YOU KNOCK THIS WHOLE THING DOWN? WE WANT TO REBUILD IT.
HEH HEH...
WE'RE GOING TO BUILD A FORTRESS THAT WILL KEEP INTRUDERS OUT...
TCH!
JEEZ... WHAT A CHANGE OF TUNE FROM YOU TWO!
CELL
CELL
Long-term effects of the novel coronavirus
Patients with novel coronavirus infection can have long-term effects of taste and smell disorders. Even if the infection was mild, some patients continue to experience effects for several months.

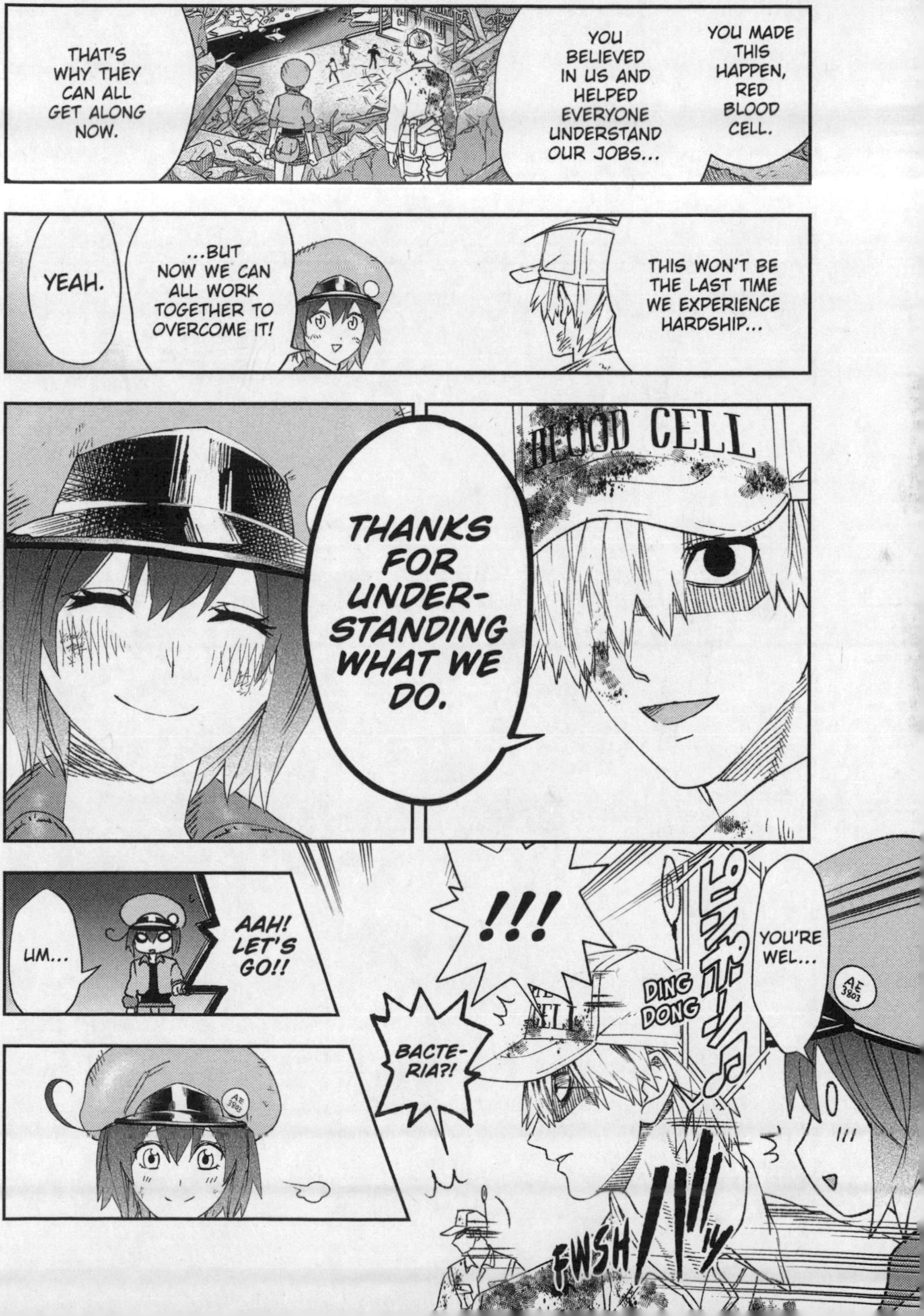
YOU MADE THIS HAPPEN, RED BLOOD CELL.
YOU BELIEVED IN US AND HELPED EVERYONE UNDERSTAND OUR JOBS...
THAT'S WHY THEY CAN ALL GET ALONG NOW.
THIS WON'T BE THE LAST TIME WE EXPERIENCE HARDSHIP...
...BUT NOW WE CAN ALL WORK TOGETHER TO OVERCOME IT!
YEAH.
BLOOD CELL
THANKS FOR UNDER-STANDING WHAT WE DO.
YOU'RE WEL...
AE 3803
DING DONG
!!!
BACTE-RIA?!
FWSH
AAH! LET'S GO!!
UM...
AE 3803

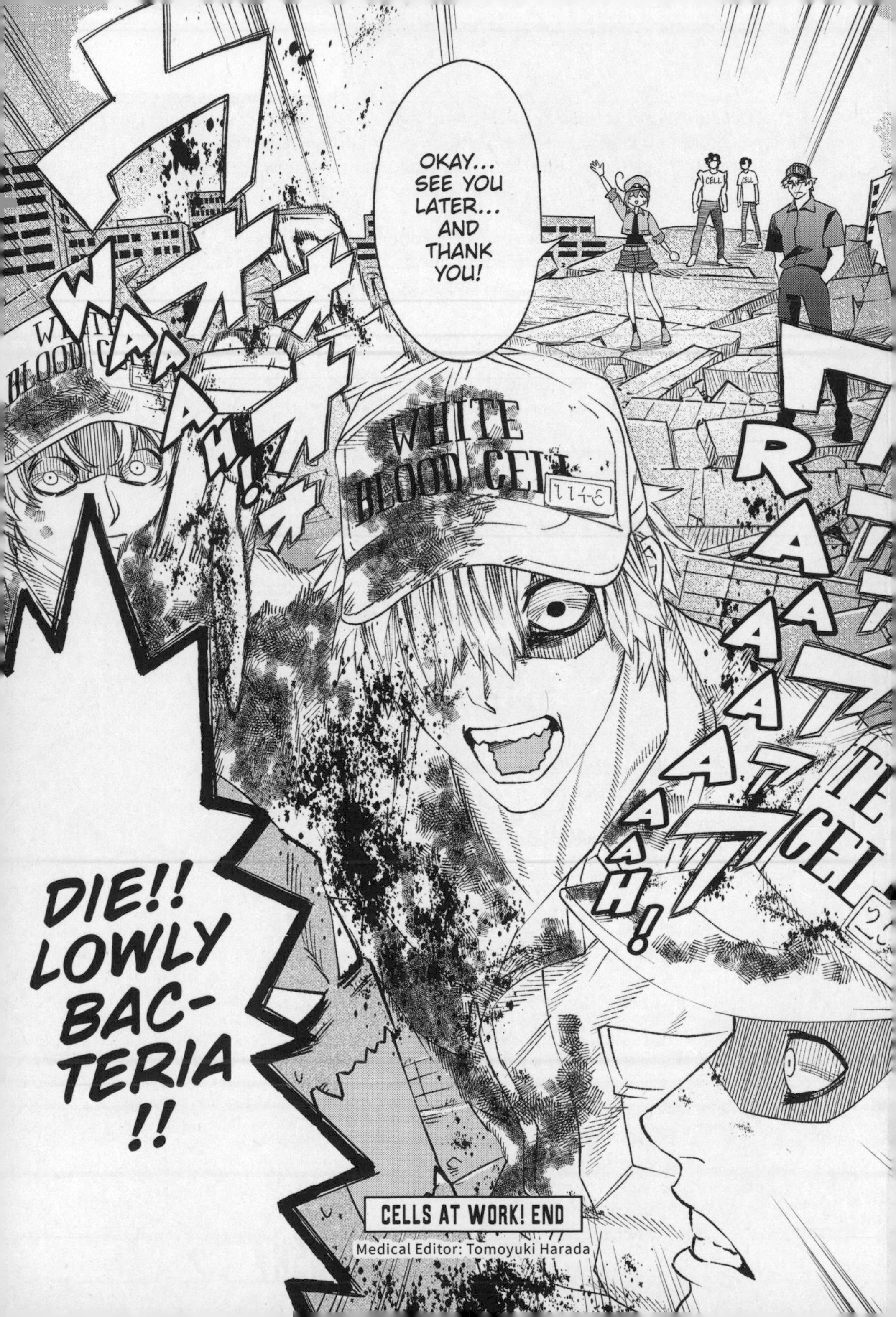
OKAY... SEE YOU LATER... AND THANK YOU!
RAAAAAAH!
WAAAH!
DIE!! LOWLY BAC-TERIA !!

CELLS AT WORK! END

Medical Editor: Tomoyuki Harada

A Kodansha Comics Trade Paperback Original
Cells at Work! volume 6 copyright © 2021 Akane Shimizu
English translation copyright © 2021 Akane Shimizu

All rights reserved.

Published in the United States by Kodansha Comics, an imprint of Kodansha USA Publishing, LLC, New York.

Publication rights for this English edition arranged through Kodansha Ltd., Tokyo.

First published in Japan in 2021 by Kodansha Ltd., Tokyo as *Hataraku Saibou*, volume 6.

ISBN 978-1-63236-427-2

Printed in the United States of America.

www.kodansha.us

9 8 7 6 5 4 3 2 1
Translation: Iyasu Adair Nagata
Lettering: Abigail Blackman
Editing: Ben Applegate
Kodansha Comics edition cover design by Phil Balsman

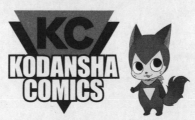

Publisher: Kiichiro Sugawara

Director of publishing services: Ben Applegate
Associate director of operations: Stephen Pakula
Publishing services managing editors: Alanna Ruse, Madison Salters
Production managers: Emi Lotto, Angela Zurlo
Logo and character art ©Kodansha USA Publishing, LLC